Die Reihe „Weltwirtschaft und internationale Zusammenarbeit“ wird herausgegeben von

Prof. (em.) Dr. Hartmut Sangmeister, Universität Heidelberg

Prof. Dr. Aurel Croissant, Universität Heidelberg

Prof. Dr. Günther Maihold, Stiftung Wissenschaft und Politik, Deutsches Institut für Internationale Politik und Sicherheit, Berlin

Volume 25

Daniel Brombacher | Günther Maihold
Melanie Müller | Judith Vorrath [Eds.]

Geopolitics of the Illicit

Linking the Global South and Europe

Nomos

This edited volume is part of the project "Transnational Governance of Sustainable Commodity Supply Chains from the Andean Region and Southern Africa", which is funded by the German Federal Ministry for Economic Cooperation and Development (BMZ).

The Deutsche Nationalbibliothek lists this publication in the Deutsche Nationalbibliografie; detailed bibliographic data are available on the Internet at http://dnb.d-nb.de

ISBN 978-3-7560-0015-9 (Print)
978-3-7489-3594-0 (ePDF)

British Library Cataloguing-in-Publication Data
A catalogue record for this book is available from the British Library.

ISBN 978-3-7560-0015-9 (Print)
978-3-7489-3594-0 (ePDF)

Library of Congress Cataloging-in-Publication Data
Brombacher, Daniel | Maihold, Günther | Müller, Melanie | Vorrath, Judith
Geopolitics of the Illicit
Linking the Global South and Europe
Daniel Brombacher | Günther Maihold | Melanie Müller | Judith Vorrath (Eds.)
411 pp.
Includes bibliographic references.

ISBN 978-3-7560-0015-9 (Print)
978-3-7489-3594-0 (ePDF)

1st Edition 2022

Published by
Nomos Verlagsgesellschaft mbH & Co. KG
Waldseestraße 3–5 | 76530 Baden-Baden
www.nomos.de

Production of the printed version:
Nomos Verlagsgesellschaft mbH & Co. KG
Waldseestraße 3–5 | 76530 Baden-Baden

ISBN 978-3-7560-0015-9 (Print)
ISBN 978-3-7489-3594-0 (ePDF)
DOI https://doi.org/10.5771/9783748935940

Onlineversion
Nomos eLibrary

Content

Abbreviations

3TG	tin, tungsten, tantalum and gold
ABNJ	Areas Beyond National Jurisdiction
AIDS	Acquired Immune Deficiency Syndrome
AIS	automatic identification systems
ALDFG	abandoned, lost or otherwise discarded fishing gear
AML	anti-money laundering
API	active pharmaceutical ingredient
APP	Africa Progress Panel
ASM	artisanal and small-scale mining
ASGM	artisanal small-scale gold mining
ATAF	African Tax Administration Forum
ATS	amphetamine-type stimulants
BCE	before the common era
BEPS	base erosion and profit shifting
BGR	German Federal Institute for Geosciences and Natural Resources
BMZ	German Federal Ministry for Economic Cooperation and Development
BKA	German Federal Criminal Police Office
BLKA	Bavarian State Criminal Police Office
BOV	Bank of Valletta
CAHRA	conflict-affected and high-risk areas
CCAMLR	Commission for the Conservation of Antarctic Marine Living Resources
CCPCJ	UN Commission on Crime Prevention and Criminal Justice
CDS	catch documentation schemes
CEO	chief executive officer
CIP	Public Integrity Center
CITES	Convention on International Trade in Endangered Species of Wild Fauna and Flora
CJNG	Jalisco New Generation Cartel
CND	UN Commission on Narcotic Drugs
COFI	FAO's Committee on Fisheries
DCIM	Directorate for Combatting Illegal Migration
DETER	deforestation detection system
DIY	do it yourself
DMRE	Department of Mineral Resources and Energy
DRC	Democratic Republic of the Congo
DRM	Domestic Resource Mobilisation
DWF	distant water fishing
e.g.	for example
EC	European Commission
EEZ	Economic and Ecological Zoning
EEZ	exclusive economic zones
EIA	Environmental Investigation Agency
EICC	Electronic Industry Citizenship Coalition
EITI	Extractive Industries Transparency Initiative
EJF	European Justice Foundation
EMCDDA	European Monitoring Centre for Drugs and Drugs Addiction
ENRC	Eurasian Natural Resources Corporation
EPRM	European Partnership for Responsible Minerals

ESAAMLG	Eastern and Southern Africa Anti-Money Laundering Group
EU	European Union
EUTR	EU Timber Regulation
FACTI Panel	High Level Panel on International Financial Accountability, Transparency and Integrity for Achieving the 2030 Agenda
FAO	Food and Agriculture Organization
FATF	Financial Action Task Force
FDI	foreign direct investment
FLEGT	Forest Law Enforcement, Governance and Trade
FOC	flags of convenience
FSC	Forest Stewardship Council
FTZ	free trade zone
GDP	gross domestic product
GFI	Global Financial Integrity
GI-TOC	Global Initiative against Transnational Organized Crime
GIZ	Deutsche Gesellschaft für Internationale Zusammenarbeit
GNA	Government of National Accord
GNU	Government of National Unity
GPDPD	Global Partnership on Drug Policies and Development
GSMS	Global Surveillance and Monitoring Systems
HIV	human immunodeficiency virus
IBAMA	Brazilian Institute of Environment and Renewable Natural Resources
ICCAT	International Commission for the Conservation of Atlantic Tunas
ICGLR	International Conference on the Great Lakes Region
ICIJ	International Consortium of Investigative Journalists
IFF	illicit financial flows
ILO	International Labor Organisation
INCB	International Narcotics Control Board
INCRA	National Institute for Colonisation and Agrarian Reform
INPE	Brazilian National Institute of Space Research
INTERPOL	International Criminal Police Organization
ISIS	Islamic State of Iraq and Syria
ISS	Institute for Security Studies
ITRI	International Tin Research Institute
iTSCi	ITRI Tin Supply Chain Initiative
IUCN	International Union for Conservation of Nature
IUU	illegal, unreported and unregulated
LMIC	low- and middle-income countries
LNA	Libyan National Army
MAS	Mobile Authentication Service
MCS	monitoring, control and surveillance
MCSD	Monitoring, Control, and Surveillance Division
MHRA	British Medicines and Healthcare products Regulatory Agency
MINEM	Ministerio de Energía y Minas (Peruvian Ministry of Energy and Mines)
MINUSMA	United Nations Multidimensional Integrated Stabilization Mission in Mali
ML/TF	money-laundering and terrorist financing
MNE	multinational enterprises
MPLA	Movimento Popular de Libertação de Angola
MPRDA	South African Mineral and Petroleum Development Resource Act
n.d.	no date
NAAM	National Association of Artisanal Miners
NAFDAC	National Agency for Food and Drug Administration and Control of Nigeria
NEPAD	New Partnership for Africa's Development
NEST	National Environmental Security Task Force
NGO	non-governmental organisation

NMRA	national medicines regulatory authorities
NOC	Libyan National Oil Corporation
NPS	new psychoactive substances
NTR	North Texas Refinery
OC	organised crime
OCG	organised criminal groups
ODA	official development aid
OECD	Organisation for Economic Co-operation and Development
PAMP	Produits Artistiques Métaux Précieux
PFG	Petroleum Facility Guards
PQM	Promoting the Quality of Medicines
PSMA	Port State Measures Agreement
RINR	Regional Initiative against the Illegal Exploitation of Natural Resources
RCM	Regional Certification Mechanism
RFMO	Regional Fisheries Management Organisations
SDG	United Nations Sustainable Development Goal
SEAFO	South East Atlantic Fisheries Organisation
SEC	Securities and Exchange Commission
SF	substandard and falsified
SGE	Shanghai Gold Exchange
SIMP	Seafood Import Monitoring Program
SOCTA	Serious and Organised Crime Threat Assessment
SVLK	Sistem Verifikasi Legalitas Kayu, timber verification system
TOC	transnational organised crime
TRIPS	Trade-Related Aspects of Intellectual Property Rights
UAE	United Arab Emirates
UK	United Kingdom
UN	United Nations
UNCLOS	UN Convention on the Law of the Sea
UNCTAD	United Nations Conference on Trade and Development
UNECA	United Nations Economic Commission for Africa
UNEP	United Nations Environment Programme
UNESCO	United Nations Educational, Scientific and Cultural Organization
UNFSA	United Nations Fish Stocks Agreement
UNGASS	UN General Assembly Special Session on Drugs
UNODC	United Nations Office on Drugs and Crime
UNTOC	United Nations Convention against Transnational Organised Crime
US(A)	United States (of America)
USAID	United States Agency for International Development
USP	United States Pharmacopeia
VMS	Vessel Monitoring Systems
VPA	Voluntary Partnership Agreement
WCO	World Customs Organization
WHO	World Health Organization
WTO	World Trade Organization
WWF	World Wildlife Fund

Part I:
Introduction

Introduction: illicit flows, criminal markets and geopolitics[1]

Daniel Brombacher[2], Günther Maihold, Melanie Müller and Judith Vorrath

Illicit flows play a growing role in the international economy and in (trans)regional and local conflict dynamics. There is a great diversity in illegal markets and criminal activities, including a broad range of products, services and resources. Among the actors involved, it is usually the more structured organisations like Italian mafia groups – with their famous secrecy, rituals and engagement in racketeering – that get a lot of attention. Most are, however, far less "glamourous" and well-known – let alone hierarchically organised. In fact, the 2021 Serious and Organised Crime Threat Assessment (SOCTA) by Europol identifies criminal networks that resemble businesses with managerial layers and field operators as the prime actors engaged. These are linked to service providers such as document fraudsters, technical experts, financial advisors or money launderers (Europol 2021: 10). Moreover, a large share of networks operating in the EU use legal business structures in their criminal activities – according to the SOCTA more than 80 % (Europol 2021: 11). This already points to the entanglement of the legal and illegal spheres which, however, has various further dimensions. These only become fully apparent when the field of view is extended beyond the EU's internal area of freedom, security and justice in order to understand how this space is connected with various parts of the world through illicit flows.

Two features stand out: first, these flows are often transnational, linking up local actors with a much broader web of players in other world regions. Second, they are far from being tied to a separate criminal underworld, but rather have linkages and overlaps with licit markets, commercial structures and even state authorities. While the use of the label of organised crime

1 The editors would like to thank Viktoria Reisch for her tireless support in the completion of the book and Felix Pahl for the thorough editing of all the contributions.

2 Head, Global Partnership on Drug Policies and Development (GPDPD) at Deutsche Gesellschaft für Internationale Zusammenarbeit (GIZ) GmbH, Berlin, Germany. The chapter reflects exclusively the opinions of the author and not those of the Federal Ministry for Economic Cooperation and Development (BMZ) or GIZ GmbH.

(OC) can rely on a group-based definition in the Palermo Convention that entered into force in 2003, it is often difficult to apply to different contexts.[3] Moreover, how the view from European countries and the EU in particular to the outside has itself undergone significant change is reflected in the EU Strategy to tackle Organised Crime 2021–2025 (European Commission 2021).

A relevant reference in the 2003 European Security Strategy strongly echoed the preoccupation with terrorism as the first key threat, followed by the proliferation of weapons of mass destruction, regional conflicts, state failure and, finally, organised crime. It stressed the external dimension of OC with reference to "cross-border trafficking in drugs, women, illegal migrants and weapons" and its possible links with terrorism (CoEU 2003: 6). Moreover, the strategy outlined the convergence of the internal and external dimension of the threat by pointing to examples like Afghanistan, from where allegedly 90 % of the heroin in Europe came while at the same time profits made in the drug trade financed "private armies" there (CoEU 2003: 7). This very much set the tone for how the view on transnational organised crime (TOC) would evolve at the interface of internal and external security. However, the wider international debate extended to organised crime as an obstacle for development and a stress factor as well as a source of violence particularly in fragile states (e.g. World Bank 2011). The Sustainable Development Goals established in 2015 include a specific target to "reduce illicit financial and arms flows, strengthen the recovery and return of stolen assets and combat all forms of organized crime" (UNGA 2015: 25), but also several targets on related matters, such as those referring to the eradication of human trafficking and exploitation. At the time, organised crime trickled into the rhetoric of foreign and security policy documents on a wider scale. The EU Global Strategy adopted the following year is no exception in this regard. It repeatedly refers to organised crime, links it to various issues (terrorism, migration, conflict prevention or border security) and calls for stronger institutional links between external and internal action to tackle it and related threats (EU 2016: 20; 36; 50). The general attention for OC has been growing, and so has the number of regional or national strategies and action plans. Yet, its understanding has remained limited, and at times the meaning of the term is controversial. Furthermore, the actual responses that follow political rhetoric are the final indicators of objectives and priorities pursued – whether in domestic or foreign policy. Beyond traditional law enforce-

---

3 See the contribution of Mark Shaw and Alex Goodwin in this volume.

ment cooperation schemes, there are many programmes by the EU and its member states to support third countries or regions in the fight against OC. Their focus is usually on establishing or harmonising regulatory frameworks, developing national or regional strategies and building capacities, particularly of security agencies. In doing so, European actors are entering settings with different legal, social and political frameworks that may not easily fit into their understanding of organised crime.

Flows, paths and spaces of the illegal have in recent years become of growing interest not only for the authorities in charge of law enforcement but also in the academic community (Hudson 2014). While the first approaches tried to define and consider the scope of illegality and crime in quantitative terms with rather mixed results (for an evaluation of the results see Andreas and Greenhill 2010), the next generation of the literature focused on the practices and logics of criminal organisations (Reuter 1983) and the criminogenic conditions for the expansion of the criminal operations (Albanese 2015) as well as on international regimes with a special emphasis on the control of drug trafficking and growing violence (Collins 2018). In recent years, the spatial and transnational dimensions of illicit flows have come under consideration with respect to the different organisational modalities that accompany illicit flows, the actors involved and the preferred locations (van Schendel and Abraham 2005a). In the context of the global crime approaches (Pearce and Woodiwiss 1993), the structure of illegal markets (Dewey et al. 2019) and the functioning of the respective supply chains have been the object of new publications (Beckert and Dewey 2017).

The circulation of illegal goods and services as well as the specifics of their international transshipment have been of major importance in research (Dávila et al. 2021), on value generation along the respective supply chain concerning the social and ecological harm that is allocated at the different stages of production, transit and consumption (Magliocca et al. 2021). The heterogeneous character of supply chains, goods and services makes it quite difficult to get a clear picture of the logics, the structural factors and the operational modalities of different supply chains. For this reason, in recent years comparative research designs have tried to generate new knowledge with respect to different supply chain arrangements and/or illicit goods and services. According to these studies, which have received major attention in the *Journal of Illicit Economies and Development*, a list of elements has been identified that should be taken into account when analysing illicit supply chains, e.g. price and spatial structures in the upstream and downstream sections of those chains, differential regulation of goods and services, varying transaction costs due to risk evaluations of possible or real detection and interdiction, the number and distribution of actors involved, volume and value assignments per shipment and the value captured along the different stages of the supply chain. What characterises these supply chains is their dynamics in space and time, with a more decentralised organisation in multi-nodal and multi-route logistics which in some cases overlap with those of licit supply chains while in others taking separate approaches due to the changing risks of detection by the authorities. So the calculus of streamlining in the supply chain management as its basic turns out more complex when dealing with illicit goods and services, as diffuse and changing trade networks will result due to the specific requirements of social embeddedness of the illicit flows in corruptible contexts. The strategies of the operators to shift routes and corridors in response to law enforcement or growing pressure from competing agents are producing additional externalities for civil society, the environment and the coexistence of legal and illegal actors.

The empirical evidence of the above-mentioned comparative studies does not show a very wide range of key similarities in the different supply chain arrangements, as the patterns of the material, financial and social interactions as well as their specific embeddedness differ. There appears to be a general consensus that the different goods and services from drugs and arms trade through illicit wildlife, illegal mining to human smuggling and organ trade represent different forms and variants of illicitness due to diverging definitions of legality in the national jurisdictions through which the respective products and services pass on their way to the consumer markets. These ways of "the making of illicitness" (van Schendel and Abraham 2005b) correspond to diverging social practices and regulatory spaces, especially when the respective goods pass through transformations and the change of meanings which lend concepts of illicitness a certain degree of fluidity (van Schendel and Abraham 2005b: 24). This does not mean that in certain moments and places illegality and illicitness coincide (as in the case of blood diamonds), but it would be analytically and politically negligent to assume the concurrence of the two dimensions in every case study. Again, as in many studies on criminal phenomena, one has to be careful to make the distinction that "congruence of behavior does not imply identity of purpose" (van Schendel and Abraham 2005b: 32), a conclusion that is supported by the different cases presented in this volume on the one hand and by the overlap of legal and illegal procedures in supply chains worldwide on the other.

Starting from these general observations, this book aims to examine different dimensions of illicit flows and asks how they can be understood through a geographical perspective that looks from the Global South to

Europe. One central dimension of its contributions refers to the study of transactions, the way in which these exchanges occur and possible repetitive trade cycles that shift objects and assets from licit to illicit and vice versa and produce market structures in varying shades of grey. Essentially this dimension is about the actors and practices embedded in illicit flows, key drivers and incentives as well as modi operandi. The main aim of the volume is to generate insights into the merging of illegal, grey and legal markets at certain points of the production chain and to trace linkages to organised crime.

Conceptual basis and cross-cutting themes

In recent years, the previously dominant interpretation of TOC as a security challenge has gradually changed. Different interpretations of harm associated with TOC have led scholars to move beyond the traditional security scheme of what has been defined as "illicit globalization" (Andreas 2011) or "deviant globalization" (Gilman et al. 2013). The study of illegal and illicit economies has taken a turn towards a multidisciplinary approach, e.g., analysing illicit economies from the perspective of development (Gillies, Collins and Soderholm 2019) or the environment (Brombacher, Garzón and Vélez 2021).

Despite the evolution of a multidisciplinary research agenda and normative efforts at the UN level, still even basic terminology lacks broad consensus. Most prominently, this includes the lack of a generalised understanding of what is considered legal/illegal or licit/illicit, which criteria are used to assess criminal endeavours as organised and transnational and how illicit flows may be distinguished from illicit markets or criminal markets. Therefore, the use of terminology has become somewhat arbitrary across the different strands of research and analysis.

Given the strongly fluctuating character of illicitness and illegality depending on legal, societal and cultural criteria and patterns (Portes and Haller 2005; De Theije et al. 2014), the editors of this volume have decided not to provide a common definition of key terminology to the authors. With the focus of this volume on geographically wide-ranging supply chains, a unified definition of illicitness and illegality would become even more difficult to apply consistently. In areas of limited or absent statehood, societal and cultural patterns of definition may fully replace legal criteria and therefore become the key determining element of legitimacy of an economic activity and thus of illicitness and licitness (Felbab-Brown 2018). Mackenzie (2002) has identified four different types of illicit supply chains, with characters of illicitness and licitness fluctuating between source, transit and destination countries. This pattern of transient forms of illicitness also applies to several case studies in this volume. Quite surprisingly, despite, at least for some goods and services, almost universal control regimes, the shifting legal character of commodities appears to be rather the rule than the exception.

The complexity stemming from changing legal characteristics of goods and services generates major difficulties for the authorities in dealing with TOC and managing to control grey areas. Evidence shows that criminal organisations are capable of exploiting the ever-changing legal definitions along supply chains. Therefore, it makes sense not to apply a pattern of clear-cut "categorical distinctions between licit and illicitness, but continuums of state practice (...), which encompass organized criminality, and enterprises that span the licit/illicit spectrum" (Hall 2013: 372).

Given these terminological challenges, this volume suggests a new framework of analysis for illicit economies. The editors have sought to apply a supply chain perspective to illicit economies. This supply chain lens builds on an analytical framework that allows for a focus on spatial aspects of illicit economies and on the convergence of licit and illicit markets instead of narrowing down the scope of the volume along the traditional dichotomy of criminality and legality. A key assumption guiding this volume is that "Underworld and Upperworld" (Galeotti 2001) are not clearly separated, but mutually dependent and converging.

The concept of supply chains appears to be promising, as it does not a priori distinguish between licit and illicit market transactions, but highlights their mutual connectedness. Hence, the scope of the book is not limited to a rather narrow definition of TOC but starts from the configuration of spatially distant corporate, state and criminal actors in a range of different illegal market activities. Furthermore, in contrast to many single-market studies, a supply chain approach does not focus merely on sections of transnational supply chains but allows the full array of transactions from source to destination to be analysed. Supply chains are economic structures where the legal and illegal flows overlap and mix, creating highly attractive environments for criminal rent-seeking, not least because of the heavy impact of illegality on price formation and because of diverging schemes of prohibition along the supply chain. The term "shadow value chain"[4] appears particularly appealing in order to describe the blending of

4 There is an entire literature on the diverging meanings of "value chains" and "supply chains"; for our purpose this is a matter of perspective, as the supply chain

legal/illegal and licit/illicit elements within a single value chain. Shadow value chains can be defined as those "that run, often in parallel, or intertwined with legal value chains" (Stridsman and Østensen 2017: 6), which fits with the fact that the diversion of resources from the legal interchange enables and sponsors other types of illicit activities. So the perspective of shadow value chains seems to correspond to the convergence view of criminal markets, with supply chains being the structures which serve these markets with goods and services. While even in shadow value chains some of the transactions may be visible, the shadowy nature of the value chain is defined by its constrained conditions of access. Criminal actors try to control access to the markets they are providing with their goods and services, thus reducing competition and participation in the value chains.

The geopolitical dimension

Independent of the legal character of the respective goods and services, all supply chains in this volume can be described as shadow supply chains. While drug crop cultivation, illegal mining and illicit logging activities are highly visible at the initial stage of the supply chain, most subsequent transactions within the respective value chain remain in the shadows or are blended with and disguised in licit trade. It is only at the end-consumer stage that these goods and services tend to resurface. A pattern of *geopolitics of the illicit* appears, in which criminal actors exploit geographical spaces and their respective legal regimes in order to maximise profit and to reduce risk along the respective supply chains. This pattern links highly diverse sets of legitimate and criminal actors with different interests, organisational features and roles in functional macro-networks of the global sphere. This perspective allows to view "pieces and nodes in recombinant chains with links that can merge and decouple as necessary" (Farah 2012: 2).

In essence, this merging and decoupling is the nature of the geopolitics of the illicit: geopolitics along supply chains are driven by rent-seeking and risk avoidance, as in classical realist geopolitical theory. However, the geopolitics of the illicit are governed by a plethora of legitimate business, criminal and state interests, while traditional approaches to geopolitics

---

perspective includes all physical logistics operations along the product creation process, while the value chain perspective focuses on the step-by-step increase in value.

are guided by state-centred assumptions. The manifestation of illicit flows relates to the state in different ways: as a space where a specific set of laws, rules and standards apply and as an actor defending this order against those challenging it, such as criminal groups or networks. Moreover, key aspects of geopolitical considerations like space, distance and resources are also clearly drivers of the routes and modi operandi of "the illicit". Yet it is important to make clear that the geopolitical terminology is not meant to convey the idea of global criminal enterprises that possess a high level of organisational capabilities that allow them to organise full-fledged supply chains from plant to plate and take geopolitical decisions on a global scale. Over the past decades, research has shown that organised crime tends to work rather locally and to control only a minor part of the transactions within a given transnational value chain (Galeotti 2001: 208; Reuter 1983: 109–117; von Lampe 2012: 183). The case of the Calabrian 'Ndrangheta, which manages to control and govern entire value chains from source countries in the Global South up to destination countries in the Global North (Catino 2019: 152–205), appears to be rather exceptional. The contributions to this book show that the geopolitics of the illicit tend to be driven by localised rationales and limited criminal capabilities, lacking centralised governance structures, in all the stages of supply chains and independent of the respective jurisdictions.

Contributions

This volume sheds light on these geopolitics of the illicit, displaying how transnational shadow supply chains oscillate between illegality and legality, illicitness and licitness, depending on time, space and involved actors. The narrative of a geopolitical nature of shadow value chains is built on a broad array of thematic contributions and disciplines. These cover relatively well-understood markets of prohibited goods and services such as drugs, counterfeit medicines and human trafficking. But the supply chain approach allows the scope of analysis to be broadened towards licit goods that are produced, harvested or trafficked illicitly and/or illegally. It covers a wide spectrum, ranging from cultural goods and conflict minerals to criminal activities such as IUU fishing, illicit logging as well as artisanal gold mining. A special focus has been placed on natural resource supply chains in order to broaden the dominant view of organised crime scholars on illicit goods and services to mostly considered licit value chains. Given the legality of the respective commodities, natural resource supply chains are usually considered licit, while potentially illicit transactions within the chain tend to be overlooked or ignored. There is a maximal convergence of licit and illicit transactions in natural resource supply chains that requires a renewed focus beyond the standard analysis of TOC.

In order to contribute to a better understanding of the geopolitical character of the organisation of shadow supply chains, this volume seeks to promote a holistic view, analysing the supply chains from the hubs and nodes of supply to transit and consumption. In most cases, the editors have come across patterns of transnational and transregional value chains that link the Global South to Northern consumer markets. This pattern prevails in the contributions to this volume. To enhance the multidisciplinary approach, the editors have decided to invite academics, policymakers and practitioners. Thus, this volume gathers contributions from international scholars from both the Global South and the Global North as well as chapters from professionals in law enforcement, development cooperation and journalism. We expect that the diversity of themes and authors adds to the quality of policy analysis and recommendations developed across this book and that the policy recommendations contribute to improving policies and programmes that aim to curb criminal business and organised crime at the national, regional and global levels.

The authors of the **first part** lay the theoretical and conceptual foundation for the volume. ***Marc Shaw and Alex Goodwin*** describe the conceptual challenges of the discussion on organised crime and illicit markets, in which different definitions are used to describe the same phenomena. They explore the differences between "legal" and "illegal" but also the shades of grey in between and show that the state of certain goods can change at different stages of the supply chain: "This interplay between what is 'legal' and what is 'illegal' is a big part of all illegal flows/markets and their regulation. This is especially noticeable in the case of grey markets when illicit flows (for example of people, gold or timber) converge with and blend into legal flows. (Alternatively, an initially legal good can become illegal when diverted from a legal supply chain)." The authors therefore also advocate an approach that takes into account the actors at the various stages of a shadow supply chain and thus opens up a broader understanding of the various interdependencies in illicit markets. They propose a policy approach that focuses first and foremost on the harm caused by criminal activities in order to outline priorities in dealing with organised crime. The second chapter by ***Günther Maihold*** investigates the connection between shadow supply chains and criminal markets. He challenges the assumption of a "geographical convergence of illicit flows and criminal networks" in which transnational networks of organised crime "have cast a net of contacts and cooperation around the globe that the authorities are not able to control". By using an approach that focuses on various stages of different shadow supply chains, the author is able to show that the individual actors are more diffusely linked and often less connected than the literature suggests. While there are linkages between powerful actors at various points, there are also different supply chain linkages that are less entangled and follow a cost-benefit logic of the actors. This chapter thus sheds light on the role of actors who are often less in the focus of discussions on supply chains but who are key connection points in transnationally organised shadow supply chains: intermediaries, transporters and criminal diasporas. To minimise the risk of shadow supply chains being established, the author suggests a number of instruments for de-risking supply chains. This could be achieved by market players making their supply chains more transparent and establishing closer relationships with their trading partners.

The **second part** is dedicated to the more classical cases of illicit flows and investigates the links between the Global North and the Global South in these established relationships. The first two chapters focus on the global drug economy, which is considered to be one of the most harmful but also the best studied illicit economy. ***Fatjona Mejdini*** focuses in her chapter on "one of the most important European suppliers of illicit cannabis throughout the continent for almost two decades": Albania. She traces the historical development of cannabis cultivation in Albania, which plays a significant economic role in the country, and sheds light on the role of criminal networks that profit from the illegal trade in the drug. The author describes the Albanian government's efforts to curb trafficking and the associated money laundering as rather timid. Enforcement and interdiction are complicated by the fact that Albanian networks are closely linked to criminal networks from other countries, which enables transnational trafficking. In the second chapter with a focus on drug value chains, ***Daniel Brombacher*** focuses on the three most relevant plant-based drug economies. He finds the non-convergence of supply and demand and weak deterrence to be key defining structural elements across plant-based drug value chains. While the global drug control regime has come under pressure in recent years, most of the global debate on drugs still relies on a set of standard supply-side indicators. Brombacher argues that supply-side indicators are essentially positivist and are often misinterpreted, which contributes to a distorted understanding of the organisational principles of transnational drug markets. Based on an analysis of structural and actor-based approaches, the chapter concludes that structural factors appear to be essential for understanding how these value chains evolve. In the last chapter of the second part of the book, ***Judith Vorrath*** investigates trafficking of Nigerian women and girls to Western and Southern European countries for sexual exploitation. Her chapter focuses on the different stages of this human trafficking and its evolution over time in order to better understand how its peculiar features are embedded in a wider set of dynamics and incentives along the chain. With this particular analytical lens on the linkages between West Africa and Europe, she highlights how illicit and licit aspects converge in the trafficking business and the multi-faceted links involved that are not merely the product of an isolated criminal phenomenon.

The **third part** investigates the illicit trade in goods which have not been the focus of academic and policy debates but have received increased attention in recent years. The first chapter by ***Jan Schubert*** examines the field of trafficking in cultural objects. This is considered to be one of the most persistent illicit trades, alongside arms and narcotics. The author describes the linkages of transnational organised groups that link actors in Europe – which has one of the most important markets for arts and cultural objects – with actors from the Global South, which is being culturally drained and where the illicit trade in cultural property is being used to fund terrorist activities. In order to tackle the criminal trade in cultural objects, Jan Schubert proposes a holistic approach. The second chapter investigates the trade in substandard and falsified (SF) medicines, which appears to be a very timely topic because the COVID-19 pandemic led to a global surge in SF medicines. ***Nhomsai Hagen, Cathrin Hauk and Lutz Heide*** show that the increasing complexity of supply chains in a globalised world and the growing popularity of e-commerce provide numerous entry points for illegal medical products in both the Global South and the Global North. The authors argue that constrained access, weak technical capacity and poor governance contribute to the emergence of SF medicines. Because this kind of trade has a multidimensional impact on public health as well as severe economic and socioeconomic consequences, the authors suggest key elements to combat SF medicines: prevention, detection and response with united, global participation of all parties involved. The last chapter in the third part by ***Peter Fabricius*** looks at illicit financial flows (IFF), focusing on the links between Africa and Europe, which have received increased attention only in recent years. Political decision-makers as well as academics have become sensitised to the problem and are more seriously trying to staunch the flows. On a global level, the G20 and the OECD have been negotiating international rules which aim at preventing multinational enterprises (MNEs) from avoiding taxes by domiciling in tax havens. On the African continent, awareness has also increased, and African countries are trying to increase coordination to prevent these practices by MNEs, which have serious economic and financial consequences for affected countries. Fabricius argues that crime IFFs (money from crimes such as trafficking of contraband or corruption) could be even more harmful than commercial IFFs such as tax fraud. He argues that more attention is need in order to combat these practices.

The fourth part of the book focuses on the illicit in natural resource supply chains. ***Ina Tessnow-von Wysocki, Dyhia Belhabib and Philippe Le Billon*** investigate the linkages between illegal fishing and markets in the European Union. While illegal, unreported and unregulated (IUU) fishing is predominantly occurring in low-income countries in the Global South, target markets are often located in countries of the Global North, including countries in the European Union. The chapter focuses on illegally caught fish within EU markets, analysing the role of different actors in illegal fishing activities and their modus operandi. The authors investigate in particular the case of illegally caught fish from Ghana making its way to the markets of the European Union and provide policy recommendations on how to approach IUU as a problem that puts marine environments and coastal populations at risk. ***Inga Carry and Günther Maihold*** analyse the illegal flow of timber products from producer countries in the Global South to consumer countries in the Global North. Illegal timber supply chains are characterised by a three-stage process: *harvesting*, during which the timber is illegally cut and transported; *laundering*, i.e. the process of making illegally cut timber indistinguishable from legal timber; and *integration*, whereby the illegal timber is introduced and integrated into the legal global timber supply chain. The authors illustrate this for the case studies of Brazil, Indonesia and Malaysia, which are global hotspots for illegal logging and timber trade. They argue for an integrated criminal justice strategy that, beyond forest management, includes strategies to counter corruption, financial crime and organised criminal networks. In the last chapter of the fourth part, ***Lorenzo Bagnoli*** follows the path of crude oil that is smuggled from Libya to the EU. According to the author, "[t]he Libyan turmoil is a perfect environment for the growth of organised crime groups. The chess game about the stabilisation of Libya between international actors such as Turkey, Russia, Egypt, the United Arab Emirates and the European Union – and the resulting split of its resources – has so far been another factor of instability". Bagnoli looks at the connections of different actors involved in the smuggling of oil and focuses on the special role of intermediaries as a link between the Global North and the Global South. In addition, the author discusses the mechanisms that allow the illicit trade to continue despite international attempts to stop it and argues that a discernible unification process is a precondition for tackling the problem of illegal smuggling in Libya. In many cases, smuggling is the only way to survive, and the current economic situation creates many incentives for people to get involved in illegal economies. Interventions should target legal actors in the Global North and the Global South who facilitate illegal trade rather than focusing on actors who get involved in smuggling in order to survive.

The **fifth part** is dedicated to illicit flows of metals, in particular the supply chain of gold, which also plays an important role in the context of high socioeconomic inequality. ***Melanie Müller*** investigates the case of South Africa, which has not yet succeeded in formalising artisanal mining. In South Africa, two parallel supply chains exist: the legal supply chain of gold that has developed around industrial mining, making South Africa one of the most important gold exporters on the African continent, and the illegal supply chain of gold from artisanal extraction that plays a central role because it ensures survival for various groups. The chapter explains how gold from artisanal mining – in South Africa that means from illicit or illegal trade – is transferred to the legal supply chain; it shows that legal and illegal practices intersect and that both legal and illegal actors are involved at various stages of the supply chain and thus enable the trade in illicit gold. The chapter further highlights the central role of international trading hubs (such as the United Arab Emirates) as facilitators of illicit gold trade. It highlights the need for a holistic view of supply chains that focuses not only on resource extraction but also on the role of transportation and trade in order to tackle the illicit trade in gold. ***Gerardo Damonte and Bettina Schorr*** observe similar patterns in the Andean region. They describe the emergence of a hybrid regime in the supply chain of artisanal gold from Peru. Artisanal mining was legalised in 2012, but some artisanal miners operate without a licence or extract gold in prohibited areas. As a result, legal, illegal and informal artisanal gold mining practices coexist and overlap at various points in the supply chain. The authors criticise existing international approaches to regulating gold supply chains as inadequate and argue for an approach that places a stronger emphasis on legal actors involved in illegal practices in addition to illegal practices and actors. In the final chapter of the fifth part of the book, ***Stefan Bauchowitz and Leopold von Carlowitz*** take a closer look at these international regulatory approaches and describe the development of "an emerging regulatory regime to fight the trade in conflict minerals". The authors describe the process of due diligence of so-called conflict minerals as a process of "norm diffusion" that first developed as a result of civil society pressure and was later taken up by governmental actors, culminating at the European level in the adoption of the EU Conflict Minerals Regulation.

The case studies across the five parts show how criminal actors employ different strategies to penetrate the licit economy, exploit weak or absent statehood, subvert public institutions and erode the rule of law in the transit of goods and services through different jurisdictions. The geopolitical calculus in the supply of (European) criminal markets from the Global South consists in using the networked environment of supply chain structures in order to profit from low state surveillance and potentiate the agility of the criminal actors to adapt to and capitalise on the changes in routes and technologies. As criminal groups avoid detection and exploit the differences of applicable national jurisdictions and legal frameworks, the authorities are encouraged to advance their cooperation frameworks beyond traditional ways of sharing information to new levels of interoperability and the confiscation of criminal proceeds. In order to keep pace with the geopolitical patterns of TOC, transnational intelligence is also needed to disrupt and dismantle criminal organisations. New instruments such as digital forensics, open source intelligence and darknet investigations are indispensable for preventing new pathways for illicit flows to the consumer markets and involve the local level in the surveillance operations from the beginning through transparency and due diligence standards. At the same time, the case studies show that enhanced law enforcement efforts as well as addressing legal loopholes created by differences between jurisdictions need to be complemented by new approaches. As much as illicit flows link Europe with the Global South, their social and economic embeddedness, as well as the opportunities and harms they produce differ significantly. Varying shades of grey characterise market structures, but also the geopolitics of the illicit in a wider sense. Therefore, inclusive approaches that engage the authorities at all levels and stages in the shadow supply chains as well as civil society are essential. In order to permit for collective action against organised crime some common ground on key objectives and priorities between partners – whether state or non-state – needs to emerge. Particularly where trade cycles shift objects and assets from licit to illicit and vice versa there might be various entry points for increasing transparency and accountability in market structures that still take into account the livelihood aspect for sections of the population that depend on income from these flows. In other cases, addressing social, economic and political conditions that fuel illicit supply chains with clearly criminal agendas should be part of any response that attempts to be sustainable.

References

Albanese, Jay (2015): Organized crime. From the mob to Transnational Organized Crime. New York: Routledge.

Andreas, Peter/Greenhill, Kelly M. (eds.) (2010): Sex, drugs, and body counts. The politics of numbers in global crime and conflict. Ithaca: Cornell University Press.

Andreas, Peter (2011): "Illicit globalization. Myths, misconceptions, and historical lessons". In: Political Science Quarterly, 126, 3, pp. 403–425.

Beckert, Jens/Dewey, Matías (2017): The architecture of illegal markets. Towards an economic sociology of illegality in the economy. Oxford: Oxford University Press.

Catino, Maurizio (2019): Mafia organizations. The visible hand of criminal enterprise. Cambridge: Cambridge University Press.

Collins, John (2018): "Rethinking 'flexibilities' in the international drug control system. Potential, precedents and models for reforms". In: International Journal of Drug Policy, 60, pp. 107–114.

CoEU, Council of the European Union (2003): "A secure Europe in a better world. European security strategy. 15895/03, Brussels, 8 December 2003". At: https://data.consilium.europa.eu/doc/document/ST-15895-2003-INIT/en/pdf (accessed 7 June 2022).

Dávila, Anayansi/Magliocca, Nicholas/McSweeney, Kendra/Rueda, Ximena (2021): "Spatialising illicit commodity chains. Comparing coffee and cocaine". In: Area, 53, 3, pp. 501–510.

Dewey, Matías/Dohmen, Caspar/Engwicht, Nina/Hübschle, Annette (2019): Schattenwirtschaft. Die Macht der illegalen Märkte. Berlin: Wagenbach.

European Commission (2021): "Communication from the Commission to the European Parliament, the Council, the European Economic and Social Committee and the Committee of the Regions on the EU Strategy to tackle Organised Crime 2021–2025. COM/2021/170 final". At: https://eur-lex.europa.eu/legal-content/EN/TXT/?uri=CELEX:52021DC0170 (accessed 7 June 2022).

EU, European Union (2016): "Shared vision, common action: a stronger Europe. A global strategy for the European Union's foreign and security policy". At: https://op.europa.eu/en/publication-detail/-/publication/3eaae2cf-9ac5-11e6-868c-01aa75ed71a1 (accessed 7 June 2022).

Europol (2021): European Union Serious and Organised Crime Threat Assessment (SOCTA). A corrupting influence: the infiltration and undermining of Europe's economy and society by organised crime. Publications Office of the European Union, Luxembourg.

Galeotti, Mark (2001): „Underworld and upperworld. Transnational organized crime and global society". In: Josselin, Daphné/Wallace/William (eds.): Non-state actors in world politics. London: Palgrave Macmillan, pp. 203–217.

Gilman, Nils/Goldhammer, Jesse/Weber, Steven (2013): "Deviant globalization". In: Miklaucic, Michael/Brewer, Jacqueline (eds.): Convergence. Illicit networks and national security in the age of globalization. Washington, DC: National Defense University Press, pp. 3–14.

Hall, Tim (2013): "Geographies of the illicit. Globalization and organized crime". In: Progress in Human Geography, 37, 3, pp. 366–385.

Hudson, Ray (2014): "Thinking through the relationships between legal and illegal activities and economies. Spaces, flows and pathways". In: Journal of Economic Geography, 14, 4, pp. 775–795.

Mackenzie, Simon (2002): "Organised crime and common transit networks". In: Trends & Issues in Crime and Criminal Justice No. 233. At: https://traffickingculture.org/publications/mackenzie-s-2002-organised-crime-common-transit-networks-trends-issues-in-crime-and-criminal-justice-no-233-canberra-australian-institute-of-criminology/ (accessed 7 June 2022).

Magliocca, Nicholas/Torres, Aurora/Margulies, Jared/McSweeney, Kendra/Arroyo-Quiroz, Inés et al. (2021): "Comparative analysis of illicit supply network structure and operations. Cocaine, wildlife, and sand". In: Journal of Illicit Economies and Development, 3, 1, pp. 50–73.

Pearce, Frank/Woodiwiss, Michael (eds.) (1993): Global crime connections. Dynamics and control. London: Palgrave.

Reuter, Peter (1983): Disorganized Crime. Illegal Markets and the Mafia. Cambridge, Mass: The MIT Press.

Stridsman, Mats/Østensen, Åse Gilje (2017): Shadow value chains. Tracing the link between corruption, illicit activity and lootable natural resources from West Africa. Bergen: U4 Anti-Corruption Resource Centre, Chr. Michelsen Institute.

UNGA, United Nations General Assembly (2015): Resolution adopted by the General Assembly on 25 September 2015. Transforming our world: the 2030 Agenda for Sustainable Development. A/RES/70/1, 21 October 2015.

Van Schendel, Willem/Abraham, Itty (eds.) (2005a): Illicit flows and criminal things: states, borders, and the other side of globalization. Bloomington: Indiana University Press.

Van Schendel, Willem/Abraham, Itty (2005b): „Introduction. The making of illicitness". In: Van Schendel, Willem/Abraham, Itty (eds.): Illicit flows and criminal things: states, borders, and the other side of globalization. Bloomington: Indiana University Press, pp. 1–37.

Von Lampe, Klaus (2012): "Transnational organized crime challenges for future research". In: Crime, Law and Social Change, 58, pp. 179–194.

World Bank (2011): World Development Report 2011. Conflict, security, and development. Washington DC.

Re-evaluating organised crime and illicit markets: a path towards a new response

Mark Shaw and Alex Goodwin[*]

Introduction

Since the early 1990s, the world has witnessed a boom in what is now referred to as "organised crime", a phenomenon that accelerated even more dramatically in the new millennium as globalisation gained pace. But effective action to combat this phenomenon has been lacking, and policy discussions have proceeded glacially in the face of rapid criminal change and innovation.

This chapter argues that the debate around the expansion of global organised crime and criminal markets and the associated response have been hamstrung by several definitional and conceptual challenges regarding "organised crime" and "illicit markets". In part, this struggle with terminology dates back to the very beginning of a coordinated response to organised crime, when states famously could not agree on a definition of "organised crime" during the negotiations for the United Nations Convention against Transnational Organised Crime (UNTOC). This reflected a wider uncertainty about the nature of the new criminal challenge: until the convention was opened for signature and ratification in the early 2000s, terms such as "organised crime group" and "mafia" were seldom used or understood outside a few national jurisdictions.

Two decades later, arguably the opposite problem exists: terminology which once applied to a few countries has now been applied to many, with some countries embracing and others rejecting the "organised crime" label for different forms of illicit behaviour and markets. "We have a serious challenge", said one senior crime intelligence official from South Africa, which scores badly on the Global Initiative against Transnational Organized Crime (GI-TOC) Global Organized Crime Index and is widely regarded as having an organised crime problem, "but we don't have an organised crime problem like with mafias".[1]

* With thanks to Tuesday Reitano and Judith Vorrath.
1 Interview with Mark Shaw.

Unfortunately, she couldn't be further from the truth. Even some academics who have built careers studying mafias in developed countries find it hard to widen their lens for the multitude of criminal and mafia-like formations that are now present elsewhere. The extent and diversity of criminal activity and the difficulty in describing that activity have resulted in some confusion among policymakers in multiple places and to some extent clouded the debate on solutions. Much of the terminology around what may be termed the 'global illicit' is often confusing, and different phrases are used to describe an array of challenges.

Furthermore, the debate over illicit markets and organised crime is characterised by a relatively high degree of fragmentation, in part because expert analysis is generally required to understand individual markets, with the result that the overall concept of organised crime and the principles of regulating the illicit are rarely discussed amongst policymakers. This is one of the reasons that this volume is important, seeking as it does to provide an analysis of multiple illicit markets within the same framework. This is especially vital since, as this chapter will argue, a comparison of harms between the various illicit markets is essential in prioritising the response.

What is clear is that the time is right for a rethink on how to deal with illicit markets and organised crime. The global policy response to organised crime is largely being built on the foundation of UNTOC, but that foundation is shaky. Due to political disagreement, the convention has taken years to gain traction, with a (weak) review mechanism only agreed quite recently.[2] There is currently little or no data to provide any accurate indication of whether or not the convention has achieved any real impact on the ground. While international cooperation is almost always urged as the prescription to fight organised crime at every UN meeting on the subject, the available evidence suggests that, in the main, it is only like-minded (generally democratic) states that achieve effective cooperation, although there are notable exceptions. There is still no clear global strategy to respond to organised crime, and meaningful state cooperation to respond to cross-border criminal activity is much less widespread than is often assumed.

While the global response remains disjointed, criminal markets are thriving. Drug production and use[3] globally are at an all-time high. Over

---

2 The Mechanism for the Review of the Implementation of the United Nations Convention against Transnational Organized Crime and the Protocols thereto was launched in October 2020 (UNODC n.d.-a).

3 There are many challenges in collecting accurate data concerning drug use, and UNODC urges caution in comparing estimates across different years, but there is

the last few years cocaine, heroin and methamphetamine production have all increased significantly.[4] The COVID-19 pandemic did little to disrupt drug markets, which have proved to be highly resilient, in part due to decades of enforcement action that have removed all but the most effective and dynamic actors (EMCDDA 2021; Shaw and Reitano 2021). Exploitation of and illegal trade in environmental commodities are also now probably more widespread and extensive than at any previous time in global history.[5] Illegal fishing fleets are decimating global fishing stocks (GI-TOC 2019), and the rate of illegal forestry clearance was perceived to have increased significantly in some places during the pandemic.[6] While illegal trade in wildlife slowed in the first months after the pandemic hit, a level of trade did resume (and online trade notably increased), and there were several large seizures in later months – including 626 kilograms of

evidence of an increase. According to UNODC's 2021 World Drug Report, between 2010 and 2019, the global number of past-year users of any drug was estimated to have increased from 226 million to 274 million. This represents a rise of 22 per cent, although UNODC cites global population growth as partially responsible for this rise, with the number of people aged 15–64 increasing by 10 % (UNODC 2021: 19).

4 Global cocaine manufacture hit record levels in 2019, despite decreasing areas of coca under cultivation, while opium production has been consistently high at around 7,400 tonnes per year since 2018 (there was a dramatic spike in 2017, when opium production reached 9,000 tonnes). Seizures of synthetic drugs soared 12-fold between 2001 and 2019, with a 30-fold increase in amphetamine-type stimulants in the same period. Cannabis seizures have declined since 2015, but the quantities of cannabis seized far outstrip seizures of other drugs, and it remains the most widely cultivated drug. The decline in seizures may also reflect changing law enforcement approaches to cannabis (UNODC 2021: 51–56).

5 According to a 2016 report by UNEP and INTERPOL, environmental crime had increased dramatically over the course of a few decades to become the fourth-largest crime market, with an annual growth of 5–7 % in the previous decade (with some sub-sectors witnessing a rise of 21–28 %). In 2018, the World Atlas of Illicit Flows estimated that environmental crime (including illegal exploitation and theft of oil) was the third-largest illicit market, after drugs and counterfeit goods, and the largest conflict finance sector (Nellemann et al. 2016; Nellemann et al. 2018).

6 There were reports of increased local illegal logging in the Congo Basin and Sulawesi, Indonesia, but it should be noted that Indonesia's overall primary forest loss rate decreased for the fourth year in a row. Globally, there was a 12 % increase in forest loss during 2020 compared to 2019, the vast majority of which occurred in Brazil. However, using a three-year trend analysis (which overcomes uncertainty of data in year-on-year analysis) shows that levels in 2020 were still in fact declining from highs in 2016 and 2017 (see Chandra 2021; Mbzibain et al. 2021; Weisse and Goldman 2021). For an analysis of the lack of a macro-level link between the pandemic and deforestation, see Wunder et al. (2021).

ivory in Cameroon – although seizures overall were well below previous years (TRAFFIC 2020). Yet this drop in seizures is not necessarily good news, as fears have grown that traffickers have been stockpiling for the time when restrictions of movement ease (Abano and Chavez 2021; Maron 2021).

The numbers of smuggled migrants also dropped during the early stages of the pandemic (INTERPOL 2020), but the widespread economic impact of the pandemic (together with conflict and poor livelihood prospects) will only incentivise more to move. Higher barriers – be it from states' fear of contagion or exclusionary nationalism – have also provided opportunities for criminal networks to hike the price they charge for those eager to move. Cybercrime has also matured into a fully fledged criminal market, driven by the exigencies of life under the pandemic when millions of people spent more time online, providing a ready market for fraudsters and scammers. There has also been a rapid expansion in sophisticated ransomware attacks – 2020 saw a 485 % increase in reports of ransomware attacks compared to 2019 (Bitdefender 2021) – with many targeting major companies, including national infrastructure. In May 2021, Colonial Pipeline, which supplies almost half of the US East Coast transport fuel, paid nearly US$5 million after a ransomware attack forced the company to shut down its pipeline (Shear, Perlroth and Krauss 2021).

As these developments show, the threat from organised crime is dynamic and rapidly evolving. To counter this threat effectively, we need to dispense with the prevailing orthodoxy over how to tackle illicit markets and return to first principles. The calls for a change in approach have grown louder in recent years, yet efforts to pioneer more innovative approaches have often been hamstrung by insufficient funds or lack of political will (or both).[7] The focus on the ground in many places remains informed by the old notions of stringent prohibition and heavy prison terms, an approach perhaps best epitomised by the US-led war on drugs, which despite its mounting number of critics continues to magnetise – and some would argue warp – attention and debate, centring the organised crime focus on drugs, violent cartels and dramatic interdiction efforts. Yet despite the trillion dollars spent over the past five decades, there is a general consensus that the war on drugs has not achieved its aims – and many would argue

---

7 To give one example, Rio's Police Pacification Units, launched in 2008, were intended as a hybrid form of on-the-ground policing and community-outreach programmes, but the latter suffered from a lack of resources from the very beginning (Clavel 2017).

that it has made the problem much worse (Farber 2021; Shultz and Aspe 2017).

The failure of such approaches should spur us to reconsider the concepts on which they are built. To this end, this chapter sets out to examine some of the conceptual challenges in the debate about "organised crime" – namely illegality, illicit markets and actors, and harms – and by doing so make an argument for changing the focus of our efforts to respond to illicit markets.

Legal, illegal and the spaces in between

At the heart of all discussions about the illicit is the notion of illegality, yet it is perhaps under-appreciated how nuanced, varied and even arbitrary a concept this is. An activity, such as trade in a particular commodity, is only illegal if a state makes it so, not because it is innately illegal. And even once declared illegal, that declaration is not universally absolute, but bound to the extent of a state's jurisdiction – a commodity or activity's legal status can vary from place to place across state borders. For instance, it may be illegal to poach or exploit a commodity in one place but quite legal to sell it in another. Similarly, legal products can form part of an illegal flow, such as precursor chemicals which are used both in the production of illicit drugs and in the legal production of other substances.

This interplay between what is "legal" and what is "illegal" is a big part of all illegal flows/markets and their regulation. This is especially noticeable in the case of grey markets when illicit flows (for example of people, gold or timber) converge with and blend into legal flows. (Alternatively, an initially legal good can become illegal when diverted from a legal supply chain.) If the laundering/diversion is successful, it may be impossible to tell the difference between a commodity that was illegal at one point (due to its production or transit, for example) and a legal one. Grey markets can arise in cases where a formerly licit product has been banned, restricted or heavily taxed, as seen in 2018, when the Kenyan government banned the production and sale of Kenyan charcoal – a vital source of fuel for many people. With demand continuing, illicit domestic production continued and was laundered into legal imports (and also smuggled flows). It is for this reason that a series of policy responses such as certification schemes to identify the sources of products have been implemented, with varying degrees of success.

The Kenya example demonstrates two things: first, the rapid rise of an illicit grey market when a commodity suddenly changes legal status, and second, how criminals can exploit differences in the legal status of a commodity between different countries (in the case of Kenya, the fact that charcoal imports from Uganda and Tanzania were still legal). This second point also reveals a major challenge in attempting to build a unified global response towards organised crime: put simply, countries often cannot agree on what is legal and what is not and how they should cooperate to regulate illegal flows.

This is because how countries respond to illicit flows is a political issue before it is a law enforcement issue – for Kenya, the decision to ban domestic charcoal production was motivated by environmental concerns, but other states may be more pragmatic. This is particularly true in cases where the illicit economy is a significant source of livelihood for domestic populations, whether in the production of illicit goods (for example in artisanal mining or logging) or the long-standing engagement of historically nomadic groups in the illicit transit trades of people and drug smuggling across the Sahel. International pressure to crack down on such activities is likely to be resisted by the states in question, given the lack of viable legitimate alternatives. These political interests are one reason why so much effort and debate in international fora is expended on determining what should be prohibited (the endless discussions about what drugs to put on what lists, for example, or what species should be on the CITES appendices/IUCN "red list").[8]

Of course, simply declaring something illegal does not make the problem go away, and can in fact make it very much worse. From the criminal's perspective, enforcement increases the risk and thus the cost of moving illegal commodities, but ironically, that may mean more profits for organised crime. (This may be due to several factors: criminals may pass the cost of moving illicit goods on to consumers, with a healthy

8 The International Union for Conservation of Nature (IUCN) Red List of Threatened Species is an inventory of the global conservation status of thousands of flora and fauna species and is used as a source for amending the three appendices of the Convention on International Trade in Endangered Species of Wild Fauna and Flora (CITES). CITES was adopted in 1973 to regulate international trade in certain species, and the convention's three appendices determine the various levels of protection and control applied to the trade of any given species. (Appendix 1, for example, includes species threatened with extinction, where trade is only permitted in exceptional circumstances.) The categorisation of flora and fauna species in these appendices therefore has real-world impacts for the 183 parties of CITES, shaping trade and conservation efforts. Of course, the listing of a species in a restrictive category does not eliminate demand, which may then be met by illicit actors.

percentage for themselves; illegality and interdiction limits supply, which may drive up prices; and restricted supply may also lead to products such as drugs being adulterated or cut with cheap filler agents, boosting profit margins (National Research Council 2010).[9]) Declaring a market illegal also removes its activities from public view and makes it much harder to monitor and research.

If we recognise that legality and illegality are essentially arbitrary, state-led terms, how can we coordinate a global response? The answer has to lie in reconfiguring the debate – not around whether some commodity or activity should be declared illegal, but on the basis of a more comprehensive discussion on the balance of harms. Doing so in the wake of a pandemic, where government decisions have been based on exactly such calculations (the harm of the spread of the virus against the economic damage caused, for example) provides an opening for rethinking our approach to illicit markets.

Effective calculations of the harms that result at different points along illicit flows may ultimately be the best way to get states to engage with the real consequences of illicit markets; if states have compelling evidence, then perhaps good policy will follow. They might be less inclined to prohibit, and more disposed to address structural drivers. We will return to this theme, but given the complexity of what is and is not considered illegal, it is necessary to first define what is regarded as a criminal market or flow and what we mean when we talk about "organised crime" actors.

Illicit markets and criminal actors

The term "organised crime" is often used to describe both illicit flows (or markets) and organised criminal groups (or actors), but it is important to distinguish between the two. The terms "illicit markets" and "illicit flows" refer to the provision or the movement across borders of commodities or services that states designate by law to be illegal. The concept can also be widened to suggest that "flow" also means delivery of illicit activities across borders – if you accept that definition, we could also talk about virtual flows through the delivery of criminal activity using the transport systems of the internet. There are of course also local criminal markets, sometimes disorganised, which do not provide any such service or commodity but

9 For an analysis of how prices respond to supply-side interdictions, see National Research Council 2010, Chapter 2, 'Markets for Drugs'.

which are merely predatory, such as robbery, kidnapping and extortion. While the generally local nature of such activities sets them apart from other forms of illicit flow, they often form part of the ecosystem of illicit markets that entrenches criminal governance. (Extortion, for example, is often 'justified' by criminals as the provision of security that the state is unable to provide, and sophisticated actors like the Yakuza may even become part of the crime-regulatory apparatus itself (Bonello, Reitano and Shaw 2021: 18).) And polycriminality is increasingly a factor: organised crime groups engaged in illicit flows may also work with local criminals who engage in extortion, racketeering and violence (UNODC n.d.-b).

An enormous diversity of commodities and services are traded in criminal markets, including people, weapons, illicit drugs, wildlife products and non-renewable resources such as oil and gold. Criminal markets and their operation are associated with increased evidence of criminalised governance, state protection of illicit activities and rent seeking, as well as violence within and between criminal groups and against communities. Criminal markets also generate a demand for a wide range of services: political protection, legal support, financial services for laundering funds, document fraud and the contracting of violence, amongst others. Consequently, illicit markets create an ecosystem of interests around them. It is little wonder that those who attempt to disrupt illegal markets face significant resistance.

The geography of the illicit for almost all commodities can be divided into three types: the point of production or supply; the trafficking or transportation of the illicit commodity in question (including through zones or countries of transit); and the markets where it is consumed. Europe is generally seen as primarily a consumer market, but the infrastructure of global trade – air travel and container shipping in particular – has helped illicit products reach an ever-increasing number of countries. The explosion in the production of synthetic drugs has also dramatically shifted which states are producer, transit and consumer locales, with production sometimes taking place in the same country as consumption. Changes in global synthetic drugs markets in the coming years will only serve to increase the number of drug production locales, diversifying supply and fuelling local markets. Growing virtual markets are also opening up new opportunities for advertising and coordinating the movement of illicit commodities on a global scale, as well as creating new forms of virtual crime.

Yet discussions of this "globalisation" of illicit flows and markets can overshadow the role of the local context. Local criminal groups with their connections to government and local networks and knowledge are much better placed than external criminal actors to ensure the control and regulation of local criminal economies. This is one reason why, despite the general policy statement that "organised crime has gone global", more granular research suggests that criminal groups don't travel well, or at least that a set of specific conditions must be fulfilled for them to do so. What has travelled well are illicit markets and flows, which have indeed gone global, in the sense that demand is equally found in developing economies and developed ones. In that sense, it is useful to see illicit markets and flows as a chain which various actors are attached to (or extract rents from). These actors engage in agreements, but the lack of trust between actors and the challenges of enforcing informal contracts mean that most criminal markets are inherently unstable.

The degree to which criminal flows are transnational and control is local is well illustrated by one subset of data in the GI-TOC organised crime index, which shows a weak correlation between the presence of criminal markets in countries across the globe and the presence of foreign actors (GI-TOC 2021: 115). Why would that be the case? The short answer is that foreign actors find it difficult to break into local criminal markets – particularly where local organised crime is dominant – and so generally are unable to maintain an extensive local presence.

Instead, foreign criminal actors generally seek to do deals with local criminals and often occupy the position of intermediaries between local and foreign groups. In the early 1990s, Italian brokers such as Roberto Pannunzi began stationing themselves in Colombia to coordinate cocaine shipments between the Medellín and Cali cartels and the Italian 'Ndrangheta and Cosa Nostra. While the mafia footprint in Latin America grew larger in later years (with the 'Ndrangheta in particular mobilising Italian migrant populations in Latin America to set up front operations), independent brokers remained important, in part because they did not raise the kind of attention that a major European mafia presence in Latin America would attract. Crucially, brokers understand both supply- and demand-side contexts: Pannunzi was among the first to realise in the early 1990s that the profit margins from selling cocaine in Europe were vastly greater than those from heroin. Later, brokers also leveraged Europe's efficient transport infrastructure (including container ports) – and the fact that European law enforcement presence and capacity in Latin America is far lower than that of the US – to supply a reliable flow of cocaine to the various European trafficking groups.[10]

For the majority of criminal markets we need to dispense with the idea that there is a 'farm-to-fork' model of organised crime, with a single organisation dominating the trade along the entire chain.[11] Instead, a range of brokers, intermediaries or violent entrepreneurs are present at different points along the chain, performing functions that essentially push the product along while drawing profit from doing so. Given that trust is in short supply in many of the transactions along illegal commodity chains, cheating and threatening others (stealing commodities, extracting rents and threatening and carrying out violent acts) are the language or signals of business. Only in the most settled criminal markets – where one group may dominate part of the production, supply or sales chain – is violence reduced.

We also need to expand our definition of what constitutes a criminal actor. The stereotype of the drug dealer on the corner or mafia don may dominate the popular perception, but in reality there are a wide diversity of actors involved in managing criminal enterprises (and thus those involved in what we term organised crime), including legal companies, militia groups, organised gangs and criminal networks.

Criminal actors particularly thrive in conflict zones. The GI-TOC organised crime index highlights the strong correlation of organised crime with countries in conflict and fragile states, as reflected in the high rankings of the Democratic Republic of the Congo, Colombia, Myanmar, Mexico and Nigeria (the top five countries affected by organised crime) (GI-TOC 2021: 18). In many places, the distinction between criminal actors and conflict actors is not clear-cut. In an important new study of organised crime and separatist movements, Danilo Mandić describes how the line between crime and war often blurs, with "[m]embers [of organised crime groups] often simultaneously serv[ing] in armies, militias, or other armed formations" (Mandić 2020: 26).

Criminals in conflict zones are well placed to exploit shortages in commodities and services during times of war and are often keen to maintain

10 This discussion of the evolution of cocaine trafficking is drawn from McDermott et al. (2021).

11 Albanian cocaine networks come close to this end-to-end model for drugs, buying cocaine from cartels in Latin America, arranging shipment and then distributing the drug through Albanian retail networks on the street in places like the UK, although they are not involved in growing coca or manufacturing cocaine (McDermott et al. 2021: 33).

the chaotic status quo. In a recent study of how mass atrocities occur, Kate Ferguson argues that "criminal markets that may predate the application of sanctions are primed to benefit when sanctions start to bite. When these criminal networks are also irregular armed groups, the vested interest in prolonging violence and crises becomes one [...] of financial gain requiring only long-term, complex solutions" (Ferguson 2020: 204). Once peace is achieved, it is highly likely that these groups will have cemented their influence in society and be able to wield real influence over the reconstruction of the state. This was seen in the 1990s during the Bosnian wars, when criminal actors grew powerful through weapons and fuel smuggling and became deeply influential actors in the post-conflict state (Andreas n.d.; see also Glenny 2009).

One consideration when talking about "organised crime" groups is how much of the total activities of the group is related to the management of a criminal market. A "pure" organised crime group is likely to be 100 % focused on obtaining illegal profit, while a legitimate company may engage in both legal and illegal activities (and if the laundering of a product like fish or wood is involved these may be closely related). A militia group or paramilitary force may only be identified as partially involved in criminal activities, usually to fund their activities and often in the form of taxing the movement of illegal goods. Very few serious organised crime groups are now only involved in illicit markets. Most have used their dirty money to buy political influence, licit businesses and vast holdings of assets. By laundering their income into the global financial system (which has aided this through either insufficient regulation or unscrupulousness), these groups have merged with the upperworld.

At the other end of the spectrum, it is important to understand that not all actors involved in illicit flows are associated with organised crime groups. Many criminal markets draw on the expertise and labour of people in informal economies, who hover between legal and illegal work. For example, the illicit gold market has at its base literally thousands of people toiling in difficult conditions, and drug cultivation involves small-scale farmers. Such groups of people may often be targeted by the authorities, as they constitute easy game and offer fast results. Crops can be destroyed and illegal miners rounded up, stats can be compiled, but in general illicit flows remain largely unaffected. (The huge coca eradication campaign in Colombia, for example, has had little impact on longer-term cocaine flows, or indeed coca cultivation, which has sporadically risen despite such attempts (Felbab-Brown 2020).)

For such people, illicit work is sometimes the only viable option for earning a livelihood, and removing that livelihood risks plunging them further into economic hardship. Policy in such cases has to focus on bringing such actors into the space of a more regulated legal economy. In the case of illegal gold miners for example, this would mean giving them the opportunity to sell their production to legal as opposed to illegal brokers. There are many ways to regulate grey or quasi-illegal actors without undermining livelihoods.

The role of state actors in criminal markets is also complex. The a priori assumption is that states act to curtail and/or regulate criminal markets. The reality, depending on the context, is that state actors are often deeply embedded in criminal activities and serve as important protectors of some criminal actors. While this is a wider debate in its own right, state attempts at enforcement may, by default or design, protect or favour some actors over others, the best example being the protection of informers within the criminal community – informers whose intelligence is often targeted against opposing criminal groups or networks.

At the extreme end of this relationship, the state may collaborate with criminals. In the context of organised crime, "state capture" refers to the phenomenon of the criminal predation of the state and the protection of criminal markets by the state, and is a critical part of understanding how criminal markets are sustained and how they benefit political elites. As well as driving corruption and distorting law enforcement, such state capture can also put independent media and civil society actors – often the last channels through which information on the activities of criminal groups and their corrupt protectors can be made public – in the firing line. It is little wonder then that civil society voices are being challenged in countries across the globe, including through state actions and criminal violence. Our own work in Africa indicates a decline in the space in which independent media voices and community activists can operate – a consequence of increasing state control and state capture.

The phenomenon of state capture constitutes the ultimate form of control around an illicit flow. The state apparatus essentially drives out the criminal competition to occupy the key position in regulating who can benefit from the criminal economy. The figures from the GI-TOC organised crime index are sobering in this regard, with state-embedded actors assessed as having a "significant or severe influence on society and state structures" in 112 out of 193 states (58 %). In other words, the majority of states (or at least state actors) are critical vectors drawing profit from global criminal flows. But even such state capture does not reduce the necessity to keep the focus on flows as the primary target for disruption, rather than actors. If flows are reduced, or reduced in value, those who rely on them to dispense patronage or extract rents will wither on the vine.

If we recognise that flows are the issue and actors merely serve the flows, we can start to move away from an antagonistic crusade against a criminal "enemy" and instead work out how to curtail demand and divert those actors involved in illicit production into licit business. The focus must be on disrupting a supply chain phenomenon, not taking down individual gangs/mafias/cartels, which will only be replaced by others – sometimes along with severe policy blowback. In 2006, recently elected Mexican President Felipe Calderón launched a 'decapitation' strategy (with US assistance) aimed at capturing or killing drug-trafficking kingpins. It worked, with 22 of the top 37 kingpins removed by 2012 (Beckhusen 2012), but also led to a fragmentation of the big cartels (which had maintained a semblance of harsh order) into hundreds of smaller factions,[12] each of which violently asserted itself in an attempt to gain turf and market share, with the Jalisco New Generation Cartel (CJNG) in particular grabbing headlines for its extraordinary brutality. Murders, kidnapping and extortion all skyrocketed (New York Times 2016), and of course, the drug markets remained intact.

Evaluating multi-market harm: a new approach to anti-crime policy

How a commodity or activity is designated as illicit is theoretically determined by a policy discussion as to the harms that would be caused by the legal trade in that commodity or activity. In theory, that perspective should be weighed with the harms of suppressing a particular market through state interventions such as law enforcement and regulation, especially as these harms are often severe. In the last ten years, action to contain illicit markets and criminal groups has proven to involve some of the most prolonged and deadly forms of violence associated with organised crime.

In reality, policy processes are often more confused than that, contain bureaucratic inheritances from the past, political grandstanding, moralising and stereotyping and often generate sets of institutional interests which make even slow change challenging. Uncreative policymakers often have an automatic default position that suggests that organised crime is about drugs, or that legitimately registered companies cannot be criminal groups. And for the most part, our assessment of the real harms done by criminal markets is poorly conceived or badly distorted. In the drug de-

12 In 2021, the Mexican consulting agency Lantia estimated that there were more than 400 gangs operating in Mexico (Chaparro 2021).

bate, for example, the term "harm reduction" has been deeply polarising. In this context the focus is on reducing harms to drug users by ensuring that responses are managed by the health sector as opposed to the criminal justice system, but some states with a strict prohibitionist approach viewed attempts to move drug control away from law enforcement as enabling crime. The term "harm reduction" became a dirty word in some quarters, and it is only recently that it has been possible to use it in UN consensus-driven resolutions.

Measuring the extent of harm as a result of criminal markets should be a priority for researchers, but this will be difficult to achieve. The harm caused by organised crime and criminal markets is multifaceted, having both direct and indirect impacts. This includes staggering levels of violence, with parts of several cities around the world having homicide rates that surpass those of war zones. It also encompasses severe environmental damage, deaths from drug overdoses and severe disruptions to economic activities. It will also be important to trace harms along the line of illicit flows to gain a full-spectrum view of the damage caused. Illicit flows to Europe, for example, may drive wars in Africa or on its periphery or reduce biodiversity and forest cover. In 2020 and again in 2021, allegations arose that Swedish homeware company IKEA had sold furniture made from wood linked to illegal logging in Siberia and Ukraine (Earthsight 2020; Earthsight 2021).[13]

While current systems to measure harm from organised crime are primitive, they do offer an important prism through which to view responses to illicit markets. Most importantly, they should be used to determine the priority and (by implication) the resources that should be brought to bear on different aspects of the wider criminal economy. The foundation for a discussion of harms caused by individual criminal markets should be determined by, amongst others, the following questions:

> *To what extent is the harm an existential crisis for people?* That question may sound dramatic, but several criminal markets fit the bill in this regard, most notably illegal fishing and forestry crimes. Organised criminal markets around resources such as sand for construction and water may also constitute existential threats to parts of humanity in future.

13 In its response, IKEA asserted that its wood was legally harvested.

To what extent is the harm a symptom of a failure of responses to deal effectively with the market itself? Not all criminal markets are violent, but some, most notably drug markets under specific conditions of criminal competition, are extraordinarily violent. In such contexts the bulk of resources or policy thinking may be targeted at the wrong thing: in this case drug trafficking or drug dealing without creative responses to violence.

Is the harm caused as a result of state and community responses to the illicit market – or lack of such responses – and is it outweighing the harm caused directly by the market itself? This is the question that has long confronted the 'war on drugs', but it may equally apply to other markets. In the last decade, thousands of migrants and refugees attempting to cross the Mediterranean Sea have resorted to human smugglers, who have routinely sent them aboard overloaded and unseaworthy vessels – a practice which has resulted in thousands of migrant deaths. At times, such tragedies have catalysed a more empathetic response and increased calls for reform, yet efforts to tackle the main driver of the smuggling market – the dearth of avenues for legal migration – have been stymied. Interdiction remains the default position, with those intercepted or rescued often returned to unsafe contexts,[14] while those who do reach Europe are often held in overcrowded and unsanitary camps in legal limbo, despite their refugee status (UNHCR 2020).

While this chapter is not intended to provide a detailed response to these questions, there are several points that may be useful to make in passing in order to stimulate discussion on issues of prioritisation around the threat that the global community faces from organised crime.

Threats from organised crime that are regarded as existential to humanity should arguably be those that are addressed most comprehensively and with the greatest allocation of resources. Several criminal activities (illegal fishing, forestry, waste dumping, etc.) which have (or ultimately will have) extreme environmental consequences and which at present only attract a paltry and under-resourced set of responses should by this rationale be pushed to the front of the queue. It is also worth emphasising that cybercrime increasingly constitutes an existential threat to patterns of economic and social activity, and potentially a threat to democracy itself. Attacks on infrastructure and social services will become increasingly common and

14 In 2020, 11,891 migrants were intercepted/rescued and returned to Libya (IOM Libya 2021).

target developing countries more extensively, in part because developed countries will over time be able to secure some of their infrastructure and institutions. And in a new age of geopolitical competition, some cybercrime networks have state links.

Based on this rationale, drug markets, given that the harms caused to citizens are in part a consequence of the state response itself, should be downgraded in seriousness, with fewer resources being provided to address interdiction and much more to address the health consequences. Also, much clearer thinking is required on how they can be regulated in the first place. Calls to modernise the international drug control system have risen in recent years, but while there have been significant developments in, among others, Portugal (which decriminalised the possession and consumption of drugs in 2001) (Ferreira 2017), Mexico (where the legalisation of cannabis is pending final approval from the Senate) (BBC 2021) and even the UN (Tennant, Collins and Eligh 2020), the focus of such efforts remains overwhelmingly on cannabis, with the debate over cocaine and heroin largely deadlocked.

The rise of new psychoactive substances (NPS) poses arguably the biggest regulatory challenge, not least because it is still unclear how to categorise them in the first place: in the words of a 2017 study, "defining psychoactivity is conceptually fraught, with great consequence for the scope of the prohibition" (Reuter and Pardo 2017: 25). Further challenges arise through the ease and speed with which these new compounds can be created (as of August 2020, more than 1,000 individual NPS had been reported, UNODC 2020: 10) and enter and leave the market, together with the fact that some (such as opioids in the US) were originally created as legal alternatives to illicit substances (indeed, some may remain legal when prescribed) (Peacock et al. 2019). Faced with this dizzyingly dynamic threat, the traditional system of drug control – in which the UN body tasked with deciding which compounds should be scheduled meets only annually (UNODC n.d.-c), and compound classes cannot be scheduled – requires fundamental overhaul.

A new approach

As with so much else, COVID-19 provides an opportunity to critically reflect on the discussion on illicit markets and organised crime. But, significantly, the pandemic is also clearly driving a wider period of instability that is greatly strengthening criminal actors in many places around the world. And while the assumption is that these changes may end when the pandemic has weakened its grip, there is no guarantee that this will be the case. A period of sustained social and political change may be upon us.

What does that mean for policies against illicit markets and organised crime? Four interrelated things:

The need for a global strategy that moves beyond law enforcement: The current response to illicit markets and organised crime remains fragmented and unsuccessful. All illicit markets continue to grow, and state responses for the most part, while perhaps constraining further growth, have been unable to reduce the growth. One of the reasons for this lack of success is that there is, despite UNTOC, no effective and agreed upon framework to confront illicit markets. While this will be difficult to achieve in light of political and geostrategic differences, there is a strong argument for seeking to develop a more strategic response – and one which moves beyond what are clearly unsuccessful law enforcement responses. Focusing on harms – especially harms that transcend national borders – may provide a means of more accurately assessing the impact of illicit markets, disrupting illicit flows and disempowering criminal actors.

Understanding that state actors are key vectors in criminal economies: The surface debate on organised crime often assumes a clear divide between state responses to organised crime and the operation of criminal markets. In many places, nothing could be further from the truth. From the funding of political parties and interests to the protection of some actors by state security personnel and the licit economic interests that develop around them with connections to state actors and regulatory decisions, government institutions are key vectors of influence within criminal markets. One of the major challenges in building an international consensus on organised crime is the incorporation and reformation of compromised state actors, as those left out in the cold will not only continue to maintain criminal economies within their own borders, but may also fuel those further afield. Such countries may also become safe harbours for increasingly mobile transnational organised crime networks.

Better measures of harm to prioritise action: Our ability to determine both direct and indirect harm from criminal markets and organised crime is poorly developed. No country has developed a sophisticated model for doing so in order to target state responses effectively. The result is predictably a focus on older markets (drugs largely) where there are established institutional bureaucratic interests. For many, the response to the fallout of the pandemic should be prioritised, and yet the impact of crime is no less pervasive. Approximately three-quarters of the world's population lives in areas of high criminality (GI-TOC 2021: 12–13) – and there is no vaccine for organised crime. The longer it is left unattended, the worse the problem will become.

More innovative research: Our understanding of illicit markets has grown substantially over the last decade. There is, however, much more to do. Central to this must be more sophisticated processes of data collection (commodity pricing and protection fees across all markets being two examples) and more work on the political economy of different illicit markets. Without such work, the policy discussion will remain trapped in narrow and often case-by-case law-enforcement-style discussions, which, while important, provide only a narrow window into the power and reach of illicit flows.

Greater policy experimentation: For too long the world has adhered to the same narrow spectrum of responses to deal with an ever-wider range of illicit markets, yet the time may now be right for a varied and imaginative approach that deals with each market on its own terms. Regulation, not enforcement, may well be the best way to limit the harms stemming from many illicit markets, although this will be uncharted territory for many, and electorates must be won over with clear and data-supported arguments, as public acceptance of a new paradigm is crucial. More collaborative efforts between state and non-state actors, including the private sector and civil society, may also help generate more holistic, comprehensive and impactful responses. The effectiveness of such an approach was seen in South Korea during the pandemic, where approximately one-fifth of all government initiatives were in formal partnership with civil society; involvement of civil society with the ministries of Foreign Affairs and of Agriculture, Food and Rural Affairs in the implementation stage reached very high levels (90 % and 87.5 % respectively) (Jeong and Kim 2021, as cited in Carnegie Civic Research Network 2021). Targeted state collaborations for specific markets may also be an effective method, as was the case with the counter-piracy coalition in Somalia, which was a rare example of an illicit market being effectively closed down, and the closure sustained, although security measures in themselves cannot be sufficient and indeed may even be counterproductive.

We have reached a critical phase in the discussion of criminal markets. Currently we are building our response on a set of old paradigms, largely shaped by how we have responded to drugs, and based upon the assumption that states are good actors. There is no evidence that this is the case. Most significantly, the lack of success in the fight against many illicit markets, which are going from strength to strength, demonstrates that we are on the wrong path when it comes to tackling organised crime in all its myriad guises.

We need a new way of thinking that is underpinned by a re-examination of the basic principles behind our current conceptions of organised crime. Declaring something illegal has consequences, many of them not planned for, and in a globalised world, state prohibition can easily be circumvented. And yet this is not to dismiss illegality as a useful and necessary tool: the harms caused by human trafficking, forced labour and violent crimes (among others) are real and serious, and there can be no room for such activities in a just society. Rather, we need to assess whether our determinations of illegality are fit for purpose and accurately comprehend the contemporary criminal landscape. The seductive myths of omnipotent kingpins and arcane criminal codes have long dominated public perception, but awareness is growing that crime as a system is driven by the same forces as licit business, and indeed, the line between the two is frequently blurred. In this light, we need to appreciate that flows create criminal actors and not necessarily the other way around: if we reduce the profits from the flows, criminal incentives will decline. But most importantly, we need to reassess the relationship between crime, harm and response. At this juncture in our history, we must seek to protect the vulnerable – whether that be people, infrastructure, wildlife or the planet's resources – from the devastating consequences of crime, while doing all we can to dismantle the contexts that allow crime to thrive.

References

Abano, Imelda/Chavez, Leilani Chavez: "Wildlife trafficking, like everything else, has gone online during COVID-19". At: https://news.mongabay.com/2021/06/wildlife-trafficking-like-everything-else-has-gone-online-during-covid-19/ (accessed 28 April 2022).

Andreas, Peter (n.d.): "Criminalized conflict. The clandestine political economy of war and peace in the Balkans". At: https://www.wilsoncenter.org/publication/261-criminalized-conflict-the-clandestine-political-economy-war-and-peace-the-balkans (accessed 3 May 2022).

BBC (2021): "Mexico marijuana. Top court decriminalises recreational use of cannabis". At: https://www.bbc.co.uk/news/world-latin-america-57645016 (accessed 3 May 2022).

Beckhusen, Robert (2012): "Killing drug cartel bosses isn't working, says top U.S. General". At: https://www.wired.com/2012/03/cartel-general/ (accessed 3 May 2022).

Bitdefender (2021): "New Bitdefender Report Reveals Top Global Cyberthreats". At: https://www.bitdefender.com/news/new-bitdefender-report-reveals-top-globa l-cyberthreats-3977.html (accessed 28 April 2022).

Bonello, Deborah/Reitano, Tuesday/Shaw, Mark (2021): "A handbook for community responses to countering extortion". At: https://globalinitiative.net/wp-conte nt/uploads/2021/05/Extortion-handbook-WEB-1.pdf (accessed 3 May 2022).

Carnegie Civic Research Network (2021): "Civil society and the global pandemic. Building back different?". At: https://carnegieendowment.org/2021/09/30/civil-s ociety-and-global-pandemic-building-back-different-pub-85446 (accessed 3 May 2022).

Chandra, Wahyu (2021): "Illegal loggers use pandemic as cover to ramp up activity in Sulawesi". At: https://news.mongabay.com/2021/05/illegal-loggers-use-pande mic-as-cover-to-ramp-up-activity-in-sulawesi/ (accessed 28 April 2022).

Chaparro, Luis (2021): "Mexico's war on cartels has created 400 new gangs that are taking on the police and cartels that are left". At: https://www.businessinsider.c om/fragmentation-in-mexico-war-on-drugs-created-400-new-gangs-2021-10?r=US &IR=T (accessed 3 May 2022).

Clavel, Tristan (2017): "What LatAm cities can learn from the failures of Brazil's UPP policing model". At: https://insightcrime.org/news/analysis/what-latam-citi es-can-learn-brazil-upp-policing-model/ (accessed 28 April 2022).

Earthsight (2020): "Flatpåcked Förests. IKEA's illegal timber problem and the flawed green label behind it". At: https://www.earthsight.org.uk/flatpackedf orests-en (accessed 3 May 2022).

Earthsight (2021): "IKEA's house of horrors. The stolen Russian forests being greenwashed into kids' furniture". At: https://www.earthsight.org.uk/news/inves tigations/ikea-house-of-horrors (accessed 3 May 2022).

EMCDDA, European Monitoring Centre for Drugs and Drug Addiction (2021): "Impact of COVID-19 on drug markets, use, harms and drug services in the community and prisons. Results from an EMCDDA trendspotter study. April 2021". At: https://www.emcdda.europa.eu/system/files/publications/13745/TD03 21143ENN_002.pdf (accessed 28 April 2022).

Farber, David (2021): "The War on Drugs turns 50 today. It's time to make peace". At: https://www.washingtonpost.com/outlook/2021/06/17/war-drugs-turns-50-to day-its-time-make-peace/ (accessed 28 April 2022).

Felbab-Brown, Vanda (2020): "Detoxifying Colombia's Drug Policy. Colombia's counternarcotics options and their impact on peace and state building". At: https://www.brookings.edu/wp-content/uploads/2020/01/FP_20200106_colombi a_drug_policy_felbabbrown.pdf (accessed 3 May 2022).

Ferguson, Kate (2020): Architectures of violence. The command structures of modern mass atrocities. London: Hurst.

Ferreira, Susana (2017): "Portugal's radical drugs policy is working. Why hasn't the world copied it?". At: https://www.theguardian.com/news/2017/dec/05/portugals-radical-drugs-policy-is-working-why-hasnt-the-world-copied-it (accessed 3 May 2022).

Glenny, Misha (2009): McMafia. Seriously organised crime. London: Random House.

GI-TOC, Global Initiative against Transnational Organized Crime (2019): "The Illegal, Unreported and Unregulated Fishing Index, January 2019". At: https://globalinitiative.net/wp-content/uploads/2019/02/IUU-Fishing-Index-Report-web-version.pdf (accessed 28 April 2022).

GI-TOC, Global Initiative against Transnational Organized Crime (2021): "Global Organized Crime Index 2021". At: https://globalinitiative.net/wp-content/uploads/2021/09/GITOC-Global-Organized-Crime-Index-2021.pdf (accessed 3 May 2022).

IOM Libya, International Organization for Migration Libya (2021): "IOM Maritime Update". Twitter, 13 September 2021. At: https://twitter.com/iom_libya/status/1437419820442599428 (accessed 3 May 2022).

INTERPOL (2020): "COVID-19 impact on migrant smuggling and human trafficking". At: https://www.interpol.int/en/News-and-Events/News/2020/COVID-19-impact-on-migrant-smuggling-and-human-trafficking (accessed 28 April 2022).

Jeong, Bok Gyo/Kim, Sung-Ju (2021): "The government and civil society collaboration against COVID-19 in South Korea. A single or multiple actor play?". In: Nonprofit Policy Forum, 12, 1, pp. 165–187.

Mandić, Danilo (2020): Gangsters and other statesmen. Mafias, separatists and torn states in a globalized world. Princeton and Oxford: Princeton University Press.

Maron, Dina Fine (2021): "Wildlife seizures are down – and an illicit trade boom may be coming". At: https://www.nationalgeographic.com/animals/article/wildlife-seizures-dropped-in-2020-but-an-illicit-trade-boom-may-be-coming (accessed 28 April 2022).

Mbzibain, Aurelian/Mohsen Mohamed, Habiba/Baur, Daniela/Jara Cazares, Cristina (2021): "Experiences from Frontline Forest Communities: Covid-19 impacts on Indigenous Peoples and Local Communities, women and forest and wildlife illegality in the Congo Basin". At: https://cidt.org.uk/wp-content/uploads/2021/01/Experiences-from-Frontline-Forest-Communities.pdf (accessed 28 April 2022).

McDermott, Jeremy/Bargent, James/den Held, Douwe/ Ramírez, Maria Fernanda (2021): "The cocaine pipeline to Europe". At: https://globalinitiative.net/wp-content/uploads/2021/02/The-cocaine-pipeline-to-Europe-GI-TOCInsightCrime.pdf (accessed 3 May 2022).

National Research Council (2020): Understanding the demand for illegal drugs. Washington, DC: The National Academies Press.

Nellemann, C./Henriksen, R./Kreilhuber, A./Stewart, D./Kotsovou, M./Raxter, P./ Mrema, E./Barrat, S. (eds.) (2016): "The rise of environmental crime – a growing threat to natural

Resources, peace, development and security. A UNEP-INTERPOL rapid response assessment". At: https://wedocs.unep.org/20.500.11822/7662 (accessed 28 April 2022).

Nellemann, C./Henriksen, R./Pravettoni, R./Stewart, D./Kotsovou, M./Schlingemann, M.A.J/Shaw, M./Reitano, T. (eds) (2018): "World Atlas of Illicit Flows". At: https://globalinitiative.net/wp-content/uploads/2018/09/Atlas-Illicit-Flows-FINAL-WEB-VERSION-copia-compressed.pdf (accessed 3 May 2022).

New York Times (2016): "Mexico's kingpin strategy against the drug cartels". At: https://www.nytimes.com/interactive/2016/02/16/world/americas/mexicos-kingpin-strategy-against-the-drug-cartels.html (accessed 3 May 2022).

Peacock, Amy/Bruno, Raimondo/Gisev, Natasa/Degenhardt, Louisa/Hall, Wayne et al. (2019): "New psychoactive substances. Challenges for drug surveillance, control, and public health responses". In: *Lancet*, 394, 10209, pp. 1668–1684.

Reuter, Peter/Pardo, Bryce (2021): "Can new psychoactive substances be regulated effectively? An assessment of the British Psychoactive Substances Bill". In: *Addiction*, 112, 1, pp. 23–31.

Shaw, Mark/Reitano, Tuesday (2021): Criminal contagion. How mafias, gangsters and scammers profit from a pandemic. London: Hurst Publishing.

Shear, Michael D./Perlroth, Nicole/Krauss, Clifford Krauss (2021): "Colonial pipeline paid roughly $5 million in ransom to hacker" At: https://www.nytimes.com/2021/05/13/us/politics/biden-colonial-pipeline-ransomware.html (accessed 28 April 2022).

Shultz, George/Aspe, Pedro (2017): "The failed war on drugs". At: https://www.nytimes.com/2017/12/31/opinion/failed-war-on-drugs.html (accessed 28 April 2022).

Tennant, Ian/Collins, John/Eligh, Jason (2020): "Smoke signals. The evolving status of cannabis under the international drug-control regime". At: https://globalinitiative.net/analysis/cannabis-status-drug-control/ (accessed 3 May 2022).

TRAFFIC (2021): "Record elephant ivory seizure of 626 kg in Cameroon". At: https://www.traffic.org/news/record-elephant-ivory-seizure-of-626-kg-in-cameroon/ (accessed 28 April 2022).

UNHCR, United Nations High Commissioner for Refugees (2020): "Act now to alleviate suffering at reception centres on Greek islands – UNHCR's Grandi". At: https://www.unhcr.org/uk/news/press/2020/2/5e4fe4074/act-alleviate-suffering-reception-centres-greek-islands-unhcrs-grandi.html (accessed 3 May 2022).

UNODC, United Nations Office on Drugs and Crime (n.d.-a): "Mechanism for the review of the implementation of the United Nations Convention against Transnational Organized Crime and the Protocols Thereto". At: https://www.unodc.org/unodc/en/organized-crime/intro/review-mechanism-untoc/home.html (accessed 28 April 2022).

UNODC, United Nations Office on Drugs and Crime (n.d.-b): "Transnational organized crime: the globalized illegal economy". At: https://www.unodc.org/toc/en/crimes/organized-crime.html (accessed 3 May 2022).

UNODC, United Nations Office on Drugs and Crime (n.d.-c): "United Nations Commission on Narcotic Drugs". At: https://www.unodc.org/unodc/en/commissions/CND/index.html (accessed 3 May 2022).

UNODC, United Nations Office on Drugs and Crime (2020): "Global synthetic drugs assessment 2020". At: https://www.unodc.org/documents/scientific/Global_Synthetic_Drugs_Assessment_2020.pdf (accessed 3 May 2022).

UNODC, United Nations Office on Drugs and Crime (2021): "World Drug Report 2021, booklet 2". At: https://www.unodc.org/res/wdr2021/field/WDR21_Booklet_2.pdf (accessed 28 April 2022).

Weisse, Mikaela/Goldman, Liz (2021): "Primary rainforest destruction increased 12 % from 2019 to 2020". At: https://www.globalforestwatch.org/blog/data-and-research/global-tree-cover-loss-data-2020/ (accessed 28 April 2022).

Wunder, Sven/Kaimowitz, David/Jensen, Stig/Feder, Sarah (2021): "Coronavirus, macroeconomy, and forests: What likely impacts?". In: Forest Policy and Economics, 131, 102536.

Shadow supply chains and criminal networks

Günther Maihold

In 2020, various governmental and civil society organisations with a strong research interest in the development of criminal activities around the world issued a white paper with the title "Criminal Market Convergence" (USAID and GI-TOC 2020). The main argument of this paper is based on 3 hypotheses: (1) An argument which comes from the literature of organisational theory argues that this convergence is increasing in situations where organised crime groups coordinate with other criminal actors across multiple illicit business lines or purchase illicit goods or services from one another. (2) The second argument is more service-oriented in the sense that criminal and legal markets may converge with licit markets when an organised crime group seeks to conceal its activities through front companies or purchases audit, banking and legal services that support its criminal activity. Finally, it is stated that (3) for the illicit economy the best hubs are states with good infrastructure and markets but weak institutions. Although the major interest of the white paper may have been to point to the overlap and mutual reinforcement of different criminal markets, especially with respect to transport, laundering, nodes and vulnerable points, the general argument promotes a view of poly-criminal networks which have cast a net of contacts and cooperation around the globe that the authorities are not able to control. By using common service providers, the same transport infrastructure and trading practices with other criminal groups, they are linking criminal markets in certain geographical areas not only, but also due to the facilitating conditions of corrupt governments or governmental agencies. This sort of geographical convergence of illicit flows and criminal markets articulates – in this view – a mapping of crime on a global scale that should orient the interventions of the law enforcement authorities in order to interrupt these networks and thus raise the costs of the criminal business.

This "convergence lens" to understand criminal activities on the one hand certainly addresses relevant elements such as the mixing of licit and illicit transactions and logistics, the international character of money laundering and complementary services, but on the other hand it suggests a view of a worldwide interconnectedness of criminal actors with an extraordinary relational power which on a global scale undermines many national action plans to counter crime and control illegal markets.

This article will try to revise some arguments of the "convergence perspective" based on an approach that treats supply chains as an analytical tool, pointing out that these connections are not uncommon in the context of international supply chains and that the different branches of organised crime are not even as interconnected as the convergence argument may insist. Supply chains can be understood as "the world economy's backbone and central nervous system" (Cattaneo, Gereffi and Staritz 2010: 7). They are an expression of a globalised economy, based on comparative advantages in production costs and resource availability around the globe, a rationale which covers legal and illegal transactions in the same way. Criminal actors have been analysed as behaving like international companies and trying to take advantage of their operations in multiple jurisdictions, with components sourced all over the world. They operate quite smoothly in a world with tariffs and taxes, as the liberalisation of trade in global terms has reduced duties and brought the entanglement of economies worldwide to a new dimension.

Shadow supply chains and illicit globalisation

One of the major topics regarding illicit flows is the demarcation of licit, (il)legal and illicit streams of goods and services. The main distinction does not refer to the harm that the production, transport or consumption of these goods may cause; their illegal dimension is due to the fact that these products or services are prohibited by law, that they are not legal and therefore not licit. From this it becomes quite clear that the category of licitness also covers elements beyond a formally legal character, including social and cultural norms. As we know from ethnological research, some communities consider determined psychoactive substances as licit for cultural uses, although they are legally forbidden (De Rios and Smith 1977). On the other hand, the term "illicit flows" does not refer in the first instance to the transfer of illegal goods or trade in illegal services but rather indicates that the illicit trade can occur – independent of the legal or illegal character of the traded goods – either in black markets or in legitimate markets, with the participation of legally established agents or informal or even criminal actors in these marketplaces. The illicit character therefore does not derive from the status of the goods but from the type of transactions that occur during the production, transport or consumption of the respective good or service. As we know from transnational crime research, this kind of trade passes through different jurisdictions, which may not be homogeneous with respect to the legal or illegal status of the different transactions. Therefore, it makes sense not to insist on clear-cut "categorical distinctions between licit and illicitness, but continuums of state practice [...], which encompass organized criminality, and enterprises that span the licit/illicit spectrum" (Hall 2013: 372).

Clandestine economic flows continue to cause concern, not only in state agencies but also in firms and enterprises, which fear the disloyal competence of illicit agents. The subversion of existing supply chains and transportation networks for illegal purposes has become one of the major threats, as part of what has been defined as "illicit globalization" (Andreas 2011) or "deviant globalization" (Gilman, Goldhammer and Weber 2013), based on the argument that both licit and illicit actors take advantage of the reduction of transaction costs. What began as the smuggling of narcotics across borders has evolved into transnational commercialisation of endangered species, counterfeit and stolen goods as well as illicit antiquities. What is being sold at international art fairs or presented in private zoos etc. may be or has been obtained by illegal extraction, excavation or simple robbery in other territories and states. In the panoply of criminal activities and illicit economies, the trade in arms and toxic waste receives high public attention (especially due to the growing interest in knowing what is happening on the darknet) (Persi Paoli et al. 2017), while other dimensions such as transborder car theft have become a more regular experience in police stations and customs offices (Felbab-Brown and Niño 2021).

Whereas cargo crime is related to theft (exiting) from the supply chain, smuggling can be viewed as 'entering' a supply chain. Whilst one destroys value in the supply chain by causing disruption, the other (smuggling) is not designed to create disruption at all. Criminals are as interested as legal shippers in ensuring that their consignments reach the destination in a timely fashion. However, countermeasures designed to intercept illicit goods have the impact of disrupting logistics systems for both legal and criminal parties.

Illicit trade that operates in the shadow of the global economy is characterised by a high diversity of illicit goods and services such as the trafficking of humans, narcotics, counterfeits, fake medicines, endangered and illegally harvested species of fauna and flora, antiquities and conventional arms. At the same time, there are various international standards in place to prohibit or regulate the different sectors of illicit trade and to promote the implementation of legal, regulatory and operational measures to combat the proceeds of illicit flows, which are supervised by the World

Customs Organization (WCO).[1] The growing number of operators who enable the illicit economies makes it even more urgent to deter their activities in order to prevent harm to persons, businesses and the environment. The negative externalities of the illicit economies range from the loss of revenue and market share up to diminished brand integrity and market reputational value, not to mention further consequences for security concerns in general, the environment or the livelihood of people.

Supply chains are economic structures where the legal and the illegal flows can overlap and mix, which is most interesting for the criminal actors. On this basis, we consider as "shadow value chains" those "that run, often in parallel, or intertwined with legal value chains" (Stridsman and Østensen 2017: 6), pointing especially to the fact that the diversion of resources from the legal interchange enables and sponsors other types of illicit activities. So at first sight, the analytical perspective of shadow supply chains seems to correspond to the convergence arguments on poly-criminal markets. But analytically we have to distinguish between the market level on the one hand and the structure which provides these markets on the other hand; then the question arises whether the supply chains also follow a convergence dynamic or whether this diagnosis should be limited to certain market segments. The central question to be answered is what differentiates "shadow supply chains" from their legal counterparts? At first sight is that they limit the participation of certain actors (e.g. competitors). Although criminal actors try to maintain control over access to the markets, they provide their own goods, displacing the legal supply by a better pricing of the products and using violence to dispel competitive supply. This includes the interest to mix legal and illegal components in the supply chain itself, following the logic of the main strategic rationale of the profit orientation in the grey market to exclude competitors from market access and foster a monopolistic position in the marketplace. In order to provide insights into the differential composition of these mixtures, I will refer to different sectors and pathways of criminal activities as examples.

1 The best known standards are: The Convention on International Trade in Endangered Species of Wild Fauna and Flora (CITES); the Montreal Protocol on Substances that Deplete the Ozone Layer; the Basel Convention on the Control of Transboundary Movements of Hazardous Wastes and their Disposal; the Stockholm Convention on Persistent Organic Pollutants; the Rotterdam Convention on the Prior Informed Consent Procedure for Certain Hazardous Chemicals and Pesticides in International Trade; the Cartagena Protocol on Biosafety; and the Minamata Convention on Mercury.

The fluid limits of the legal/illegal and illicit in supply chains: the central role of intermediaries

With a perspective on the specific role of intermediaries, it is necessary to distinguish different forms of governance in supply chains. The extended literature on this topic cannot be reviewed in this text, but to address the illicit dimension in the chains it seems helpful to distinguish between chain coordination of the individual linkages ("forms of coordination") and the governance of the entire chain ("modes of governance"). The latter refers to defining rules and conditions of chain participation (Ponte and Gibbon 2005) and the functional dimensions of the different actors. From the start, one has to recognise the difficulties of clearly separating the legal from the illegal, looking at illicit dimensions of flows with respect to a certain good. For example, the dual nature of cigarette consumption (i.e. the coexistence of a legal and an illegal market) causes the illegality of a cigarette to depend on its supply chain, which complicates the identification of illegal products. To some degree, the intensity of enforcement efforts reflects the difficulties in those dual markets where smuggled items are not easily discernible from legal ones. The knowledge about the transnational flows is therefore rather limited, and in many cases it is only on the basis of an extrapolation of seizures that an estimation of the size of markets and the value of traded goods has been possible. A different approach is to use social network analyses to identify the extension of criminal networks by the density of communicational contacts between certain nodes or intermediaries in order to counter suspicious transactions, an approach which has proven most fertile on the micro level (Giommoni, Aziani and Berlusconi 2017). Which are the elements that differentiate illicit supply chains from legal or licit ones?

In his report on illicit supply chains, Mackenzie (2002) identifies four different types:

- Illicit at source, transport and destination (narcotics)
- Illicit at source and transport, but licit at destination (diamonds, antiquities and certain minerals). Audit and certification systems have been put in place in order to prove the provenance of the goods and their legality.
- Licit at source, but illicit transport and at destination (firearms, people smuggling)
- Licit at source, but illicit transport and then licit at destination (cigarettes)

This complexity that certain goods at one moment in the supply chain have the characteristics of "legality" generates major difficulties for the authorities in dealing with those illicit supply chains and managing to control grey areas. For our analysis, the legal-illegal interface is a general problem due to its changing character in the different stages of the supply chain and depending on the concrete product which is being processed. For this reason, we prefer to look at some empirical evidence that can give us further orientation. In cases such as timber exploitation or wildlife trafficking, intermediaries play the decisive roles in this interface (Lavorgna 2014; Kleinschmit et al. 2016). Their roles are important in the supply chain, as they not only bring together supply and demand but 'make things happen'. Without the intermediaries, the illegal chain would be weak or even broken, as they "transform" the product or create the conditions for it to move from origin to destination.

In the case of wood from the Colombian Amazon, for example, it must be taken into account that in the process of exploitation and for subsistence purposes, indigenous and peasant communities carry out logging, slash-and-burn agriculture, cattle farming in reserved zones etc. Intermediaries interested in the product, such as "gasteros", are those who have financed these activities over the years and who help the communities obtain exploitation permits and other requirements, as well as loans (with high interest) and machinery necessary for the activity. Gasteros give the community a minimum profit or some assets such as school supplies, food or provisions. What deserves special attention is how these intermediaries usually profit not only from the product they obtain, but also by obtaining signatures and documents to "apply for forestry permits and safe-conducts in the name of the communities" (own translation), although this is to be understood as fraud from a legal point of view; however, for many community members this practice appears legitimate and accepted, in part because the profits and goods obtained meet the needs that the state unfortunately does not fulfil (EIA 2019: 32).

In addition to the "gasteros", there is another type of intermediary: the proxies. Their work consists of paying fixed amounts to the owners and holders of lands, whether communities or peasants, for signing documents that allow them to obtain logging permissions and legal representation of those territories before the environmental authorities. These proxies can use strategies such as obtaining authorisations to log certain areas and then carrying out the actual logging in others.

Referring specifically to wildlife trafficking, Phelps, Biggs and Webb (2016) describe different types of intermediaries; however, they can be transferred to other supply chain contexts as they fit them all, forming a conceptual framework:

- Logistician: involved in ordering, aggregation and transport, as well as financing and planning trade
- Specialised smuggler: specialised in actions to evade detection or negotiate access
- Government colluder: involved in using an official government position to facilitate trade, whether for financial (corruption), social or personal gain
- Third party: external services hired to support trade, potentially unknowingly.
- Processor: involved in product transformation (e.g. skinning, medicine preparation)
- Launderer: involved in laundering illegal wildlife into legal supply chains
- Vendor: involved in direct sales to consumers or sales to other intermediaries

In the process of illegal trafficking of goods, the criminal patterns that can be applied to different supply chains can vary, but in many cases they also have an overlapping dimension. As mentioned, organised crime networks may overlap with intermediaries but are not necessarily involved in the entire chain. This typological exercise suggests a certain caution in applying the organised crime framework as the only lens through which illegal traffic can be analysed. Empirical evidence hints at the multiple influences exercised inside the supply chain: organised crime networks are by no means isolated from producers; they can overlap them in some way or be a part of them but may also influence them, as in the case of gold and drug trafficking in Colombia (see the respective chapters in this volume). On the other hand, corruption and laundering processes depend on the intermediaries, whether they are directly involved with organised crime or not.

The illegal traffic of products and goods and the black market are not isolated from legal markets and goods; in fact, what allows them to exist is the coexistence with legality and the diffuse frontier between actors (state institutions, people, companies and their documents) and legal processes on the one hand and the illegal terrain on the other. A study on the convergence between legality and illegality in wildlife trafficking showed that more than 30 % of actors involved in that market are registered animal traders (Van Uhm and Moreto 2018).

The links between legality and illegality are not necessarily direct. Indeed, there are different degrees of directness and factors such as risks and benefits that affect both parties involved in this relationship (Passas 2002: 15); in fact, these are of various types, grades and functions, ranging from antithetical to symbiotic relationships.

Table 1: The nature of the legal-illegal interface (Passas 2002)

ANTITHETICAL RELATIONSHIPS	Antagonistic: competition between legal and illegal actors.
	Injurious: when actors undermine, attack or harm each other.
	Parasitical: when the aim is to preserve the viability of the target, such that illegal benefits can be extorted on a more or less regular basis.
SYMBIOTIC RELATIONSHIPS	Outsourcing: division of labour between legal and illegal actors, where one party offers specialised services to the other.
	Collaboration: legal and illegal enterprises or actors actually work together for the commission of the same offense.
	Co-optation: involves mutual benefits; there are uneven power relations between the parties.
	Reciprocity: deliberately mutual benefits between the legal and illegal actors.
	Synergy: when legal and illegal actors benefit each other while they go about their business independently promoting their interests and objectives.
	Funding: legitimate organisations providing, knowingly or not, essential financial support for the operation of criminal groups.
	Legal interactions: Diversification not only for money laundering purposes, but also for the reduction of risk and maximisation of benefits.
	Legal actors committing organised crimes: legal actors engage in well-organised and sophisticated crimes on their own.

Dimensions and dynamics of shadow supply chains

Illicit supply chains, just like legal ones, are organised to be secure, redundant and resilient to disruption. In many supply chains, subcontracting has become the dominant organisational rationale regarding transport specialists, assassins for hire, corruption nodes, money launderers and legal actors like lawyers, accountants and bankers (MacDermott 2021). Criminal supply chains "are often designed with an extensive compartmentalization of operational knowledge throughout the layers of the various organizations involved [...] with redundant nodes and simplified roles to limit the potential negative impact" (Deville 2013: 65) when competing actors or law enforcement agencies try to intervene in the network. While in earlier articles (Neumann 2013) the expectation of a convergence of criminal organisations to form illicit networks was stated, this view had to be revised due to growing rivalries and violent confrontations between different networks, especially when they compete for the control of routes, border crossings or other places and nodes. One of the approaches to interpreting different places and nodes is the concept of "criminogenic asymmetries" (Hall 2013: 374) which depend on diverging economic conditions and regulatory regimes and are exploited in the organisation of illegal flows from South to North as well as from East to West. In order to identify the different dynamics and dimensions of shadow supply chains, especially with respect to uncovering the strategies of criminal actors, it is advisable to proceed with a mixed approach which combines three dimensions: products, activities and networks (Anzoom, Nagi and Vogiatzis 2022: 145).

Places and nodes

In applying the network approach, it is analytically fruitful to identify "hubs and nodes" which articulate networks, partnerships and interactions of the illicit. As a recent analysis puts it for the cocaine supply chain: "Different criminal nodes will align for a particular shipment, then drift apart, searching for new opportunities and trafficking constellations" (MacDermott 2021). Also, within the EU, a decentralised pattern of rather disorganised supply chains with manifold individual transactions is prevalent, especially in internet-based transactions (Europol 2021). Moreover, illicit flows have changed in the context of the pandemic; cyber marketplaces and internet online shopping have become a new venue where supply meets demand. This has created new opportunities for the commercialisation of counterfeit products or otherwise fraudulent goods. What has been detected is a new surge in the distribution of pirated assets over the internet. There is empirical evidence that the distribution of drugs on the surface web and the darknet and supported by the postal services has become a new dimension in this transnational illegal business (EMCDDA 2016).

This new marketplace complements the established nodes used for mixing licit and illicit trade activities, as do the free trade zones (FTZs), where strategic actors have placed their facilities in order to interconnect their international presence in relevant markets and establish their logistic networks. In these hubs, goods are landed, handled and manufactured but also repacked, reconfigured and reexported without the intervention of the customs authorities. So this type of procedure permits changes in the status of the goods in terms of their licit/illicit character, e.g. by introducing counterfeit and pirated products, which permits a stage of metamorphosis of the product. Although these key transhipments points produce economic benefits for host countries and hosted companies alike, they can also compromise both actors in their reputation when they are not managed according to due diligence and transparency standards. The pure numbers of these nodes for global trade are impressive: The OECD/EUIPO report (2018: 16) mentions more than 3,500 free trade zones, which are often located at key ports, in 130 countries or economies in North and South America, the Asia-Pacific region, Europe and Africa. In these nodes, enterprises take advantage of the interconnection of supply chains, using the FTZs' special offer of low tariffs and lighter regulation on financing, ownership, labour, immigration and taxes in these areas. At the same time, FTZs serve as places for concealing the origin of illicit products which are repacked and relabelled to enter the legal supply chains. For this reason, in order to reduce illicit trade risks in the FTZs (OECD 2019) these conduits of illegal trade are subject to joint efforts by the authorities to improve compliance with international standards of transparency. For these efforts to be effective, it is recommended to also include shell companies that mask the beneficial owners in these corporate structures.

International hubs of communication are also relevant nodes in the transformation of the supply chains or their management. New markets have been configured for illicit goods due to their future centrality: Most obviously, this is visible in emerging markets in the Gulf states, Russia, East Asia and beyond for antiquities (Brodie et al. 2022); China as well as India are major actors in the production of counterfeit and substandard medicines (OECD and EUIPO 2017: 6). By exploiting the fragmented character of these supply chains, the "continuous change of hands can mask the provenance of counterfeit medicines, making tracing almost impossible and making it hard to identify who is making the counterfeit drugs" (OECD and EUIPO 2020: 42).

These examples give a clear indication of the hubs and nodes that are central to the configuration of different shadow supply chains, which has to be identified in each case. Not to forget, there are also hubs for "cooling off" stolen products or maintaining some sort of safety stock and thus trying to control the inventory in order to avoid detection or control prices. But we can infer at this point the essential role that intermediation plays in the functioning of these structures, as the respective transactions may vary rapidly and can change without more in-depth traceability. The new dimension we can identify looking at supply chains beyond the reconstruction of series of individual transactions is to trace "pieces or nodes as a part of a series of recombinant chains with links that can merge and decouple as necessary" (Farah 2012: 2). This is also valid for interdiction in shadow supply chains: as we know from drug trafficking, rivalry or even enmity is an element of the criminal scenery. Instilling intensifying conflict between nodes or clusters of nodes has been a rather efficient way for law enforcement agencies to disrupt criminal networks.

As we know from research on bribery, intermediate structures or persons are of critical importance for the organisation of illegal/legal procedures and the "transformation" of the status of goods. The supply chain literature has shown that intermediate structures such as smelters for raw materials or sawmills in the illicit trade of wood are essential points where transparency and traceability will come to a chokepoint and even to a rapid stop (Muirhead and Porter 2019). So these points in a supply chain are of major concern in the tracking of illicit proceeds and of the participants in those stages of the supply chain.

Intermediation and disintermediation: the role of the middlemen

In the literature on organised crime, the "fixer-centric understanding" of the phenomenon has taken into perspective the facilitators as central agents for empowering the network structure in the shadow supply chains. The term "intermediaries" has been defined to refer to "all parties who act as a conduit in international business transactions, e.g. agents, sales representatives, consultants or consulting firms, suppliers, distributors, resellers, subcontractors, franchisees, joint venture partners, subsidiaries and other business partners including lawyers and accountants. Both natural and legal persons, such as consulting firms and joint ventures are included" (Working Group 2009: 5). The concrete form of the agency of the middlemen varies from facilitators to complicit actors, which may range from customs officials, appraisers and dealers to lawyers, who may routinely facilitate the illicit market simply by being reluctant to exercise the oversight they could apply. The services that they are providing as middlemen include issuing fake documents, organising auction mechanisms and facilitating the movement of the goods through numerous jurisdictions by identifying loopholes. The expectation concerning the role of the intermediaries is that they support the matching of buyers and suppliers and create trust in the process, functioning as certifiers of the quality of the product. In illegal or illicit transactions, the relationship between demand and supply is essentially characterised by a deficit of trust due to the surveillance strategies generated by the security agencies or possible competitors. Experience shows that no one in the chain of supply is likely to inform on the intermediaries. For these reasons, some criminal actors might prefer disintermediation, bypassing the middlemen, especially when their commitment is not credible or when they overstretch their bargaining power (Biglaiser and Li 2018: 18).

For this reason, actors in illegal markets may rely on different strategies concerning the organisation of their ties, seeking to establish weak links with customers for security reasons or opting for strong linkages with their partners in order to maintain control of the marketplace. The concrete selection of the preferred strategy will depend on the products and the structure of the market, in particular its mono- or oligopolistic characteristics. Also, in some product categories we will face conditions of monopsony or oligopsony which determine the presence or dispensability of middlemen. As we know from Granovetter's (1973) seminal analysis of network structures, more dispersed, nonredundant, open networks have greater access to information and power than smaller, denser, and more interconnected ones, resumed in the thesis of the "strength of weak ties", which also applies to the dark field of business relations.

For the organisation of the shadow supply chain, the criminal actors can opt on the one hand for a redundant chain of different intermediary structures with compartmentalised operations which don't know the "owner" of the supply chain for whom they are acting (multiple intermediary case) and try to guarantee by this anonymous character of the intermediation agents that interventions by state authorities or competing providers of their goods or services cannot cause major damage to the entire supply chain and its management. On the other hand, criminal actors might opt for a low-risk environment by adopting a disintermediation strategy that reduces the number and the role of the intermediaries, pushing the established intermediaries out of a market niche. Instead, they can rely e.g.

on electronic commerce via the internet or on the darknet, implementing a model of online dealing that has been developing most successfully in medicines and online drug marketplaces (EMCDDA 2015). Anonymous transactions have been facilitated by hiding IP addresses and operating with Bitcoins, thus reducing violence and face-to-face contacts as well as hiding identities. This sort of 'disorganised' crime in de-centralised markets based on encryption strategies is expanding rapidly and represents a new variant of hybridisation of illicit supply chains which combine surface web stores, social media contacts and cryptomarkets (Aldridge and Décary-Hétu 2016).

The transport dimension: illegal trafficking

Modes and routes of transportation, especially the number of transshipment points, are essential in the determination of profits and the distribution of risks (Basu 2014). Shifting routes is one of the most widely practiced instruments for avoiding interdiction and the presence of adversaries such as rival organisations, concealment capability being the second most employed tactic.

Most illicit markets are transnational, and the goods are not consumed where they are produced. The flow of illicit products is one of the preferred intervention points for the authorities in order to detect the trafficking. Although in many cases the concrete routes of transport are not exactly known, in the most studied case of illicit flows, which is drug trafficking, drug consumption and prices and especially their dynamics are used as a predictor where the product will be shipped. The demand for cocaine and the size of the markets in the US or Europe are employed to infer the direction of trafficking flows. The main interest of the law enforcement agencies at the international and national levels is to identify the major hubs or transit countries in order to exert pressure on them and try to prevent the products from reaching the own national territory (Giommoni et al. 2017).

But it is not always feasible to clearly distinguish between the country with 'outflows' and the one with 'inflows', in part due to complex market structures and product specifications or branding as well as unclear product descriptions in macrodata models and categories, especially in simulations for political purposes. Moreover, all deliveries of goods rely on transportation networks for the exchange of legal and illegal goods, a variable which is also influenced by lower-tax or higher-tax regimes, as in the case of cigarette smuggling. It is also assumed that the geographical scope is influenced by a double "neighbouring effect", in the sense of (1) the existence of geographical clusters served by the same routes chosen by traffickers to ship the illicit product and (2) a "spillover effect" of the same criminal networks using the same transport facilities for other illegal goods in order to minimise their costs. Empirical studies suggest a high density of illicit goods flowing on few transport routes (Aziani, Berlusconi and Giommoni 2021). Apart from geographically given conditions with fixed flows of licit goods, there are complementary factors such as established opportunities to bribe customs officers, the use of kinship and ethnic ties in foreign trade and knowledge about the routines of law enforcement agencies in specific countries. All these elements are helpful in reducing the risks of being discovered and in maximising the profits in the transactions. Comparative studies have shown that in the trafficking of different types of illicit goods, for example drug trafficking or antiquities smuggling, the flows show a clear distinction between source and destination countries, which means mostly unidirectional flows, while in cigarette trafficking a very complex network of multidirectional movements seems to exist (Meneghini, Aziani and Dugato 2020: 18) as well as different roles that countries play in these markets.

Another aspect which constitutes the interface between illegitimate and legitimate is transport, where legal and illegal products are often mixed and shipped to the consumer markets without distinction according to their legal status. Transport and access to central places where logistics are organised are paramount for allowing crime to profit from free market conditions. For example, the grey market nature of the antiquities trade, where illicitly obtained objects become effectively laundered by insertion into legitimate streams of supply, is a case characteristic of this type of procedure. The same is true for the sector of counterfeit goods, where China has been identified as the top producer, while Hongkong, Singapore and the United Arab Emirates serve as the global transit hubs for this type of illicit trade. By obfuscating the provenance in the chains of supply, the consumer market for certain products like antiquities transforms into a grey market of "those who do not know, or do not want to know" (Mackenzie 2011: 79).

In order to understand the role of transport, it is of central importance to calibrate the nature of the trade, especially its organisation and operation. The extension of the criminal network and the size of cross-border illicit flows are the critical variables for estimating the volume, the scope of the transport facilities as well as the capacities to control illicit trafficking. The traditional view of identifying the trafficking routes is becoming obsolete due to the growing importance of the internet trade. It is becoming more difficult to discover identities through a mapping of the structure in a transnational illicit network, especially for certain small and easily portable products and amounts, given a nearly infinite and easily multipliable number of storefronts and very differentiated transport facilities to serve them. This kind of decentralised and retail distribution exists in parallel with the more traditionally organised high-value supply chains headed up by well-connected dealers.

The trade is also related to traditional ways of transport (maritime, land- and air-based), which allow for different forms of concealment and are subject to sudden rerouting if obstacles arise: "(1) false information on the container's manifest, claiming that the container carries legitimate items; (2) false legal documentation such as import licenses (e.g. false declarations, consignee's contact details, etc.); (3) fraudulent packaging (e.g. illegal products have been hidden in boxes labelled as commercial products); (4) concealment of illicit goods among legally imported products; and (5) the use of transit places, which can serve several purposes depending on the stage of the journey" (as has been shown for the case of Tramadol trafficking in UNODC 2021: 32).

Stages and participants

Supply chains are always associated with production, (internal) trade, distribution and consumption, organized in the different roles of supplier, manufacturer, distributor, retailer and consumer. All these stages are related to products, which in passing through them undergo some sort of transformation, be it in the product itself or in the value assigned to it due to a greater geographic proximity to the final consumer. The architecture of the supply chain, its network character, is determined by the distribution channels or the (illicit) actors who are able to manage the structure to ensure high levels of connectivity. The factors that drive illicit supply chains, i.e. the transactions and interactions inside of the supply chain, may have a legal or illegal character, which means that the trade itself need not be illegal in general (due to smuggling or counterfeiting, product piracy, miscoding, evasive route selection, document forgery, corruption of officials). Also, at the different stages of the chain the distribution of revenues is unequal, the most typical case being that a substantial share is extracted at the level of distribution, while producers and retailers receive less benefits along the chain (Aguiar de Medeiros and Trebat 2017).

Shadow supply chains and illegal trafficking should not be considered a phenomenon that necessarily corresponds to organised crime and/or vice versa, nor should the actors involved be considered to belong to organised crime structures; although the relationship is close, it should be analysed to what extent and in what phases they belong to organised crime frameworks. This is because in the production/smuggling there are stages and individual actors with their own interests (who do not belong to any organised structure) that play a role in these dynamics and cannot be ignored.

The first essential stage is the local level, where the actors have to know the territory and be accepted in some way in an environment that can turn extremely hostile to outsiders. This applies to wildlife traffickers who act locally and on a small scale as well as in the trading market for antiquities and cultural items. According to the perception of some archaeologists, who are experts in this business, organised crime networks are not necessarily involved as long as the trafficking operates at the local level (Proulx 2011). In fact, the author states that situating the trafficking of antiquities and cultural goods solely within the framework of organised crime may be erroneous, insofar as "it overlooks the micro-level social and organizational complexities of the antiquities trade; that is, the local realities of looting and trafficking are lost within broader global abstractions" (Proulx 2011: 24). In this way, at the local level, providers, producers or even communities have to be treated differently than the operators of the international trade.

The second stage includes the concealment of the origin. In the case of timber trafficking, the greatest cases of corruption and fraud have been found in the Amazon region. Several reports by Greenpeace have provided detailed evidence of how this phenomenon occurs. Since 2014, this NGO has warned that legal documentation does not guarantee the legal origin of timber; this is due to the dynamics of fraud and corruption both in obtaining licenses and in the extraction and commercialisation processes, which make it difficult for the authorities to determine the legality of the timber (Greenpeace 2018). Estimates of the volume of timber to be cut are made fraudulently, mostly by increasing the numbers through fake identification of the trees and inclusion of non-existent trees (size and quantity), due to the activities of the logging companies which carry out the exploitation; in this way, "imaginary trees" are created, giving the firms the chance to legalise illegally cut timber. This is one of the strategies for illegal extraction.

Once the illegal timber is camouflaged in the legally felled timber, with false documents and transport and sales authorisations, it goes directly to the sawmills, which then saw the timber. After this processing step, it is impossible to distinguish its legal or illegal origin. The foreign companies that import this timber accept the documents, in many cases without asking about its legal status and omitting audits or independent legality tests (wood laundering). One of the sawmill companies investigated for dubious domestic and international sales is Rainbow Trading, which exports to companies in Belgium, China, Denmark, France, Germany, Italy, the Netherlands, Portugal, Spain, Sweden, the United Kingdom and the United States (Greenpeace 2014; 2015).

With respect to the third stage (export, transport and trade), it cannot be ignored that consumers and importers are involved as well. Exporting companies obtain wood from sawmills, or process it themselves, satisfying specific needs of buyers in terms of species and types of wood (Greenpeace 2015). This also applies to the case of cultural property. One of the ways to "launder" cultural property is to exhibit or present it to the public through displays and exhibitions and even by opening private museums (García 2013: 27). This artifice of promotion and public diffusion allows society to assume or know about its existence, but above all it seemingly "legalises" the property of the goods.

It is important to note, as stated above, that for smugglers, routes and methods are associated with other types of trafficking. This seems to be in line with the convergence argument, but each market has particular markers regarding the product and the actors involved in the supply chain. In fact, "[c]riminals who engage in the illegal wildlife trade are often merely transferring the skills, connections, transport routes, counterfeiting and concealment techniques they have developed in the areas of drugs, small arms or human trafficking" (Cowdrey 2002: 4); nevertheless, shadow supply chains and their respective markets are product-specific. This applies to the antiquities trade the chain/process as well as in the case of wildlife trafficking, which varies according to the type of product or species being transported (animals, live or dead plants, parts of unprocessed animals, such as skins, tusks or bones, or processed goods, such as ivory carvings, traditional Asian medicines or sawn timber), which have their own features for multiple re-exporting in order to cover offences (Schneider 2008).

According to Campbell (2013: 114), the antiquities trade has similarities with other goods trafficked through networks. A common pattern is the demand in wealthy countries that drives individuals in economically depressed countries to export goods abroad. This transnational trade requires sophisticated strategies and organisation in order to succeed, and this is not necessarily due to a hierarchical structure but to "fluid network structures", generally with personal interactions and no other obligations. Different kinds of actors play roles in this process, from farmers and looters to trained professionals and experts in this matter "whose only connection is a shared opportunity" (Campbell 2013: 115).

The antiquities trade, according to Campbell (2013), seen through the lens of role specialisation shows the need to collaborate and accept a smaller portion of profits in exchange for a higher success rate.

Diagram 1: Based on Campbell (2013); stages in illegal antiquities trade

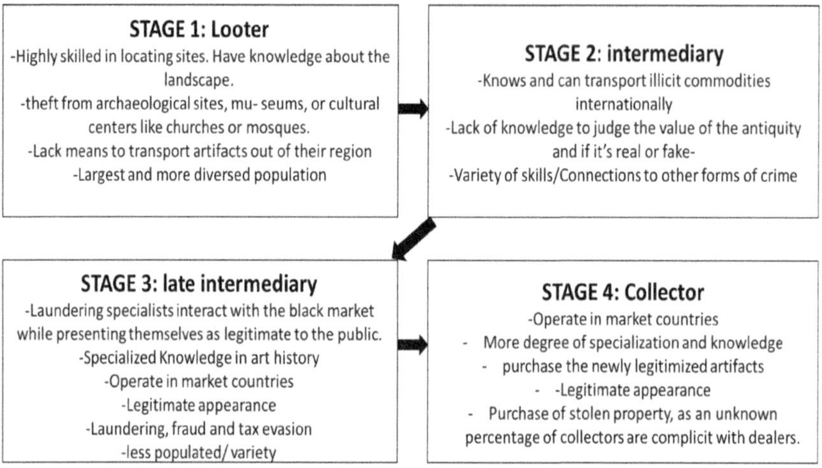

This diagram shows that the later the stage and the more specialisation in art and antiquities is invested, we can identify an increase in the profit rate for the criminal actors active in the chain, ending up in auction houses, museums and the houses of private collectors (Alderman 2012) which pay high prices for illegal products.

The organisation of shadow supply chains: criminal diasporas

In the discussion on the organisational aspects of illicit supply chains, one of the dominant approaches is to analyse the factors that contribute to organised crime spreading beyond national borders and being able to develop transnational dimensions. Again, the convergence argument is presented as a general explanation, as the expansion of illegal flows may contribute to the corresponding organisational patterns of the criminal actors that permit their operativity in multidimensional markets and the movement of different goods and services. For this reason, attention is predominantly given to the type of linkages that criminal organisations are able to establish, be it by migrating the respective networks, spreading out or linking up with other organisations. The decision whether to invest in the development of local markets or in expanding the network into new markets seems to depend on the specific structure of the markets and the corresponding supply paths, their profitability and the methods of expansion that are at hand (Santamaría 2013).

As illicit markets can prove to be very complicated due to the multiplicity of (violent) actors and the offensives of state agencies, the criminal actors will prefer to rely on established structures such as "criminal diasporas" which have been established or can be activated on short notice. These diasporas are constituted by ethnic bonds and family and kinship structures but are also the result of governmental offensives against criminal organisations. Examples of this kind can be found in the spread of criminal activities to regions with less capacity to resist illegal activities due to the "balloon" and the "cockroach" effects (Garzón et al. 2013: 11–12) that expanded the presence of criminal actors to new areas. This collateral effect has been present in the drug trafficking of cartels in Colombia, Mexico and Central America, but also in the metropolitan areas of Brazil. The deportation of criminals from the US to Mexico and Central America has also contributed to the diffusion of criminal patterns, in some ways reproducing the experience of the youth gangs (Maras) in the region. This new type of geography induced by illicit flows has seen an expansion to West Africa in the 2000s (Brombacher and Maihold 2009) and has been changing in transit countries as well the transport facilities over time (Bird 2021). The initial connections between Brazilian traffickers and Nigerian criminal groups are expanding from Senegal through the Gambia and Guinea-Bissau to Guinea and Cape Verde (UNODC 2005; Bird 2021). This reflects the capacity to adapt to new conditions in the flows of drugs as well as the inherent fragility and instability of illegal supply chains, which always have to be adjusted to external pressure, internal redesign and new market dynamics. One of the major challenges in these dynamics of internal re-regulation is the asymmetric distribution of profits along the supply chain, where in many of the chains one can identify those actors which are closest to the final consumer markets and able to realise the largest profits all along the supply chain. As backward linkages in illicit supply chains are less developed and the transaction costs are realised at each stage of transaction, the final stage of delivery in the consumer market offers the best conditions for the accumulation of the value added and the profits generated by the successful passing of the product through different borders and distributing hands.

Tracking shadow supply chains and illicit networks

Tracing shadow supply chains is one of the most difficult tasks of law enforcement, in part due to the subversion of existing supply chains and of the corresponding transportation networks for illegal purposes. One possible approach is to distinguish between criminal procedures for "exiting" the supply chain (e.g. cargo theft) on the one hand and those centred on its "entering" side, that is, smuggling of products and persons, on the other hand. The measures taken by law enforcement agencies in order to intercept illicit flows cause the same disturbances as the theft of products in so far as they interrupt the logistics systems for all the market participants. The main discussion is therefore centred on the issue at which point the supply chain interruption should occur, as illegal goods as well as legal ones pass through processes of added value as they are moved along the supply chain (as was mentioned earlier in the description of the role of intermediaries). The convergence argument reappears here very prominently, as law enforcement agencies claim that illicit supply networks can just as easily be used for other goods (e.g. in the trade of illicit cigarettes it may be most appropriate to also move drugs or antiquities), making use of the corruption of the same border officials and customs agents. The use of legitimate carriers and freight forwarders is of central importance for "piggybacking" illicit supply chains on mainstream transport networks (Manners-Bell 2018: 247ff.), covering traces and thus making products untraceable.

Law enforcement agencies have considerable difficulties in tracking the complex structures of illicit networks, especially when they try to disrupt the entire network structure. On the one hand, they can focus on the flows of illicit goods and services in the shadow supply chains with the limitation that they cannot really grasp the entire network; on the other hand, they can try to intervene in the flow of payments by surveillance of money laundering activities. While finance is a critical resource in supply chains, the traditional way of transferring money in cash is being substituted by non-cash payments such as cryptocurrencies that guarantee anonymity and security to the criminal actors (Foley, Karlsen and Putniņš 2019). Again we meet the convergence argument, as a linkage of actors and networks around certain common methods and instruments in money laundering and "barter trade" has been identified. But this kind of relationship lies more in the area of activity appropriation for a certain stage of a criminal network and does not reach the level of a symbiotic relationship.[2]

Illegal trafficking and common patterns in supply chains

The configuration of vast illegal markets for legal as well as illegal goods and products such as drugs, timber, gold and other minerals, antiquities and other cultural goods, medicines and even human beings or parts of them (organs such as kidneys) is very complex, as the interactions as well as the goods or products can continuously change their status as legal or illegal. With this growing and mutable problem, an important question arises: How do networks of illegal trafficking continue to exist and operate successfully even when the authorities make multiple efforts to combat this phenomenon? In order to arrive at an answer, in a first approach we will try to identify common patterns involving actors, processes and dynamics in the trafficking chains, independent of the product or good. Also, the relationships between legality and illegality, and the practices that allow this phenomenon to persist, can provide some analytical elements to come closer to a comprehension of this phenomenon. We will therefore try to show common elements of different supply chains of illicit goods in order to compare their functioning and composition.

Illegal trafficking: common patterns

According to a UNEP (United Nations Environment Programme) report, approximately 30 % of the timber traded in the world is of illegal origin. In the same vein, WWF (2021) indicates that each year, approximately 100 tigers, 20,000 elephants and more than 1,000 rhinos are killed for trafficking in their bones, skin, tusks or horns. Moreover, an Athar Project (2019) investigation showed that almost two million people are members of groups on the social network Facebook that are dedicated to the illegal trafficking of cultural goods and antiquities, mostly from the Middle East. While these are different markets, with substantial differences in terms of

2 In the debate on the crime-terror nexus there have been identified operational dynamics with different levels of relationships, representing "activity appropriation" one of the lower levels (Dishman 2001) and pointing to the adoption of methods used by other criminal organizations.

processes, actors and methods, as well as consumers, it is worth analysing common elements that occur in the context of illegal trafficking.

Diagram 2: Illegal trade process (author's design)

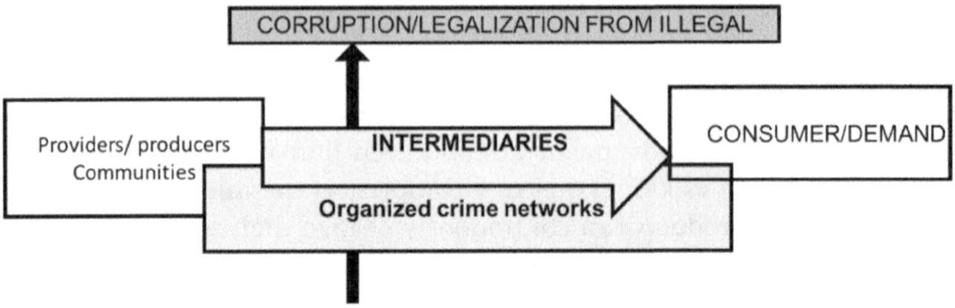

An interesting case to review is wildlife trafficking, which is currently believed to be widely penetrated by organised crime groups (Wyatt, van Uhm and Nurse 2020). This is where an issue of interest to this study comes in: the convergence of various illegally trafficked products in certain organised groups. That is, certain actors (usually dedicated to drug or weapons trafficking) participate in the illegal trade of other products such as minerals, wildlife or timber, thus exploring new markets and with them new ways to make profits, reduce risks and exercise control over territories. An example is the case of gold exploitation in Colombia: the criminal infrastructure that organised crime groups have developed to exercise control over illegal drug plantations can easily be used for other activities and provide income for criminal actors when such an opportunity exists; hence these organisations develop a broad portfolio of criminal activities, increasing profits, expanding territorial control and managing similar dynamics with associated actors (Rettberg and Ortiz-Riomalo 2016). As for the trafficking of art and antiquities, close relationships of this market with other types of goods and products, such as drugs, have been mentioned. As Tijhuis (2006: 139) writes, first, "precious stolen works of art are supposedly used as collateral or means of payment in major drug deals"; second, "stolen art or looted antiquities are trafficked together with drugs from source to market country"; and third, "stolen art is thought to be used to launder proceeds from drug trafficking or other criminal activities".

At the same time, it is important to note that illegal markets and crime dynamics highly depend on the context of each country regarding economic, legal and even cultural conditions, which impact on their configuration in some way or another. For example, the market conditions, the supply chains and the actor profiles are quite different in arms trade and wildlife crime, but criminal actors might use similar tactics and instruments or even share hubs in certain moments and segments of their criminal activities. Also, violence and coercive methods as well as the structure of criminal networks in each country are diverse due to links with the global dimension/markets, which require specific ways of delivery and supply. Another fundamental issue is the role that the internet and social media are assuming in different shadow supply chains; electronic interactions have become a central platform for the transfer of goods, services and resources of illegal origin, demanding a new type of specialist skilled at internet marketing. For example, Mexican cartels and other criminal organisations used encrypted devices for their operational communications and international trade, which was uncovered in 2021 by the operation known as Trojan Shield that coordinated police agencies in 16 nations. More than 800 suspects were arrested, and more than 32 tonnes of drugs – including cocaine, cannabis, amphetamines and methamphetamines – were seized, along with 250 firearms, 55 luxury cars and more than US$148 million in cash and cryptocurrencies (Davis 2021).

Conclusions: de-risking supply chains

Preventing supply chains from being undermined by criminal actors is one of the central challenges in developing greater robustness and operational resilience of the production networks. Research has shown that the disruption of supply chains is having major impacts on the economies of industrialised countries (Maihold and Mühlhöfer 2021); this finding shows that supply chains compromised by criminal interests are very difficult to recover for the legal actors involved without causing bottlenecks and economic costs for legal flows. Only through better risk management strategies at the company level, greater transparency and "know your customer/supplier" procedures in sourcing strategies can possible risks be minimised. As governments can support the efforts of companies by collecting and sharing information, the joint action of both levels of responsibility is an essential element of de-risking. But supply chains imply high levels of complexity, especially when different manufacturing stages and separate components are combined. For this reason, one approach has been that law enforcement agencies should focus on key or central nodes in the chain, which make the largest contribution to the criminal activities (Ballester, Calvó-Armengol and Zenou 2006), while other authors suggest targeting the most prominent criminals or emergent leaders or disrupting associated networks in order to eliminate their capability to distribute goods and resources (e.g. in the case of precursors) (Carley, Lee and Krackhardt 2002). Generally, it can be assumed that the more complex the product, the higher the costs of transparency and effective traceability of the supply chain. For example, establishing redundancy as a strategy of resilience in shadow supply chains may appear easy, but the costs may expand considerably during execution. The need to identify additional channels and persons increases network communications, raises the network's visibility and makes it more vulnerable to interdiction by the authorities. Therefore, the expansion of the scope of interdiction is one of the challenges that authorities confront in their efforts to disrupt criminal networks and avoid rapid replacement of nodes and actors.

In the end, redundancy goes against one of the basic management paradigms of supply chains: efficiency. In order to achieve higher standards of safety and reduce risk factors, additional capital may be necessary to arrive at strong oversight with respect to the participating actors. Criminal strategies like shifts in the geography of production and transport in response to higher law enforcement capacities are one of the factors which can affect the entire supply chain and imply an internal reorganisation of the established links as well as a reconfiguration of the complete (even non-criminal) supply chain. But realising vulnerabilities due to criminal participation in supply chains is essential to risk management plans (including tools to monitor possible risks) that enterprises will have to establish. Therefore, the main pathway should lead to greater robustness of the supply chains, especially in certain vulnerable stages like transportation, repackaging, logistics etc. At the end of the day, all measures of surveillance and control can be summarised in two basic options: reducing the flows and increasing the costs. Both options have considerable effects also on the legal side in supply chains, due to the mixture of illicit actors in the supply chain who are difficult to identify and remove.

Analysing illegal markets reveals common patterns, in part because both routes and actors may either be interconnected or belong to different types or sectors of markets, with profit being their primary motivation. However, the different particularities of each market cannot be ignored and should be analysed in detail, as actors, roles and specialties that determine each supply chain in each market have specific characteristics. In this view, the convergence argument is valid in terms of activity appropriation in different shadow supply chains by criminal actors who try to cover different markets or market segments. Similarities and convergences are possible, maybe frequent, but this does not imply a general trend towards symbiotic relationships or even hybrid groups. An example of this is the antiquities trade, where actors in the final stages are people with highly specialised knowledge about art, often specialists, historians and archaeologists, who are vital in the process in order to determine higher profit margins and interest in the products trafficked. In the case of trade in wildlife, antiquities and timber, the product is transformed as its value increases, and the actors gain as it moves toward the final consumer. This is one of the proofs that illegal markets are solid sources of income that provide incentives to stay in the market with specialised roles and profiles of actors and processes.

Finally, it is important to point out that governments and their legal systems and law enforcement agencies are determining factors in the existence and success of processes such as looting and illegal logging. Intermediaries play crucial roles at different levels, sometimes due to their weak capacities in the configuration of the chains, in other cases more prominent ones as brokers between important hubs for (il)legal markets. The weakness of some legal systems, in the face of which the methods and processes for concealing and transporting illegal goods continue to exist, is compounded by the lack of institutional interest in filling these gaps; the roots can be found in the profit obtained by those who participate in and facilitate the existence of shadow supply chains from their institutional positions. The efforts to de-risk have to extend from the company level to the final consumer, all along the supply chain, in order to reduce its "shadowy" segments.

Note: The author wants to express his gratitude to Diana Cortés for her research support in the preparation of this chapter.

References

Aguiar de Medeiros, Carlos/Trebat, Nicholas (2017): "Inequality and income distribution in global value chains". In: Journal of Economic Issues, 51, 2, pp. 401–408.

Alderman, Kimberly L. (2012): "Honor amongst thieves. Organized crime and the illicit antiquities trade". In: Indiana Law Review, 45, 3, pp. 601–627.

Aldridge, Judith/Décary-Hétu, David (2016): "Cryptomarkets and the future of illicit drug markets". In: EMCDDA, European Monitoring Centre for Drugs and Drug Addiction (2015): The internet and drug markets. Lisbon, pp. 23–32.

Amineddoleh, Leila (2013): "The role of museums in the trade of black market cultural heritage property". In: Art, Antiquity and Law, 18, pp. 227–254.

Andreas, Peter (2011): "Illicit globalization. Myths, misconceptions, and historical lessons". In: Political Science Quarterly, 126, 3, 403–425.

Anzoom, Rashid/Nagi, Rakesh/Vogiatzis, Chrysafis (2022): "A review of research in illicit supply-chain networks and new directions to thwart them". In: IISE Transactions, 54, 2, pp. 134–158.

Athar Project (2019): "Facebook's black market in antiquities". At: http://atharproject.org/report2019/ (accessed 20 December 2021).

Aziani, Alberto/Berlusconi, Giulia/Giommoni, Luca (2021): "A quantitative application of enterprise and social embeddedness theories to the transnational trafficking of cocaine in Europe". In: Deviant Behavior, 42, 2, pp. 245–267.

Ballester, Coralio/Calvó-Armengol, Antoni/Zenou, Yves (2006): "Who's who in networks. Wanted: the key player". In: Econometrica, Econometric Society, 74, 5, pp. 1403–1417.

Basu, Gautam (2014): "Concealment, corruption, and evasion. A transaction cost and case analysis of illicit supply chain activity". In: Journal of Transportation Security, 7, pp. 209–226.

Biglaiser, Gary/Li, Fei (2018): "Middlemen: the good, the bad, and the ugly". In: Rand Journal of Economics, 49, 1, 3–22.

Bird, Lucia (2021): "West Africa's cocaine corridor. Building a subregional response". At: https://globalinitiative.net/wp-content/uploads/2021/04/West-Africas-Cocaine-Corridor-GITOC.pdf (accessed 7 June 2022).

Brodie, Neil/Kersel, Morag M./Mackenzie, Simon/Sabrine, Isber/Smith, Emiline/Yates, Donna (2022): "Why there is still an illicit trade in cultural objects and what we can do about it". In: Journal of Field Archaeology, 47, 2, pp. 117–130.

Brombacher, Daniel/Maihold, Günther (2009): Cocaine trafficking to Europe. Options of supply control. Berlin: SWP Research Paper 10.

Campbell, Peter B. (2013): "The illicit antiquities trade as a transnational criminal network. Characterizing and anticipating trafficking of cultural heritage". In: International Journal of Cultural Property, 20, 2, pp. 113–153.

Carley, Kathleen M./Lee, Ju-Sung/Krackhardt, David (2002): "Destabilizing networks". In: Connections, 24, 3, pp. 79–92.

Cattaneo, Olivier/Gereffi, Gary/Staritz, Cornelia (2010): Global value chains in a postcrisis world. A development perspective. Washington, DC: World Bank.

Cowdrey, David (2002): "Switching channels: wildlife trade routes into Europe and the UK. A World Wildlife Fund/TRAFFIC Report". At: http://assets.wwf.org.uk/downloads/switchingchannels.pdf (accessed 7 June 2022).

Davis, Nicholas (2021): "The FBI's operation Trojan shield. Infiltrating criminal groups through their phones". At: https://www.american.edu/sis/centers/security-technology/operation-trojan-shield.cfm (accessed 7 June 2022).

De Rios, Marlene Dobkin/Smith, David E. (1977): "Drug use and abuse in cross cultural perspective". In: Human Organization, 36, 1, pp. 14–21.

Deville, Duncan (2013): "The illicit supply chain". In: Miklaucic, Michael/Brewer, Jacqueline (eds.): Convergence. Illicit networks and national security in the age of globalization. Washington, DC: National Defense University Press, pp. 63–74.

Dishman, Chris (2001): "Terrorism, crime, and transformation". In: Studies in Conflict and Terrorism, 24, 1, pp. 43–58.

EIA, Environmental Investigation Agency (2019): "Condenando el bosque. Ilegalidad y falta de gobernanza en la Amazonía colombiana". At: https://www.condenandoelbosque.org/ (accessed 7 June 2022).

EMCDDA, European Monitoring Centre for Drugs and Drug Addiction (2015): The internet and drug markets. Summary of results from an EMCDDA Trendspotter study. Lisbon.

EMCDDA, European Monitoring Centre for Drugs and Drug Addiction (2016): The internet and drug markets, Lisbon.

Europol (2021): Internet Organised Crime Threat Assessment (IOCTA) 2021. Luxembourg: Publications Office of the European Union.

Farah, Douglas (2012): "Fixers, super fixers and shadow facilitators. How networks connect" At: http://www.strategycenter.net/docLib/20120423_Farah_FixersSuperFixersShadow.pdf (accessed 7 June 2022).

Felbab-Brown, Vanda/Niño, Catalina (2021): "Legalizing drugs and illegal economies is no panacea for Latin America and the rest of the world". At: https://www.brookings.edu/on-the-record/legalizing-drugs-and-illegal-economies-is-no-panacea-for-latin-america-and-the-rest-of-the-world/ (accessed 7 June 2022).

Foley, Sean/Karlsen, Jonathan R./ Putniņš, Tālis J. (2019): "Sex, drugs, and bitcoin: How much illegal activity is financed through cryptocurrencies?". In: The Review of Financial Studies, 32, 5, pp. 1798–853.

García, Tania (2013): "Dimensión social del tráfico ilícito de bienes culturales". In: Revista De Museología, 3, pp. 20–34.

Garzón, Juan Carlos/Olinger, Marianna/Rico, Daniel M./Santamaría, Gema (2013): The criminal diaspora. The spread of transnational organized crime and how to contain its expansion. Washington, DC: Woodrow Wilson International Center for Scholars.

Gereffi, Garry (2001): "Shifting governance structures in global commodity chains, with special reference to the internet". In: American Behavioral Scientist, 44, 10, 1616–1637.

Gilman, Nils/Goldhammer, Jesse/Weber, Steven (2013): "Deviant globalization". In: Michael Miklaucic/Jacqueline Brewer (eds.): Convergence. Illicit networks and national security in the age of globalization. Washington, DC: National Defense University Press, pp. 3–14.

Giommoni, Luca/Aziani, Alberto/Berlusconi, Giulia (2017): "How do illicit drugs move across countries? A network analysis of the heroin supply to Europe". In: Journal of Drug Issues, 47, pp. 217–240.

Granovetter, Mark (1973): "The strength of weak ties". In: American Journal of Sociology, 78, 6, pp. 1360–1380.

Greenpeace (2014): "Amazonía, una crisis silenciosa". At: https://archivo-es.greenpeace.org/espana/es/Informes-2014/Mayo/Amazonia-una-crisis-silenciosa/ (accessed 7 June 2022).

Greenpeace (2014): “The Amazon's silent crisis. Night terrors”. At: www.greenpeace.de/files/publications/gp_amz_silent_crimefile_v6.5.pdf (accessed 7 June 2022).

Greenpeace (2015): “The Amazon's Silent Crisis. License to Launder”. At: https://www.greenpeace.org/usa/wp-content/uploads/legacy/Global/usa/planet3/PDFs/Amazon5Ways.pdf (accessed 7 June 2022).

Greenpeace (2018): “Árboles imaginarios, destrucción real”. At: https://es.greenpeace.org/es/wp-content/uploads/sites/3/2018/03/INFORME-Arboles-imaginarios-destrucci%C3%B3n-real-20mar2018-2.pdf (accessed 7 June 2022).

Hall, Tim (2013): “Geographies of the illicit. Globalization and organized crime”. In: Progress in Human Geography, 37, 3, pp. 366–385.

Kleinschmit, Daniela/ Mansourian, Stephanie/Wildburger, Christoph/Purret, Andre (2016): Illegal logging and related timber trade. Dimensions, drivers, impacts and responses: A Global Scientific Rapid Response Assessment. Vienna: IUFRO.

Lavorgna, Anita (2014): “Wildlife trafficking in the Internet age. The changing structure of criminal opportunities”. In: Crime Science, 3, 5, pp. 1–12.

MacDermott, Jeremy (2021): “Cocaine to Europe. An underestimated threat”. At: https://insightcrime.org/investigations/cocaine-europe-underestimated-threat/ (accessed 7 June 2022).

Mackenzie, Simon (2002): “Organised crime and common transit networks”. In: Trends & Issues in Crime and Criminal Justice No. 233. At: https://traffickingculture.org/publications/mackenzie-s-2002-organised-crime-common-transit-networks-trends-issues-in-crime-and-criminal-justice-no-233-canberra-australian-institute-of-criminology/ (accessed 7 June 2022).

Mackenzie, Simon (2005): Going, going, gone. Regulating the market in illicit antiquities. Leicester: Institute of Art and Law.

Mackenzie, Simon (2011): “The market as criminal and criminals in the market. Reducing opportunities for organised crime in the international antiquities market”. In: Manacorda, Stefano/Chappell, Duncan (eds.): Crime in the art and antiquities world. Illegal trafficking in cultural property. New York: Springer, pp. 69–86.

Maihold, Günther/Mühlhöfer, Fabian (2021): Supply chain instability threatens security of supplies. Options for industry and policymakers. Berlin: SWP Comment 2021/C 60.

Manners-Bell, John (2018): Supply chain risk management. Understanding emerging threats to global supply chains. London/New York: Kogan Page.

Meneghini, Cecilia/Aziani, Alberto/Dugato, Marco (2020): “Modeling the structure and dynamics of transnational illicit networks. An application to cigarette trafficking”. In: Applied Network Science, 5, 21, pp. 1–27.

Muirhead, Jacob/Porter, Tony (2019): “Traceability in global governance”. In: Global Networks, 19, pp. 423–443.

Neumann, Vanessa (2013): “Grievance to greed. The global convergence of the crime-terror threat”. In: Orbis, 57, 2, pp. 251–267

OECD, Organisation for Economic Co-operation and Development (2019): Recommendation on countering illicit trade. Enhancing transparency in free trade zones. Paris.

OECD, Organisation for Economic Co-operation and Development/EUIPO, European Union Intellectual Property Office (2017): Trade in counterfeit pharmaceutical products. Paris: OECD Publishing.

OECD, Organisation for Economic Co-operation and Development/EUIPO, European Union Intellectual Property Office (2018): Trade in counterfeit goods and free trade zones. evidence from recent trends. Paris: OECD Publishing.

OECD, Organisation for Economic Co-operation and Development/EUIPO, European Union Intellectual Property Office (2020): Trade in counterfeit pharmaceutical products, illicit trade. Paris: OECD Publishing.

Passas, Nikos (2002): "Cross-border crime and the interface between legal and illegal actors". In: van Duyne, Petrus C./von Lampe, Klaus/Passas, Nikos (eds.): Upperworld and underworld in cross-border crime. Nijmegen: Wolf Legal Publishers, pp. 443–462.

Persi Paoli, Giacomo/Aldridge, Judith/Ryan, Nathan/Warnes, Richard (2017): "Behind the curtain. The illicit trade of firearms, explosives and ammunition on the dark web" At: https://www.rand.org/pubs/research_reports/RR2091.html (accessed 7 June 2022).

Phelps, Jacob/Biggs, Duan/Webb, Eduard L. (2016): "Tools and terms for understanding illegal wildlife trade". In: Frontiers in Ecology and the Environment, 14, 9, pp. 479–489.

Ponte, Stefano/Gibbon, Peter (2005): "Quality standards, conventions and the governance of global value chains". In: Economy and Society 34, 1, pp. 1–31.

Proulx, Blythe Bowman (2011): "Organized criminal involvement in the illicit antiquities trade". In: Trends in Organized Crime, 14, 1, pp. 1–29.

Rettberg, Angelika/Ortiz-Riomalo, Juan Felipe (2016): "Golden opportunity, or a new twist on the resource–conflict relationship. Links between the drug trade and illegal gold mining in Colombia". In: World Development, 84, pp. 82–96.

Santamaría, Gema (2013): "La difusión y contención del crimen organizado en la región México-Centroamérica". In: Olson, Eric/Garzón, Juan Carlos (eds): La diáspora criminal. La difusión transnacional del Crimen Organizado y cómo contener su expansión. Washington D.C: Woodrow Wilson Center, pp. 59–100.

Schneider, Jacqueline L. (2008): "Reducing the illicit trade in endangered wildlife. The market reduction approach". In: Journal of Contemporary Criminal Justice 24, 3, pp. 274–295.

Stridsman, Mats/Østensen, Åse Gilje (2017): Shadow value chains. Tracing the link between corruption, illicit activity and lootable natural resources from West Africa. Bergen: U4 Anti-Corruption Resource Centre, Chr. Michelsen Institute.

Tijhuis, Antonius Johannes Gerhardus (2006): Transnational crime and the interface between legal and illegal actors. The case of the illicit art and antiquities trade. Nijmegen: Wolf Legal Publishers.

UNODC, United Nations Office on Drugs and Crime (2005): Transnational organized crime in the West African region. Vienna/New York.

UNODC, United Nations Office on Drugs and Crime (2021): At the Crossroads of Licit and Illicit. Tramadol and other pharmaceutical opioids trafficking in West Africa. UNODC: Vienna.

USAID/GI-TOC, Global Initiative against Transnational Organized Crime (2020): "Strengthening Rule of Law approaches to address organized crime. Criminal Market Convergence". At: https://globalinitiative.net/analysis/strengthening-rule-of-law-approaches-to-address-organized-crime-criminal-market-convergence/ (accessed 7 June 2022).

Van Uhm, Daan P./Moreto, William D. (2018): "Corruption within the illegal wildlife trade. A symbiotic and antithetical enterprise". In: The British Journal of Criminology, 58, 4, pp. 864–885

Working Group, Working Group on Bribery in International Business Transactions (2009): Typologies on the role of intermediaries in international business transactions. Paris: OECD-DAF.

WWF, World Wildlife Fund (2021): "Paremos el negocio de la extinción". At: https://traficoespecies.wwf.es/ (accessed 22 December 2021).

Wyatt, Tania/van Uhm, Daan/Nurse, Angus (2020): "Differentiating criminal networks in the illegal wildlife trade. Organized, corporate and disorganized crime". In: Trends in Organized Crime, 23, pp. 350–366.

Part II:
The "classic" flows of criminal business

Cannabis cultivation and trafficking in and from Albania

Fatjona Mejdini

An overview

Cannabis is the most commonly used drug in the world today, with an estimated 192 million consumers in 2018, corresponding to 3.9 per cent of the global population aged 15–64 (UNDOC 2020: 11). A study undertaken in the EU countries estimates cannabis use in 2020 among those aged 15–34 at 15.4 %, ranging from 3.4 % in Hungary to 21.8 % in France (EMCDDA 2021: 16). Albania, in Southeastern Europe, has been one of the most important European suppliers of illicit cannabis throughout the continent for almost two decades. Albania borders two European Union members, Italy and Greece, and its outdoor-grown cannabis reaches these countries and then other parts of Europe. Via the so-called Balkans route, Albanian cannabis reaches Central Europe. Furthermore, illicit Albanian cannabis has also been supplying the markets in the eastern part of the continent and its surroundings, most notably Turkey (Mejdini and Amerhauser 2019: 8–9).

The cultivation of illicit cannabis in Albania has a long history and started immediately after the collapse of the communist system that left the country in poverty and isolation from the rest of the world for more than four decades. The weak and inexperienced institutions of the country were not ready to lead a successful fight against drug cultivation. Continued political crises, especially the civil unrest that swept Albania in 1997, took a toll on security institutions, leading to weak performance in the fight against drugs. From the early 1990s on, the cultivation of cannabis in Albania helped many families across the country to secure a living in a time when the prolonged and painful political and economic transition left many without access to the formal economy. But mainly, the cultivation and trafficking of cannabis helped Albanian criminal organisations to strengthen their position, become more sophisticated and develop the ability to be active in the trafficking of other drugs as well, such as heroin and cocaine. They often used cannabis as a currency, regularly exchanging it for heroin coming from Afghanistan and entering the Balkan region via Turkey.

Figure 1: Transnational cannabis trafficking routes to and from Albania

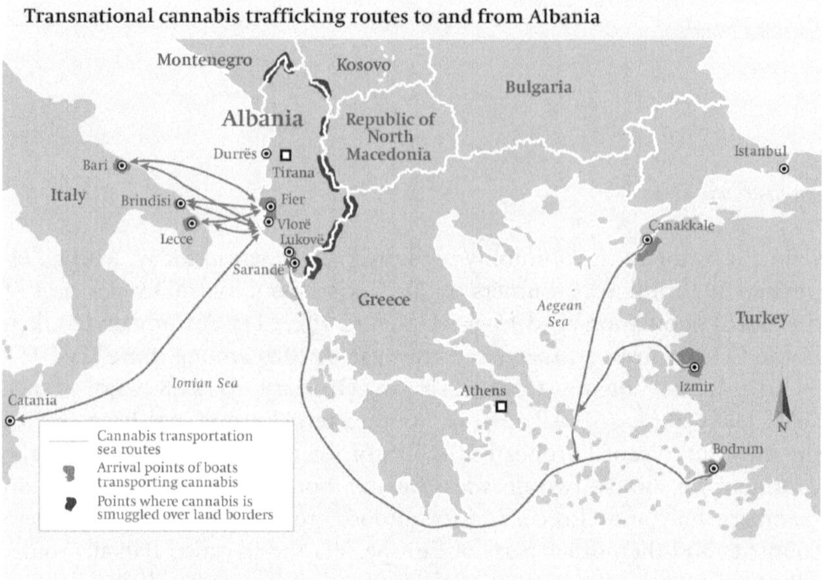

These criminal organisations were not only able to create large networks within Albania but soon started to do so throughout the European continent. Their experience in trafficking cannabis and heroin in Western Europe and the networks of distribution that they were able to create opened the door for their involvement in the lucrative cocaine market. Creating direct connections with the criminal groups in Latin America, these organisations were soon able to transport tonnes of cocaine to some of the main ports in EU countries and also take care of its distribution in the streets of Europe's largest cities. Towards the end of the first decade of the 21st century, cannabis became merely one of the illicit commodities that they had a grip on (Kemp 2020: 31). They were also able to launder money generated from the cultivation and trafficking of drugs, mainly in the construction boom that swept Albania after the fall of communism (Reitano and Amerhauser 2020: 27).

For three decades, cultivation and trafficking of cannabis in the country has been aided also by the corrupt governments and their collusion with criminal organisations (Transparency International and IDM 2021: 2–3). Criminal groups provide money and muscle in election campaigns (for example by buying votes or encouraging local constituencies to vote for a particular individual or party), and in return, once elected, the individual or party provides political protection for criminal activities, as well as jobs and favours for their constituents (GI-TOC 2019: 31). Widespread corruption in the judicial system (Council of Europe: Commissioner for Human Rights 2014: 5–6) was also considered one of the main reasons why illicit cannabis cultivation and drug trafficking remained a persistent culture in the country.

As a result, cannabis eradication in Albania was a tough road. In 2014, police cracked down on the cultivation in the village of Lazarat, a two-decade symbol of massive cultivation. However, just two years later, in 2016, the country saw an unprecedented spread in cultivation. The government pledged to end the culture of cultivation in 2017 and adopted a new national action plan against cultivation which, together with efforts on the ground, was able to bring the cultivation to a historic low for three years (2017–2019) (Albanian Interior Ministry n.d.).

But with the reduction of cultivation within the country, Albanian criminal groups intensified their efforts to 'save the business'. As a result, more effort was put into the indoor cultivation of cannabis in EU countries, a move that is keeping Albanian criminal groups present in this illicit market. Experience in cultivation and drug trafficking and good connections with the criminal underworld throughout the continent helped them to establish their presence in indoor cannabis cultivation in many European countries, including the United Kingdom, the Netherlands, Belgium, Germany, France, Spain and Italy (Europol 2020). This move, however, is still negatively impacting Albania and stimulating human smuggling. Youngsters who used to cultivate cannabis outdoors in the country are now looking for criminal opportunities abroad. The Albanian criminal groups already established in the EU and in the UK, which are characterised by fluid clan structures based on kinship or neighbourhood relations, facilitate the process, offering these youngsters with experience in drug cultivation a place where they can carry on the cultivation. These groups are also able to pay for their travel and accommodation and settle them in housing where indoor cannabis is cultivated, and the youngsters can pay off the groups with their work. These youngsters usually turn into valuable members of criminal organisations. In this way, the cannabis economy triggers human trafficking.

Though cultivation has been low in Albania during the time frame 2017–2020, it is still too early to say whether the trend will continue. As mentioned above, during 2020 an increase in cultivation was noted compared with the three previous years. The COVID-19 crisis, with police in Albania having to perform duties during the pandemic that reduce the spread of the virus, is considered one of the major factors behind the increase. Besides the lack of the necessary police power to tackle the problem, law enforcement alone is unlikely to break the cannabis culture cycle, and a rethinking of the approach is needed (Mejdini and Amerhauser 2019: 11). It is very important to discourage drug use through social and economic initiatives that provide alternative legitimate income. This is especially important for youngsters engaged or prone to be engaged in this illicit activity, at home or abroad.

Historical background

In March 1991, Albania held the first pluralist elections, after more than four decades of being ruled by a communist dictatorship. The collapse of communism started in December 1990, when students in Tirana initiated protests against the regime, demanding freedom and democracy, pushing the regime to accept pluralism. However, the change in power happened only in March 1992, when the newly formed Democratic Party of Albania won the parliamentary elections. At a time when many believed that the fall of communism would finally lead Albania towards democracy and prosperity, the transformation from totalitarianism to democracy turned out to be a difficult task. Lack of political and technical experience in successfully transitioning from a centralised to a market economy led to a severe economic crisis in the country. The breakup of the agricultural cooperatives at the beginning of the 1990s and the confusion over property rights led to food shortages. Also, most industrial enterprises ceased their activity or were operating far below their capacity from the beginning of 1991 (Muço 1997: 19–20).

The economic plight combined with the urge to explore the world – after 45 years of isolation – led to a massive wave of emigration, mainly to the two neighbouring EU countries, Greece and Italy. By the end of December 1991, more than 200,000 Albanians were estimated to have left their country since the exodus began in July 1990 (Parliamentary Assembly of the Council of Europe 1992). The chaotic political and economic transition left a large part of the population without sufficient means for living, turning many to the illicit economy. Amidst this reality, according to people interviewed,[1] at the beginning of the 1990s, the first seeds of cannabis began to be smuggled from Greece by Albanian migrants who

1 Interviews with former cultivators of cannabis in southern Albania, January 2021, Tepelenë and Këlcyrë.

learned how to cultivate the plant in the neighbouring country. In Albania, they could easily plant the seeds without much risk, at a time when law enforcement agencies were weak and inexperienced and the country was facing other major problems. The areas near the Greek border became the first ones in the country to try out cannabis cultivation, which was usually done on the farmers' own land. Greece was not only a place where the seeds and practice of cultivating illicit cannabis came from, but also a place where it could be sold after having been harvested in Albania.

Soon, Albanians explored other lucrative markets for the illicit cannabis that they had started to grow. Italy became a favourite destination because of the short distance that connects the two countries by sea. The sea distance between Vlorë in Albania and Brindisi on the Apulian coast is only 72 nautical miles. From the beginning of 1993, people from Vlorë started to cross the Adriatic Sea illegally in speedboats.

Italy soon turned into not only a destination but also an important transit point for the further distribution of Albanian cannabis to Western Europe. Illegal migrant flows and drug trafficking via the sea pushed the Italian Guardia di Finanza in October 1997 to establish a presence in Albania and collaborate closely in the fight against organised crime (Museo Storico Guardia di Finanza n.d.). This opened up a major new route for cannabis smuggling and also raised the demand for Albanian outdoor illicit cannabis. In order to fulfil the rising demand, cultivation expanded in terms of both the number of hectares under cultivation and the number of locations where cannabis was grown. In the mid-1990s, cultivation began to be present all over the country, and farmers started to specialise in its cultivation. In parallel, smugglers also started to gain experience and create important networks, not only in Greece and Italy but also in many other countries across Europe. At the end of 1996, the Albanian police reported having been able to eradicate within that year alone 383,968 plants across the country, which showed that the phenomenon was widespread and that the police was aware of the need to crack down on cultivation. However, the country's political situation was not in their favour. In 1997, Albania was swept by civil unrest as citizens angrily reacted to losing their savings in failed financial pyramid schemes (The New York Times 1997). The unrest was accompanied by civilians looting ammunition depots, and hundreds of thousands of arms were in the hands of the population. The crisis took a heavy toll on the country's institutions and led to a collapse of the security sector. As a result, tackling cannabis cultivation in the country was deprioritised in the aftermath, since the government focused its resources on the overall crisis in the country.

One of the most negative impacts that the civil unrest brought was the creation of dangerous armed gangs in the south of Albania that terrorised and extorted local communities, as the state was far from able to provide order and punish them. Dealing with powerful local gangs with a strong influence in local communities remained one of the biggest challenges of the new government formed after the election of June 1997.

Cannabis strongholds and cultivation peaks

The creation of armed gangs because of the crisis of 1997 impacted many communities throughout the country. These gangs recruited vulnerable young men, gained control of large parts of the country and terrorised their communities. Over time, these gangs started to transform into organised crime groups and to also engage, besides extortion, in the trafficking of people and drugs, especially from the shores of Vlorë, the city at the centre of the unrest, to Italy. The newly created government, however, did not show any enthusiasm for fighting these criminal groups. In many cases, there was collusion instead, with political parties using the influence of these groups in communities for political gain (Zhilla and Lamallari 2016: 25–26). In return, they turned a blind eye to their criminal activities. The collusion was further facilitated by the widespread corruption in the late 1990s and early 2000s.

It was also at this time that one of the most notorious sites of illicit outdoor cultivation of cannabis in Europe was created in Albania, the village of Lazarat. This village with less than 5,000 residents lies along the national road that connects Gjirokastër with the Greek border, 27 kilometres from the border crossing point of Kakavia. During the 1997 civil unrest, armed criminals robbed the bank of Gjirokastër in southern Albania and sought refuge in Lazarat.[2] Despite pressure from the police, the fugitives were not handed over, and from that moment the village gained a 'stronghold' reputation. As a result, illicit activities began to take place, and for almost two decades cannabis was cultivated on a large scale. This is also an illustration of the transformation of the gangs formed in 1997 into organised crime groups.

Lazarat was an open secret. In 2013, the Italian Guardia di Finanza, who were patrolling by air, reported 500 plantations of cannabis throughout the country, estimated to produce 1000 tonnes of cannabis (Guardia di

2 Interview with a police officer in south of Albania, February 2020, Gjirokastër.

Finanza 2013). Most of these plantations were in Lazarat. Organised crime groups throughout the country had their share of cultivation within the village. Around 300–500 people were also engaged every year as a workforce, while bribes were used to keep the police away. However, Lazarat was not the only place in Albania were massive cultivation was taking place. Another important area at that time were the Dukagjini Highlands, a steep terrain in the northern municipality of Shkodër, where tonnes of cannabis were harvested every year.

Although the massive cultivation in these areas was a public secret, no police intervention happened until 2014. In June of that year, police undertook a major operation to eradicate cultivation in both areas. In Lazarat, the police operation lasted for days, as heavy ammunition was fired towards police. Police forces were able to seize not only

3 tonnes of marijuana and 133,000 cannabis plants but also five drug-processing laboratories. Heroin was also found in the village, together with arms and ammunition. Two months later, in August, the police also undertook a major operation against cannabis in the Dukagjini Highlands, also seizing large amounts of cannabis stored and also planted in the fields.

In 2014, many believed that the massive cultivation of cannabis in Albania had come to an end. However, it soon became apparent that this was far from the truth. In 2016, the entire country was swept by a massive new wave of cannabis cultivation. Cannabis was not only cultivated in so-called 'traditional' and remote areas but also very close to urban ones. The massive cultivation also engaged people without criminal records or experience in cultivation, including even professionals, university students and vulnerable groups in society. As a result of the extensive cultivation that year and the large number of people engaged in it, conflicts about the land used for cultivation, the price of cannabis and its trafficking became widespread. Conflicts over cannabis led to killings and injuries. Many analysts believe that the widespread cultivation during 2016 came as a result of collusion between senior officials and criminals. In a report on the crime situation in Albania, the Office of the General Prosecutor emphasised that elements of state police and local governments had colluded with criminals and were involved in cultivation (Republika e shqipërisë Prokuroria e përgjithshme 2017).

Political implications also arose as a result of the widespread cultivation in 2016. In October 2017, the prosecution started an investigation against former interior minister Saimir Tahiri and two high police officials, accusing them of abuse of office, drug trafficking and also being part of a criminal group. On September 2019, the court cleared Tahiri and his associates of drug trafficking charges but sentenced him to three years of probation for abuse of office (Koleka 2019). The case, however, further eroded the trust of citizens in the government and reinforced their perception that cannabis cultivation and its trafficking were facilitated by the collusion of parts of the state with criminals. Also, during 2020 and 2021 there were court cases against people with power who had facilitated the cannabis cultivation, but only local police and community administrators were accused.

Trafficking opportunities

Over the last 20 years, cannabis cultivation in Albania has largely been controlled by organised crime groups that took advantage of the country's dire economic situation and lack of a serious state response to tackle the phenomenon. With the outdoor production of cannabis in Albania that has been estimated at up to 1000 tonnes in productive years, groups have become more powerful and expanded their portfolio of criminal activities. The Guardia di Finanza estimates that the annual production of cannabis in Albania yields around €4 billion in revenue for criminal groups. In the late 1990s and early 2000s, these groups not only had control of its cultivation but were also able to establish important trafficking lines from Western Europe to Turkey. Some of the members of these organised criminal groups were already placed in EU member states to coordinate and facilitate this illicit business. The majority of trafficking was directed towards Italy, Greece and Turkey, using both maritime and land borders. In Italy, several groups partnered with the Italian mafia, especially in Sicily. The speedboats loaded with cannabis (and sometimes also weapons) were handed over to the local mafia (Catania Today 2017). From this point, the mafia took on its distribution within Italy and in Western and Northern Europe. But in many cases, Albanian criminal groups had their own members on the other side of the Adriatic, who secured distribution in that country and beyond.

Cannabis trafficking opened important criminal channels and opportunities for Albanian criminal groups. Connections with the Italian mafia, but also other criminal organisations, were important for them also to gain access to the international trafficking chains of cocaine. First employed as drivers of Italian organisations in bringing the cocaine from the ports of Antwerp and Rotterdam to Italy, soon they started to create their own ties with cartels in South America. Soon cannabis became merely one illicit commodity in the hands of Albanian criminal groups, who had not only established a strong presence in the country but were also able to create sophisticated criminal networks throughout Europe and beyond. They did so in countries that are considered important hubs where drugs are being shipped and consumption rates are high, such as Spain, the Netherlands, Belgium and the UK.

One of the most important criminal operations of these groups was to establish direct trafficking lines with organised crime groups in Latin America in early 2000 that helped them secure large amounts of cocaine from the source countries (Kemp 2020: 2–3). In the decade that followed, the collaboration between criminal organisations of Albania mainly active in Western Europe with these groups in Latin America was intensified. Countries like Ecuador have been used by these groups to secure deals on cocaine and its transport to central ports of Europe. In September 2020, Europol announced the takedown of a complex Albanian-speaking cocaine trafficking network after five years of investigations (Europol 2020). The cocaine, secured in countries like Colombia, Peru and Bolivia, was shipped to Ecuador and arrived in European ports, to be further trafficked and distributed on the streets of several EU countries. According to Europol, the entire chain, from securing the cocaine in Latin America to its distribution on the streets, was controlled by Albanians. The network also used a sophisticated alternative remittance system of Chinese origin, known as *fei ch'ien*. This system is similar to *hawala* and uses a large network of operators that deposit and withdraw equivalent amounts of money in different parts of the world in order not to leave traces in the legal financial channels. In this way, also aided by encryption technology used for communication, criminal groups have laundered large amounts of money.

Opportunities for these criminal organisations also came from the East. Collaboration with criminal organisations in Turkey and the Eastern Balkans not only gave Albanians an important market for their cannabis. It often involved the exchange of cannabis for heroin and thus also helped them expand their grip on heroin going from east to west via the Balkan route. This collaboration soon turned the country into an important route for heroin trafficking.

Figure 2: Cannabis seized by Albanian police

Money laundering

The money generated by cannabis trafficking was used by criminal groups to expand their criminal operations and also to invest in entering more lucrative illicit businesses, such as cocaine trafficking for the EU market. On the other hand, the criminal income gained through drug trafficking has also allegedly entered the licit economy of Albania, mainly through laundering in the construction sector (Reitano and Amerhauser 2020: 27). Albania emerged from communism with a severe shortage of housing for its citizens, and the first decade of its prolonged transition was characterised by a chaotic construction process, with people mainly building their own houses. However, in the last two decades, the city of Tirana has been characterised by a massive wave of construction, mainly of luxury and high-rise buildings. Despite this wave, the real estate prices doubled from 2017 to 2020 (Kemp, Amerhauser and Scaturro 2021: 59), creating difficulties for citizens who want to buy apartments. It is believed that a way has been found to launder the money being generated by the trafficking of cannabis and other, more potent drugs like cocaine in the growing tourist sector in Albania. In recent decades, the country's 362-kilometre coastline has seen an increase in luxury bars and restaurants, as well as hotels and accommodation capacities. Experts estimate that hundreds of millions of euros were laundered every year in the construction business in the country during the last five years (Reitano and Amerhauser 2020: 28). The money generated from illicit activities flows outside banking channels and infiltrates the legal construction companies, facilitated by the fact that this industry remains largely cash-based in Albania.

A shift in cultivation

In 2016, Albania faced a difficult situation regarding cannabis cultivation. In the summer of that year, the phenomenon became widespread throughout the country. This situation created political tensions in the country, as well as international pressure. Intensifying the fight against organised crime was made a condition for progress on the path of Albania's accession to the EU (European Western Balkans 2019). Understanding the risk that it could bring for the country if this situation were to continue, in 2017 the government took strong measures to stop the cultivation, also implementing a three-year national plan that reinforced the fight against the phenomenon (Official Journal of the Republic of Albania 2017). This new plan took the approach of identifying and tackling cannabis especially in its early stages of cultivation instead of only focusing on eradicating grown plants. Also, the plan emphasised the need to identify and seize the assets created by this criminal activity. It also pledged to support economic activities in areas and communities affected by cannabis cultivation.

As a result, the cultivation of illicit cannabis in Albania has been significantly reduced since 2017. However, the year 2020 saw an increase in the number of cases of cultivation, according to data of the Ministry of Interior. Many believe that this is related to the COVID-19 situation and the fact that the police were put in charge of securing the imposed lockdown (March – June 2020) during the period in which cannabis is planted.

It seems that after the cultivation of cannabis in Albania was reduced since 2016, criminal groups have found alternatives to maintain their grip on drug trafficking. Transferring the cultivation to the EU and the UK is seen as an opportunity to stay in the business, avoid some of the risks of trafficking from one country to another and produce near the main cannabis markets (GI-TOC 2020: 4–7). The so-called "cannabis indoor houses" throughout Europe have become popular among Albanian organised crime groups. In the last five years, UK law enforcement has raised awareness about Albanian criminal groups being active in the country, especially in indoor cannabis cultivation (Weaver 2017). In addition, the Albanian criminal groups in the UK are also present in the cocaine market, which is considered one of the most lucrative in the world.

Conclusions

Illicit cannabis cultivation has been a widespread phenomenon in Albania, although from 2017 to 2019 cultivation decreased after authorities got alarmed by the widespread cultivation in 2016 and took effective measures to crack down on it.

Cannabis cultivation has helped the Albanian criminal groups win experience and financial power and shift to trafficking more potent and lucrative drugs like cocaine throughout Europe.

In 2020, during the COVID-19 crisis, an increase in the cultivation of cannabis was noted, while police were at the forefront of safeguarding lockdowns in urban centres and less engaged in rural areas where cannabis is cultivated.

A decrease in opportunities for cannabis cultivation in Albania is pushing criminal groups to expand their foothold in cultivation of indoor cannabis in the EU and the UK, alongside their other criminal activities like cocaine trafficking.

This shift is also luring young people from Albania to illegally migrate to the EU and the UK and engage in indoor cultivation. Organised criminal groups push and sponsor this illegal migration.

References

Albanian Interior Ministry (n.d.): "Raporti Mujor". At: https://mb.gov.al/raporti-mujor/ (accessed 20 December 2021).

Catania Today (2017): "Traffico di droga tra l'Albania e la Sicilia. Chiuse le indagini". At: https://www.cataniatoday.it/cronaca/droga-albania-sicilia-concluse-indagini-18-dicembre-2017.html (accessed 10 December 2021).

Council of Europe: Commissioner for Human Rights (2014): "Report by Nils Muižnieks Commissioner for Human Rights of the Council of Europe. Following his visit to Albania from 23 to 27 September 2013". At: https://rm.coe.int/ref/CommDH(2014)1 (accessed 10 December 2021).

EMCDDA, European Monitoring Centre for Drugs and Drug Addiction (2021): "European drug report. Trends and developments". At: https://www.emcdda.europa.eu/system/files/publications/13838/TDAT21001ENN.pdf (accessed 10 December 2021).

European Western Balkans (2019): "Bundestag adopts nine conditions for Tirana and general guidelines for negotiations". At: https://europeanwesternbalkans.com/2019/09/27/bundestag-adopts-nine-conditions-for-tirana-and-general-guidelines-for-negotiations/ (accessed 10 December 2021).

Europol (2020): "Joint investigation team leads to dismantling of one of Europe's most active Albanian-speaking networks trafficking cocaine into Europe". At: https://www.europol.europa.eu/newsroom/news/joint-investigation-team-leads-to-dismantling-of-one-of-europe%E2%80%99s-most-active-albanian-speaking-networks-trafficking-cocaine (accessed 10 December 2021).

GI-TOC, Global Initiative Against Transnational Organized Crime (2019): "Hotspots of organized crime in the Western Balkans. Local vulnerabilities in a regional context". At: https://globalinitiative.net/wp-content/uploads/2019/05/Hotspots-Report-English-13Jun1110-Web.pdf (accessed 5 May 2022).

GI-TOC, Global Initiative Against Transnational Organized Crime (2020): "The civil society observatory to counter organized crime in South Eastern Europe. Risk Bulletin". At: https://globalinitiative.net/wp-content/uploads/2020/10/SEEObs-Risk-Bulletin-1.pdf (accessed 5 May 2022).

Guardia di Finanza (2013): "Individuate 500 piantagioni di marijuana". At: https://www.gdf.gov.it/chi-siamo/organizzazione/specializzazioni/comparto aeronavale/servizio-aereo/reparti/lazio/sezione-aerea-pratica-di-mare/notizie/individuate-500-piantagioni-di-marijuana (accessed 10 December 2021).

Kemp, Walter (2020): "Transnational tentacles. Global hotspots of Western Balkan organized crime". At: https://globalinitiative.net/wp-content/uploads/2020/07/Transnational-Tentacles-Global-Hotspots-of-Balkan-Organized-Crime-ENGLISH_MRES.pdf (accessed 5 May 2022).

Kemp, Walter/Amerhauser, Kristina/Scaturro, Ruggero (2021): "Spot Prices. Analyzing flows of people, drugs and money in the Western Balkans". At: https://globalinitiative.net/wp-content/uploads/2021/05/Spot-Prices-Analyzing-flows-of-people-drugs-and-money-in-the-Western-Balkans.pdf (accessed 10 December 2021).

Koleka, Benet (2019): "Albanian ex-minister cleared on drug charges, guilty of abuse of office". At: https://www.reuters.com/article/us-albania-minister-corruption-idUSKBN1W5005 (accessed 10 December 2021).

Mejdini, Fatjona/Amerhauser, Kristina (2019): "Growing like weeds? Rethinking Albania's culture of cannabis cultivation". At: https://globalinitiative.net/wp-content/uploads/2019/12/AlbaniaCannabis.14.12.web_.pdf (accessed 5 May 2022).

Muço, Marta (1997): "Economic Transition in Albania. Political Constraints and Mentality Barriers". At: https://www.nato.int/acad/fellow/95-97/muco.pdf (accessed 10 December 2021).

Museo Storico Guardia di Finanza (n.d.): "Le missioni internazionali della Guardia di Finanza (1899 – 2009)". At: http://museostorico.gdf.it/mostre/mostra-storica-interforze/missione_internazionale.pdf (accessed 10 December 2021).

Official Journal of the Republic of Albania (2017): "Decision of the Council of Ministers No. 248, dated 29.3.2017, for the approval of the action plan against cultivation and trafficking of cannabis 2017–2020 [own translation]". At: https://mb.gov.al/wp-content/uploads/2018/02/Plani_Kombetar_i_Veprimit_kunder_kultivimit_te_kanabisit_2017_-_2020-1.pdf (accessed 10 December 2021).

Parliamentary Assembly of the Council of Europe (1992): "Report on the Exodus of Albanian nationals. Rapporteur Wilfried Böhm, Germany, CDU". At: https://assembly.coe.int/nw/xml/XRef/X2H-Xref-ViewHTML.asp?FileID=6888&lang=EN (accessed 10 December 2021).

Reitano, Tuesday/Amerhauser, Kristina (2020): "Illicit financial flows in Albania, Kosovo and North Macedonia. Key drivers and current trends." At: https://globalinitiative.net/wp-content/uploads/2020/08/IFFs-Balkans-English-WEB-Nov2020-1.pdf (accessed 5 May 2022).

Republika e shqipërisë Prokuroria e përgjithshme (2017): "Raport i prokurorit të përgjithshëm mbi gjendjen e kriminalitetit për vitin 2016". At: http://www.pp.gov.al/rc/doc/raporti_pp_2016_07_03_2017_1160.pdf (accessed 5 May 2022).

The New York Times (1997): "Violent Protests of Pyramid Schemes Spread in Albania". At: https://www.nytimes.com/1997/01/27/world/violent-protests-of-pyramid-schemes-spread-in-albania.html (accessed 10 December 2021).

Transparency International/IDM, Institute for Democracy and Mediation (2021): "Deconstructing state capture in Albania. An examination of grand corruption cases and tailor-made laws from 2008 to 2020". At: https://images.transparencycdn.org/images/2021_Report_DeconstructingStateCaptureAlbania_English.pdf (accessed 10 December 2021).

UNDOC, United Nations Office on Drugs and Crime (2020): "World drug report 2020". At: https://wdr.unodc.org/wdr2020/field/WDR20_Booklet_2.pdf (accessed 10 December 2021).

Weaver, Matthew (2017): "Albanian gangs have significant control over UK cocaine market, says crime agency". At: https://www.theguardian.com/uk-news/2017/jun/29/albanian-gangs-control-uk-cocaine-market-says-agency (accessed 10 December 2021).

Zhilla, Fabian/Lamallari, Besfort (2016): "Evoluimi i strukturave të organizuara kriminale në shqipëri". At: https://www.osfa.al/sites/default/files/evolimi_i_strukturave_te_organizuara_kriminale_ne_shqiperi.pdf (accessed 10 December 2021).

Organisational principles of the global drug economy

Daniel Brombacher[1]

1. *Introduction: dissecting the narcotics value chains*

The global drug economy can be considered one of the most studied illicit economies, if not the best studied. It is highly visible in media coverage and popular culture. While legal and ethical considerations on internationally scheduled drugs may vary widely, general attention on the issue is constantly high across countries and regions. The drug economy is arguably the largest and most harmful of all illicit economies, considering prevalence rates across the globe, estimated financial turnover, factors such as homicide and overdose-related death rates, the spread of blood-borne diseases, the relationship with armed conflict in source countries or corruption related to the drug market. More recently, the massive negative impact of drug markets on the environment is also receiving more attention (Brombacher, Garzón and Vélez 2021). Analysis shows that roughly 10 % of all UN Security Council resolutions over the past two decades have made reference to drug trafficking, only surpassed by arms trafficking, another highly problematic form of organised crime (Reitano 2020: 127). According to a recent report, almost 40 % of all organised crime groups reported in the European Union are running operations in the field of illegal drugs (Europol 2021: 18). Given the long-standing relevance of the issue, the international drug control regime, based on three UN conventions (1961, 1971, 1988), is built on a basis of almost universal ratification.

However, this regime has come under heavy pressure. The UN drug control system as such is frequently understood to be synonymous with the war on drugs and its high costs (Collins 2016: 10). As a consequence of this perception, the regime is being increasingly challenged by reformist governments, critical media and a powerful global civil society movement.

---

1 Head, Global Partnership on Drug Policies and Development (GPDPD) at Deutsche Gesellschaft für Internationale Zusammenarbeit (GIZ) GmbH, Berlin, Germany. The chapter reflects exclusively the opinions of the author and not those of the Federal Ministry for Economic Cooperation and Development (BMZ) or GIZ GmbH.

Mostly, yet not exclusively, the reformist impetus focuses on decriminalisation or regulatory efforts in the field of recreational and medical cannabis, even though the latter is within the scope of the 1961 UN Single Convention on Narcotic Drugs, while the former is not.

The normative monopoly of the international drug control system and its main proponents is being tested by increasingly bold domestic legal deviations and an ever-growing spectrum of drug policy positions between the rather extreme positions of a war on drugs and regime collapse. At the UN level, drug policy decision-making is traditionally governed by consensus and unanimity rule. The heterogeneous range of positions and attitudes of member states towards drugs, spanning from death penalty and life-long sentences for minor narcotics offences to complete decriminalisation, has made decision-making more challenging. While some take record opioid overdose-induced death rates, record amphetamine seizures and rampant violence as a justification for reinforcing the drug control system, others interpret this evidence as a sign of regime failure.

Despite the 24/7 coverage of drug issues around the globe, the intense political debates and the campaigning around the matter, this chapter argues that most of the global awareness is still focusing on a rather limited section of the real nature of the global illegal drug economy. Our picture of why drug value chains partly or entirely emerge in one country and not in another, what the key organisational principles behind the supply chains are and how the market is being governed is still incomplete and based on a small set of standard indicators. A major share of the attention is focusing on cannabis as the most widely used drug, as well as other plant-based substances. There are countless reports, documentaries, press articles and studies on drug value chains that form a global economy, following a logic from plant to plate, from source countries to retail markets. However, both the popular and the scientific accounts of the global drug trade are per se predominantly positivist, as they focus on the most visible elements of the global drug economy, i.e. the cultivation of drug crops such as coca leaf and opium poppy, substance seizures, drug market-related violence and clinically relevant problematic drug use. Detected drug crop fields, seizures, captures and homicides along the supply chain work like a light switch that is turned on and off, briefly shedding light on individual transactions of an otherwise shadowy business. However, only in a few cases does such ad hoc illumination allow a thorough understanding of the functional conditions of this economy to be developed. Furthermore, these indicators tend to be misinterpreted, and partly weak conclusions are being drawn.

The common notion of the global drug trade is thus rather simplistic and is mostly a consequence of a lack of evidence, reducing the actual complexity of the drug value chains to their perceptible segments. A pabloescobarised cliché of the global drug economy is still prevalent, replicating the idea of a highly controlled and criminally regulated global narcotics business in which power, income and risk are monopolised by a few. While such popular patterns of interpretation apply to most illicit economies, they seem to be particularly harmful in the field of drugs, as policies also frequently draw on these notions.

At times, the current international debate on drugs creates the impression that the one-size-fits-all solution of the world drug problem lies either in the legal status of cannabis or in the detention of all drug kingpins from Barranquilla to Berlin. This chapter seeks to show that this impression is misleading and distorts the most pressing structural issues underlying the global drug economy and its high costs, such as the relationship between armed conflict and the drug trade, the massive effects on public health, corruption and the undermining and even capture of state institutions. There is a clear link between flourishing drug markets in countries of origin and transit and development conditions; however, these structural development factors mostly remain a "blind spot" in the global discussion around drugs (Buxton 2020), despite some recent changes in the discourse.

After a brief overview of the state of affairs of the global drug economy and drug policies, the chapter starts with an introduction to the common structural features of the global drug value chains, focusing on the three most relevant plant-based drug value chains, cannabis, coca-cocaine and opium poppy-heroin. In the following section, the key supply-side indicators prevalent in any effort to map the global narcotics trade are analysed: Seizures, price and purity data as well as drug market-related violence. The purpose is to gain a better understanding of the evidence they actually provide and what conclusions on the nature of the global drug economy can be drawn from them. Finally, the subsequent section contrasts structural and actor-based models to understand what the relevant drivers of global drug markets are. Based on this analysis, the conclusion briefly contrasts currently dominant global supply-side policies with the findings of this discussion, assessing potentially new directions of the global drug control efforts.

2. *The global drug economy and the global response: state of affairs*

The current UN drug control regime is built on the three UN drug control conventions of 1961, 1971 and 1988; however, its origins date back to the Shanghai Opium Commission in 1909 as the first multilateral effort with regime-building intent (Buxton 2010: 62). Its prohibitionist character was originally based on public health concerns. These concerns are manifest in the narrative to build a drug-free world, the overall goal of the UN General Assembly Special Session on Drugs (UNGASS) 1998 and the frequent commitment to a society free of drug abuse, as enshrined in countless resolutions of the UN Commission on Narcotic Drugs (CND). While public health concerns are still a guiding foundation of the UN drug control regime, the normative scope of the regime has constantly evolved in the past decades, linking the drug issue to a plethora of other global challenges, including violence, organised crime, armed conflict, corruption, human rights abuses as well as racial and gender inequalities linked to drug enforcement.

The implementation of the UN drug control regime and of the respective domestic legislation is costly. In 2008, the annual costs of the war on drugs were estimated to amount to up to US$100 billion (Open Society Foundations and Transform Drug Policy Foundation 2008). Some estimates of the cost to the US alone come up with a potential cost of US$ one trillion by summing up the different strands of counternarcotic efforts since 1971 (Pearl 2018). While most of these estimates focus on public budgets for law enforcement efforts and are limited to the US, similar though lower investments are to be expected from other countries along the major drug value chains.

Usually, the performance of the drug control regime is measured against supply- and demand- side indicators. On the supply side, this includes the seizures of illegal drugs, captures of traffickers and dealers, price and purity data, drug-related offences and violence, the area under cultivation of drug crops and the number of detected production sites for both plant-based and synthetic drugs. On the demand side, overdose rates, infection rates of blood-borne diseases, prevalence data on drug use or wastewater analysis are taken as indicators of how the global drug economy evolves.

In 2019, around 275 million people were reported by UN member states to have used drugs at least once in the past year. This number is more than 20 % higher than in 2010. In 2019, almost 50,000 died of an opioid-related overdose in the US alone, almost tenfold the figure of 2010. A total of 18 million people died of drug-related disorders in 2019 worldwide. While coca cultivation in the Andes has recently stabilised and even slightly decreased, cocaine production is at a historical high due to improved production methods that doubled the production output from 2015 to 2019. The cultivation of opium poppy, the key ingredient for heroin production, has been mostly stable at high levels in Afghanistan. The volume of cocaine seized in the European Union is at unprecedented levels, even though prices remain low and purity is high on average. Drug market-related violence is consistently high in major producing and trafficking hubs such as Colombia, Brazil and Mexico, while European countries have also lately faced an increased level of drug market-inherent violence, for instance Belgium and the Netherlands, a tendency that has intensified during the global COVID-19 pandemic (Europol 2021: 22; UNODC 2021a: 22–68; EMCDDA/Europol 2019: 127; EMCDDA/Europol 2020: 8).

Against most of these indicators, global drug control seems to fare poorly in its efforts to curb the supply of and reduce the demand for illegal drugs. However, while these indicators are widely used to assess global drug control efforts, an analysis built solely on these indicators tends to be misleading. While demand-side indicators, at least in a certain share of countries that annually report them to the UN, tend to be based on actual surveys and therefore on a sound quantitative basis, supply-side data are less robust. This chapter will show that the sole use of positivist indicators, i.e. seizures, captures and narcotics-related offences in general, tends to be of little use for an analysis of the true nature and development of drug markets and their inherent value chains. The same applies to drug market-related violence, as it does not provide any evidence for the volume of a drug market but is mostly a dependent variable of the structure of organised crime groups and of the markets in which they interact. Wholesale and retail prices as well as data on purity reflect the risk associated with illegal markets well, and not merely the supply and demand.

The following section will analyse these concerns in more depth, as they lie at the core of the understanding of the organisational principles of drug economies that connect the Global South with Europe and other major consumer markets. The analysis focuses on three major drug value chains that connect Europe to source countries in Asia, Latin America and Southeastern Europe, namely those for heroin, cocaine and cannabis.

3. The organisation of the drug value chains: common features

3.1. Terminology

In this chapter, the term "global drug economy" reflects the totality of market transactions that involve internationally scheduled narcotic drugs, including those cases where the legal character of a substance may fluctuate depending on jurisdictions. Therefore, the global drug economy is understood here as being composed of a highly diverse set of individual drug markets that may be local, national, regional or global by nature.

At the same time, drug markets as constitutive elements of the global drug economy are supplied by value chains that reflect the entire range of transactions from cultivation, production and manufacturing to wholesale and retailing. The organisation of these value chains is the key focus of this chapter. While most of the attention on the global drug economy is directed towards the illegal segments of the drug markets, the global drug economy is based on a blending of both legal and illegal as well as licit and illicit transactions. In the case of the global cocaine economy, with special legal regimes for coca cultivation in Bolivia and Peru, a certain share of production is legal but widely considered illicit at the national and international level. In the case of opium poppy and cannabis cultivation, there are frequently situations where traditional cultivation is illegal *de iure* but widely perceived to be licit. In the Dutch cannabis economy, use of cannabis is legally accepted by authorities and therefore licit, while the back-door supply of coffee shops is delivered through an illegal value chain run by organised crime groups. In the case of synthetic opioids like tramadol, the product and trade are legal in general terms, trafficking and counterfeiting are illegal, but its use is considered licit in many African countries. Furthermore, while drug value chains frequently combine legal/licit and illegal/illicit elements, their structural embedding in the economy also creates a continuum of legality and illegality, most visibly in the area of the financial flows that link the illegal drug markets with legal economies. Therefore, a value chain perspective on the global drug economy and its (sub)markets allows the organisational nature of supply chains and their potential interaction with legal markets to be analysed.

3.2. Geographical non-convergence of supply and demand

There is no such thing as a singular world drug problem. There is rather a plethora of local and national challenges that are directly or indirectly linked to the production, trafficking or use of scheduled narcotic drugs. While in Colombia, in Myanmar and formerly in Afghanistan the drug issue has been a major concern within counterinsurgency strategies, in Western Europe most of the attention lies on problematic use, while in Mexico the drug issue is rather considered to be a problem of organised crime, rampant violence and corruption. However, moving away from the traditional "problem perspective" on drugs towards a drug economy analysis shows that beyond the visible symptoms there a few common denominators of the global drug markets that to a certain degree replicate themselves across different regions and substances.

The bulk of the either most used or most problematic drugs are plant-based substances: cannabis as the most widely used drug at both the global and the EU level, cocaine, heroin and other opiates. At the EU level, cannabis has by far the highest lifetime prevalence (almost 80 million citizens in 2019). The prevalence of heroin is comparatively low, but in 2019 heroin accounted for 76 % of fatal overdoses in Europe. Cocaine has the second highest lifetime prevalence in Europe, reaching 14 million persons who used cocaine at least once. At the same time, the demand for treatment for cocaine-related problems is on the rise in Europe, potentially related to the increased level of purity and general availability (EMCDDA 2021a: 5–20). While synthetic drug use on a global and European scale has been increasing in recent years, there is also a growing production and market of plant-based methamphetamine, i.e. the harvesting of endemic ephedra in Afghanistan as a key herbal ingredient for methamphetamine (Mansfield and Soderholm 2020).

In the value chains of plant-based drugs, a pattern of geographical non-convergence of production and use or supply and demand prevails. Coca cultivation and cocaine production are concentrated in Colombia, Peru and Bolivia, with some anecdotal evidence of minor plantations that were lately detected in neighbouring countries as well as in Honduras and Mexico[2] (Insight Crime 2020; UNODC 2021a: 51). At the same time, the use of cocaine and other derivates of the coca plant is, compared to major cocaine markets, a limited phenomenon in the major source countries. Also, the actual volume of traditional coca leaf usage is rather negligible

2 See Janowitz (2021).

in overall terms. The user populations are comparatively small, while the massive consumption of cocaine-based substances is concentrated in North America, southern South America and Europe as well as Oceania, which has the highest prevalence of cocaine use on a global scale (UNODC 2021a: 24). Therefore, given the huge geographical distance between the hubs of supply and demand, a set of globally organised supply chains is an essential characteristic of the global cocaine market.

A similar pattern applies to heroin, with some limitations. Afghanistan is the major opium poppy growing country in the world and thus the major source of supply for opiates on a global scale. According to UNODC, the second and third largest suppliers of opium-based substances are Myanmar and Mexico.[3] There is certain evidence of opium poppy cultivation in more than 50 countries (UNODC 2021a: 51). Furthermore, in contrast to coca (with the exception of certain regions in Bolivia and a minor share of cultivation in Peru and Colombia), there is legal production of opium poppy for medical industrial purposes in a handful of countries, where a partial diversion of the harvest for illicit purposes is being reported (Brombacher 2013: 279–283), another example of the mingling of legal and illegal value chains within the global drug economy. While it is quite clear that coca cultivation is more concentrated than opium poppy cultivation, the massive extent of cultivation in Afghanistan makes it unlikely that any similar level of cultivation could remain undetected anywhere else. While prevalence of opiate use is extremely high in Afghanistan and also widespread in its neighbouring countries and Myanmar (UNODC 2021b), it is to be assumed that a major share of heroin production is trafficked to main consumer markets, including Europe. Therefore, the geographical reach of the heroin value chain is as wide as in the case of cocaine, though not divided by oceans. A similar pattern seems to apply to plant-based methamphetamine originating in Afghanistan. While there is evidence of user communities within neighbouring countries and the region, there has been increasing evidence of supply chains of Afghan methamphetamine to Eastern and Southern Africa, using well-established heroin trafficking routes out of the region (Mansfield and Soderholm 2020: 23; GI-TOC 2020).

3 However, the UN data reflects the data reported to the UN by its member states. While annual crop monitoring surveys are available for the major coca and opium producing countries, there is anecdotal evidence for relevant levels of opium poppy cultivation in other countries in Asia and Latin America that is not surveyed annually.

While cannabis is reported to be grown almost all over the world (UNODC 2021a: 51), still massive cultivation for transnational trafficking purposes is concentrated in a few source countries supplying adjacent major consumer markets. In the case of Europe, adding to the domestic, mostly indoor production within the EU, a key supply hub for herbal cannabis in the EU is Albania, while Morocco is considered to be the most important source country for cannabis resin trafficked into the EU (EMCDDA and Europol 2019: 82–83; Europol 2021: 47, EMCDDA 2021b: 5). In 2019, Spain and Morocco reported the globally highest levels of intercepted Cannabis resin (UNODC 2021a: 54). Even less nuanced than in the case of cocaine and heroin, the cannabis value chains also tend to span several countries and a major geographical area, thus establishing a more limited but still transnationally organised supply chain.

3.3. State authority, deterrence and illegal drug economies

At first glance, the plant-based drug value chains may appear to be similar to those of other agrarian commodities that are linked to Europe through transcontinental value chains, e.g. coffee, cocoa or bananas. However, the only true common denominator of legal and illegal commodity chains is the geographical divergence of main producer and consumer hubs, i.e. of supply and demand. The illegal markets constitute themselves in a very different manner than their legal peers. While on legal markets the stakeholders seek to reduce costs within their value chains (e.g. for labour, land, production, packaging, warehousing, transport) and to maximise profit, within illegal markets actors prioritise risk reduction in the way the value chain is organised, i.e. the risk of detection, seizure and legal sanctions. This is especially true for the narcotics trade, where a tight legal regime is imposed on trafficking in most of the world. Therefore, risk avoidance appears to be a key driving principle of illegal drug markets. The plant-to-powder chain in the drug economy is quite complex and requires many intermediary steps, all of which need to be low-risk in order not to put the entire production and commercialisation process at risk (Thoumi 2010: 198).

While even massive trafficking activities can rather easily be concealed in global trade logistics, the cultivation of drug crops is more difficult to hide, at least when major quantities are to be produced. Hence, massive cultivation of drug crops can only be run with an either weak or non-existent level of territorial control by public authorities. Formal laws and norms appear to be partly replaced in major source countries by competing informal norms that legitimise involvement in the drug economy (Thoumi 2010: 197), i.e. that define the involvement in the illegal drug economy as legitimate. The fluid limits between illegal and legal coca or opium poppy growing in some countries where traditional or industrial production is legal (e.g. Bolivia, Peru; India, Turkey) reinforce the normative diversity that allows for the interplay of licit and illicit elements within the cocaine value chain as described above. A similar pattern is currently evolving through the proliferation of medical and recreational cannabis industries around the globe, sometimes with competing legal regimes even within the same jurisdiction and highly fluctuating perceptions of licitness and illicitness.

The expectation of impunity for narcotics offenses, partly based on normative diversity, appears to be the single most important explanatory factor for the emergence and persistence of an illegal drug economy. It is of secondary relevance how impunity is attained. Impunity, i.e. weak deterrence, may be established through a lack of territorial control, corruption, intimidation, organisational features of organised crime groups or concealment strategies. In major drug economies, most of the above-mentioned factors converge in a complex interplay, creating a "criminogenic environment" (Morselli, Turcotte and Tenti 2011: 166) and serving as pull factors for organised crime activities. All major source regions for illegal outdoor cannabis, coca and opium poppy are concentrated in areas with poor government control and weak deterrence capabilities or, as in the case of drug economies in conflict zones, sometimes no government control at all. This pattern applies to most of the coca cultivation on the eastern slopes of the Andes and in the Amazon basin and to cannabis cultivation in the Rif in Morocco, the Albanian Alps, Kandahar and Helmand in Afghanistan as well as Shan State in Myanmar, just to name a few. In these settings, the distinctive legal and illegal elements of the drug value chains become blurred.

Absence of territorial control by the government and therefore a lack of enforcement capabilities – and thus reduced risk – create a permissive environment where other productive factors of drug economies, such as cheap labour, expertise, proximity to trafficking hubs, organised crime or armed groups as commercial partners may develop their potential to build massive drug economies as in the case of cocaine, heroin and cannabis. Weak deterrence and an expectation of impunity paired with instable assessments of licitness and illicitness thus form the second defining structural condition of global drug value chains.

4. *How to trace the illicit drug value chains: the positivist bias*

If the geographical non-convergence of supply and demand and risk avoidance are key defining characteristics of global drug economies, how can the character and scope of drug value chains be described? Three of the most commonly applied supply-side indicators in the global debate are seizures of drugs, price and purity of illegally trafficked substances as well as drug market-related violence.

4.1. Seizures

While drug crop cultivation as territorially extended agriculture is usually visible and therefore more prone to be reported even under conditions of weak territorial state authority, drug shipments are harder to detect, despite their transnational reach. Usually hidden in containers, in lorries or on planes, mingled with legitimate goods or even transported in semisubmersibles and submarines, once they leave the cultivation areas illegal drugs tend to remain invisible until they reach their final destination retail markets. Even though frequent reports of seizures may convey a different message at first glance, only a minor share of the global drug trade can be assumed to be seized. Estimates of up to 20 % of all cocaine being intercepted along the supply chain seem to be quite optimistic (GI-TOC and Insight Crime 2021: 10). The probability of identifying even a multi-tonne drug shipment on commercial vessels is low, considering the sheer volume of maritime commerce. The four major ports of the EU, i.e. Rotterdam, Antwerp, Hamburg and Dover, handled a total of roughly 13,000,000 containers in 2019, corresponding to a total of roughly 18,000,000 TEU.[4] Contrasting this with the estimated overall annual production of cocaine and heroin in the same year – around 1800 tonnes of cocaine and 7400 tonnes of opium (as a basis for heroin) (UNODC 2021a: 18, Booklet 1) – leaves little doubt that searching for drug shipments is like looking for a needle

4 Figures on annual container volumes; port of Hamburg at: https://www.hafen-hamburg.de/en/statistics/containerhandling (accessed 3 May 2021); port of Rotterdam at: https://www.portofrotterdam.com/sites/default/files/2021-06/facts-and-figures-port-of-rotterdam.pdf. (accessed 3 May 2021); port of Antwerp at: http://web.archive.org/web/20220318140034/https://www.portofantwerp.com/sites/default/files/Statistisch%20Jaarboek%202020_1.pdf (accessed 20 May 2021); port of Dover at: https://www.gov.uk/government/statistical-data-sets/port-and-domestic-waterborne-freight-statistics-port#all-port-traffic-totals-major-and-minor (accessed 3 May 2021).

in a haystack. When the commercial volumes of outgoing cargo in the key departure ports for cocaine are analysed, the overall relations may be slightly less striking, but they are still quite clear. Only three notorious departure ports for cocaine, Santos in Brazil, Callao in Peru and Barranquilla in Colombia, together handled around 1,600,000 containers in 2019.[5]

Around 83 % of all cocaine seizures in 2019 took place in the Americas. This may partly be explained by the worse cocaine-to-container ratio, partly by the tendency in the drug trade to gradually reduce shipment sizes along the supply chain. While there was an increase in the volume of seized drug shipments during the first months of the COVID-19 pandemic, including an all-time record seizure of 12 tonnes of cocaine in the port of Hamburg, this may be understood as a transitory phenomenon and be explained by the reduced number of cargo vessels at sea (UNODC 2020: 12). All over Europe, in 2019 1.1 million individual seizures across all types of drugs were reported in 2019, mostly in small quantities on retail markets. Around two-thirds of seizures in 2019 pertained to herbal cannabis and cannabis resin, 11 % to cocaine and crack cocaine, 5 % to amphetamines and 3 % to heroin (EMCDDA 2021a: 14–15), which also reflects the above-mentioned prevalences of drug use within the EU.

The control capabilities are even more limited on land transportation routes. While the transatlantic cocaine trade is bound to maritime or aerial routes, a good share of the heroin and cannabis trafficking routes to Europe are by land. The busiest border in the world, the US-Mexican border, hosts more than 50 land border crossings along more than 3000 km. According to official data, around 56 million personal vehicles, trucks and trains crossed the US-Mexican border in 2020. Before the pandemic, in 2019, the overall number of vehicles, trucks and trains reached almost 80 million (US Bureau of Transportation Statistics n.d.).

Both the data on container handling at leading European ports and the border crossing data from the US leave little doubt about the enforcement and deterrence capabilities of authorities even in economically powerful Western nations. Considering the ratio of the overall production to the volume of containers being processed, fortuitous seizures are statistically improbable. Law enforcement and customs agencies need to rely on intel-

5 Port of Santos at: http://www.portodesantos.com.br/informacoes-operacionais/estatisticas/mensario-estatistico/ (accessed 3 May 2021); port of Callao at: https://www.apn.gob.pe/site/estadisticas.aspx (03.05.2021); port of Barranquilla at: https://www.supertransporte.gov.co/index.php/superintendencia-delegada-de-puertos/estadisticas-trafico-portuario-en-colombia/ (accessed 3 May 2021).

ligence, prediction and selection strategies to enhance their capabilities to identify shipments.

Still, despite the needle-in-a-haystack logic in the global drug control efforts along the illegal value chains, our understanding of the global drug trade beyond the identified source countries relies heavily on seizure data. There are few articles and reports on the global drug economy without a map with arrows from source countries to seizure spots to destination markets. The seizures are interpreted as nodes in the global web of trafficking routes that is mapped through the GPS points of seizure. While seizures do indeed reflect a certain trafficking pattern at a certain time (or a certain law enforcement strategy at a certain time), the sum of all seizures does not yield a correct model of the geography of the drug trade. The essentially clandestine character of drug value chains (as with other illegal markets) makes it difficult to map its spatial extension. Even in cases like Italy, where the evidence base on organised crime tends to be better developed, geographical mapping exercises are hardly robust (Calderoni 2011: 41–52).

Beyond chance, seizures and successful interception efforts require law enforcement and intelligence capabilities. The number of successful interceptions therefore first of all reflects law enforcement capabilities and actions. There is little doubt that these capabilities are not equally distributed within the drug value chains. While there may be a certain degree of control in standard departure and destination ports, e.g. Santos and Antwerp, there may be a plethora of alternative routes that simply remain undetected. Less frequent but sizable seizures in other European ports, e.g. Gioia Tauro in Italy (Europol 2019), Durrës in Albania and Istanbul in Turkey (Daily Sabah 2021), allow for transitory spotlights on the potential abundance of less prominent trafficking routes (GI-TOC 2021: 5). What is quite clear: The geographical points of seizures of illegal drugs are not necessarily also the hubs and nodes of the corresponding value chains, just a potential subset of them detected by chance or strategy.

At the same time, seizure data may also indicate production, not just trafficking, which further hampers their analytical value. Seizure data do not per se provide the information whether a shipment is outgoing or incoming, whether it is intercepted while in transshipment through a country or whether the country is its final destination (Reuter 2010: 101). Even though we know that probably all cocaine in the world has its origin in the Andes and the Amazon area, a potential seizure in Rotterdam does not indicate its final destination. Especially for synthetic drugs, Europe is both a source and a destination region (EMCDDA 2021a: 14). Seizure data should therefore be used with caution. While individual case analyses may provide additional information, overall aggregated seizure data do not allow trafficking routes to be mapped from wholesale source to retail destination level, as is often suggested by standard narratives.

4.2. Price and purity

What other indicators may provide to gain a better understanding of the nature of the global drug market? Given the essentially secretive nature of the transnational drug trade, there is a limited number of potential alternative supply-side indicators. Price and purity data on drug markets as proxy indicators help to sustain assumptions on variations in market dynamics. Following the logic of legal markets, an increase in purity or a decrease in (wholesale or retail) price is considered to signal an increased supply of a certain good and vice versa. At the beginning of the global pandemic, at the same pace as overall legal commerce was significantly reduced, there were reports of temporary increases in the price of certain drugs on European retail markets as well as temporary decreases on wholesale markets in source countries such as Peru (UNODC 2020: 19; EMCDDA and Europol 2020 : 7–10). This example may show how scarcity of certain drugs may impact pricing, even though this effect was only temporary.

However, price formation mechanisms in illicit markets are distorted, as prices not only take into account the costs of labour, production and logistics or scarcity, but reflect first of all the risk associated with the involvement in the drug trade and seek to compensate this risk. Some estimate risk to account for more than 50 % of drug prices (Caulkins and Reuter 1998: 597), but such estimates are hard to verify on a shadow market. Price formation is therefore highly complex, as legal penalties and enforcement pressure directly impact the cost of market engagement and thus wholesale and retail prices. This logic appears to be behind the impressively high prices for illegal drugs, even though tougher enforcement and higher risk may be offset by criminal adaptation (Pollack and Reuter 2014: 1964), which reduces the impact on price. Production costs are minimal in the drug economy, and the highly diverging market prices of agrarian products like cannabis, cocaine and heroin cannot be explained by supply volumes, production costs or demand alone. In median terms, in 2018 in Belgium a gram of herbal cannabis cost €10, a gram of cocaine €50 and a gram of heroin €20 (EMCDDA 2021e). Risk perception along the supply chain may play a central role in these dynamics, but this may be difficult to prove.

With risk appearing to be the key determinant of price, the steeply increasing value of plant-based drugs along the supply chain may also be explained. Borders tend to multiply the price of an illegal drug, as borders imply control and enforcement efforts and therefore increase risk. While a South American coca farmer gets around €50 to €100 for the amount of coca leaves required to produce a kilogram of cocaine, the same kilogram of cocaine is sold for €54,000 to €83,000 on retail markets in the EU, reflecting the current medium price range as reported by the EMCDDA (2021c). Purity is not reflected in these numbers. The bulk of the revenue is created at the end of the value chain, i.e. on retail markets, and purity has by then decreased by a considerable ratio. The refined cocaine is sold for around €1,500 to €2,000 in the source country, and for €15,000 to €20,000 in transit, depending how many individual transactions are conducted and whether an organised crime group controls several intermediary steps, as in the case of the 'Ndrangheta or formerly the cartels of Cali and Medellín.

There is little doubt that the price range along the value chain does not exclusively communicate production costs, state of supply or demand, but also risk perception that is to be compensated by those that are part of the value generating process. Distribution and trafficking drive prices up (Reuter 2010: 103), as growing drug crops is less risky due to weak territorial control while also being less penalised in most source countries. Beyond logistics, production, labour and risk there are also domestic or even local features of drug markets that apparently have an impact on price. The variation of prices with time and location is a familiar pattern on drug markets (Caulkins and Reuter 1998: 598). On average, in 2019 a gram of cannabis resin was sold for €16 in Austria, while it was worth €22 in Germany and €28 in Norway (EMCDDA 2021e). The differences for other substances across European countries tend to be even more pronounced. Factors such as local supply shortages, differing enforcement levels and penalties, local demand and purchasing power are also to be considered when seeking to dissect price formation on drug markets.

Given the complex interplay of factors and the clandestine mechanisms in price formation, price and purity data may well serve to better understand the state of overall supply and the perception of risk on a drug market but offer few insights into the dynamics and driving factors of this illegal value chain.

4.3. Violence

In order to counter deterrence and to enhance the chances of impunity, actors in illegal drug value chains resort to self-help instruments. Key instruments to attain this goal, yet not the only ones, are corruption and intimidation, i.e. the threat or actual use of violence to deter interventions in the illegal value chain. While corruption as a crime without a direct victim is per se highly clandestine and difficult to trace, violence creates high visibility, usually triggering a public response and media coverage. Since corruption linked to organised crime and drug trafficking can only be traced on a case-by-case basis, this section focuses on drug market-related violence as an indicator that is potentially useful for understanding the evolution and nature of drug value chains.

Given that there are few visible signs of covert drug markets, the frequent violence associated with them is often taken as an indicator of the emergence of trafficking patterns. However, in public perception there is little differentiation between the nature of drug market-related violence and how it relates to actual transactions on these markets. Contrary to expectations, violence is the exception on illegal markets, as it puts criminal transactions and rent-seeking at risk. While some studies estimate that up to 60 % of organised crime groups in the EU resort to violence and as many to corruption (Europol 2021: 18), there may be a bias in such accounts due to the higher visibility of violent behaviour. In the vast majority of countries, criminal justice penalties for violence are high and, in the case of homicide, the highest. Violence provokes legal and enforcement responses that are diametrically opposed to business interests. It is important to note that violence is distributed unequally along drug value chains. While retail markets are more prone to violence due to the higher level of competition, wholesale markets tend to be more peaceful, as does production, even though the prevalence of armed conflict in some of the major source countries may distort this assumption.

Still, drug economies tend to be particularly violent (Catino 2019: 199) as compared to other illegal economies. What might explain this pattern, and what can we learn from this indicator to assess global drug value chains? We may distinguish between two very basic types of violence on drug markets. First, regulatory violence within criminal markets and second, communicative violence towards non-participants in the criminal markets, i.e. authorities or the broader public (Brombacher and Maihold: 2013).

Due to the lack of formal mechanisms of conflict settlement on illicit markets as compared to their licit peers, criminal markets frequently choose violence to regulate disagreements and conflicts of interest emerging in market transactions. On illegal markets, there are usually no written rules or universally accepted legally binding systems for dispute settlement. This applies to all the illegal elements along the drug value chain. Only federation models of organised crime groups build up "higher-level bodies of coordination", such as the *mandamenti* and the *crimini* in the case of the Calabrian 'Ndrangheta, that seek to organise the value chain in a rule-based and therefore peaceful fashion. Based on a cross-comparative approach between the three major Italian mafias, Catino shows that the differences in violent behaviour "are due to different ways of organizing cooperation among [...] various criminal groups, and to the different organizational orders adopted" (Catino 2019: 203). Catino shows that those organised crime groups that follow the model of a "clan-based federation" have historically managed to avoid violence within their overarching criminal network while groups that follow "clan-based models" such as the Campanian Camorra tend to compete within the same criminal system, being more prone to engage in mafia wars and armed feuds (Catino 2019: 152–205). According to this analysis, building a coordination structure to organise value chains provides an advantage on illegal markets, as it reduces regulatory violence and thus reduces the expectation of impunity, allowing for flourishing criminal businesses.

The endemic violence on the Mexican drug market since 2006 is a well-known case of the opposite situation, i.e. a highly competitive and therefore conflict-prone illicit market in which a plethora of clans without any overarching coordinating body participate and organise often competitive value chains. The polypolistic order of the Mexican drug market has constantly produced high levels of homicides for the past 15 years, partly due to competition and partly due to the frequent disruption of the market and arrests of market participants in the course of the massive countercampaign (Behrens and Brombacher 2015: 139–142).

The wide geographical scope of drug economies due to the non-convergence of supply and demand described above increases the amount of transactions between country of origin and country/ies of destination. Value chains are therefore geographically stretched. For the US retail market, Caulkins and Reuter (1998: 598) estimated five to six separate sales transactions of cocaine between the source country and the hands of the user. Every transaction increases the probability of conflict, especially given the constantly high level of risk and the countless possibilities of what may possibly go wrong. The violent character of drug value chains may therefore be explained on the one hand by the way in which the organised crime groups involved cooperate, on the other hand by the usually long series of individual transactions between the starting and ending points of the global drug supply chains.

Still, the organisational character of the organised crime groups involved appears also to have a taming effect on the use of violence. Clan-based federation models as in the case of the 'Ndrangheta manage to reduce and settle disputes even along long supply chains, as in the case of the European cocaine value chain, heavily dominated by the 'Ndrangheta, with its influence spanning the entire supply chain up to source and transit countries (GI-TOC 2021 and Insight Crime: 24–26). Similar clan-based federation models were historically also identified in Colombia and Mexico. However, with the disappearance of major drug trafficking operations like the Medellín cartel, the atomisation of competing clans has favoured the current explosion of violent behaviours. What may be seen in Mexico after 2006 and partly in Colombia after the demobilisation of the FARC guerrilla in the aftermath of the 2016 peace accords may be described as a process of camorrisation, i.e. the restructuring of an oligopolistic drug market towards a polypoly with competing clans. Catino shows that since the 1980s, in Italy almost 50 % of all mafia-related homicides were concentrated on Camorra territory, i.e. an area governed by a clan structure without overarching coordination systems like in the case of Sicilian and Calabrian mafia organizations (Catino 2019: 208). Poor deterrence capabilities and the expectation of impunity, described as key characteristics of drug markets, also reduce the costs and risk of violent behaviour, which contributes to explaining the endemic violence in some drug markets, like in Mexico. According to estimates of the US Department of State (2020: 2), 94 % of all crimes in Mexico are either not reported or not investigated, which leads to a very high level of expectation of impunity.

Hence, contrary to what is frequently reported by the media and assumed by the broader public, violence within drug markets cannot be used as an indicator to draw conclusions on the transactional volume of these markets. Violence out of control on the Mexican drug market does not mean that more drugs are being handled as compared to the pacific times of the PRI governments. At the same time, the relative absence of drug market-related homicides in Albania, Bolivia or Peru is not to be interpreted as the absence of drug market transactions. The absence of regulatory violence could possibly mean that there are fewer disputes on the market, that functional overarching coordination structures for organising the value chain are in place or that efficient bribery systems have been set up. The clandestine character of these markets, especially of the less violent and therefore less visible ones, makes a thorough analysis beyond guesswork difficult.

In addition to the previously described patterns of regulatory violence directed towards market participants, functional participants within the drug value chains also tend to resort to violence that is directed towards society, the government and judicial authorities. While the concept of regulatory violence may explain the quantity of violence on competitive drug markets, it is not helpful in analysing the quality of such violence. Especially in Latin America, drug-related violence tends to be highly visible due to its quality. Extreme brutality such as frequent beheadings and public exposure of tortured bodies like in Mexico seems to be at odds with the wish to avoid public response and interventions in the criminal markets. This kind of violence has an instrumental character and therefore appears irrational only at first glance (Brombacher and Maihold 2013: 88). This communicative violence seeks to deter authorities, competitors or even the broader public from intervening in the illicit markets, sowing intimidation and fear as a strategy to enhance the expectation of impunity. This pattern is quite well known from the concept of terrorism, where not the actual victim is the target but a broader audience. The killed and tortured body is bound to convey a message to third parties. The result of this pattern of communicative violence is to build a reputation, a key success factor in illicit markets to enhance obedience and predictability of interpersonal behaviour (Reuter 2009: 280). However, the parallel emergence of both regulatory and communicative violence as in Mexico appears to be rather exceptional. While other organised crime groups like the Sicilian Cosa Nostra or more recently Belgian and Dutch organised crime groups have sometimes resorted to highly visible targeted killings, such violence does not appear to be functional in the long term, given the usually heavy sanctioning response of enforcement agencies and judicial systems. While for Mexico some estimates relate one-third to half of all homicides to organised crime (Bergmann 2018: 140), such a pattern is less common for other source or transit countries of illegal drugs, where periods of intense violence seem to be of a short-term and transitory character.

As in the case of regulatory violence, the existence of communicative violence does potentially allow for some insights into the structure of drug markets and the strategies of their participants but does not provide any information about the true scope and organisation of a global value chain. All three supply-side indicators discussed here are positivist, are therefore reduced to the visible elements of the global drug economy and are highly dependent on sufficient enforcement capabilities. These indicators help to trace certain elements and patterns of the global drug value chains following the key determinants of geographical non-convergence of supply and demand as well as high levels of expectation of impunity. They provide certain information about trafficking patterns, about the risk perceptions underlying pricing and about the nature of the organised crime networks involved and how they interact with each other. The global narrative of drug economies heavily relies on these three indicators, yet they only serve to indicate *what* is happening in the global drug economy, not *why* it is happening.

There are two sets of potential explanations of how the geography of the global drug markets evolves and why, namely structural and actor-oriented approaches.

5. *What drives illicit drug economies?*

5.1. The structural dimension: demand and enabling structural conditions

As for any market, the interplay of supply and demand creates drug markets. The emergence of markets requires the establishment of value chains, defined by geographical conditions, deterrence and expectation of impunity and by the nature of the organised crime groups involved. Demand drives supply, while the reverse relationship is less clear. Demand is a prerequisite for drug markets. Drug use patterns and prevalence rates are highly divergent between countries. Even in Europe, despite similar societal conditions, there are partly massive differences in prevalence rates. While in France the adult lifetime prevalence for cannabis is 45 %, in Malta it is reported to be only 4 % (EMCDDA 2021a: 12). The adult last-year prevalence of cocaine is 2.7 % in the United Kingdom and 1.1 % in Germany (EMCDDA 2021d). As in the case of the highly divergent retail prices on the European drug market, in the case of prevalences there is also a broad range of potential explanations for these differences. However, as they are not conclusive, they are of little help in explaining global trafficking patterns. In the following, an existing range of demand is taken as a fixed variable for global drug economies.

The geographical divergence of supply and demand was discussed above as a key factor that explains the emergence and persistence of transnational drug value chains. The physical distance of supply hubs and main user markets is the simplest but most relevant factor for emerging transnational supply chains. But if demand drives supply, why do drug crop cultivation and production not move closer to consumer markets? This would reduce costs, risk and time. Partly this pattern is to be seen in the field of cannabis. Indoor production of cannabis within the EU has been on the rise in recent years (Europol 2021: 47; 99). Synthetic drug production is also massive in some European countries. As stated above, main supply hubs for outdoor cannabis can be found in close vicinity to the EU, e.g. in the Western Balkans and North Africa. However, these examples seem to be rather the exception. Even though theoretically coca cultivation and in fact also opium poppy production is technically possible within European countries with a certain technical investment (Reuter 2010: 103), the global value chains seem to stick to supply originating in the Global South.

The limited yet quite stable group of countries that dominate most of the global production of plant-based drugs appear to share features that make them more prone to evolve as central nodes of the global drug economy under a given level of continuous demand. Geography certainly helps to explain why drug crop cultivation may remain undetected. Most of the known global drug crop growing hotspots lie either in dense tropical forests or in remote mountainous areas, frequently in regions that had previously been favoured by substantial infrastructure and colonisation efforts but were then marginalised and abandoned (Gootenberg 2021; Davalos et al. 2021). Geographical marginalisation thus helps to enhance the expectation of impunity and to avoid state intervention by inaccessibility. Geography certainly also helps to understand why some countries become trafficking hubs and transshipment routes, as a spill-over effect is quite common in many cases. Seizure data show that countries neighbouring key source countries like Ecuador, Venezuela, Iran and Pakistan frequently become natural transshipment nodes for the drug value chains (UNODC 2021c).

Geography does *not*, however, explain the location of main production hubs. While moving closer to destination markets, as in the case of indoor cannabis, may be a risk-reduction strategy, this does not seem to apply to the major consumer markets for heroin and cocaine. Afghanistan and Colombia are neither well connected to the EU, nor is there a particularly large volume of legitimate commerce between the regions where boundaries between legal and illegal value chains easily blur. The supply chains span many different jurisdictions, borders and coastal waters. Mexico with its long border with the US might be expected to develop its own cocaine industry, yet coca fields have hardly ever been detected. The domination of the US market for fentanyl and its precursors by Chinese supply (Felbab-Brown 2020) cannot be explained by geographical proximity. The region in the world with the highest current prevalence of cocaine use, Oceania, is also the most remote from its South American centres of supply, even though historically coca bush was grown in Indonesia and Taiwan (Reuter 2010: 103).

As geography thus offers a limited ability to predict where massive drug economies emerge, a closer look at structural conditions in source countries is needed. A low level of risk and a high level of expectation of impunity have been identified as a second common denominator for global drug supply chains. While this variable is certainly ubiquitous in all major source *countries*, it is also ubiquitous all over the source *regions*. A similar pattern is to be found in the case of major transshipment hubs, i.e. transit countries. Weak statehood, a certain responsiveness to bribery, absence of border control, existing smuggling networks or related organised crime and armed groups seem to create an attractive enabling environment in both source and transit countries. West Africa, the Balkans and the Sahel routes all share a suitable mix of these factors to make them become part of drug value chains and participate in their attractive rewards. Again, seizures are not a conclusive indicator to assess the real volume of drug shipments across these regions, as the very root causes of their involvement in the drug business decrease the probability of seizures, i.e. the weakness or absence of deterrence and state control.

Hence, suitable geography and weak deterrence do not lead to a drug economy by themselves. The set of "competitive advantages" (Thoumi 2010: 197–199) or "pull factors" (Morselli, Turcotte and Tenti 2011: 171) for drug economies and the organised crime groups involved goes beyond these two broadly defined common denominators of drug economies. Since the drug economies at issue here are all plant-based, appropriate climate and soil conditions need to be in place with sufficient agricultural land being available and economically accessible (Reuter 2010: 106). However, this factor appears less relevant than previously assumed. In Afghanistan and Colombia, the main source countries for opium poppy and coca, respectively, less than 0.5 % of all agricultural land is dedicated to drug crop growing, though in cultivation hotspots like Helmand in Afghanistan this share rises above 20 % (UNODC 2021a: 51–52). Often, though, drug crop farmers do not legally own the plots used for cultivation but use public land either beyond the agriculture frontier or in protected areas (Grimmelmann et al. 2017). Beyond climate and land, cheap labour for the labour-intense growing, harvesting and processing of drug crops is essential, again a ubiquitous prerequisite across the key countries with low income and high inequality where the major share of supply is originating. While (extreme) poverty appears to be a main structural feature of drug crop growing areas, the deficits in development go beyond narrow income-related indicators. For Afghanistan, UNODC has identified a "development gap" in poppy-growing villages as compared to other villages. The comparison shows that access to health, schooling, security and government presence is markedly lower in poppy-growing villages, though with some variation across the country (UNODC 2019: 46–47). The marginalised character of drug crop growing communities frequently precludes access to legal markets for licit products, often making drug crops the only real alternative for small-scale farmers (Gutiérrez-Sanín 2021).

The combination of suitable geographical and climatic factors with cheap labour and land, absence of state services, low deterrence and a high expectation of impunity appears to be the complex mix of enabling factors that allows drug value chains to emerge and persist: "Low opportunity costs for factors of production in conjunction with low enforcement risks result in very modest prices for the refined product, and they also ensure that production does not move upstream" (Reuter 2010: 106).

Again, while this set of structural conditions appears to apply to all major source countries of illegal drugs, this mix can also be found in many other countries around the globe, even ones closer to the main consumer markets. Thoumi (2010: 195) estimates that climatic and soil conditions would allow coca bush to be grown in at least 30 countries and opium poppy in at least 90, yet the number of main producer countries has varied little. Reuter (2010: 107) suggests that path dependencies may explain the relative stability of drug crop cultivating countries, i.e. the otherwise high costs for setting up new global trafficking networks and the decreasing transactional costs and risks for corruption when transactions are iterated. Another key path dependency may lie in the historically evolved availability of expertise to run plant-to-powder production processes, where technical capabilities cannot be easily acquired on the labour market. At the same time, "illegal skills" to organise illegal business transactions, enforce criminal contracts, dissuade competitors and law enforcement agencies and make bribery arrangements are essential capabilities for running drug value chains (Thoumi 2010: 198). This sort of expertise tends to be available in countries with a long-standing history of armed conflict or similar forms of intrasocietal violence. The frequent albeit not universal convergence of countries with temporary or protracted internal armed conflict and massive drug economies (e.g. Afghanistan, Colombia, Myanmar) may well be explained by a set of competitive advantages that encompass the above-mentioned structural conditions and also sufficient availability of the relevant expertise and skills to initiate and run drug supply chains. It is estimated that 28 % of all revenues of non-state armed groups at a global scale stem from the drug economy (GI-TOC, INTERPOL and RHIPTO 2018: 111), which sustains the argument.

As case studies show, there is a pattern that illegal drug economies tend to grow and proliferate once established (Thoumi 2010: 198–200). The "criminogenic environments" that enable massive drug economies tend to be stable over time, while the organised crime groups seizing the opportunities of these structural conditions tend to vary considerably

(Morselli, Turcotte and Tenti 2011: 166). Therefore, even in countries that may have overcome plant-based drug production, such as Pakistan or Thailand, ongoing high levels of seizures of both synthetic and organic drugs indicate persistence of illegal drug value chains, even though the cultivation element no longer forms part of the chain. State fragility as a central enabling factor is further aggravated by the presence of drug economies, as indicated by examples like Guinea-Bissau and Mali (Reitano 2020: 131). In general terms, accumulated global seizure data indicate a relative stability of global drug markets, potentially reflecting rather the demographic growth of consumer markets than massive overall changes within the global drug markets (UNODC 2021a: 53).[6]

The summary of potential structural variables to explain the emergence and persistence of drug markets makes clear that this set of variables can be found in varying degrees in all major source countries and potentially also in most major transit countries, at least at a local scale. While it is quite clear that these variables positively influence the persistence and expansion of drug economies over time, their emergence rather appears to be rooted in specific national path dependencies or individual historical incidents such as the Soviet invasion of Afghanistan, Colombian drug trafficking organisations switching to pay Mexican intermediaries with cocaine instead of cash, the emergence of the Cali-Galicia cocaine pipeline due to joint jail time of the respective criminal leaders in Madrid or the existence of century-old traditional growth and use of coca in the Andes paired with state-led colonisation efforts (GI-TOC 2021 and Insight Crime: 8–13; Gootenberg 2021; Thoumi 2010: 241). However, the evidence base remains too weak to find a one-size-fits-all answer to the highly relevant question of why a major share of the global drug economy still heavily relies on a limited number of source countries.

5.2. The actor dimension: organised crime within the drug market

The structural factors discussed in the previous section may be complemented by actor-based explanatory factors, contributing to a more coherent understanding of the nature and scope of global drug value chains.

The predominant positivist paradigm in contouring the global drug economy as outlined above is frequently entangled with a simplistic un-

6 A notable exception is the global seizure rate of amphetamine-type stimulants (ATS), which has grown dramatically since 2008 (UNODC 2021a: 53).

derstanding of how organised crime actors run value chains. The focus on seizures appears to be accompanied by a fixation on the capture of leading figures in the global drug economy, fed by kingpin strategies and popular culture. A "pabloescobarised" cliché of the global drug economy is still prevalent in the public, replicating the idea of a highly controlled and criminally regulated global drug value chain in which control, power, income and risk are monopolised by a few, as connoted by the misleading term "cartel". According to this narrative, the emergence and persistence of drug markets are a direct consequence of deliberate and strategic decisions by organised crime groups seeking to move into regions with attractive structural conditions or "criminogenic environments" to maximise profits and minimise risks, similar to global enterprises that invest in products and markets according to meticulous business plans.

Drug value chains are composed of a highly complex set of different actors, spanning drug crop farmers in source countries, wage labourers, production staff, chemists, intermediaries, packers, sellers, traffickers, couriers, bribed officials, brokers, insurgents, drivers, sailors, pilots, hitmen, money launderers, decision-makers, retailers and users, just to name a few. All of these take individual decisions, make choices and act based on their own rationales. It would go beyond the scope of this chapter to categorize the interplay of all these actors, but the key actors in this long illegal global value chain appear to be organised crime groups and networks that cover the entire range of the supply chain between production and consumption hubs.

The illegal (and in some cases partly legal and licit) supply chain take the form of large chain-style networks (Kenney 2007) connected mostly horizontally through their nodes, the independent criminal actors. Organised crime groups arrange all the relevant transactions that connect these nodes, sometimes with the involvement of legitimate actors within legal trade or of government or military actors. Most case studies show that the global drug value chains are predominantly organised in a decentralised and often ad hoc fashion, with a high level of intermediary transactions and the involvement of a broad array of criminal organisations. These cooperate through networks, frequently outsourcing and subcontracting individual service providers, with the drug sometimes sold on several occasions along the supply chain. This latter aspect may partly explain the sometimes unexpected geographical turns of the drug supply chains. As a recent analysis put it for the cocaine supply chain: "Different criminal nodes will align for a particular shipment, then drift apart, searching for new opportunities and trafficking constellations" (GI-TOC 2021 and Insight Crime: 5). The decentralised pattern of rather disorganised supply chains with manifold individual transactions is also prevalent within the EU (Europol 2021: 22–24). There are many examples for drug shipments criss-crossing all over continental Europe before reaching their final destination. The highly flexible organisation of these value chains creates a high level of vulnerability to interruptions of supply and interception for all parties involved.

Thus, the character of the organisation and evolution of the value chain may indeed be enabled by the structural conditions in source and transit countries, but it is defined by the nature and choices of the organised crime groups involved, working within the structural conditions discussed above and adapting to them through iterative learning. The still widespread notion of a monopolised value chain from crop to retailer, from plant to powder, is rooted in historical situations where the global drug economy was perceived to be dominated by a few criminal masterminds. Notorious drug traffickers like Pablo Escobar, the Rodríguez Orejuela brothers, Joaquín Guzmán and Khun Sa did indeed exercise control over several elements of drug value chains, but never over the full set of individual transactions. Even at the height of their power, the Medellín and Cali cartels always coexisted with countless other criminal operations in the field of drugs across Colombia, interacting through informal networks that allowed for patterns of flexible transactional adaptations. Even the alleged Colombia-based global drug enterprises were in fact rather small to medium-sized business operations with never more than a few dozen members or affiliated actors (Kenney 2007: 247–258).

In the aftermath of the decapitation of these organisations, the drug supply chains have never been permanently interrupted. While on an individual case basis tackling drug trafficking networks by targeting key nodes within them appears to be the most efficient disruptive strategy (Bright et al. 2017: 433–437), from an overall market perspective the drug economy shows a high level of resilience (Morselli and Petit 2007: 111).

While the flexible organisation of value chains also increases vulnerability, at the same time it contributes to their potential to reorganise quickly and to recover functionality. As the cases of Colombia and more recently Mexico show, taking out kingpins rather favours the development of more decentralised value chains with an increased level of regulatory violence without actually disrupting the overall market. It may seem obvious at first glance that "small is beautiful" in drug trafficking operations, but evidence from single-case studies shows that small-scale drug trafficking operations are not necessarily less prone to government disruption (Bouchard and Oullet 2011: 83). This result may also prove to apply to the case of the 'Ndrangheta, which provides a high level of organisation and coordination structures for its members. Another example from the Mexican drug market shows that hierarchically structured organised criminal operations – such as the Sinaloa Cartel – apply more risk-adverse strategies in money laundering practices than flatter wheel networks with a higher level of exposure and therefore a higher risk of enforcement interventions (Farfán-Méndez 2019: 300–305).

Setting up centralised criminal operations across several countries and continents is highly risky and faces countless logistical and communicative constraints (Morselli, Turcotte and Tenti 2011: 168–169). Thus, only organised crime groups structured on a clan-based federation model may be capable of doing so. In the global cocaine economy the 'Ndrangheta seems to be a notable exception, as this organisation has apparently managed to control several intermediate transactional nodes up to the source countries with a presence in situ across Latin America and permanent structures in place, controlling a major share of the transatlantic cocaine value chain (GI-TOC 2021 and Insight Crime: 22–25). The 'Ndrangheta model of organising supply and transit hub presence is reported to be replicated by Mexican and Western Balkan organised crime groups, though not permanently but through brokers and the organisation of ad hoc crowdfunding of shipments to bridge intermediary transactions (GI-TOC 2021 and Insight Crime: 33).

Despite these accounts of changing business patterns along drug value chains, the interpretation of these developments should avoid *post hoc ergo propter hoc* pitfalls. Evidence shows that the global drug value chains are organised in a decentralised and multi-transactional manner, not strategically planned by powerful and farsighted global criminal enterprises. Within the existing range of pull factors such as the essential geographical, socio-economic and legal conditions discussed above, chance and opportunity appear to be the main causal factors to explain how the global drug value chains are organised and evolve. The frequent overrating of criminal brains underrates the lack of information and predictability on clandestine markets as well as the costs of mobility. Organised crime groups do not float freely seeking to maximise profit but organise transactions within the value chains according to the enabling conditions described above. As summarised by Morselli, Turcotte and Tenti:

> In many ways, the criminal groups and organisations that are identified in local and transnational networks are not the product of intentional organising by offenders. Instead, offenders are as reactive as law-enforcement agents. The forms and sizes of criminal groups are the product of offenders' adaptation to the constraints surrounding

> them. They are self-organising and emergent in settings where there are ample vulnerable opportunities to seize and interact across a variety of cross-border, cross-market and cross-industry settings. (Morselli, Turcotte and Tenti 2011: 167)

Hence, structural factors appear to prevail in the shaping of global drug supply chains, including the interplay of legal and illegal segments of those chains. While structures appear to be stable over time, organised crime groups handling the drug value chains fluctuate strongly. There is an astonishing level of stability of overall production and trafficking patterns. The rise and fall of the most notorious drug trafficking kingpins and their respective organisations, e.g. in Mexico, Colombia, Albania and Myanmar, did not permanently change the geographical patterns of the supply chain of cocaine, heroin and cannabis in the respective countries. Yet the manner in which the value chain is organised and the roles taken by criminal and legitimate actors in it did. The infamous Balkan route for heroin, the transadriatic trafficking patterns for cannabis and the transatlantic routes for cocaine have shown a high level of resilience and stability over the past decades (Europol 2021: 50). But the resilience only applies to geographical patterns of the market, not to functional elements within the supply chain. However, overall stability does not imply inflexibility, and new trafficking patterns may emerge, as the case of West Africa and the rather recent methamphetamine routes from Afghanistan to East Africa show. Still, the mobility of organised crime groups and supply chains appears to be far more limited and less strategic than usually assumed.

6. *Towards a more sustainable supply control policy: prioritising structural approaches*

The previous discussion gives grounds to assume that not actors but structural conditions are the key driving principle for the emergence and persistence of global drug value chains. Yet, the major efforts to control the global drug supply chain heavily rely on actor- or substance-oriented efforts, i.e. seizure-and-capture strategies, and are not directed towards structural variables. Given the disastrous effects of the global drug economy in terms of health, security, the environment, armed conflict, corruption and violence, it may be necessary to reassess this actor-focused approach. As overall legal regulation of scheduled drugs and a complete regime collapse are unlikely, a potential reorientation of global drug policies and their metrics within the current drug control regime may help to mitigate some of the most pressing harms related to the global drug economy.

While demand and geography as well as some of the historical path dependencies discussed above seem to be fixed variables in this equation, the structural enabling factors for global drug value chains are in principle responsive to actions by governments and the international community. The highly decentralised architecture of drug value chains appears to follow a rather spontaneous order instead of criminal masterplans as frequently assumed.

Organised crime groups come and go; the enabling structures remain. Criminogenic environments and the underlying root causes may be addressed by tackling the development deficits entangled within them, by increasing the costs of criminal endeavours and reducing the expectation of impunity across the key nodes of production and trafficking. While law enforcement capabilities and territorial and border control do play a key role in such a strategy, the role of the state goes beyond the repression of illicit flows, as shown by the development gaps identified in Afghanistan by UNODC and by the relevance of competing norms creating legitimacy for illicit economies as analysed by Thoumi.

There have been recent shifts within the global drug control regime that may allow for more structure-oriented strategies. A new approach to drugs and development has emerged over the past years that puts development interventions to address the root causes of illicit drug economies at the forefront (Diskul, Collins and Brombacher 2021: 86), gradually widening the scope for a more structural and development-oriented approach in international drug policy (Brombacher and David 2020: 70–72). However, the interplay of addressing development deficits that drive illicit drug economies, tackling crime and illicit markets and, in some cases, settling armed conflicts is not necessarily mutually reinforcing. A "drugs-development-peacebuilding trilemma" (Goodhand et al. 2021) may make it difficult to pursue these goals all at once, given the trade-offs between the diverse objectives intertwined within this trilemma.

A good share of the global debate on how to address the root causes of drug economies focuses on the approach of alternative development, which consists in addressing the developmental factors underlying drug economies and creating licit sources of income for drug crop farmers. Beyond the cultivation element in the drug value chains, there is a lack of technical approaches to addressing the structural factors that enable trafficking hubs and routes to flourish. When it comes to the issue of armed conflict and drug economies or state failure in a broader sense, few policy options are available so far (Reitano 2020: 131). The lack of other instruments has often led to exaggerated expectations towards the alternative development approach, which is sometimes "trying to be all things to all people" (Mansfield 2020). While the UN General Assembly Special Session on Drugs (UNGASS) 2016 widened the scope of alternative development beyond drug crop growing to drug trafficking settings, there are only a few practical experiences in this area so far (Diskul, Collins and Brombacher 2021). Moving away from the traditional actor- and substance-oriented supply-side indicators of global drug policy towards the realm of structural enabling factors is a difficult task, since short-term statistical achievements are politically more attractive than progress on long-term developmental indicators such as the measurement of development gaps as suggested by UNODC, poverty reduction or state-building efforts. Frequently, data on structural conditions favouring drug economies are available but are not used for orienting drug policy efforts (Bewley-Taylor 2016: 4–8).

Nonetheless, if harm is integrated into the equation as an indicator, a reorientation of policies beyond seizures and captures may appear possible. The concept of harm reduction is widely acknowledged in the field of demand-side drug policies. Needle and syringe exchange programmes, supervised drug consumption facilities and opioid substitution treatment are common practices to reduce the individual and societal harm associated with drug use. However, the supply-side-related harms of drugs and drug policies, e.g. violence, corruption, environmental degradation or protracted armed conflict, have not been widely considered to be addressed by harm reduction strategies. Shaw (2019) suggests applying such a strategy to drug policies, replacing the current supply control paradigm by one that seeks to reduce violence and impunity and protects political processes at risk of being undermined and corrupted by drug economies.

The global drug economy is first of all perceived through the harms it inflicts on individuals and societies. Nonetheless, how drug markets are measured and subsequently how counterstrategies are defined is not driven by the issue of harm, but by positivist actor-driven rationales. Structural approaches appear to explain the emergence, quality and persistence of drug value chains better than actor-oriented methods, yet structural indicators do not play a relevant role in global drug policy debates yet. There are no commonly acknowledged structural indicators that would allow the vulnerabilities of countries or regions to organised crime to be measured and predicted. Both structural and harm-related indicators could allow for a better measurement of the whereabouts of global drug value chains and the associated policies than the dominant standard indicators. Reorienting global drug policies towards a structural approach would imply rethinking their metrics. This may prove to be a challenging endeavour, yet worthwhile.

References

Behrens, Timo/Brombacher, Daniel (2015): „Transnationale Organisierte Kriminalität". In: Jäger, Thomas (ed.): Handbuch Sicherheitsgefahren. Wiesbaden: Springer, pp. 135–145.

Bergmann, Marcelo (2018): Illegal drugs, drug trafficking and violence in Latin America. Berlin/Heidelberg: Springer.

Bewley-Taylor, Dave (2016): "Towards metrics that measure outcomes that matter". At: https://www.swansea.ac.uk/media/Towards-Metrics-that-Measure-Outcomes-that-Matter.pdf (accessed 2 July 2021).

Bouchard, Martin/Ouellet, Frédéric (2011): "Is small beautiful? The link between risks and size in illegal drug markets". In: Global Crime, 12, 1, pp. 70–86.

Bright, David/Greenhill, Catherine/Britz, Thomas/Ritter, Alison/Morselli, Carlo (2017): "Criminal network vulnerabilities and adaptations". In: Global Crime, 18, 4, pp. 424–441.

Brombacher, Daniel/Garzón, Juan Carlos/Vélez, Maria Alejandra (2021): "Introduction Special Issue: Environmental impacts of illicit economies". In: Journal of Illicit Economies and Development, 3, 1, pp. 1–9.

Brombacher, Daniel/David, Sarah (2020): „From alternative development to development-oriented drug policies". In: International Development Policy, 12, pp. 64–79.

Brombacher, Daniel/Maihold, Günther (2013): „Das Gewaltparadox im mexikanischen Drogenkampf: Erklärungsversuche und ihre Folgen". In: Brombacher, Daniel/Maihold, Günther (eds.): Gewalt, Organisierte Kriminalität und Staat in Lateinamerika. Opladen/Berlin/Toronto: Barbara Budrich, pp. 85–97.

Brombacher, Daniel (2013): „Illegal drug cultivation and legal regulatory options in the UN drug control framework. Comparing coca and opium poppy". In: Matthieu, Hans/Nino, Catalina (eds.): From repression to regulation. Proposals for drug policy reform. Bogotá: FESCOL, pp. 253–289.

Buxton, Julia (2010): "The historical foundation of the narcotic drug control regime". In: Keefer, Philipp/Loayza, Norman (eds.): Innocent bystanders. Developing countries and the war on drugs. Washington D.C.: The World Bank, pp. 61–95.

Buxton, Julia (2020): "Drug control and development. A blind spot". In: International Development Policy, 12, pp. 13–42.

Calderoni, Francesco (2011): "Where is the mafia in Italy? Measuring the presence of the mafia across Italian provinces". In: Global Crime, 12, 1, pp. 41–69.

Catino, Maurizio (2019): Mafia organizations. The visible hand of criminal enterprise. Cambridge: Cambridge University Press.

Caulkins, Jonathan/Reuter, Peter (1998): "What price data tells us about drug markets". In: Journal of Drug Issues, 28, 3, pp. 593–612.

Collins, John (2016): "Development first. Multilateralism in the post-'war on drugs' era". In: After the drug wars. Report of the LSE expert group on the economics of drug policy. London: LSE Press, pp. 9–18.

Daily Sabah (2021): "Turkey seizes more than 1 ton of cocaine in 'biggest bust'". At: https://www.dailysabah.com/turkey/investigations/turkey-seizes-more-than-1-ton-of-Cocaine-in-biggest-bust (accessed 04 July 2021).

Davalos, Liliana/Davalos, Eleonora/Holmes, Jennifer/Tucker, Clara/Armenteras, Dolors (2021): "Forests, coca, and conflict. Grass frontier dynamics and deforestation in the Amazon-Andes". In: Journal of Illicit Economies and Development, 3, 1, pp.74 – 96

Diskul, Dispanadda/Collins, John/Brombacher, Daniel (2021): "Drugs and development in the urban setting – expanding development-oriented interventions beyond illicit drug crop cultivation." In: Journal of Illicit Economies and Development, 2, 2, pp. 80–90.

EMCDDA, European Monitoring Centre for Drugs and Drug Addiction (2021a): European Drug Report. Lisbon: EMCDDA.

EMCDDA, European Monitoring Centre for Drugs and Drugs Addiction (2021b): Illicit drug markets and supply in the Western Balkans. Impact of COVID-19. EMCDDA Trendspotter Briefing. Lisbon: EMCDDA.

EMCDDA, European Monitoring Centre for Drugs and Drugs Addiction (2021c): "Statistical Bulletin. Cocaine price and purity in the European Union". At: https://www.emcdda.europa.eu/media-library/Cocaine-price-and-purity-european-union-updated-june-2021_en (accessed 3 July 2021).

EMCDDA, European Monitoring Centre for Drugs and Drugs Addiction (2021d) Statistical Bulletin 2021. Prevalence of drug use. At: https://www.emcdda.europa.eu/data/stats2021/gps_en (04 July 2021).

EMCDDA European Monitoring Centre for Drugs and Drugs Addiction (2021e): "Statistical Bulletin 2021. Price, purity and potency". At: https://www.emcdda.europa.eu/data/stats2021/ppp_en (accessed 12 July 2021)

EMCDDA, European Monitoring Centre for Drugs and Drug Addiction/Europol (2019): EU Drug Markets Report. Lisbon/The Hague: EMCDDA, Europol.

EMCDDA, European Monitoring Centre for Drugs and Drug Addiction/Europol (2020): EU Drug Markets. Impact of Covid-19. Lisbon/The Hague: EMCDDA, Europol.

Europol (2019): "News: 1 176 kg of cocaine hidden in bananas seized in Italy". At: https://www.europol.europa.eu/newsroom/news/1-176-kg-of-Cocaine-hidden-in-bananas-seized-in-italy (accessed 4 July 2021).

Europol (2021): Serious and organized crime situation assessment (SOCTA). The Hague: Europol.

Farfán-Méndez, Cecilia (2019): "The structure of drug trafficking organizations and money laundering practices. A risk appetite hypothesis." In: Journal of Illicit Economies and Development, 1, 3, pp. 294–311.

Felbab-Brown, Vanda (2020): Fentanyl and geopolitics. Controlling opioid supply from China. Washington D.C.: Brookings.

GI-TOC, Global Initiative against Transnational Organized Crime (2020): Civil Society Observatory of Illicit Economies in Eastern and Southern Africa, Risk Bulletin, 12.

GI-TOC, Global Initiative against Transnational Organized Crime (2021): Observatory of illicit economies in Southeastern Europe, Risk Bulletin, 7.

GI-TOC, Global Initiative against Transnational Organized Crime/Insight Crime (2021): The Cocaine Pipeline to Europe, Research Report. Vienna/Bogotá: 2021.

GI-TOC, Global Initiative against Transnational Organized Crime/INTERPOL/RHIPTO, Norwegian Center for Global Analysis (2018): World Atlas of Illicit Flows. Vienna/Oslo/Lyon.

Goodhand, Jonathan/Meehan, Patrick/Bhatia, Jasmine/Ghiabi, Maziyar/Gutiérrez Sanín, Francisco (2021): "Critical policy frontiers. The drugs-development-peacebuilding trilemma". In: International Journal of Drug Policy, 89, 103115.

Gootenberg, Paul (2021): "Chicken or eggs? Rethinking illicit drugs and 'Development'". In: International Journal of Drug Policy, 89, 102985.

Grimmelmann, Klaas/Arning, Nike/Arnold, Jana/Espinoza, Jorge (2017): "The land-drugs nexus. How illicit drug crop cultivation is related to access to land". In: Bulletin of Narcotics, 61, LXI, pp. 75–105.

Gutiérrez-Sanín, Francisco (2021): "Tough Tradeoffs. Coca crops and agrarian alternatives in Colombia". In: International Journal of Drug Policy, 89, 103156.

Insight Crime (2020): „Honduras proves fertile ground for coca". At: https://insightcrime.org/news/brief/coca-crops-flourish-honduras/ (accessed 30 June 2021).

Kenney, Michael (2007): "The architecture of drug trafficking. Network forms of organisation in the Colombian Cocaine trade". In: Global Crime, 8, 3, pp. 233–259.

Mansfield, David (2020): "Trying to be all things to all people. Alternative development in Afghanistan". In: International Development Policy, 12, pp. 79–105.

Mansfield, David/Soderholm, Alexander (2020): Emerging evidence of Afghanistan's role as a producer and supplier of ephedrine and methamphetamine. Lisbon: EMCDDA.

Morselli, Carlo/Turcotte, Mathilde/Tenti, Valentina (2011): "The mobility of criminal groups". In: Global Crime, 12, 3, pp. 165–188.

Morselli, Carlo/Petit, Katja (2007): "Law-enforcement disruption of a drug importation network". In: Global Crime, 8, 2, pp. 109–130.

Open Society Foundations/Transform Drug Policy Foundation (2008): The alternative world drug report. Counting the costs of the war on drugs. New York/London: Open Society Foundations.

Pearl, Betsy (2019): Ending the war on drugs. By the numbers. Washington D.C.: Center of American Progress.

Pollack, Harold/Reuter, Peter (2014): "Does tougher enforcement make drugs more expensive?". In: Addiction, 109, pp. 1959–1966.

Reitano, Tuesday (2020): "Making war. Conflict zones and their implications for drug policy". In: International Development Policy, 12, pp. 127–141.

Reuter, Peter (2009): "Systemic violence in drug markets". In: Crime, Law and Social Change, 52, pp. 275–284.

Reuter, Peter (2010): "Can production and trafficking of illicit drugs be reduced or only shifted?". In: Keefer, Philipp/Loayza, Norman (eds.): Innocent bystanders. Developing countries and the war on drugs. Washington D.C.: The World Bank, pp. 95–135.

Shaw, Mark (2019): "What could an asymmetrical strategy against organised crime look like? A lesson from the drug policy debate". In: Journal of Illicit Economies and Development, 1, 1 pp. 99–106.

Thoumi, Francisco (2010): "Competitive advantages in the production and trafficking of Coca-Cocaine and Opium-Heroin in Afghanistan and the Andean Countries". In: Keefer, Philip/Loayza, Norman (eds.): Innocent bystanders. Developing countries and the war on drugs. Washington D.C.: The World Bank, pp. 195–253.

UNODC, United Nations Office on Drugs and Crime (2019): Afghanistan opium survey 2019. Socio-economic survey report. Drivers, causes and consequences of opium poppy cultivation. Vienna/Kabul: UNODC.

UNODC, United Nations Office on Drugs and Crime (2020): Research Brief. COVID-19 and the drug supply chain: from production and trafficking to use. Vienna: UNODC.

UNODC, United Nations Office on Drugs and Crime (2021a): World Drug Report 2021, Booklet II. Vienna: UNODC.

UNODC, United Nations Office on Drugs and Crime (2021b): "UNODC World Drug Report 2021. Statistical Annex: Prevalence of drug use in the general population including NPS". At: https://www.unodc.org/unodc/en/data-and-analysis/wdr2021_annex.html (accessed 11 July 2021).

UNODC, United Nations Office on Drugs and Crime (2021c): UNODC World Drug Report. Statistical Annex: Global seizures of Cocaine and Heroin. At: https://dataunodc.un.org/data/drugs/Global%20Seizures (11 July 2021).

US Bureau of Transportation Statistics (n.d.): "Border Crossing Data". At: https://explore.dot.gov/views/BorderCrossingData/Annual?:isGuestRedirectFromVizportal=y&:embed=y (accessed 4 July 2021)

US Department of State (2020): "Mexico Human Rights Report". At: https://www.state.gov/wp-content/uploads/2021/03/MEXICO-2020-HUMAN-RIGHTS-REPORT.pdf (accessed 2 July 2021).

Janowitz, Nathaniel (2021): "Are Mexican cartels trying to make their own cocaine?". At: https://www.vice.com/en/article/epdwd7/are-mexican-cartels-trying-to-make-their-own-cocaine (accessed 30 June 2021).

Peculiarity and persistence of a transregional flow: the evolution of human trafficking for sexual exploitation from Nigeria to Europe

Judith Vorrath

1 Introduction[1]

The specific type of human trafficking analysed in this chapter has been linking an area in the Global South with Europe over an extended period of time. The persistence and some (supposedly) peculiar features of the trafficking of Nigerian women and girls for sexual exploitation to European destinations have led to an increasing interest in the phenomenon. Most notably, a substantial rise in Nigerian females entering Europe around 2013–2015 led to growing attention from policymakers, law enforcement and civil society (Pascoal 2018: 2–3).

Clearly, there have been different perspectives on how to approach the issue – from a human rights, feminist or criminal justice point of view or led, for example, by considerations related to migration and development. However, as this chapter argues, it has been the focus on some particular features of this trafficking that has at times obstructed a better understanding of the dynamics and incentives along the chain – even more so as these keep changing and data on the phenomenon is naturally limited. Several aspects of this kind of trafficking have been at the centre of attention, namely that the Nigerian perpetrators prosecuted in Europe also tend to be female, that there seems to be something like an "end-to-end" control of the trafficking process despite rather flexible criminal networks involved and that so-called juju rituals – usually performed at shrines in Nigeria – are frequently used to bind recruited girls and women to the traffickers. The chapter will start out by placing this particular human trafficking flow[2] in the larger regional and global picture and, more importantly, in

---

1 I would like to thank my colleagues Paul Bochtler, Viktoria Reisch and Corinna Templin for their support in putting together the data for the graphics in this chapter.

2 The reference to "flows" is not meant to degrade human beings to goods traded across borders, even though this ultimately is what human trafficking amounts

the context of the evolution of this particular business model over time. Moreover, it analyses the different stages of the human trafficking process and more recent changes before discussing grey zones of the "licit" and "illicit" along the chain and the types of actors involved.

Before such an assessment, though, it is essential to shed some light on the terminology. In this chapter, "human trafficking" is simply used as a short form of the terms "trafficking in human beings" and "trafficking in persons" that are commonly found in official documents. An almost universally accepted definition is provided by the Protocol to Prevent, Suppress and Punish Trafficking in Persons, Especially Women and Children that supplements the United Nations Convention against Transnational Organized Crime and entered into force in 2003[3]:

> "'Trafficking in persons' shall mean the recruitment, transportation, transfer, harbouring or receipt of persons, by means of the threat or use of force or other forms of coercion, of abduction, of fraud, of deception, of the abuse of power or of a position of vulnerability or of the giving or receiving of payments or benefits to achieve the consent of a person having control over another person, for the purpose of exploitation. Exploitation shall include, at a minimum, the exploitation of the prostitution of others or other forms of sexual exploitation, forced labour or services, slavery or practices similar to slavery, servitude or the removal of organs" (Art. 3 (a): UN 2001: 32).

Accordingly, human trafficking is not only defined by the actual act and the means employed, but also by the purpose of exploitation, meaning the intention. The purpose of exploitation remains a sufficient criterion even if a victim is rescued before the actual exploitation begins (IOM 2020: 3, 5). If the person concerned is a child (under eighteen years of age according to Art. 3(d) of the Protocol), the means used are not relevant, as underage victims are seen as dependents who cannot make a free decision on such an arrangement. While these criteria might appear relatively clear, the following discussion of the trafficking of Nigerian women and girls will reveal a

---

to, nor should it suggest that flows of persons are "flooding" European countries. It rather indicates the direction and fluidity of actions and actors in a criminal market that converge along a specific route.

3 The EU, its member states as well as West African states are signatories of the Convention, including the Protocol. The key elements of the definition are also part of the definition under the Nigerian Trafficking in Persons (Prohibition) Law Enforcement and Administration Act (NAPTIP) from 2003, subsequently revised in 2005 and 2015.

significant grey zone, especially where historical, social and economic drivers come into play.

2 *The larger picture of a transregional flow*

Among victims of trafficking across the world, a minority seems to cross regional boundaries. In fact, less than one victim out of ten identified in 2016 had been trafficked transregionally (UNODC 2018: 42). Usually persons are exploited in the country or (sub)region they are from (according to their nationality). Yet, Western and Southern Europe[4] as well as North America and the Middle East stand out as target regions of significant flows of trafficked human beings from other world regions (UNODC 2020: 59).

As indicated in the map in Figure 1, the respective human trafficking flows largely originate in the Global South.[5] Apart from victims coming from European countries, including Central and South-Eastern Europe, the largest group of victims detected in Western and Southern Europe came from West Africa: about 16 per cent overall in 2016 (UNODC 2018: 54) and 13 per cent in 2018 (UNODC 2020: 135). Moreover, this transregional flow is not a recent phenomenon, as the share of victims from Sub-Saharan Africa detected in Western and Southern Europe has remained largely stable over the last ten years (UNODC 2020: 135).[6]

---

4 According to the UNODC 2020 Global Report on Trafficking in Persons, the region of Western and Southern Europe consists of the following countries: Andorra, Austria, Belgium, Cyprus, Denmark, Finland, France, Germany, Greece, Ireland, Italy, Liechtenstein, Luxembourg, the Netherlands, Norway, Portugal, Spain, Sweden, Switzerland, Turkey and the United Kingdom.

5 The 2020 Global Report on Trafficking in Persons by UNODC (2020: 136) shows very similar patterns on its global map as the 2018 Report.

6 There is not yet sufficient data on changes due to the COVID-19 pandemic. But there are indications that the routes have changed and Nigerian women and girls are trafficked more within the West Africa region (Interview Precious Diagboya (online), 9 December 2021).

Figure 1: Main transregional human trafficking flows

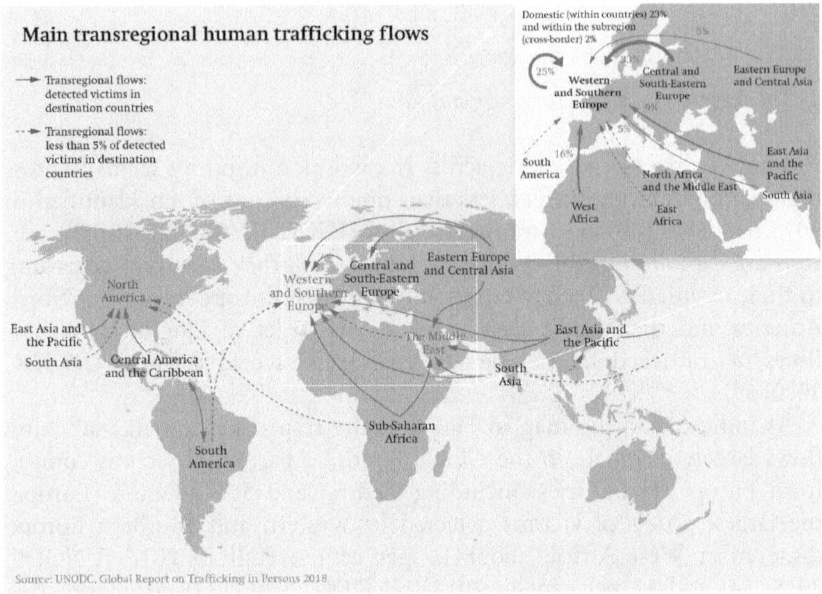

This raises the question of what the drivers behind these flows are. There are general factors, most notably those linked to dynamics in an illegal market. The way in which supply and demand link up may change over time, as may the cost-benefit analyses for certain transit routes. Specific factors make countries or areas particularly vulnerable to human trafficking; they fall into categories like governance, socio-economic and political inequality or effects of armed conflict.[7] For transregional flows, the difference in wealth and economic opportunities between countries of the Global South and Europe clearly plays a central role.

However, such factors alone can hardly explain the pattern that the vast majority among West African victims detected in European countries are Nigerian women and girls trafficked for sexual exploitation. For example, Nigerian nationals were the most commonly recorded trafficking victims in the EU in 2015, apart from intra-European trafficking (US DoS 2020: 382). At the time, hardly any victims from other West African countries were detected in the EU. This is supported by other data, for example

7 The Global Slavery Index 2018 is based on a vulnerability model that uses different dimensions and variables of this kind, see p. 154ff.

numbers of persons assisted by the International Organization for Migration (IOM). In 2016, almost 60 % of the 768 victims assisted in the EU were of Nigerian nationality, followed by Bulgaria (11 %), Romania (8 %), Hungary (3 %) and Thailand (2 %) (IOM 2017: 6). While this is not a complete picture of human trafficking in the EU, it clearly shows that no other significant transregional links come up among assisted victims.

Figure 2: Identified human trafficking victims in European destination countries for 2015- 2016

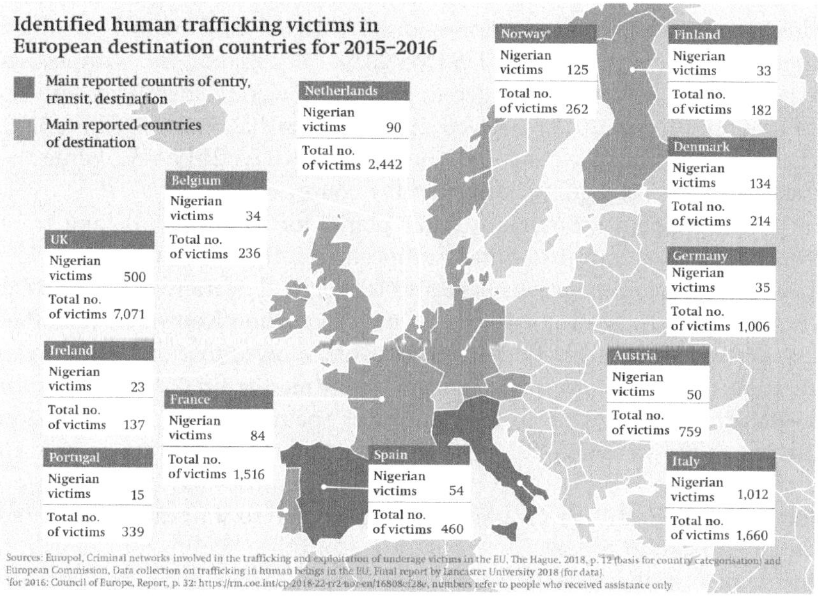

While comparisons of numbers between European countries should be taken with a grain of salt due to different legal definitions and/or standards of recording and reporting data, what is consistent across most of the countries in Figure 2 is the fact that the number of Nigerian victims detected is the highest registered after European nationalities. Moreover, the Nigerian victims are largely or almost exclusively female – where gender has been reported, which is the case for most countries displayed in Figure 2. This also holds true for countries like Germany, where the overall number of Nigerian victims has been fluctuating at relatively low levels.[8]

The map in Figure 2 clearly shows that the trafficking of Nigerian women and girls is no longer a phenomenon linked to one specific country in Western and Southern Europe. At the time, Italy still recorded one of the highest shares with almost 61 % (and by far the highest absolute number) of Nigerian victims, closely behind Denmark (with a 62.6 % share of Nigerian victims) and ahead of Norway (almost 50 %). In absolute terms, countries such as the UK are clearly relevant destinations as well. Obviously, the map is a snapshot, and relevant shifts have occurred over time. Italy continues to be a major destination country with 72 % of victims identified there in 2019 being Nigerian (US DoS 2020: 277). France, for example, has reported a higher share of Nigerian trafficking victims identified with up to around 50 % in 2018 (US DoS 2020: 382), as has Austria with a 37 % share among female victims the same year (GRETA 2019: 45), while the percentage has been going down in other countries.

Italy and Spain are relevant entry points for human trafficking from Nigeria, also for transit to other European countries (Europol 2018a: 12). Law enforcement operations have also revealed other transit hubs, such as the Netherlands. Most notably, the Dutch Operation Koolvis in 2008 that exposed an entire Nigerian criminal network showed that the country was their port of entry into the Schengen area while the final destinations for sexual exploitation were usually Italy and Spain (European Commission 2015, as cited in EASO 2015: 34). Thus, while the trafficking of women and girls from Nigeria to several European countries has been going on for a long time, the exact routes and features tend to shift due to increased attention from European law enforcement or other reasons for changes in operations by Nigerian traffickers. This fluid nature with a largely persisting business model at its core becomes fully visible in an analysis of the evolution of the trafficking, its modus operandi and the actors involved.

8 The German Federal Criminal Police Office (BKA) reported the following numbers of Nigerian victims in recent years, referring to cases in investigations completed by the police: 25 out of 488 (2016), 39 out of 489 (2017), 61 out of 430 (2018) and 16 out of 427 (2019) (BKA 2016, 2017, 2018, 2019). The 2020 report does not provide a specific number for Nigerian human trafficking victims because the number was even lower than in 2019.

3 *Trafficking of women for sexual exploitation from Nigeria: following the chain*

The chain of human trafficking includes recruitment, the transport of those being trafficked and finally their exploitation. Various activities facilitating the illegal business along this chain are required. These can range from forging documents for those being trafficked to facilitating the flows of money associated with moving the persons to protecting the business of sexual exploitation at the destination. While human trafficking can be undertaken by single persons or very small networks of individuals with loose connections, the type of transregional trafficking discussed in this chapter tends to be more elaborate and organised. While a common modus operandi has been identified in the trafficking from Nigeria to Western Europe, it has evolved over time.

Some peculiarities of this trafficking flow have drawn much attention, as already mentioned. While these features are clearly relevant, especially with regard to effective countermeasures and protection of victims, they are often presented out of context. Instead, they should be discussed as part of the complex chain and against the historical and spatial background in order to better understand today's trafficking of women and girls from Nigeria to Europe for sexual exploitation.

3.1 Understanding recruitment patterns

The most striking point about the background of Nigerian women and girls trafficked to Europe, at least at first sight, is that the vast majority are from the southern part of Nigeria, mostly from Edo State. And this is not a new observation. Already in the period from 1999 to 2001, an incredible 86 per cent of the 800 sex workers deported to Nigeria from Italy were from Edo State and 7 per cent from neighbouring Delta State (Ellis 2016: 135). More recently, Edo State still figures as the main area of origin. According to an IOM assessment, out of the 5,425 Nigerian women who arrived as migrants in Italy in 2017, an estimated 80 % were potential victims of trafficking and 94 % were from Edo State (IOM 2019). Other federal states of Nigeria have been named as areas of origin in cases exposed or in interviews conducted e.g. by IOM, but these also tend to be in the southern part of the country (IOM 2017: 13).

This observation defies simple explanations. Clearly, factors used to measure vulnerability to human trafficking are relevant. For example, the Global Slavery Index 2018 ranks Nigeria 12th out of a total of 167 countries. For this ranking, the factor "effects of conflict" has a particular impact (Walk Free Foundation 2018: 156). This might be due to the huge trafficking issue linked to internal displacement in the northeast and other parts of the country, including the abduction of women and girls for domestic servitude and forced labour by Boko Haram and ISIS-West Africa (US DoS 2020: 382). However, Edo State is not a particular "hot spot" of insecurity, though violent conflict is an issue in parts of Nigeria's south as well (see e.g. the Nigeria Security Tracker, CFR n.d.). Other factors like poverty can also hardly explain the prominence of this state of origin. This suggests that human trafficking from Southern Nigeria to Europe must have additional drivers.

Historical evolution

Three common aspects are mentioned in the literature when it comes to how human trafficking from Southern Nigeria has evolved: first, the history of slave trading in Nigeria's southeast and the development of a prostitution business at the time of colonial rule; second, the appearance of the business model of sexual exploitation of Southern Nigerian women in Italy in the 1980s; and third, the evolution of the underlying recruitment and exploitation patterns that reproduced this type of trafficking and extended it to other European countries.

On the first point, Stephen Ellis states in his book on Nigerian organised crime that "[p]eople-trafficking and people-smuggling in the twentieth century reflect the deep historical legacy of slavery and the slave trade" (Ellis 2016: 216). Amongst others, he refers to the particularly developed system of slave trading in the southeast of Nigeria and its underground continuation with shifting patterns after it was banned by the British (Ellis 2016: 35–36). Others rather stress that the continuing slavery in parts of Nigeria under colonial rule veiled the existence of a well-organised type of trafficking linked to forced prostitution called "white slave traffic" at the time (Aderinto 2012: 16). Irrespective of the exact interpretation of the role of slavery, by the 1940s colonial officials confirmed a common organised scheme by which girls from the southeast were forced into prostitution in Lagos or even Ghana, at the time the Gold Coast (Apard, Diagboya and Simoni 2020: 55). This scheme even seems to date back as far as the 1920s (Aderinto 2012: 10). By the end of the 1930s, estimates amounted to thousands of Nigerian women and girls working as prostitutes in the Gold Coast alone and generating significant profits for their communities in Southern Nigeria (Aderinto 2012: 2). Another important observation is that the core business model seemed to be similar to today's, as women with experience in prostitution were returning to their areas of origin to recruit girls under false promises or pretexts of marriage, only to coerce them into the sex business afterwards and take money from them (Ellis 2016: 37).

This model reemerged decades later in Europe, most notably in Italy. However, the initial reasons for Nigerian women to go to Europe seem to have been others than simply transferring an existing practice to a new location. There are different accounts of why Nigerian women particularly from the south started to come to Italy before engaging in prostitution. Some say the stays were linked to the pilgrimage to Rome by Nigerian Christians from the south (Ellis 2016: 134), others refer to relationships between Italians working in the petrol industry in Lagos and the periphery of Benin City with Nigerian women who followed them to Italy (Carchedi 2000, as cited in Pascoal 2018: 9). Other explanations are that Nigerian women went to Italy on visas to work in agriculture, for example picking tomatoes (EASO 2015: 14; Myria 2018: 62) or engaged in legitimate businesses like trading in fabrics, clothes and jewelleries (Braimah 2013: 12). Sometimes these explanations are combined.

What almost all accounts refer to are worsening economic situations of the women while they were in Italy that led them to work in prostitution. Thus, they started to gain an (additional) income by selling sex, often reinvesting their profits back home, for example by trading in fashion items. Apparently, the demand by Italian clients increased at the time, creating incentives for other Nigerian women to come to Italy for prostitution (Myria 2018: 62). This first generation of women not only served as an example for others who saw the wealth some had acquired in Europe, but also started to directly recruit women back in their home area of Benin City – the capital of Edo State – and thus established some control over the entry to this kind of business (Ellis 2016: 134).

This model gained particular traction from the 1990s onwards, supposedly linked to the increasing difficulty of Nigerians to get visas for travelling to Italy. While women could previously often organise the trip by themselves, they became dependent on logistical support and larger loans to pay for the journey. By this time, women who had arrived earlier could earn significant profits from recruiting others back home and facilitating their travel to Italy, where they lived on their earnings from prostitution (Plambech 2014: 34; Ellis 2016: 134). This setup resembled the known patterns, but restrictions on migration to Europe and other factors, such as a lack of economic opportunities in Nigeria, particularly for women, most likely led to the extension and professionalisation of this model while keeping the particular connection to Nigeria's southern states.

Social aspects of recruitment

Overall, social and ethnic ties have been central in the recruitment. A study based on interviews with trafficked women found that 72 % of women had been recruited by someone they or their family knew quite well (Cherti, Pennington and Grant 2013: 5). Some girls also seek ways to migrate to Europe themselves using known contact points in their southern home areas (EASO 2015: 22). The key role of women in the trafficking is also rooted in the tradition in the region that the less privileged place their children with richer relatives (Ebo'o and Tite 2019: 34). These ties and the underlying business model can help explain why victims and those involved in trafficking today still predominantly come from the same region in Nigeria.

Even with trafficking becoming more organised, the so-called "madams" – who were usually trafficked and exploited themselves before – remained central figures in the process. While the women and girls are under their authority in the destination country and they collect their profits from prostitution, the "madams" also order the recruitment of new girls. Sometimes they undertake the recruitment themselves, but it has become common practice to rely on recruiters and sponsors in Nigeria (EASO 2015: 21–22). They offer support for the girls or women to migrate to Europe, including financing the transport as well as providing all necessary (forged) documents and arrangements along the route, though the "madam" can also be the sponsor to cover the costs in advance (EASO 2015: 23). More recently, recruiters often seem to be young men who had to return from Europe and so have a certain experience in migration and contacts along the routes (Henriksen and Jesperson 2019: 27). To make sure that debts are repaid after arrival, an agreement is sealed, commonly involving the visit to a shrine where a juju ritual is performed (Ellis 2016: 182).

More recently, recruitment patterns have shifted towards even younger girls, particularly from rural areas, many only 13 to 15 years old. This seems to be due to the increasing awareness of the trafficking phenomenon and the risks it involves for women and girls in and around Edo State (EASO 2015: 15; Myria 2018: 67). Young girls may also be more likely to believe promises of well-paid jobs abroad as hairdressers, shop workers, babysitters or the like that recruiters commonly make (Europol

2018a: 14). In the process of recruitment, the family tends to play a key role. Many are approached with an offer to arrange taking their daughter to Europe for work. This is not only promising due to the prospect of an income for the family, but sending a child abroad is also linked to a higher status in the local community (EASO 2015: 23).

Whether the kind of work waiting for the girl in Europe is known or families are deceived, the pressure on girls to agree to the deal proposed is often high. Not only poor but also middle-class families tend to see prospects of social advancement. The "madams" as wealthy and powerful persons in their community set an important example here – and this despite prostitution still being stigmatised in Southern Nigeria (Apard, Diagboya and Simoni 2020: 57, 68). These social aspects are highly relevant to understanding how the system of trafficking women and girls from Southern Nigeria tends to reproduce itself.

3.2 Transiting from origin to destination

In the process of transporting women or girls to Europe, illicit means usually have to be employed since legal ways of entry to Europe are hardly available. For this reason and due to the long distance victims have to travel, a higher degree of organisation is needed than for trafficking a person within West Africa, particularly as the Free Movement Protocol by the Economic Community of West African States (ECOWAS) supports intra-regional mobility.[9] For the transfer of women and girls to Europe, there are brokers or agents on the ground in Southern Nigeria, all kinds of facilitators, persons organising the movement along the route and those bringing the women or girls to their final destination. While Nigerian actors are said to be connected in networks with specialised roles, there has been some kind of "end-to-end" control of the trafficking process. Apart from being in charge of recruitment and exploitation, the "madam" may also pay for the journey and keep in touch with traffickers along the way while outsourcing the transport of the girls and women. Thus, the general assessment is that they are in charge of the core business while (mostly Nigerian) men are having rather supportive or facilitating roles (Europol 2018: 13). Yet, the routes and modi operandi have changed over time.

---

9 For details see: Economic Community of West African States Protocol on Free Movement of Persons, Right of Residence and Establishment, 1979, Protocol A/P.1/5/79.

Shifting routes

As mentioned in the last section, the initial scheme – maybe not (yet) amounting to human trafficking – involved travel of Nigerian women by air to Italy. As the model evolved, travelling by air remained the most common way to bring women and girls to Europe until about the mid-2000s (EASO 2015: 32). The mentioned hurdles to obtain proper visa meant that fraudulent passports and visa were increasingly used for these journeys. Moreover, with increasing controls by Nigerian authorities, traffickers started to send women to Europe via other West African countries like Ghana or the Gambia in order to attract less attention upon departure; but these journeys were usually still by plane (Myria 2018: 64–65).

Over the last 15 years, Nigerian victims of human trafficking have increasingly travelled by land and sea – passing several transit countries before crossing the Mediterranean Sea along the Western or Central route, mostly landing in either Spain or Italy. The reasons for the change in route are the more restrictive migration controls and the intensification of passenger and document checks at airports after 9/11 and thus higher costs for "madams" to bring new recruits to Europe (Myria 2018: 64–65; EASO 2015: 32). According to a common estimation, the difference is substantial, as transporting women and girls by plane would cost an average of €10,000 per victim while the alternative route by land/sea through Libya, for example, only requires an investment of about €2,500 (Myria 2018: 65).

IOM noted that in 2016 the largest group of migrants arriving in Italy by sea were Nigerians, with a particular increase of women and unaccompanied children (respectively 11,009 and 3,040 in 2016, compared to about 5,000 and 900 in 2015). The assessment by IOM that approximately 80 % of these Nigerian women and children were likely to be victims of trafficking for sexual exploitation in the EU (IOM 2017: 9) has been cited widely in the literature to underline the extent of the phenomenon. It should be noted, however, that these numbers dropped in the following years, with a significant decrease of Nigerian arrivals in Italy by sea in absolute and relative terms (UNHCR 2018). Though after a steep decline the overall number of arrivals by sea in Italy from Libya went up again from 2020 to 2021, Nigerians were no longer among the top ten nationalities arriving via that route (UNHCR 2021). The further evolution remains to be seen, particularly in light of the impact of the COVID-19 pandemic on smuggling routes and human trafficking more generally.[10]

Overlap of human trafficking and migrant smuggling

The overland and sea journey – despite being generally less costly for traffickers – still requires quite a sophisticated logistical process. While a transport agent may plan the travel stages, a male person who is called "boga" ("trolley") can accompany several women or girls, usually up to Libya. The same term can be used for men picking up women in migration centres, where they usually end up after entering Europe (IMO 2017: 7). When travelling by air it has also been common for the women or girls to be accompanied by a man on the flight to provide a cover (e.g. as a husband or brother), but also to collect the passport provided to the victim before immigration controls at her destination for further use by others back in Nigeria. These papers are not necessarily fraudulent, but can be authentic ones issued to women who look like the victims travelling. In this scheme, once the passport is taken from them, the victims present themselves without papers to the authorities at the destination (Ellis 2016: 183).

For the women and girls travelling by land through Libya, the journey can take months or even years. The supervisors on their way can change, yet "bogas" tend to be in close contact with the "madam" in Europe. As a European law enforcement official stated: "Over the past few years, probably hundreds of Nigerians have set up a network composed of intermediaries, drivers and staging posts to take people (generally young girls) to the Libyan coast. The Nigerian 'madam's' choice of network depends on her previous experiences (good or bad), the price, the operation's chances of success, the reputation of those involved, etc." (Franz-Manuel Vandelook, Police Superintendent, Head of the Human Trafficking group, Brussels federal judicial police, External contribution, in: Myria 2018: 79).

Recruited females are very vulnerable to abuses and exploitation along these routes. Those transporting or accompanying them may physically assault or sexually exploit them (EASO 2015: 31). Furthermore, the women are easy victims for armed groups or criminals along the way (Europol

10 In 2018, it was still assumed that the most common itinerary for Nigerian women and girls to reach Europe was via Agadez in Niger on to Zuwara, Sabha or Tripoli in Libya (Myria 2018: 65).

2018a: 14). In particular, once they reach the Libyan coast and have to wait for the opportunity to get on a boat across the Mediterranean, they are often exposed to all kinds of abuses and frequently forced into prostitution (IMO 2017: 7).[11] It has been argued that ironically Nigerian women and girls may have smoother journeys than those "only" being smuggled through Libya, as Nigerian traffickers still control the itinerary and "madams" or sponsors have a high interest in the victims reaching Europe in order to repay their debts (DIIS 2021: 43).

Yet, women and girls still get trapped in North Africa for extended periods of time. There have also been clear indications that Nigerian and Libyan traffickers sell and buy them (UNICRI 2010: 83). When women or girls fall into the hands of armed groups, these can demand ransom payments to let them move on, which have to be paid either by families or by the "madams". Otherwise they will have to engage in prostitution to pay for making their onward journey (BAMF 2020: 11). In Morocco, women have been found to be forced into begging by traffickers (EASO 2015: 33). These patterns illustrate the link between human trafficking and migrant smuggling, which by definition are distinct phenomena. But the exploitation of Nigerian women and girls as an integral part of the smuggling process has also been interpreted as an indication of the waning influence of "madams" in transit countries, especially in Libya, and thus of a diminishing direct link between the area of origin and European destinations (Pascoal 2018: 14, 18).

Entering and moving around Europe

If women and girls ultimately make it by boat from Libya to Italy or another European country, they are placed into a refugee reception centre or camp. This is where they are usually picked up by another "boga" or trafficker who takes them to their destination country, where the "madam" is waiting for them (Myria 2018: 80). But they may also only be recruited in the centre after arrival. In fact, it has been concluded that the different phases in trafficking have become blurred, so that women arrive in Italy without an understanding of the different stages or knowledge about the identity of their traffickers (Pascoal 2018: 19).

11 Of course, violence and exploitation is similarly faced by male migrants from Nigeria in Libya. Male applicants accounted for the majority of asylum claims by Nigerians in Italy for most years between 2008 and 2019 (Cohen 2021: 19–21).

Yet, women have still entered Europe through other countries by air if more structured networks are implicated and have then been taken to Italy or Spain as well as other countries for sexual exploitation (Ellis 2016: 181, 185). More importantly, the movement of women or girls within Europe has apparently become a frequent practice (Europol 2016b). Two factors have been named as an explanation for this evolution. One is learning from other criminal networks e.g. Bulgarian ones. Their scheme was apparently mimicked by "madams", who now tend to be more connected with each other and exchange victims internationally, for example between Belgium, Italy, Spain and Sweden (Myria 2018: 64, 89). The other, complementary reason is that Nigerian networks simply respond to increasing pressure by law enforcement in some countries. Thus, victims are moved around once they are tracked by the police, and thus women tend to disappear before authorities are able to establish closer contact (Myria 2018: 73). Additional reasons may play a role, such as declining profits in this kind of sex business. The movement of women and girls around Europe can also be linked to the use of asylum claims upon arrival that will be discussed below.

3.3. Exploitation and control

Apart from expanding links and operations across European countries, the "madams" do not work alone at the destination. They may have several assistants, who may be women who are working for them in prostitution. Moreover, they usually work with a male enforcer or warden (Ellis 2016: 183; Europol 2016a: 17) as well as others working as couriers or money launderers (EASO 2015: 22; Europol 2018a: 15). The control of women and girls by the "madam" is based on their obligation to repay debts from their travel arrangements. This amount, which tends to be much higher than the actual expenditure, has to be "paid back" by engaging in prostitution and leaving all earnings to the "madam". The amounts used to be up to €50,000 or €60,000 but have apparently declined to sums between €20,000 and €30,000, which is explained by lower prices in human trafficking that are partly due to a larger number of exploited girls (Pascoal 2018: 15, 18).[12]

---

12 The prices in prostitution also seem to have gone down on European streets, e.g. in France, where "a hard discount in prostitution" has been noticed due to low prices taken by Nigerian sex workers (Pascual/Tilouine 2020).

Debt bondage and juju rituals

The victims usually have to engage in the sex business for years to pay back the money, especially as the amount tends to increase due to living expenses or fines being added to the debt over time. For example, women and girls have to pay fines for abortions and pregnancies or if they try to hide earnings to send them back to their families in Nigeria while still in debt with the "madam" (BAMF 2020: 7; EASO 2015: 25). Often the victims are aware that some money has to be repaid upon arrival but barely know the size of the debt in advance – either because they are deceived about the real amount or because they do not understand how much money it actually is (if only because they have no idea about exchange rates between Nigerian naira and euros) (EASO 2015: 24). Moreover, some women learn only at this point that they will actually work in prostitution. Others may have realised this along the trafficking route; still others may have been aware even before.

An essential aspect of human trafficking is the coercion, dependence and/or deception used to bind victims to their traffickers and make sure they do not run away, potentially cooperating with law enforcement. In the case of Nigerian women and girls forced into prostitution in Europe, there are several ways to control them. The basic means to make women and girls obey and stick to the arrangement have been specified in a Human Rights Watch report. Apart from violence and threats against the victims and their families in Nigeria, this can be anything from "threats of selling them to other traffickers, surveillance, passport confiscation, confinement, and isolation to keep them trapped and terrified, and to avoid law enforcement detection" (HRW 2019: 5). Another, more exceptional means has been the use of the mentioned juju rituals that victims usually undergo before leaving Nigeria. In this ceremony they mainly have to pledge allegiance to their "madam" and swear to repay their debts and not to cooperate with third parties. During these rituals, women and girls often have to drink a mixture including herbs and/or blood from animals while hair, nails or body fluids are taken from them and kept by the juju priest (Aluko-Daniels 2015: 80).

Usually the girls and their families – most commonly their mother – have to be present, while the "madam" participates either physically or by phone, with the priest being the guarantor of the agreement (Apard, Diagboya and Simoni 2020: 63). Not all women and girls undergo this ritual, but apparently it has become common practice. For example, in France among a group of interviewed Nigerian women working in prostitution the share who had undergone such a ceremony was at least 75 % for the period between 2011 and 2013 (Simoni 2013, as cited in EASO 2015: 29). The ritual itself can be fear-inducing in a way that many women have not experienced before (Baarda 2016: 265). Ultimately, the ceremony becomes a core part of psychological control and intimidation once the girls and women start to question the arrangement or do not repay their debts (quickly enough) (EASO 2015: 26–27). The juju priests can threaten "under-performing" or "unruly" victims with physical harm, madness or death (or that of their relatives) (EASO 2015: 25).

In general, juju is an expression of the belief that power comes from the spiritual world, and it is by no means limited to its use in human trafficking. Shrines have exercised judicial functions and have been linked to (secret) societies led by political and traditional leaders in Benin City for a long time (Ellis 2016: 48). In the scheme discussed here, juju priests tend to be accomplices of the traffickers and act in their interest (EASO 2015: 28). In fact, a study has found that according to many observations in different temples in Benin City between 2017 and 2019 the priest or his assistants in almost all cases of disagreement about the accord later on ruled in favour of the "madam" (Apard, Diagboya and Simoni 2020: 76). They have a direct interest in keeping the arrangement going and making women pay back their debts because they tend to receive a percentage of the amount the traffickers receive (Cohen and Diagboya 2018).

After this instrument of control aroused increasing attention, in March 2018 the Oba of Benin, the most powerful traditional ruler in the area, made a declaration for all people from Edo that juju rituals shall no longer be used in human trafficking in the future. He issued a curse on sex traffickers and annulled existing oaths taken in the context of trafficking (Apard, Diagboya and Simoni 2020: 76; US DoS 2020: 382). The results so far seem to be mixed. Some girls and women may have felt encouraged to come out as victims and seek help after the oaths had been revoked. But traffickers seem to be using the limited territorial and ethnic reach of the declaration by the Oba as a loophole and, for example, simply hold the rituals outside his area of authority. In recent cases, victims were apparently also asked to undergo some kind of spiritual ritual that did not involve an oath but was still used to intimidate them (Interview Diagboya 2021). In general, the trafficking and exploitation of Nigerian women and girls has apparently not been significantly interrupted (Apard, Diagboya and Simoni 2020: 78).

Coercion and enforcement

The strong focus on the use of juju may also have disguised other means of coercion. First of all, concrete physical threats and violence are used against victims as well as their families back home, involving not only juju priests but also relatives or assistants of the "madam" in Nigeria. Ultimately, the repayment of the debts is not just a way of making profits for traffickers, but the key instrument of control. As a starting point, it holds the promise of a potential (social and material) advancement after debts have been repaid – personified by the "madams" themselves – even though most women do not turn into a wealthy "madam" after repaying their debts and are obliged to continue with prostitution to make a living (EASO 2015: 25; Apard, Diagboya and Simoni 2020: 80).

Moreover, social pressure plays an important role. Families tend to openly welcome back women and girls who have made money, but if someone comes back without a visible financial gain, e.g. because they have been deported from Europe, they are often rejected by the family (Pascoal 2012: 24, as cited in EASO 2015: 36). Thus, deported women returning to Nigeria have a high likelihood of being re-trafficked to Europe, particularly if their debts have not been entirely repaid (EASO 2015: 47). Obviously, fear of reprisals against the family and/or the victim plays a key role here as well. Again, social relations are relevant, as the "madam" has relatives or accomplices on the ground in Nigeria. They can transmit real threats and commit acts of violence, including even murders of family members, in order to make families pay remaining debts and/or bring women in line with the trafficking networks (Apard, Diagboya and Simoni 2020: 66). In a prominent trafficking investigation in Belgium, it became clear that the mother of a girl back home was severely beaten by Nigerian police officers who had been paid by the brother of the "madam", as a punishment for the girl's escape (Myria 2018: 72). There can also be considerable pressure from the group of trafficked and exploited women surrounding a victim in the country of destination (Apard, Diagboya and Simoni 2020: 71). Moreover, as outlined above, the "madam" herself may actually be related to trafficked girls, which has been a major obstacle for victims coming forward to testify. In general though, unpaid debts have proven to be more risky for victims than testifying against traffickers (EASO 2015: 45).

Beyond their network of enforcers and assistants, the "madams" can have other support structures within Europe. In Belgium, for example, investigations uncovered contacts by the "madam" to the Nigerian embassy (Myria 2018: 71). Furthermore, Nigerian networks have cooperated with

European organised crime groups. The victims work as prostitutes in the streets or in brothels, where particularly underage girls are easier to hide from public attention. At this point, profits may flow to local criminals, for example in Italy, where "madams" may pay a certain fee per month for their girls working in a particular spot out on the street (Ellis 2016: 183). Interestingly, there seems to be cooperation with and a certain compensation of European mafias and other groups, for instance in Spain, rather than outright competition (US DoS 2020: 222–223). These arrangements, as well as the role of Nigerian "cult" groups or confraternities, will be discussed in Section 5 below.

4 Illuminating the grey zone: intersections of the licit and illicit in the trafficking chain

In contrast to some illicit trade flows, humans – or rather the control over persons (Campana 2016: 69) – can hardly be traded as "goods" in a legal way these days. Since the adoption of the protocol under the UN Convention, human trafficking has been criminalised almost globally: over 90 % of the UN member states have established a specific offence, and the definition is almost universally based on the protocol (UNODC 2020: 23).

But the illegality of human trafficking may still be disputed or concealed at different stages. Basically, there can be a grey zone around the crime of human trafficking – when (potentially) legal acts or means are part of the business model and/or when a legal setting is used for cover, such as recruitment agencies set up as a façade for labour exploitation (UNODC 2020: 14). In the first case, the actual categorisation of an activity as human trafficking may even be called into question; in the second case, trafficking is simply masked by a legal cover. To the outside, including those using the services of exploited victims, both categories may appear legal.

In the case of Nigerian women and girls who are trafficked to Europe, questions are repeatedly raised about the aspect of coercion or deception during the recruitment phase. Several publications state that Nigerian women sometimes know they will be working in prostitution and be linked to a pimp – if only from the example of other women from the same area. The essential point of this claim is that women are not necessarily tricked or coerced into the arrangement. Stephen Ellis (2016: 183–184) has pointed out that "[t]he system thrives on the fact that recruits for the sex industry are not actually trafficked – meaning, taken against their will – but are socially obliged to take part in a very exploitative business".

Many girls and women themselves supposedly also see prostitution as a transitional phase and one – if not the only – way to advance in society (Apard, Diagboya and Simoni 2020: 60).

While this is crucial for assessing motivations, such circumstances of recruitment do not by themselves "legalise" this business model or make it anything less than human trafficking. First, as outlined in the introduction, the aspect of informed consent does not apply to underage girls, which is increasingly relevant as victims have become, on average, much younger. Second, even if those recruited are adults and know about the nature of the work waiting for them in Europe, they barely know about the real conditions. This applies to the working conditions in prostitution, the actual size of the debt they will have to repay as well as the pressure and violence that may be applied against them. As the debt is often raised for living expenses and as a punishment, the "deal" also keeps changing once they are in Europe. In addition, risks on their way as well as in the sex business in Europe are often unknown to women. These points are acknowledged across the relevant literature (EASO 2015: 17, 26; Apard, Diagboya and Simoni 2020: 60–61; Aluko-Daniels 2015: 79). However, the kind of relationship between trafficker and victim as well as the psychological means of coercion used have posed significant challenges for law enforcement (Pascoal 2018: 72).

The second aspect – using legal façades in the process of trafficking – has many facets. Apart from the mentioned covers used in transporting women, there are several relevant aspects upon arrival in Europe. Victims have been provided with falsified residence permits allowing them to travel within the Schengen zone (EASO 2015: 35). More recently, however, traffickers have tended to push victims to apply for asylum once they enter a European country and tell girls to claim an older age in order to be placed in a shelter for adults, where it is easier to escape (Myria 2018: 1, 74; Frontex 2018: 37; US DoS 2020: 279). They may provide the victims with a fake backstory, and even if the asylum claim is ultimately not successful, it does enable applicants to stay in Europe with a legal status for a longer period of time. Another advantage may be that authorities take care of food and lodging for the women and girls (Pascoal 2018: 42; Wallis 2019). However, the victims usually do not stay in the reception centres for long, but are told to call a trafficker who will then pick them up and transfer them to their destination, which can be in another European country (Europol 2018a: 15).

Another cover may come with legal ways to engage in prostitution as exist in some European countries. There is a general assumption that liberal prostitution laws can be a pull factor. Indeed, an analysis including

150 countries showed that countries where prostitution is legal have larger reported human trafficking inflows (Cho, Dreher and Neumayer 2013). There are known cases, e.g. in Germany and Austria, where legal covers have been used by Nigerian traffickers, for example women being registered in brothels by their "madam" with a forged passport (Milborn 2020; BAMF 2020: 13). Yet, in view of the most common destinations and ways of sexual exploitation in the EU, these kinds of covers have not (yet) been used extensively by Nigerian traffickers.

Finally, there are different methods to hide and launder the profits of Nigerian networks. The money transfers, usually to Nigeria, can be made in small amounts via official transfer services, but these days the most common way seems to be via systems like the "Black Western Union". This scheme resembles the "hawala" system, and in contrast to the actual Western Union it has the advantage that the money transfer can hardly be traced (Myria 2018: 64). In a case revealed in Belgium, a shop was the hub for sending cash that was later transferred to a beneficiary in Benin City. Basically, those behind this scheme in Belgium frequently travelled to Nigeria with the collected cash and took a 10 % commission for the service (Myria 2018: 92–93). Generally, couriers tend to transfer the money to Nigeria and claim it is for legitimate business purposes when they get caught (Europol 2018a: 15).

In the past, there were indications that the "madams" invested their profits in the legal trade, for example with fabrics. They also opened businesses like hotels or shops in larger cities of their Nigerian home areas and invested in real estate. It has been stated that the "richest generally belong to the first generation of Nigerian women who left for Europe in the early 1980s to work as prostitutes and who, having settled mainly in Italy, were nicknamed 'Italos' on their return" (Apard, Diagboya and Simoni 2020: 57–58, own translation). These investments not only serve money-laundering purposes but are also symbols of wealth and status.

5 A Nigerian mafia?

There is frequent reference to a Nigerian mafia supposedly involved in human trafficking. Clearly, there has been a professionalisation of trafficking to Europe by specialised networks. But the organisation has usually not been centralised and not run along ethnic and family ties, as a deep study of an exposed trafficking network has confirmed. This particular ring was rather a business operation, with transporters acting as service providers to the "madams" (Campana 2016: 80, 82). The study also found that "there is no evidence of a global mafia that is able to internalise trafficking activities across continents, or to provide services like dispute settlement and contract enforcement in every stage of the process" (Campana 2016: 82). The supply of protection (including the enforcement of agreements) beyond simply engaging in extortion is considered a characteristic of organisations like the Calabrian 'Ndrangheta, the Russian mafia or the Japanese Yakuza (Varese 2014: 343, 353).

While the mentioned study found that "madams" largely operated independently of each other, these days they may be more connected, as in the "exchange scheme" mentioned above. In a case exposed in France in 2018, ten "madams" ran a trafficking and exploitation network called "Authentic Sisters" together (BAMF 2020: 6). Moreover, they have set up support structures that link them beyond simply exchanging girls or women within Europe. There are clubs set up by "madams" with branches in Nigeria and Europe that organise events and provide financial support while overall strengthening the ties between the women and their trafficking networks. At events, there is a club code that includes wearing a certain outfit, performing dances and engaging in "money spraying" (Apard, Diagboya and Simoni 2020: 58–59). But these groups hardly conform with the characteristics of a mafia as mentioned above. The traditional European organised crime groups that impose certain fees on Nigerian actors, including for example the Camorra in Naples, are apparently not engaged in the actual prostitution activities (Campana 2016: 82).

The reference to a Nigerian mafia in human trafficking mostly seems to be due to another link, namely the one to Nigerian confraternities, also called "cult" groups. They started out as confraternities at universities and colleges within Nigeria but are today mostly known for being engaged in all types of serious crimes like kidnapping, robbery as well as drug and human trafficking and thus might be seen as "a fully structured crime network" (Ellis 2016: 191). Codes and initiation rites of confraternities are often compared to gang culture, but they have cells and structures far beyond their core areas in Nigeria. As they are often described as being hierarchically organised and particularly violent, they have also been likened to mafia organisations (EASO 2018b: 43). Nigerian media are full of reports about violent clashes among such groups and the major problem "cultism" poses for public security.

With regard to human trafficking, the presence of confraternities along trafficking routes up to the destinations in European countries is relevant (EMSC 2020: 21–22). UNODC has reported that confraternities like Supreme Eiye and Aye have also been active in parts of Spain since at least 2007 and in Italy since 2008 (UNODC 2014: 56). The German Federal

Criminal Police Office also named three Nigerian confraternities that were active in Germany in 2019 (BAMF 2020: 16–17), and the German Federal Intelligence Service, according to a leaked internal report, warned that groups like Black Axe and the Supreme Eiye Confraternity are trying to extend their criminal activities to the country (Diehl 2019). Links of the groups to human trafficking have been reported by authorities in Spain and Italy, but also in France, most notably in the mentioned case of the "Authentic Sisters" (UNODC 2020: 44; Apard, Diagboya and Simoni 2020: 66). The Spanish Guardia Civil, the Nigerian National Agency for the Prohibition of Trafficking in Persons (NAPTIP) and the UK's National Crime Agency together dismantled a Nigerian network in one of the largest operations against human trafficking in Europe. It was operating across multiple EU countries and was linked to the Supreme Eiye confraternity (Europol 2018b). In Italy, there were operations against Black Axe and the Supreme Eiye Confraternity in Sicily and Sardinia around the same time (Wallis 2019). However, it needs to be clarified what character the link between human trafficking and confraternities really has in these cases.

Most often, members of Nigerian "cults" have been seen as recruiters, facilitators or enforcers for the "madams" while also engaging in other types of crimes like credit card fraud, counterfeiting of documents, money laundering or drug trafficking (Pascual and Tilouine 2020; EMSC 2020: 21). More recently, changes in this pattern have been reported, most notably a more important (and violent) role of these groups in human trafficking in Europe. Several reports interpret this evolution as an indication of a declining position of the "madams", partly linked to the withdrawal of the juju oaths by the Oba of Benin effectively taking away this instrument of psychological control and thus empowering more violent groups like the confraternities (Pascual and Tilouine 2020). In a media report, the commander of NAPTIP in Lagos was cited as saying that "cult" groups apparently had even taken over the entire business, leading to endless exploitation rather than repayment of debts (BAMF 2020: 14).

It has also been noticed that "madams" have relocated to other countries like France and Germany, apparently to avoid being arrested. During the first lockdown of the COVID-19 pandemic, Nigerian women in Italy were reported to have been abandoned by traffickers, only with someone around for control and punishment in case they did not continue to work (The Guardian 2020). To what extent these recent observations indicate a greater role of confraternities in human trafficking remains unclear. Yet, even if their influence should have increased, the European chapters can hardly be categorised as mafias. A recent study by Corentin Cohen confirms that confraternities like the Black Axe, Supreme Eiye and the

Maphites have established a presence across different continents, but in Europe they mostly function as social institutions (Cohen 2021: 2, 23). He also describes the role of their members in human trafficking as similar to that of subcontractors, without visible involvement of the organisation as such, not even when it comes to the flows of related revenues (Cohen 2021: 26–27). From this perspective, the specific role of Nigerian confraternities in human trafficking to Europe needs further investigation with regard to specific cases, yet without criminalising their members in general.

6 *Conclusion*

Human trafficking has attracted increasing attention at the international level. The Sustainable Development Goals of the Agenda 2030 include two targets with references to eliminating trafficking and exploitation of women and girls (5.2) or children (16.2) as well as one on eradicating forced labour and human trafficking, in particular the worst forms of child labour (8.7). At the regional level, the European Commission just came out with a new Strategy on Combatting Trafficking in Human Beings for 2021 to 2025 (EC 2021).

The specific trafficking flow analysed in this chapter has increasingly been addressed by law enforcement operations and cooperation. Since 2012, a European project within the EMPACT framework has been focusing on tackling Nigerian trafficking networks and identifying victims across the EU. Apart from pan-European operations coordinated by Europol, there are also efforts to increase cooperation between authorities in the EU and Nigeria. Various countries in Europe collaborate with Nigerian law enforcement in joint investigations, intelligence sharing and/or prosecutions (US DoS 2021: 426). There are also efforts at the regional level, for example an EU programme[13] supporting the Economic Community of West African States (ECOWAS) and its members in addressing different types of trafficking in West Africa – mostly human and arms trafficking. The Nigerian government also issued a National Referral Mechanism in 2016, defining roles and responsibilities of different stakeholders in support of victims of trafficking (EASO 2018a: 58). The Nigerian strategy is essentially based on the four Ps, namely prevention, protection, prosecu-

13 Co-funded by the German Federal Foreign Office.

tion and partnership (Ebo'o and Tite 2019: 33). Thus, the focus is not exclusively on a criminal justice response.

Yet, this particular type of trafficking has proven quite persistent, as actors involved adapt to changing conditions. The shifting patterns along the chain and the grey zone around human trafficking of this kind clearly pose challenges for a straightforward implementation of the UN Protocol. More importantly, however, certain features and practices that gain particular attention need to be placed in the context of the historical, social and economic background. Therefore, dynamics and incentives along the trafficking chain have to be better understood – if only to avoid unintended negative consequences of countermeasures.

Finally, the agency of the women and girls, who should not be seen merely as passive victims, needs to be acknowledged. Even if a range of organisations support victims, the ultimate outcome may often be far from satisfactory. As long as the conditions in their area of origin do not change significantly, the situation remains difficult for returning women, especially when they are deported from Europe. In fact, deportation appears to be more stigmatised in Southern Nigeria than working in prostitution, as it is seen as downward social mobility (Plambech 2017: 150). Therefore, these women are at high risk of being re-trafficked. There are different schemes in European countries for them to get the permission to stay – temporarily or permanently – once they have been identified as victims. In France, victims of trafficking from Southern Nigeria are even considered a specific social group and can obtain refugee status, provided they can show that they have been leaving the network (Apard, Diagboya and Simoni 2020: 51). Yet, the right to legal residency for women cooperating with law enforcement is not always coherently implemented. Apart from the need for improvement in this area, it will certainly remain key to counter the more structured networks – without risking to worsen the plight of those being exploited. But ultimately, the links involved in a trafficking chain are multi-faceted and not merely the product of an isolated criminal phenomenon.

References

Aderinto, Saheed (2012): "'The problem of Nigeria is slavery, not white slave traffic': Globalization and the politicization of prostitution in Southern Nigeria, 1921–1955". In: Canadian Journal of African Studies/La Revue canadienne des études africaines, 46, 1, pp. 1–22.

Aluko-Daniels, Olufunke (2015): "At the margins of consent. Sex trafficking from Nigeria to Italy". In: Massey, Simon/Coluccello, Rino (eds.): Eurafrican migration. Legal, economic and social responses to irregular migration. Basingstoke: Palgrave Macmillan, pp. 74–87.

Apard, Élodie/Diagboya, Precious/Simoni, Vanessa (2020): "'La prostitution, ça ne tue pas!' projets d'ascension sociale familiale dans le contexte de la traite sexuelle (Nigeria–Europe)". In: Politique africaine, 159, 3, pp. 51–82.

Baarda, C.S. (2016): "Human trafficking for sexual exploitation from Nigeria into Western Europe. The role of voodoo rituals in the functioning of a criminal network". In: European Journal of Criminology, 13, 2, pp. 257–273.

Braimah, Tim S. (2013): "Sex trafficking in Edo State. Causes and solutions". In: Global Journal Of Human Social Science, 13, 3, pp. 17–29.

BAMF, Bundesamt für Migration und Flüchtlinge (2020): „Länderreport 27: Nigeria – Menschenhandel zum Zwecke der sexuellen Ausbeutung. Stand: 06/2020". Nürnberg. At: https://www.bamf.de/SharedDocs/Anlagen/DE/Behoerde/Informationszentrum/Laenderreporte/2020/laenderreport-27-nigeria.pdf?__blob=publicationFile&v=3 (accessed 13 April 2022).

BKA, Bundeskriminalamt (2016, 2017, 2018, 2019): „Bundeslagebild Menschenhandel und Ausbeutung". At: https://www.bka.de/DE/AktuelleInformationen/StatistikenLagebilder/Lagebilder/Menschenhandel/menschenhandel_node.html (accessed 13 April 2022).

Campana, Paolo (2016): "The structure of human trafficking. Lifting the bonnet on a Nigerian transnational network". In: British Journal of Criminology, 56, 1, pp. 68–86.

Carchedi, Francesco (2000): "La prostituzione straniera in Italia. Analisi dei risultati dell'indagine sulle protagoniste e i modelli relazionali". In: Carchedi, Francesco/Picciolini, Anna/Mottura, Giovani/Campani, Giovanna: I colori della Notte. Migrazioni, sfruttamento sessuale, esperienze di intervento sociale. Mailand: FrancoAngeli, pp. 100–163.

Cherti, Myriam/Pennington, Jenny/Grant, Peter (2013): "Beyond borders. Human trafficking from Nigeria to the UK". London: Institute for Public Policy Research. At: https://www.ippr.org/files/images/media/files/publication/2013/01/nigeria-trafficking_Jan2013_10189.pdf (accessed 13 April 2022).

Cho, Seo-Young/Dreher, Axel/Neumayer, Eric (2013): "Does legalized prostitution increase human trafficking?" In: World Development, 41, 1, pp. 67–82.

Cohen, Corentin (2021): "Les confraternités nigérianes á la conquête du monde?" In: Les études du CERI, 258. At: https://www.sciencespo.fr/ceri/sites/sciencespo.fr.ceri/files/Etude_258.pdf (accessed 13 April 2022).

Cohen, Corentin/Diagboya, Precious (2018): "Le rôle des acteurs religieux dans la traite d'êdes humains entre le Nigéria et l'Europe". Sciences Po: Centre de Recherches Internationales. At: https://www.sciencespo.fr/ceri/fr/oir/le-role-des-acteurs-religieux-dans-la-traite-d-etres-humains-entre-le-nigeria-et-l-europe (accessed 13 September 2021).

CFR, Council on Foreign Relations (n.d.): "Nigerian Security Tracker". At: https://www.cfr.org/nigeria/nigeria-security-tracker/p29483 (accessed 13 April 2022).

Diehl, Jörg (2019) „BND warnt vor nigerianischer Mafia“. At: https://www.spiegel.de/panorama/justiz/bundesnachrichtendienst-warnt-vor-nigerianischer-mafia-a-1254963.html (accessed 13 April 2022).

DIIS, Danish Institute for International Studies (2021): “Does information save migrants' lives? Knowledge and needs of West African migrants en route to Europe”. At: https://pure.diis.dk/ws/files/4209801/Does_information_save_migrants_lives_DIIS_Report_2021_01.pdf (accessed 13 April 2022).

Ebo'o, Agnes/Tite, Naomi (2019): “Transnational organised crime in West and Central Africa. The case of the Nigerian ‘madams’”. In: Hilsdon, Anne-Marie (ed.): Gender and human security. African perspectives”. Institute for Security Studies: Monograph 198, pp. 27–37.

Ellis, Stephen (2016): This present darkness. A history of Nigerian organised crime. London: Hurst & Company.

EASO, European Asylum Support Office (2015): “Country of Origin Information Report: Nigeria – Sex trafficking of women, October 2015”. At: https://coi.euaa.europa.eu/administration/easo/PLib/BZ0415678ENN.pdf (accessed 13 April 2022).

EASO, European Asylum Support Office (2018a): “Country of Origin Information Report: Nigeria – Key socio-economic indicators, November 2018”. At: https://coi.euaa.europa.eu/administration/easo/PLib/2018_EASO_COI_Nigeria_KeySocioEconomic.pdf (accessed 13 April 2022).

EASO, European Asylum Support Office (2018b): “Country of Origin Information Report: Nigeria – Targeting of individuals, November 2018”. At: https://coi.euaa.europa.eu/administration/easo/PLib/2018_EASO_COI_Nigeria_TargetingIndividuals.pdf (accessed 13 April 2022).

European Commission (2015): “Koolvis Case, last update 19 August 2015”. At: https://ec.europa.eu/anti-trafficking/legislation-and-case-law-case-law/koolvis-case_en (accessed 19 August 2015).

European Commission (2021): “Communication from the Commission to the European Parliament, the Council, the European Economic and Social Committee and the Committee of the Regions on the EU Strategy on Combatting Trafficking in Human Beings 2021–2025”. At: https://op.europa.eu/en/publication-detail/-/publication/94bfb18f-9e13-11eb-b85c-01aa75ed71a1/language-en (accessed 13 April 2022).

EMSC, European Migrant Smuggling Centre/Europol (2020): “4th Annual Activity Report – 2020”. At: https://www.europol.europa.eu/cms/sites/default/files/documents/emsc_4th_annual_activity_report_-_2020.pdf (accessed 13 April 2022).

Europol (2016a): “Situation Report. Trafficking in human beings in the EU”. The Hague, February 2016, Document Ref No: 765175. At: https://www.europol.europa.eu/sites/default/files/documents/thb_situational_report_-_europol.pdf (accessed 13 April 2022).

Europol (2016b): “Joint action to tackle West African Human Trafficking Networks”. Press Release, 4 May 2016. At: https://www.europol.europa.eu/newsroom/news/joint-action-to-tackle-west-african-human-trafficking-networks-0 (accessed 24 September 2021).

Europol (2018a): "Situation Report. Criminal networks involved in the trafficking and exploitation of underage victims in the European Union". The Hague, October 2018, Document Ref No: 1001370. At: https://www.europol.europa.eu/sites/default/files/documents/23-11_report_child_trafficking.pdf (accessed 13 April 2022).

Europol (2018b): "Trafficked by Voodoo threats: one of the largest operations in Europe rescues 39 Nigerian women". Press Release, 22 March 2018. At: https://www.europol.europa.eu/newsroom/news/trafficked-voodoo-threats-one-of-largest-operations-in-europe-rescues-39-nigerian-women (accessed 13 April 2022).

Frontex (2018): Risk Analysis for 2018, Warsaw, February 2018, Frontex reference number: 2671 / 2018.

GRETA, Group of Experts on Action against Trafficking in Human Beings/Council of Europe (2019): "Reply from Austria to the Questionnaire for the evaluation of the implementation of the Council of Europe Convention on Action against Trafficking in Human Beings by the Parties, submitted on 1 April 2019". At: https://rm.coe.int/greta-2018-26-aut/168094b570 (accessed 13 April 2022).

The Guardian (2020): "Sex traffickers left thousands of women to starve during Italy lockdown". At: https://www.theguardian.com/global-development/2020/jul/10/sex-traffickers-left-thousands-of-women-to-starve-during-italy-lockdown-coronavirus (accessed 14 September 2021).

Henriksen, Rune/Jesperson, Sasha (2019): "Nigeria. Community complicity for wealth". In: Jesperson, Sasha/Henriksen, Rune/Barry, Anne-Marie/Jones, Michael (eds.): Human Trafficking. An organised crime? London: Hurst & Company, pp. 19–39.

HRW, Human Rights Watch (2019): "'You pray for death': Trafficking of women and girls in Nigeria". At: https://www.hrw.org/report/2019/08/27/you-pray-death/trafficking-women-and-girls-nigeria (accessed 13 April 2022).

IOM, International Organization for Migration (2017): "Human trafficking through the Central Mediterranean Route: Data, stories and information collected by the International Organization for Migration". At: https://reliefweb.int/sites/reliefweb.int/files/resources/IOMReport_Trafficking.pdf (accessed 13 April 2022).

IOM, International Organization for Migration (2019): "'Voodoo Curses' keep victims of trafficking under bondage". At: https://www.iom.int/news/voodoo-curses-keep-victims-trafficking-under-bondage (accessed 13 April 2022).

IOM, International Organization for Migration (2020): "Trafficking in persons. Victim identification and assistance-training guide". At: https://publications.iom.int/system/files/pdf/trafficking-in-persons-training-guide.pdf (accessed 13 April 2022).

Interview Diagboya, Precious, French Institute for Research in Africa, Nigeria (online), 9 December 2021.

Milborn, Corinna (2020): „Wenn das Opfer bestraft wird". At: https://www.zeit.de/2020/46/asylpolitik-wien-menschenhandel-nigeria-abschiebung-aufenthaltsgenehmigung (accessed 13 April 2022).

Myria, Federal Migration Centre (2018): "Trafficking and smuggling of human beings: Minors at major risk". At: https://www.myria.be/files/RATEH-EN-2018-DEF.pdf (accessed 13 April 2022).

Pascoal, Rafaela (2012): The situation of the Nigerian human trafficking victims and their children in Italy, 19 December 2012.

Pascoal, Rafaela Hilário (2018): Stranded: The new trendsetters of the Nigerian human trafficking criminal networks for sexual purposes. CISS – Cooperazione Internazionale Sud Sud.

Pascual, Julia/Tilouine, Joan (2020): "Sur les trottoirs de Paris, des jeunes Nigérianes victimes de la cruauté de leurs proxénètes". At: https://www.lemonde.fr/afrique/article/2020/08/04/sur-les-trottoirs-de-paris-l-enfer-de-la-prostitution-nigeriane_6048084_3212.html (accessed 13 April 2022).

Plambech, Sine (2014): Points of departure. Migration control and anti-trafficking in the lives of Nigerian sex worker migrants after deportation from Europe. PhD Dissertation, Department of Anthropology, University of Copenhagen and Danish Institute for International Studies (DIIS).

Plambech, Sine (2017): "Sex, deportation and rescue. Economies of migration among Nigerian sex workers". In: Feminist Economics, 23, 3, pp. 134–159.

Simoni, Vanessa (2013): "'I swear an oath', serments d'allégeances, coercitions et stratégies migratoires chez les femmes nigérianes de Benin City". In: Lavaud-Legendre, Bénédicte (ed.): Prostitution nigériane. Entre rêves de migration et réalités de la traite. Paris: Karthala, pp. 33–60.

UNHCR, United Nations High Commissioner for Refugees (2018): "Italy. Sea arrivals dashboard – December 2018". At: https://data2.unhcr.org/en/documents/details/67555 (accessed 24 September 2021).

UNHCR, United Nations High Commissioner for Refugees (2021): "Arrivals in Europe from Libya – September 2021". At: https://data2.unhcr.org/en/documents/details/90198 (accessed 7 January 2022).

UNICRI, United Nations Interregional Crime and Justice Research Institute (2010): "Trafficking of Nigerian girls in Italy. The data, the stories, the social services". At: https://unicri.it/sites/default/files/2021-06/trafficking_nigeria-italy.pdf (accessed 13 April 2022).

UN, United Nations (2001): "Resolution adopted by the General Assembly, Annex II: Protocol to Prevent, Suppress and Punish Trafficking in Persons, Especially Women and Children, supplementing the United Nations Convention against Transnational Organized Crime". A/RES/55/25, pp. 31–39. At: https://www.un.org/en/development/desa/population/migration/generalassembly/docs/globalcompact/A_RES_55_25.pdf (accessed 13 April 2022).

UNODC, UN Office on Drugs and Crime (2014): "Global Report on Trafficking in Persons 2014." At: https://www.unodc.org/documents/data-and-analysis/glotip/GLOTIP_2014_full_report.pdf (accessed 13 April 2022).

UNODC, UN Office on Drugs and Crime (2018): "Global Report on Trafficking in Persons 2018". At: https://www.unodc.org/documents/data-and-analysis/glotip/2018/GLOTiP_2018_BOOK_web_small.pdf (accessed 13 April 2022).

UNODC, UN Office on Drugs and Crime (2020): "Global Report on Trafficking in Persons 2020". At: https://www.unodc.org/documents/data-and-analysis/tip/2021/GLOTiP_2020_15jan_web.pdf (accessed 13 April 2022).

US DoS, US Department of State (2020) "Trafficking in Persons Report, June 2020". At: https://www.state.gov/wp-content/uploads/2020/06/2020-TIP-Report-Complete-062420-FINAL.pdf (accessed 13 April 2022).

US DoS, US Department of State (2021) "Trafficking in Persons Report, June 2021". At: https://www.state.gov/wp-content/uploads/2021/07/TIP_Report_Final_20210701.pdf (accessed 13 April 2022).

Varese, Federico (2014): "Protection and Extortion". In: Paoli, Letizia (ed.): The Oxford Handbook of Organized Crime. New York: Oxford University Press, pp. 343–358.

Walk Free Foundation (2018): "The Global Slavery Index 2018". At: https://downloads.globalslaveryindex.org/ephemeral/GSI-2018_FNL_190828_CO_DIGITAL_P-1649854280.pdf (accessed 13 April 2022).

Wallis, Emma (2019): "Tricked, trafficked and sold. How criminal gangs are bringing Nigerian women to Italy". At: https://www.infomigrants.net/en/post/14725/tricked-trafficked-and-sold-how-criminal-gangs-are-bringing-nigerian-women-to-italy (accessed 19 September 2021).

Young, Mary Alice (2011): "Human cost. Nigerian criminal networks in the UK". In: Jane's Intelligence Review, September 2011, pp. 44–47.

Part III:
“New kids on the block” in illicit trade

Out of Africa. Following the money: uncovering illicit financial flows from Africa to Europe

Peter Fabricius

Introduction

Illicit financial flows (IFFs) cost honest citizens around the world a great deal. They siphon off from us to criminals huge amounts of money which could and should be used for the development of countries, e.g. for better schools, hospitals, roads and railways. This is why combatting IFFs has now been included under target 16.4 in the 17 United Nations Sustainable Development Goals (SDGs) to be attained by 2030 – just eight years away. For Africa, IFFs are especially relevant because this continent has a very large financing shortfall – which could largely be wiped out if IFFs were eliminated. The African Union Commission noted in December 2020 that the amount of US$88.6 billion in annual IFFs from Africa (as recently estimated by the United Nations Conference on Trade and Development (UNCTAD)) was almost as high as the combined capital inflows from official development aid (ODA) of US$48 billion and foreign direct investment (FDI) of US$54 billion (AU Commission 2020).

This was why former South African president Thabo Mbeki, as chair of the United Nations Economic Commission for Africa (UNECA) High Level Panel on Illicit Financial Flows from Africa, wrote in the panel's 2015 report that "Africa was a net creditor to the rest of the world" and not the mendicant debtor it was generally presented to be (Mbeki et al. 2015: 2).

Yet even if all can agree that IFFs are a very large problem for Africa, it is not easy to get a firm conceptual grasp on the problem. There are grey areas. For one thing, the term "illicit financial flows" is not easily defined. The word "illicit" is used instead of "illegal" mainly to include tax avoidance – such as registering companies in tax havens – which may be legal but is considered immoral. Moral and other ambiguities also arise about whether the proceeds of some illicit activities – like informal gold mining – which don't cross borders but are spent to the benefit of local communities should be considered as IFFs.

Quantifying IFFs also presents problems. The large estimates of IFFs which UNCTAD, Mbeki's UNECA panel and other analysts have made seem to contain a lot of guesswork. Moreover, they may reflect certain preconceptions about the roots of the problem. Both UNCTAD and Mbeki's panel lay most of the blame for IFFs on multinational corporations for tax evasion and avoidance or mispricing exports or imports. In the 2015 UNECA High Level Panel report, Mbeki and his co-authors – probably not well disposed towards global capital anyway – estimated the sources of IFFs as 65 % commercial, 30 % criminal and 5 % corruption (Mbeki 2015: 24). Yet some analysts have suggested this ratio is a very rough estimate. Marcena Hunter of the Global Initiative against Transnational Organized Crime (GI-TOC) has written that not only Mbeki and UNCTAD but most analysts have focused on commercial IFFs because they are more easily quantified. This is basically like a person looking for their lost keys under a street light – not because they think that's where they dropped them but just because that's where the light is (Hunter 2018). Hunter suggests that IFFs from the other two broad categories, crime and corruption, may be much larger than most analysts propose, but they are much harder to quantify (Hunter 2018).

Clearly, the commercial aspects such as tax avoidance and evasion and trade misinvoicing must be addressed, and this must be done at the highest level, perhaps through a global pact to be administered by the United Nations, as the FACTI Panel (the High Level Panel on International Financial Accountability, Transparency and Integrity for Achieving the 2030 Agenda) proposed in February 2021. The panel also proposed greater global cooperation on money laundering, which is vital as so much money laundering crosses international borders.

But the international community should not lose sight of the fact that vast quantities of money are generated by transnational crimes such as trafficking in various types of contraband – and that these are very often facilitated by corruption. So combatting this type of more conventional crime and corruption must enjoy equal attention with commercial crimes and unethical practices such as tax avoidance in the fight against IFFs.

"Follow the money" is the advice often given to those investigating non-commercial crime. Transfers of money often lead to those complicit in such crimes. But we should also move in the opposite direction, by starting our search for illicit financial flows at the point of these non-commercial crimes. For example, when law enforcement authorities in Guinea-Bissau intercept a large cache of cocaine and discover a whiteboard showing all the senior government figures who have been bribed, this should be a clue to possible IFFs. And if South African police break into a house in

Johannesburg and discover an Indian national tied up in the basement, evidence that he has been kidnapped for ransom and ISIS literature all around, this should prompt suspicion that IFFs are flowing out of the country to finance ISIS.

UNECA panel sets a benchmark by estimating that Africa is losing at least US$50 billion annually in IFFs

Six years ago, the UNECA IFF report said the continent was losing at least US$50 billion a year in illicit financial flows comprising about 65 % from tax evasion and avoidance and other questionable practices of multinational enterprises (MNEs), about 30 % from ordinary crime and 5 % from corruption. The panel said curbing IFFs would greatly help Africa to become financially independent of foreign donors by mobilising its own domestic resources. Aid dependence, indeed, remains high. According to World Bank statistics, the unweighted average for African countries of net official development assistance (ODA) as a proportion of central government spending is about 40 %. The percentage is as high as 291.9 % for the Central African Republic, 178.7 % for the Gambia, 144.49 % for Guinea and 70.4 % for the Democratic Republic of the Congo (DRC) (World Bank n.d.).

Conversely, African governments raise comparatively little tax. The latest figures of the unweighted average of central government tax revenues as a percentage of GDP was 15.10 for the 45 African countries for which the IMF has statistics (IMF Data n.d.). The Organisation for Economic Co-operation and Development (OECD) gives an unweighted average tax-to-GDP ratio of 16.6 % for 30 selected African countries in 2019, compared to 22.9 % for the Latin American and Caribbean countries and 33.8 % for the OECD countries (OECD 2021: 1). Moreover, "African countries are particularly vulnerable to IFFs due to deriving a large part of their revenue from corporate income tax", as Lee Corrick, technical adviser on international tax at the African Tax Administration Forum (ATAF), said in an interview with this author (Corrick 2021). He said ATAF had calculated that the average share of corporate income tax in the total revenues of 35 ATAF member countries had risen from 15.6 % in 2010 to 17.8 % in 2019. "This compares to around 9 % in OECD countries" (ATAF 2020).

There could of course be many reasons why African countries raise so little tax and are so dependent on foreign aid. But Mbeki's UNECA panel focused on the role of IFFs. The panel's report was a watershed moment, bringing much wider attention to IFFs in Africa and renewing the call for efforts to counter them.

Tackling IFFs globally

The OECD and the G20 have taken the lead with a broad and comprehensive agenda of reform of the international tax system. Loopholes in that system have allowed MNEs – in Africa these are particularly mining and energy companies – to relocate their profits to tax havens to avoid paying higher taxes in the countries where they actually make their money ("profit shifting"). Other loopholes have permitted MNEs to avoid taxes by claiming deductions on a variety of dubious costs such as interest and royalties. This practice is labelled as "base erosion".

The OECD has estimated that up to US$240 billion in tax is being lost annually by countries due to base erosion and profit shifting (BEPS) by MNEs (OECD n.d.-a).

The OECD and G20, joined by many other countries, have tackled IFFs via several initiatives. First, as part of the Global Forum on Transparency and Exchange of Information for Tax Purposes, in which 163 countries and jurisdictions are participating, 90 jurisdictions started automatically exchanging tax information in 2017 and 2018. In this way, they are providing tax administrations with data on more than 84 million offshore accounts with a value of €10 trillion, for example. Anticipating these disclosures, almost half a million individuals have come forward to disclose their hidden assets. Over €107 billion in taxes has been recovered so far, and foreign-owned offshore bank deposits have been reduced by 20–25 % (OECD n.d.-b).

Second, 141 countries and jurisdictions are working together in another major OECD/G20 initiative, the Inclusive Framework on BEPS, which is tackling tax avoidance through measures such as combatting harmful tax regimes; prevention of tax treaty abuse and countering "treaty shopping";[1] and country-by-country reporting to reveal the tax jurisdictions in which companies actually make specific profits. The OECD (2020: 3) calls this "the first substantial – and overdue – renovation of the international tax standards in almost a century". The OECD is helping developing coun-

1 "Treaty shopping typically involves the attempt by a person to access indirectly the benefits of a tax agreement between two jurisdictions without being a resident of one of those jurisdictions." (OECD/G20 BEPS 2020: 19).

tries implement these measures against tax avoidance through technical assistance. For example, between 2016 and 2020, the Inclusive Framework reviewed 287 suspect tax regimes to ensure that companies conducted substantial business activities in the jurisdiction offering the tax regime to justify domiciling themselves there for tax purposes. Of these, 76 were abolished, 50 were amended, 15 were in the process of being abolished or amended, 59 were found not to be harmful, four were considered harmful, seven were assessed as potentially harmful but not actually harmful, 35 remained under review and the rest were mainly considered beyond the scope of the review (OECD 2020: 14–15).

Over three-quarters of the Inclusive Framework members, including all G20 countries, have introduced or are in the process of introducing an obligation for large MNEs to report their accounts country by country, to show where exactly they make their money (OECD 2020: 3). And in October 2021, the G20 leaders endorsed an OECD deal for a global minimum corporate tax of 15 %, which 136 member countries of the OECD/G20 Inclusive Framework on Base Erosion and Profit Shifting had agreed on earlier that month. It was believed to be aimed, among others, at internet giants like Google, Amazon, Facebook, Microsoft and Apple which had been accused of avoiding taxation by domiciling in tax havens (Reuters 2021).

Africa addresses IFFs

Meanwhile, Africa has also stepped up its own efforts to combat IFFs. In December 2020, the African Union Commission launched a "Multi-Donor Action against Illicit Financial Flows in Africa" as a follow-up to the UNECA report by Mbeki's panel. The AU noted that the COVID-19 pandemic had exacerbated the fiscal deficit of some African countries, underscoring the urgency to address illicit outflows. The new initiative is being financed by the EU and the German Federal Ministry for Economic Cooperation and Development (BMZ) and implemented by the Deutsche Gesellschaft für Internationale Zusammenarbeit (GIZ) through the Good Financial Governance in Africa programme. The strategy is to strengthen the AU's capacity to coordinate anti-IFF policies on the continent. The strategy also supports the implementation of country pilot measures being undertaken through the leadership of the ATAF. The AU noted that "Domestic Resource Mobilisation (DRM) is one of the most promising sustainable development financing sources. However, tax-to-GDP ratios in most [...] African countries have remained extremely low – averaging only 18 percent in 2018. Tax revenue under-collection is largely associated with considerable IFF in the region" (African Union Commission 2020). ATAF, which advises African countries on how to counter tax avoidance, mainly through revising tax treaties, has helped its members assess additional tax of more than US$2.2 billion and collect additional tax of over US$900 million in the past six years (Corrick 2021).

Towards a global pact?

Some African and other analysts have questioned whether the OECD and G20 can be depended upon to really tackle IFFs from Africa thoroughly since their members often look for benefits for themselves. UNCTAD complained that though the OECD/G20 initiatives had closed or reformed many smaller and well-known tax havens, they had not touched financially more powerful states such as the US, Switzerland, Ireland, Luxembourg or the Netherlands. Some African tax havens, notably Mauritius and Seychelles, also continued to operate. UNCTAD also chided African states for not really participating in international negotiations to reform international taxation, despite having so much to gain from them (UNCTAD 2020).

Current international negotiations mainly address the thorny problem of how to tax digital commerce. This requires going beyond the established principle of taxing companies in countries where they have a physical presence to taxing them in markets where they generate revenue. The Tax Justice Network Africa advocacy group recently complained that the latest OECD/G20 draft proposals for taxing digital commerce are biased in favour of rich countries and urged developing countries to seek a different forum for negotiating a global agreement (Tax Justice Network Africa 2020). The UNECA IFF panel had also recommended in its 2015 report that the IFF problem be taken up by a more representative body, preferably the UN (Mbeki 2015: 86).

There are now signs of such a wider forum evolving. In its report, Mbeki's panel had also lamented that curbing IFFs had not been included among the Millennium Development Goals and recommended that it be included in the successor regime (Mbeki 2015: 79). Indeed it was included under target 16.4 in the 17 SDGs adopted in 2015 and meant to be reached by 2030. Target 16.4 states that by 2030, the world should "significantly reduce illicit financial and arms flows, strengthen the recovery and return of stolen assets and combat all forms of organized crime" (SDSN n.d.). Curbing IFFs is important to help African countries mobilise capital to finance the achievement of all the SDGs and other national priorities, especially in the wake of the COVID-19 pandemic, which increased Africa's financing shortfall.

"Official development assistance (ODA) to Africa has stagnated for a decade at around $30 billion per year and donor countries are unlikely to increase their aid commitments as they spend on COVID-19 recovery packages at home" according to Paul Akiwumi, Director for Africa and Least Developed Countries at UNCTAD. "Meanwhile, UNCTAD predicts that foreign direct investment (FDI) in Africa will plunge from $45 billion in 2019 to between $25 and $35 billion in 2020, with a recovery not expected until 2022" (Akiwumi 2020). UNCTAD (2020) calculated that the US$88.6 billion in annual IFFs could bridge half of Africa's gap in financing the implementation of the SDGs.

Clearly, what was needed was a truly global approach to combatting IFFs.

In 2020, the FACTI panel was created to that end jointly by the President of the United Nations General Assembly and the President of the United Nations Economic and Social Council. Chaired by former Nigerien Prime Minister Ibrahim Mayaki, now CEO of the New Partnership for Africa's Development (NEPAD), in February 2021 the FACTI Panel recommended 14 "ambitious [...] measures to reform, redesign and revitalise the global architecture, so it can effectively foster financial integrity for sustainable development" (FACTI Panel 2021: III). These would be based on a global pact under the auspices of the UN. Beyond an impact on the well-being of people and planet, the panel stressed the potential contribution of such a pact to improving multilateral and national governance.

Such a global pact would include establishing common standards of financial transparency to eliminate the secrecy jurisdictions which encourage money laundering. It would also include a universal approach to oblige all taxpayers, especially multinational corporations, to pay their fair share of taxes. Fairer rules and stronger incentives would be established to combat tax competition, tax avoidance and tax evasion[2], starting with an agreement on a global minimum corporate tax. To avoid profit shifting, multinationals would have to declare their taxes on a country-by-country basis, showing where their income was earned. While some of these mea-

2 "Tax competition" here refers to countries competing with each other for investment by offering foreign companies better tax terms than other countries. This easily becomes a "race to the bottom". "Tax evasion" is illegal action by a taxpayer to escape tax, such as hiding income. "Tax avoidance" refers to legal but ethically questionable actions to escape taxation, such as registering businesses in tax havens.

sures are already being implemented by the OECD and G20 (as described above), the 14 recommendations of the panel constitute an ambitious proposal to make the response to IFFs more universal. If implemented, the FACTI Panel's recommendations would certainly make a substantial impact on IFFs. However, we need to bear in mind that tackling the full scope of IFFs – including those deriving from corruption and crime – will require much more than reforming the financial system.

Beyond commercial IFFs

There are big questions about the quantity of IFFs and the relative contribution of different sources, with some analysts casting doubt on the sorts of statistics being published in the UNECA IFF panel report by UNCTAD and others. In a 2018 study commissioned by the G20, the World Customs Organization (WCO) was unable to put a reliable figure on IFFs and said that the many existing large estimates should be regarded only as "risk indicators" rather than as hard facts (WCO 2018: 5). The UNCTAD estimate of a US$88.6 billion IFF outflow – of which about US$40 billion was from extractive industries – was largely based on UN Comtrade data comparing exports of commodities from Africa with imports of the same commodities in other countries. But this method has been questioned before.

In particular, doubts were expressed in South Africa about the conclusions of a July 2016 UNCTAD (2016a) report entitled "Trade Misinvoicing in Primary Commodities in Developing Countries: The cases of Chile, Côte d'Ivoire, Nigeria, South Africa and Zambia". The UNCTAD report found purported widespread underinvoicing[3] of commodity exports which, it alleged, was deliberately designed by commodity producers to evade taxes and other payments due to the fiscal authorities. For South Africa, the report calculated cumulative underinvoicing over the period 2000–2014 to have amounted to US$102.8 billion (in constant 2014 US dollars): US$621 million for iron ore; US$24 billion for silver and platinum; and US$78 billion for gold (UNCTAD 2016a: 26, Table 9; 27, Table

---

3 "Underinvoicing" refers to the practice of invoicing for a lower amount than the real value of the particular goods (in this case of alleged trade misinvoicing, primary commodity exports) to avoid taxation or other moneys due to the state or for other illegal purposes. Overinvoicing is the practice of invoicing for a higher amount than the real value of the goods. This is done, for example, to illegally export money or to launder it.

10; 30, Table 11). UNCTAD revised the report in December 2016, but its fundamentals remained unchanged (UNCTAD 2016b).

The Chamber of Mines of South Africa (tralac 2017), representing the mining industry, firmly denied these allegations. It pointed out that many of its gold and platinum exports are not classified by South Africa as such because they originate in other African countries and are merely refined in South Africa. But they are registered by importers as South African products, hence the discrepancy. The chamber also claimed that the UNCTAD claims of underinvoicing of iron ore exports were simply based on wrong statistics.

If the Chamber of Mines (now called Minerals Council South Africa) is right, such errors in UN Comtrade data could have large implications for global estimates of IFFs from Africa. The data would overstate the contribution of commercial IFFs to overall IFF figures, including in the report of the UNECA IFF panel. That panel relied heavily on UN Comtrade data. And its 65:30:5 breakdown of IFFs into commercial, criminal and corruption sources, respectively, seems to have been based largely on that of the think tank Global Financial Integrity (GFI). GFI director Raymond Baker was a prominent member of the UNECA panel. In the GI-TOC report "Measures that Miss the Mark" of June 2018, Marcena Hunter dismisses GFI's breakdown of the sources of IFFs as largely guesswork (Hunter 2018). Part of the reason she gives is that GFI simply transposed the global 65:30:5 ratio to Africa without evidence that it was locally applicable. She asserts that IFFs deriving from commerce – such as trade misinvoicing or tax avoidance and evasion – have been overemphasised simply because they are easier to measure – for example by analysing the discrepancies between exports and imports. As we have seen in the case of African mineral exports, these discrepancies can be misleading.

In any case, the measures fail to give proper weight to the IFFs which derive from crime and corruption. And IFFs from the least developed countries are at even higher risk of being underestimated, largely because crime and corruption are harder to measure in poorer than in richer countries. Hunter suggests this is because poorer countries have less developed financial systems, rely more on cash transactions and generally have lower bureaucratic capacity to maintain crime statistics. Hunter notes, nevertheless, that crime IFFs have a significant impact on lives, even if they cannot be quantified. "In fact, the Global Initiative Against Transnational Organized Crime found that organized crime could directly and significantly impair the ability to achieve 23 of the 169 SDG targets. IFFs, together with the underlying activities, distort economic and political competition, subvert government institutions, generate conflict and violence, and undermine the integrity of legal and financial systems." (Hunter 2018)

Money laundering is often the financial manifestation of other non-financial crime, but it is hard to quantify. The United Nations Office on Drugs and Crime (UNODC) calculated in 2011 that the proceeds of all crimes amounted to about US$2.1 trillion or 3.6 % of global GDP in 2009, of which about US$1.6 trillion, or 2.7 % of global GDP, was laundered (UNODC 2011). The latter is about the total size of Africa's current economy. This tallied with the International Monetary Fund's estimate in 1998 that global money laundering could represent somewhere between two and five percent of the world's gross domestic product (IMF 1998).

UNODC has estimated, very roughly, that the proceeds of all crimes could amount to about 3.6 % of global GDP per annum, which would have been about US$2.1 trillion in 2009. Of this, it estimated that about 1.5 % of global GDP (i.e. about US$870 billion) emanated from transnational organised crime – mainly drug trafficking, counterfeiting, human trafficking, oil bunkering, environmental crimes and arms trafficking. Of this in turn about 1 % of GDP (i.e. US$580 billion) was laundered. And UNODC estimated that about half of the proceeds of transnational organised crime were from drug trafficking (UNODC 2011: 7). The biggest drug trade was in cocaine, estimated to be worth about US$85 billion in 2009, of which about US$84 billion was profits of traffickers all along the supply chain, leaving only US$1 billion to the Andean growers of the coca plants (UNODC 2011).

Gauging crime IFFs from Africa: the looting continues

By UNODC's measure, money laundering in or from Africa, if proportional to GDP, would currently total about US$70 billion a year – i.e. more than the UNECA panel's estimate of total annual IFFs of around US$50 billion. UNODC has also estimated that most of the money invested offshore by Africa – including laundered money – goes to Europe. It said that of the US$7.4 trillion invested offshore by all countries in 2009 (legally and illegally), about US$1.3 trillion came from Africa and the Middle East. Of this, about US$490 billion was invested in the United Kingdom and US$460 billion in Switzerland (UNODC 2011: 44, Table 35). The assumption is that offshore money launderers would choose about the same investment destinations. The share of drug-trafficking in the proceeds of transnational organised crime may be even higher in the largely informal economies of West Africa than it is globally (OECD 2018: 62). West Africa is the drug-trafficking fulcrum of the continent, the conduit for three major illicit drug flows, cocaine, cannabis and methamphetamines (OECD 2018: 62).

The most lucrative of these is the cocaine trade, with West Africa emerging from about 2007 as the main transit region for the flow of this narcotic from Latin America to Europe – channelling about one quarter of Europe's cocaine supply (Shaw 2015: 339–340). "Because of the flow's high value and the lack of an indigenous market, cocaine trafficking has had the greatest impact of all drug flows on the region's illicit economy and stability" (OECD 2018: 62). While cocaine trafficking generated US$34.8 billion in North America and US$27.5 billion in Europe in 2009, the value of the trade in Africa was a mere US$1.6 billion, with only US$600 million of that remaining on the continent and US$1 billion being laundered abroad. This was nevertheless a large amount of money by regional standards. Most of the African cocaine trade goes through West Africa, with just a small amount transiting South Africa, the report added. It estimated that West African actors earned only US$40 million per year from the drug trade, with the rest staying in the hands of Colombian and other Latin American drug dealers (OECD 2018: 62).

Of the US$40 million, the authors estimate that about 80 % remain in the region and is spent on local operations and patronage systems. "The remaining 20 % enter the formal banking system and are laundered through the region's larger economies, i.e. Ghana, Senegal or Nigeria." (OECD 2018: 65) The OECD report documents how Latin American drug cartels have captured some West African states by finding partners or at least protectors at the highest level of these states, especially those who could control transport hubs or deploy military power to protect the trade (OECD 2018: 64). Most of the local proceeds remain with these elites, and for the rest of the population the drug trade has largely been an unmitigated disaster, corrupting politics and law enforcement and sparking instability (OECD 2018: 65).

A narco-state with strong links to Portugal

As the classic example of state capture by drug traffickers, the OECD report cites Guinea-Bissau, the former Portuguese colony widely reputed to be a "narco-state". Shaw disapproves of applying this term and prefers to describe the state as being run by an "elite network with mafia-like attributes" (Shaw 2015: 339–340). However, the term remains useful for our purposes. Shaw describes how police discovered evidence in August

2007 that Columbian drug traffickers were paying off all the key figures in the government, including national President Nino Vieira. Greed for drug money then led to a bust-up between Vieira and his military chief General Batista Tagme Na Waie, who was killed in a bomb blast in 2009, provoking his soldiers to beat Vieira to death in his home in retaliation the next day (Shaw 2015: 352–353). The US designated the navy chief Admiral José Américo Bubo Na Tchuto and the air force chief Papa Camará as drug kingpins in 2010, imposed sanctions on them and managed to arrest Na Tchuto in a daring offshore sting operation in 2013 (Shaw 2015: 359). Since then, the government of Guinea-Bissau has shown renewed commitment to engage in the fight against drug trafficking and organised crime, as evidenced by the two largest ever cocaine seizures in the country in 2019 (UNODC 2020).

A local analyst nonetheless said that rumours were still very strong that Guinea-Bissau "is still an important point of transshipment of drugs and that business is just as good, if not even better for the traffickers" (Guinea-Bissau analyst 2021). This analyst said it was generally believed that about 10 to 15 % of the cocaine that enters Guinea-Bissau stays in the hands of locals and the rest transits to Europe. The cocaine seizure operations had revealed many wire transfers of drug proceeds to Europe, particularly Portugal, Spain, the UK and France (Guinea-Bissau analyst 2021). Portugal is evidently the money laundering centre of choice. "The so-called elite has tight links with Portugal, children are sent away to study and they live in expensive areas in Lisbon. It is impossible for a public servant from Guinea-Bissau to buy a 5-bedroom apartment for example in Cascais city only with their salary, yet that is something common." (Guinea-Bissau analyst 2021)

The US State Department's 2018 International Narcotics Control Strategy Report agreed, stating that "Portugal is a transit point for narcotics entering Europe. Portugal's long coastline, vast territorial waters, and privileged relationships with countries in South America and Lusophone Africa make it a gateway country for South American cocaine and a transshipment point for drugs coming to Europe from West Africa. Portugal has a significant number of dual-nationals who move wealth between Angola and Portugal." (US State Department 2018: 168) "Suspicious funds from Angola continue to be used to purchase Portuguese businesses and real estate." (US State Department 2018: 167)

Luanda Leaks: how Isabel dos Santos, the former president's daughter, became the richest woman in Africa

This last observation was sharply vindicated in 2019 by the "Luanda Leaks", a trove of more than 715,000 secret emails, contracts and other documents which were passed on to the International Consortium of Investigative Journalists (ICIJ) and other media representatives.

These documents confirmed the widely held belief that over the last few years of his tenure, which ended in 2017, President José Eduardo dos Santos had basically made his daughter Isabel probably the richest woman in Africa by awarding her companies, public contracts, tax breaks, telecom licences, diamond-mining rights, insider deals and preferential loans (ICIJ 19 January 2020). This blew her cover story that she was a self-made business tycoon. "Over the last two decades, she acquired valuable stakes in every important Angolan industry, including oil, diamonds, telecom and banking" (ICIJ 19 January 2020). Her most important position was as CEO of the state oil firm Sonangol. And large quantities of these ill-gotten moneys – which the ICIJ quantified at about US$2.1 billion – flowed beyond Angola's borders as IFFs, mainly to Europe but also to the US and Asia.

Dos Santos and her late husband, Sindika Dokolo, amassed a vast foreign empire of more than 400 companies and subsidiaries in 41 countries and bought up assets such as high-priced real estate in London and Lisbon (ICIJ 19 January 2020). The heart of dos Santos's business empire was in Europe. The ICIJ found that she had interests in 17 companies in Portugal, including Banco BIC Português, S.A., 14 in Malta, nine in the Netherlands, seven in the British Virgin Islands, five in Madeira, three in Switzerland and one in each of Italy, the UK, Luxembourg, Cyprus and France (ICIJ 19 January 2020). European and American consulting firms, accountants and lawyers such as Boston Consulting, PwC (formerly PricewaterhouseCoopers), KPMG and others also helped sustain the dos Santos empire for years, the ICIJ said. This included helping her set up shell companies to move hundreds of millions of US dollars in public money out of Angola, one of the poorest countries in the world (ICIJ 7 December 2020).

Dos Santos and Dokolo denied wrongdoing, and she claimed to be the victim of a political "witch hunt" and "political persecution" by the new President João Lourenço (ICIJ 19 January 2020). Lourenço did indeed precipitate her downfall by firing her as CEO of Sonangol in November 2017, but the Luanda Leaks accelerated her demise. Days after the leaks, Angola's prosecutor general charged dos Santos with money laundering and embezzlement committed when she headed Sonangol in Angola (Africanews 2020). That precipitated an avalanche of reactions in Europe as courts and regulatory authorities in Portugal, the Netherlands and Germany froze dos Santos's and Dokolo's assets and bank accounts or seized their businesses (ICIJ 17 March 2020). These actions followed a request from the Lourenço administration, which was pursuing more than US$1 billion that it claimed she, her husband and associates had siphoned off from Angola (ICIJ 7 April 2020).

In June 2020, dos Santos closed down her business offices in Portugal, the heart of her offshore business empire, complaining that the asset freeze had made it impossible for her to continue paying staff salaries (ICIJ 18 June 2020). The European authorities also turned their attention to locals complicit in dos Santos's gigantic money laundering enterprise. In July 2020, the European Banking Authority launched an inquiry into whether EU financial supervisors had failed to perform their duty to monitor her money laundering (ICIJ 20 July 2020). On 2 October 2020, the Portuguese Securities Market Commission CMVM opened investigations against nine auditing companies that had worked with dos Santos (ICIJ 2 October 2020). In September 2021, German authorities fined the state-owned KfW-Ipex-Bank US$178,000 for indirectly lending about $55 million to dos Santos's brewery Sodiba through an Angolan state-owned bank (ICIJ 3 September 2021). The dismantling of the vast business empire of Isabel dos Santos seems to be continuing indefinitely, a measure in part of how deeply the many tentacles of that giant enterprise penetrated, mainly into European economies.

It is proving to be a case study of crime IFFs from Africa, a rare glimpse into what everyone had long suspected but no one could prove, that the dos Santos family was pillaging the state and exporting the proceeds. No amount of international tax reform was ever likely to address this problem. The dos Santos empire is falling firstly for political reasons, because Angola's ruling MPLA finally decided it had had enough of José Eduardo dos Santos and his children and forced him to stand down in 2017. And then because of good investigative journalism – which may well have been aided in turn by the change of political power in Luanda. Nevertheless, there is reason to suspect that Lourenço's pursuit of the dos Santos family has more to do with asserting his own personal political power than with cleaning out the state. It would probably take a change in the ruling party, not just a change in the president, to really root out Angola's deep corruption and staunch the flow of illicit finances. The Luanda Leaks have also exposed the interface between African corruption and hitherto apparently respectable and legal professionals and businesses in Europe which helped dos Santos launder her loot. It is hardly surprising that crime IFFs from Africa are vast on a continent where the reach of the law is often limited, as are democratic constraints on corruption.

Especially in countries like Angola, Gabon, the Republic of the Congo or Mozambique, where the same leader, family or party has been in power for a long time, one often finds sustained and systematic looting of state coffers or national resources. And Europe seems to be the destination of choice for the proceeds of this pillaging, which are often deposited in bank accounts or invested in fixed property or other valuable assets. The Middle East and the US also feature prominently as destinations. The IFFs are often facilitated by European or American bankers, tax accountants, lawyers, estate agents and other financial officers who enable these transactions to occur clandestinely, in defiance of money laundering laws or just commonsense ethics.

How African leaders stash their loot abroad

The 2013 report of the Africa Progress Panel (APP) chaired by the late UN Secretary General Kofi Annan also gave a snapshot of how the leaders of some of Africa's most resource-rich countries stash loot abroad (APP 2013). It noted that lawsuits filed in foreign countries had revealed that the Republic of the Congo's President Denis Sassou-Nguesso allegedly owned 24 estates and operated 112 bank accounts in France while then Gabonese President Omar Bongo Ondimba and his relatives allegedly owned 30 luxurious estates on the French Riviera and in Paris. Sassou-Nguesso and Bongo featured again in the Pandora Papers, another huge trove of secret emails revealed by the ICIJ in October 2021, which showed that they had secretly stashed millions of US dollars offshore.

The exposé also fingered Kenyan President Uhuru Kenyatta and his family (ICIJ 3 October 2021). The APP report also said that the US Justice Department had seized several assets which Equatorial Guinea president Teodoro Obiang Nguema Mbasogo's son Teodoro Obiang Mangue, a government minister, had acquired offshore. These included "a Gulfstream jet, a variety of cars – including eight Ferraris, seven Rolls-Royces and two Bugattis – a 12-acre estate in Malibu valued at US$38 million, and white gloves previously owned by Michael Jackson" (APP 2013: 29). Transparency International noted that in 2017, Obiang junior had his €107 million (US$118 million) mansion in Paris confiscated after he was found guilty by a court in France of money laundering and embezzlement. It also noted that President Obiang was at the time hosting Yahya Jammeh, the exiled former Gambian president. "Jammeh and Obiang owned luxury mansions next door to each other in Maryland, USA" (Transparency International 2019).

And it cited the case of James Ibori, once a shop assistant in a DIY store in London and later governor of Delta State in Nigeria from 1999 to 2007, who was sentenced to 13 years in prison in London in 2012 after admitting fraud of nearly £50 million (US$66 million). Ibori used shell companies to buy luxury goods around the world, including six houses in London, one a Hampstead mansion. "Around the world, buying property is a favourite method for the corrupt to launder their ill-gotten gains." (Transparency International 2019) The Financial Action Task Force (FATF) found that "[r]eal estate accounted for up to 30 % of criminal assets confiscated in the last two years [between 2011 and 2013], demonstrating this as a clear area of vulnerability" (FATF 2013: 24). Transparency International and FATF have recommended various measures to combat money laundering through the purchase of real estate, most of which entail an obligation on estate agents, lawyers and other professionals involved to know their customers. Yet Transparency International found in a study of the US, UK, Canada and Australia, that relevant officials were not following their own guidelines to avoid money-laundering through property purchases (Maira 2017).

Smuggling gold through the souks of Dubai

As the APP revealed, the extractive industries are particularly vulnerable to IFFs, and gold and diamonds are often the products of choice for money laundering and smuggling, as they are more portable because of their high value relative to weight. Hunter has noted: "Gold is a desirable financial vehicle to move and hide wealth because it is almost untraceable, the exact amount or value can be easily concealed, it possesses a high level of liquidity, and it holds its value." (Hunter 2019: 16) She has estimated that in 2016 at least US$4.1 billion worth of gold mined by artisanal and small-scale gold miners (ASGM) was smuggled abroad from Sudan, South Africa, Zimbabwe, Mali, Burkina Faso, the Democratic Republic of the Congo, Ghana and Libya (Hunter 2019: 14). Most of this went to Dubai, which Hunter and other researchers have identified as the money laundering capital of the world because of its lax import and export controls (Blore and Hunter 2020).

According to Hunter (2021), Dubai serves as a buffer for European nations, providing "a level of plausible deniability because they aren't as directly engaged with these supply chains or financial flows". "The process of reselling ASGM gold freely exported from red-flagged sources to Dubai jewellers and refiners (via the emirate's bustling souk) essentially launders illicit ASGM gold into a refined product that is acceptable to the world's most reputable gold hubs." Switzerland was one of the largest buyers of this partly processed gold from Dubai, importing 148,423 tonnes in 2016, valued at just under US$6 billion (Blore and Hunter 2020: 37–38).

Hunter has also noted that in places like the Democratic Republic of the Congo and Sudan, ASGM gold is sometimes taxed by, or otherwise used to benefit, illegal armed groups conducting insurgencies or is implicated in gross human rights violations. "For this reason, ASGM gold is sometimes characterized as a conflict mineral" (Blore and Hunter 2020: 36). Though these "taxes" mostly stay in the country, other beneficiaries may be laundering some of the proceeds abroad. Though conflict (or "blood") diamonds have received the most global attention – such as through the Kimberley Process – the international community has begun to widen the scope of its efforts to combat conflict minerals, e.g. through the EU's 1 January 2021 Conflict Minerals Regulation to help stem the trade in tin, tantalum, tungsten and gold – which sometimes finance armed conflict (European Commission n.d.).

The DRC: a smugglers' and looters' paradise

The DRC has been one of the most lawless and corrupt countries on the continent for decades, particularly in view of its lax control over minerals. The Enough Project has estimated that more than US$600 million in gold leaves the DRC annually, and greed for gold provokes fighting among armed groups trying to control mines and trading routes (Enough Project n.d.). As Hunter (2019) notes, there is strong evidence that large volumes of gold are being smuggled from unstable Eastern DRC to Uganda and Rwanda in particular but also to Burundi and Tanzania. This also applies to many other minerals, such as coltan, which is used extensively in high-tech electronics like cell phones and in jewellery, as well as tin, tantalum and tungsten, according to the UN Group of Experts on the DRC (UN 2021: 19). Several foreign trading companies were also suspected of having bought these minerals directly from small artisanal miners.

These IFFs are depriving the DRC of large revenues, firstly to the benefit of Rwanda in particular but also to the benefit of foreign traders, as well as manufacturers of cell phones, jewellery and other products beyond Africa who obtain valuable minerals at smuggled prices. The DRC has also lost billions of US dollars through the official but clearly corrupt sale of its state-owned mines at bargain prices to foreign mining companies which then sell them on at large profit. The obvious assumption is that Congolese officials – probably all the way up the president – benefit from large kickbacks from these mining companies. In the process, of course, Congolese citizens have also lost hundreds of millions of US dollars from the proceeds of what were supposed to be state assets. According to the APP report, the DRC lost US$1.36 billion between 2010 and 2012 as a result of the alleged undervaluation of state assets in just five selected mining deals. This was equivalent to more than double the combined annual budget of the DRC for health and education in 2012. The report said the five companies it investigated – all listed on the London Stock Exchange and most registered in the British Virgin Islands – had paid just a sixth of the real price of the mining assets they had bought and had then sold them at average rates of return of 512 per cent. This generated a return of US$1.63 billion on assets purchased for US$275.5 million, the APP calculated. "Under these deals, the DRC sold copper and cobalt assets to offshore companies linked to an offshore-registered holding company called Fleurette. [...] Glencore and the Eurasian Natural Resources Corporation (ENRC) subsequently purchased assets acquired by offshore concession holders – both are FTSE100 companies listed on the London Stock Exchange." (APP 2013: 100, Annex 1) The implication of the APP report was that Fleurette had acted as an intermediary in these privatisations of the DRC's minerals at bargain-basement prices. Fleurette is owned by the notorious Israeli businessman Dan Gertler, who was close to the previous DRC president Joseph Kabila. In 2017, the US slapped sanctions on Gertler and some of his companies, including Fleurette, for "hundreds of millions of dollars' worth of opaque and corrupt mining and oil deals" in the DRC (U.S. Department of the Treasury 2017).

These examples from the DRC, probably Africa's richest country in natural resources, show that stealing from Africa's citizens does not necessarily require the sophisticated BEPS techniques of clever tax accountants and lawyers. It can be done more simply and more crudely by physically smuggling gold or coltan across the border into Rwanda or "selling the family silver", i.e. entire mines (though in this case more likely gold and copper mines), to corrupt European and other foreign companies at bargain-basement prices – and then recycling some of that back into one's personal bank account. In a country – and on a continent – where democratic oversight of government spending and selling is in short supply, why cook the books when you can simply steal the loot directly?

Hidden debt: Mozambique reels from the consequences of looting of state coffers and neglect of its own people

Crime IFFs may be harder to quantify than commercial IFFs, but they are probably even more costly to a state and its people (Hunter 2018). Mozambique is a case in point. It is currently experiencing a devastating insurgency which is jeopardising the exploitation of its vast liquid natural gas reserves. It is also reeling from the long-term impacts of a US$2 billion "hidden debt" scandal which has seriously undermined its international standing and economy. Both have arguably been at least in part consequences of the looting of national resources and the government's failure to deliver basic services. The Mozambique government secretly contracted US$2 billion in loans from Credit Suisse and the Russian company VTB Capital in 2013 and 2014 to buy a tuna trawler fleet and maritime patrol craft, ostensibly to both exploit its fishing waters and guard them against illegal exploitation by foreign fishing interests. The late exposure of this debt, which had not been approved by parliament nor included in the budget, by the Wall Street Journal in April 2016 prompted the IMF and all other international donors to halt direct budget support in 2016, with a huge knock-on effect on the economy. The fleet of tuna trawlers and patrol boats was supplied by the Abu Dhabi-based Privinvest Group and built in Cherbourg, France. Credit Suisse and VTB Capital, unusually, disbursed the US$2 billion loans directly to Privinvest rather than to the Mozambique government.

In a 2017 analysis of the deal, the risk assessment company Kroll calculated that Privinvest had overcharged Mozambique US$713 million for the vessels and back-up equipment (Kroll 2017: 16). This was an example of overinvoicing to perpetrate IFFs. Kroll also found that the tuna fishing enterprise was not fully operational and so had been able to generate only "negligible revenue" instead of the combined operating revenues of US$2.3 billion it had been expected to generate by December 2016 to be able to start repaying the loans (Kroll 2017: 17). Though some media reports have put the figure higher, Kroll said it could not account for at least US$500 million of the $2 billion loans (Kroll 2017: 16). The US$2 billion loan scandal has generated enormous controversy and litigation. After long delays, a corruption case against 19 Mozambican officials and other individuals – including the son of previous President Armando Guebuza – began in Maputo in August 2021. The US indicted several people involved, and three Credit Suisse officials pleaded guilty. Both Mozambique and the US government have indicted former finance minister Manuel Chang, who signed off on the loans, for receiving a bribe. He is in jail in South Africa. In November 2021, the Johannesburg High Court ordered the South African government to extradite him to the US, though Mozambique has requested leave to appeal this ruling. Meanwhile, the Mozambique government is fighting in a London court to avoid having to repay the $2 billion in loans because it says these were fraudulently contracted.

The "hidden debt" scandal provides another glimpse into the possible scale and impact of crime IFFs on the continent, though it is possibly just the tip of the iceberg. In a study published in May 2021 and reported by Mozambique's official news agency AIM, Mozambique's anti-corruption NGO, the Public Integrity Center (CIP), calculated that the "hidden debt" had already cost the country at least US$11 billion and had plunged an additional two million people into poverty (CIP/Chr. Michelsen Institute 2021: 6).

CIP arrived at this larger figure by taking into account interest on the debt, the cancellation of foreign aid by all foreign donors – which has not been resumed – as a result of the fraud as well as the huge blow to Mozambique's international credibility and reputation. This scandal caused a financial crisis, "making the government unable to pay its bills, there was a major currency devaluation, foreign debt became unpayable, the economy slowed down sharply, real GDP per capita fell, unemployment soared, and poverty increased" (CIP/Chr. Michelsen Institute 2021: 6).

The "hidden debt" scandal exhibits some of the same features as Angola's Luanda Leaks saga. For one thing, it took investigative journalists to uncover both scandals. The official oversight bodies of Angola and Mozambique did not initiate the exposures of the scandals, though they got on board eventually. And foreigners – including some in Europe – were major beneficiaries of both corruption scandals, while ordinary locals were the big losers. Though much has been made of the bribes paid to the likes of Manuel Chang and former President Armando Guebuza's son Ndambi in the Mozambique looting, the big winner was the shipbuilder Privinvest. Clearly, corruption runs deep in the Mozambique state and the Frelimo ruling party. FATF, operating through its local branch, the Eastern and Southern Africa Anti-Money Laundering Group (ESAAMLG) has been trying for years to get the government to comply, at least at the theoretical level, with international benchmarks for combating money laundering and terrorist financing. In its latest report of June 2021, it noted that "Mozambique has not yet assessed its ML/TF [money-laundering and terrorist financing] risks" (ESAAMLG 2021: 11). Mozambique's reluctance to tackle ML/TF may well derive from the complicity of very senior government officials in those money laundering offences.

Conclusion

It is clear that illicit financial flows are a highly complex problem with little in the way of absolutely hard facts to grasp onto and many grey areas. These include difficulties in quantifying IFFs, or even defining them. The word "illicit" is part of the problem. "Illegal" would be straightforward and objective. "Illicit" is complicated and subjective. In the commercial areas, the word "illicit" brings into the definition activities such as tax avoidance – rather than evasion – by multinational corporations: avoiding tax by domiciling companies in offshore tax havens can be legal but is considered morally wrong. As we have seen, trying to give appropriate weight to different types of IFFs is also difficult. Commercial IFFs – such as tax avoidance and misinvoicing exports – are easier to quantify, so they have received greater attention, at the expense of crime IFFs, the proceeds of non-financial crimes such as trafficking contraband or corruption. Yet the latter are arguably larger and also have a huge impact on development.

Some of the ambiguity about the illicitness of IFFs also pertains to Africa's extremely vast informal business sector, such as ASGM, which can be good or bad.

Hunter notes that in some areas of Sierra Leone, financial contributions by the ASGM sector to local communities, such as the payment of teachers' salaries, have been reported to far outstrip the financial support provided by government programmes, civil society organisations or development organisations. This gives ASGM stakeholders, which might include criminal actors, a substantial degree of legitimacy with the local population. Thus, efforts to counter criminal networks or break down markets might be met with considerable resistance – or even harm development and undermine state authority. One might add that investing the revenues of such illicit activities in the local economy is better than exporting them abroad. But it is not ideal either, as it unfairly competes with legitimate businesses and creates an environment for more serious crime and also an opportunity to buy political influence and protection.

In any case, we have seen that Europe is the favourite destination for IFFs from Africa, including crime IFFs, though it seems to be impossible to put anything but the roughest figure on this. It is clear that commercial aspects of IFFs are damaging Africa's development prospects and so must be addressed, in part through raising them to the level of a global responsibility and therefore one to be undertaken under UN control.

But the international community must never lose sight of the fact that a very large part of IFFs apparently derives from "ordinary" transnational crime, such as corruption and trafficking of drugs, minerals, other contraband and people – and that these must be tackled with just as much vigour as commercial IFFs. Ultimately, the only way to do this is through greater democracy and much better and more efficient governance.

References

Africanews (2020): "Angola charges Isabel dos Santos with fraud, embezzlement". At: https://www.africanews.com/2020/01/23/angola-formally-charges-isabel-dos-santos-with-fraud-embezzlement (accessed 12 May 2022).

APP, Africa Progress Panel (2013): "Africa progress report 2013 – Equity in extractives. Stewarding Africa's natural resources for all". At: https://reliefweb.int/report/world/africa-progress-report-2013-equity-extractives-stewarding-africa-s-natural-resources (accessed 12 May 2022).

ATAF, African Tax Administration Forum (2020): "African tax outlook. 2020 edition." At: https://events.ataftax.org/index.php?page=documents&func=view&document_id=121# (accessed 12 May 2022).

African Union Commission (2020): "African Union Commission set to launch a Multi-Donor Action against Illicit Financial Flows in Africa". At: https://au.int/en/pressreleases/20201201/african-union-commission-set-launch-multi-donor-action-against-illicit (accessed 12 May 2022).

Akiwumi, Paul (2020): "Curbing illicit financial flows to finance sustainable development in Africa". At: https://unctad.org/news/curbing-illicit-financial-flows-finance-sustainable-development-africa (accessed 12 May 2022).

Blore, Shawn/Hunter, Marcena (2020): "Dubai's problematic gold trade". In: Page, Matthew T./Vittori, Judi (eds.): Dubai's role in facilitating corruption and global illicit financial flows. Washington D.C.: Carnegie Endowment for International Peace, pg. 35–47.

CIP, Centro de Integridade Pública Moçambique/Chr. Michelsen Institute, Norway (2021): "Costs and Consequences of the Hidden Debt Scandal of Mozambique". At: https://www.cipmoz.org/wp-content/uploads/2021/05/Costs-and-consequences-of-the-Hidden-Debt.pdf (accessed 12 May 2022).

Corrick, Lee, technical adviser on international tax at the African Tax Administration Forum (AFAF) (22 September 2021): Email interview with author.

ESAAMLG, Eastern and Southern Africa Anti-Money Laundering Group (2021): "Anti-money laundering and counter-terrorism measures. Mozambique mutual evaluation report, June 2021". At: https://www.esaamlg.org/reports/MER%20of%20Mozambique-June%202021.pdf (accessed 12 May 2022).

Enough Project (n.d.): "Conflict Gold 101". At: https://enoughproject.org/files/ConflictGold101_ActivistBrief.pdf (accessed 12 May 2022).

European Commission (n.d.): "Conflict Minerals Regulation. The regulation explained". At: https://policy.trade.ec.europa.eu/development-and-sustainability/conflict-minerals-regulation/regulation-explained_en (accessed 12 May 2022).

FACTI Panel, High Level Panel on International Financial Accountability, Transparency and Integrity for Achieving the 2030 Agenda (2021): "Financial integrity for sustainable development". At: https://uploads-ssl.webflow.com/5e0bd9edab846816e263d633/602e91032a209d0601ed4a2c_FACTI_Panel_Report.pdf (accessed 13 May 2022).

FATF, Financial Action Task Force (2013): "Money laundering and terrorist financing vulnerabilities of legal professionals, June 2013". At: https://www.fatf-gafi.org/media/fatf/documents/reports/ML%20and%20TF%20vulnerabilities%20legal%20professionals.pdf (accessed 12 May 2022).

Guinea-Bissau analyst, anonymous (6 February 2021): Email exchange with author.

Hunter, Marcena (2018): "Measures that miss the mark. Capturing the proceeds of crime in illicit financial flow models". At: https://globalinitiative.net/wp-content/uploads/2018/06/TGIATOC-Illicit-Financial-Flows-report-1941-hi-res-2-1.pdf (accessed 12 May 2022).

Hunter, Marcena (2019): "Pulling at golden webs. Combating criminal consortia in the African artisanal and small-scale gold mining and trade sector". At: https://enactafrica.org/research/research-papers/pulling-at-golden-webs-combating-criminal-consortia-in-the-african-artisanal-and-small-scale-gold-mining-and-trade-sector (accessed 12 May 2022).

Hunter, Marcena (21 February 2021): Interview with author.

ICIJ, International Consortium of Investigative Journalists (19 January 2020): "How Africa's richest woman exploited family ties, shell companies and inside deals to build an empire". At: https://www.icij.org/investigations/luanda-leaks/how-africas-richest-woman-exploited-family-ties-shell-companies-and-inside-deals-to-build-an-empire/ (accessed 21 September 2021).

ICIJ, International Consortium of Investigative Journalists (17 March 2020): "Portuguese 'super judge' orders total seizure of dos Santos assets". At: https://www.icij.org/investigations/luanda-leaks/portuguese-super-judge-orders-total-seizure-of-dos-santos-assets/ (accessed 12 May 2022).

ICIJ, International Consortium of Investigative Journalists (7 April 2020): "Isabel dos Santos condemns 'abusive' seizure of $442m stake". At: https://www.icij.org/investigations/luanda-leaks/isabel-dos-santos-condemns-abusive-seizure-of-442m-stake/ (accessed 12 May 2022).

ICIJ, International Consortium of Investigative Journalists) (18 June 2020): "Isabel dos Santos blames asset freeze for Lisbon retreat and failure to pay staff". At: https://www.icij.org/investigations/luanda-leaks/isabel-dos-santos-blames-asset-freeze-for-lisbon-retreat-and-failure-to-pay-staff/ (accessed 12 May 2022).

ICIJ, International Consortium of Investigative Journalists (20 July 2020): "European banking regulator to probe Luanda Leaks' allegations". At: https://www.icij.org/investigations/luanda-leaks/european-banking-regulator-to-probe-luanda-leaks-allegations/ (accessed 12 May 2022).

ICIJ, International Consortium of Investigative Journalists (2 October 2020): "Portuguese regulator calls for criminal prosecution of auditors following Luanda Leaks". At: https://www.icij.org/investigations/luanda-leaks/portuguese-regulator-calls-for-criminal-prosecution-of-auditors-following-luanda-leaks/ (accessed 12 May 2022).

ICIJ, International Consortium of Investigative Journalists (7 December 2020): "After Luanda Leaks, a billionaire's empire falls, but her enablers carry on". At: https://www.icij.org/investigations/luanda-leaks/after-luanda-leaks-a-billionaires-empire-falls-but-her-enablers-carry-on/ (accessed 12 May 2022).

ICIJ, International Consortium of Investigative Journalists (3 September 2021): "German state-owned bank fined for Angolan loan exposed in Luanda Leaks". At: https://www.icij.org/investigations/luanda-leaks/german-state-owned-bank-fined-for-angolan-loan-exposed-in-luanda-leaks/ (accessed 12 May 2022).

ICIJ, International Consortium of Investigative Journalists (3 October 2021): "As Kenyan president mounted anti-corruption comeback, his family's secret fortune expanded offshore". At: https://www.icij.org/investigations/pandora-papers/kenya-uhuru-kenyatta-family-offshore-wealth/ (accessed 12 May 2022).

IMF, International Monetary Fund (1998) "Money laundering. The importance of international countermeasures. At: http://www.imf.org/external/np/speeches/1998/021098.htm (accessed 12 May 2022).

IMF Data (n.d.): "Government Finance Statistics". At: https://data.imf.org/?sk=A0867067-D23C-4EBC-AD23-D3B015045405 (accessed 29 May 2022).

Kroll (2017): "Independent audit related to loans contracted by ProIndicus S.A., EMATUM S.A. and Mozambique Asset Management S.A. Prepared for The Office of the Public Prosecutor of the Republic of Mozambique". At: https://reflekt.ch/wp-content/uploads/2019/09/Kroll-Report-Juni-2017-redacted.pdf (accessed 12 May 2022).

Maira, Martini (2017): "Doors wide open. Corruption and real estate in four key markets". At: https://images.transparencycdn.org/images/2017_DoorsWideOpen_EN.pdf (accessed 12 May 2022).

Mbeki, Thabo/Lopes, Carlos/Apata, Olusegun/Baker, Raymond/ElBakri, Zeinab Bashir et al. (2015): Track it! Stop it! Get it! Illicit Financial Flows. Addis Ababa: United Nations Economic Commission for Africa.

OECD, Organisation for Economic Co-operation and Development (n.d.-a): "BEPS, Inclusive Framework on Base Erosion and Profit Shifting". At: https://www.oecd.org/tax/beps/ (accessed 12 May 2022).

OECD, Organisation for Economic Co-operation and Development (n.d.-b): "Global Forum on Transparency and Exchange of Information for Tax Purposes". At: https://www.oecd.org/tax/transparency/ (accessed 12 May 2022).

OECD, Organisation for Economic Co-operation and Development (2018): "Illicit financial flows. The economy of illicit trade in West Africa". At: https://www.oecd.org/dac/illicit-financial-flows-9789264268418-en.htm (accessed 12 May 2022).

OECD, Organisation for Economic Co-operation and Development (2020): OECD/G20 Inclusive Framework on BEPS. Progress report July 2019 – July 2020". At: https://www.oecd.org/tax/beps/oecd-g20-inclusive-framework-on-beps-progress-report-july-2019-july-2020.pdf (accessed 13 May 2022).

OECD, Organisation for Economic Co-operation and Development (2021): "Revenue Statistics in Africa 2021". At: https://www.oecd.org/tax/tax-policy/brochure-revenue-statistics-africa.pdf (accessed 12 May 2022).

Reuters (2021): "G20 leaders endorse global minimum corporate tax deal for 2023 start". At: https://www.reuters.com/business/g20-leaders-endorse-global-minimum-corporate-tax-deal-2023-start-2021-10-30/ (accessed 13 May 2022).

Shaw, Mark (2015): "Drug trafficking in Guinea-Bissau, 1998–2014. The evolution of an elite protection network". In: The Journal of Modern African Studies, 53, 3, pp. 339–364.

SDSN, Sustainable Development Solutions Network (n.d.): "Indicators and a Monitoring Framework. Launching a data revolution for the sustainable Development Goals". At https://indicators.report/targets/16-4/ (accessed 13 May 2022).

Tax Justice Network Africa (2020): "The OECD inclusive framework is not that inclusive". At: https://taxjusticeafrica.net/wp-content/uploads/2020/02/Press-release-OECD-tax-inclusive-framework-not-that-inclusive-9.pdf (accessed 13 May 2022).

tralac, Trade Law Centre NPC (2017): "Chamber of Mines releases final independent report on trade misinvoicing". At: https://www.tralac.org/news/article/12033-chamber-of-mines-releases-final-independent-report-on-trade-misinvoicing.html (accessed 12 May 2022).

Transparency International (2019): "Three ways to stop money laundering through real estate". At: https://www.transparency.org/en/news/three-ways-to-stop-money-laundering-through-real-estate (accessed 13 May 2022).

UN, United Nations (2021): "Letter dated 10 June 2021 from the Group of Experts on the Democratic Republic of the Congo addressed to the President of the Security Council". At: https://www.ecoi.net/en/file/local/2053905/S_2021_560_E.pdf (accessed 13 May 2022).

UNCTAD, United Nations Conference on Trade and Development (2016a): "Trade misinvoicing in primary commodities in developing countries. The cases of Chile, Côte d'Ivoire, Nigeria, South Africa and Zambia. Advanced copy July 2016". At: https://www.tralac.org/images/docs/10103/trade-misinvoicing-in-primary-commodities-in-developing-countries-unctad-july-2016.pdf (accessed 13 May 2022).

UNCTAD, United Nations Conference on Trade and Development (2016b): "Trade misinvoicing in primary commodities in developing countries. The cases of Chile, Côte d'Ivoire, Nigeria, South Africa and Zambia (date of issuance: 23 December 2016)". At: https://unctad.org/system/files/official-document/suc2016d2_en.pdf (accessed 13 May 2022).

UNCTAD, United Nations Conference on Trade and Development (2020): "Tackling illicit financial flows for sustainable development in Africa". At: https://unctad.org/system/files/official-document/aldcafrica2020_en.pdf (accessed 13 May 2022).

UNODC, United Nations Office on Drugs and Crime (2011): "Estimating illicit financial flows resulting from drug trafficking and other transnational organized crimes. Research report". At: https://www.unodc.org/documents/data-and-analysis/Studies/Illicit_financial_flows_2011_web.pdf (accessed 13 May 2022).

UNODC, United Nations Office on Drugs and Crime (n.d.): "Guinea Bissau" At: https://www.unodc.org/westandcentralafrica/en/guinea-bissau.html (accessed 13 May 2022).

US State Department, United States Department of State Bureau of International Narcotics and Law Enforcement Affairs (2018): "International Narcotics Control Strategy Report Volume II. Money laundering. March 2018". At: https://www.state.gov/wp-content/uploads/2019/04/2018-INCSR-Vol.-II.pdf (accessed 13 May 2022).

U.S. Department of the Treasury (2017): "United States sanctions human rights abusers and corrupt actors across the globe". At: https://home.treasury.gov/news/press-releases/sm0243 (accessed 13 May 2022).

World Bank (n.d.): "Net ODA Received (% of central government expense)". At: https://data.worldbank.org/indicator/DT.ODA.ODAT.XP.ZS?view=map (accessed 28 September 2021).

WCO, World Customs Organization (2018): "Illicit financial flows via trade mis-invoicing. Study report 2018". At: http://www.wcoomd.org/-/media/wco/public/global/pdf/media/newsroom/reports/2018/wco-study-report-on-iffs_tm.pdf?la=en (accessed 13 May 2022).

Trade in substandard and falsified medicines

Nhomsai Hagen, Cathrin Hauk and Lutz Heide

Introduction

The spread of substandard and falsified (SF) medicines is one of the most urgent health challenges of our time. In 2017, the World Health Organization (WHO) estimated that 1 in 10 medicines in low- and middle-income countries (LMICs) is substandard or falsified. Constrained access to medicines through the legal supply chain, low standards of governance with regard to medicine regulation and weak technical capacities e.g. in national medicine quality control laboratories are related to a high prevalence of SF medicines (Fig. 1) (WHO 2017a).

Figure 1: Factors that contribute to the emergence of substandard and falsified medical products. Modified from: WHO (2017a).

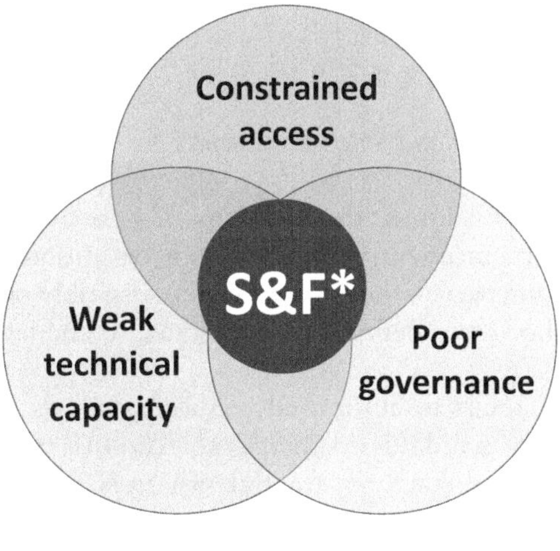

About one third of the world's population lacks access to medicines, vaccines and other essential health products (WHO 2020a). To achieve universal health coverage, which is part of Sustainable Development Goal

3 of the United Nations (UN), equitable access to safe, effective, quality and affordable essential medicines and vaccines (target 3.8) is of key importance. SF medicines pose a serious threat not only to public health but also to family and government budgets by prolonging or even causing illness and hospitalisation, in addition to loss of wages. They undermine trust in health services and contribute to the emergence of drug-resistant pathogens. The growing complexity of supply chains in our globalised world and the increasing popularity of e-commerce provide numerous entry points for illegal medical products. Even trained professionals often have difficulties to detect SF medicines, and if detected these products are often not reported (WHO 2017a).

According to the International Criminal Police Organization (INTERPOL), the trade in falsified medicines may have become more attractive to organised criminal networks than trafficking in illegal drugs due to high profits, a very low risk of detection and prosecution as well as penalties that are small compared to the penalties for illegal drug trafficking (INTERPOL 2014). The profits made with falsified medical products may also become a resource to fund other types of illegal activities (INTERPOL 2014; WHO 2017a). The outbreak of the COVID-19 pandemic led to a worldwide increase of SF medical products as criminals took advantage of the high demand for personal protection and hygiene products, medicines and vaccines (INTERPOL 2020a).

Definition of substandard and falsified medicines

To understand and address the problem of substandard and falsified medicines, a common understanding of their definitions is crucial. After many years of controversy, the World Health Assembly of 2017 finally introduced an authoritative definition of substandard and falsified medicines (WHO 2017b).

"Substandard" refers to authorised medical products that fail to meet either their quality standards or their specifications, or both. "Falsified" medical products deliberately or fraudulently misrepresent their identity, composition or source. These definitions are mutually exclusive, and samples can either be classified as substandard or as falsified (WHO 2017b; UNODC 2019).

"Substandard" medicines may result from unintentional shortcomings in the manufacturing of the products and/or from deterioration occurring after manufacturing. Medicines that are sensitive to high temperatures and humidity can easily become "substandard" e.g. if subjected to poor transport and/or poor storage conditions. However, the stability of medicines depends not only on storage conditions but also on the formulation of the products, e.g. on the choice of excipients and stabilising agents. Therefore, the manufacturing procedures as well as the packaging play a crucial role for the stability of medicines.

A product is considered not as "substandard" but as "falsified" if an authorised manufacturer deliberately fails to meet the quality standards or specifications due to misrepresentation of identity, composition or source (WHO 2017b). Obviously, however, it is not always possible to obtain information on the intention of the manufacturer, and chemical analysis for the identity and quantity of the active pharmaceutical ingredient (API), as well as additional pharmacopeial analyses like dissolution testing, are not sufficient to unequivocally classify a medical product as substandard or as falsified. Packaging inspection and requests to the manufacturers and distributors for authentication of the products in question can be helpful to obtain additional information (Hauk, Hagen and Heide 2021).

The term "counterfeit" has been used as a synonym for falsified medical products, or even for "poor-quality" medical products in general. However, the term "counterfeit" should only be used for products that infringe on registered trademarks or intellectual property rights, and this term is no longer used in the WHO definitions. WHO tries to focus on public health problems and not on the protection of trademarks and intellectual property rights. Therefore, the terms "trademark counterfeit goods" and "pirated copyright goods" are defined under the Agreement on Trade-Related Aspects of Intellectual Property Rights (TRIPS) (WHO 2017b).

Previously, the United Nations Office on Drugs and Crime (UNODC) used the terms "fraudulent medicines" and "falsified medicines" interchangeably (UNODC 2011). However, in its 2019 guide on "Combating falsified medical product-related crime", UNODC now also adopted the recent WHO terminology and uses the term "falsified medical products" (UNODC 2019).

Concerning the definition of "substandard" medicines, it should be noted that the tolerance limits for acceptable deviations, e.g. of the actual content of the API from the declared content, may vary between different pharmacopoeias, e.g. the International Pharmacopoeia, the United States Pharmacopeia or the British Pharmacopoeia. Therefore, a given product may be "in specification" under the criteria of one pharmacopoeia, and "out of specification" under the criteria of another one. This may quite strongly influence the prevalence rates of "substandard" medicines reported in different medicine quality studies, even more so as some studies use arbitrary rather than pharmacopeial tolerance limits (WHO 2017c; Hauk, Hagen and Heide 2021).

Prevalence of substandard and falsified medicines

From a review of one hundred scientific studies published between 2007 and 2016 and selected for their scientific quality by an Expert Working Group, WHO estimated that around 10.5 % of the medicines in LMICs are substandard or falsified (WHO 2017c). However, the reported prevalence data vary strongly between different studies, and reliable estimates on the prevalence for different regions, for different parts of the supply chain and for different types of medicine are still urgently needed. Systematic reviews of medicine quality studies by Ozawa et al. (2018), Almuzaini, Choonara, and Sammons (2013) and McManus and Naughton (2020) reported prevalences of SF medicines between 13.6 % and 28.5 % in LMICs. Notably, none of these studies was able to differentiate substandard medicines from falsified medicines, due to the heterogeneity of methodologies and definitions used in the reviewed studies. Guidelines and checklists for the conduct of medicine quality studies have been published and may help to reduce the heterogeneity of methodologies in future (Hauk, Hagen and Heide 2021; WHO 2016; Newton et al. 2009).

To gather more information on the magnitude of the problem, WHO launched a Global Surveillance and Monitoring Systems (GSMS) Portal (WHO 2021d). National medicines regulatory authorities (NMRAs) can report suspect medical products to this portal and check if similar products have been found elsewhere. 1,500 reports of SF medical products were submitted to WHO between 2013 and 2017. Antimalarials and antibiotics seem to be the most affected therapeutic classes, according to the number of reports (19.6 % and 16.9 % of the overall reports, respectively) and the prevalence rates in published studies. Most of the reports to the GSMS portal come from the WHO African Region (42 %). However, this does not mean that other regions and therapeutic classes are not affected. The GSMS database shows that all types of medical products, from cancer medicines to contraceptives and painkillers, including branded as well as generic products, expensive as well as cheap medicines, and all regions of the world are affected by the problem of SF medicines (WHO 2017a). Reports on negative health impacts caused by falsified medicines also come from high-income countries and concern falsified sedatives, hypnotics, narcotics and medicines for sexual dysfunction (Rahman et al. 2018). The rising number of substandard and falsified medical products in times of the

COVID-19 pandemic impressively shows how constrained access through the legal supply chain is linked to an increase in the number of SF products (Van Assche, Caillet and Newton 2021a).

Impact of substandard and falsified medicines

SF medicines have a multidimensional impact on public health as well as severe economic and socioeconomic consequences, and they thereby impede the achievement of the Sustainable Development Goals. Death by intoxication or other serious health consequences resulting from SF medicines that contain the wrong API or toxic chemicals are among the most serious health impacts on the individual patient. Much more frequently, SF medicines which lack the correct API, or contain an insufficient amount of the API, lead to treatment failures resulting in prolonged morbidity, disease progression and even death (WHO 2017c). Only few reports of SF medicines have attracted worldwide attention, such as the death of children from acute kidney failure due to toxic diethylene glycol in teething syrup in Nigeria (Akuse et al. 2012) or the hospitalisation of 930 patients (11 of whom died, including 5 children under five years of age) due to an intentional mislabelling of haloperidol tablets as diazepam tablets in the Democratic Republic of Congo (Peyraud et al. 2017). WHO estimated that every year treatment failures resulting from SF medicines lead to the death of 72,000 to 169,000 children with pneumonia worldwide and to the death of 31,000 to 116,000 patients from malaria in Sub-Saharan Africa alone (WHO 2017c). Treatment with SF antimicrobials may also lead to an increase of antimicrobial resistances. For example, the use of SF antimalarials containing only subtherapeutic doses of the active ingredients was associated with increases in the resistance to antimalarials in several studies (WHO 2017c). Furthermore, founded or unfounded reports about the occurrence of SF medicines can lead to mistrust of patients towards medications and the health system in general, resulting in underutilisation of health facilities, non-adherence to prescribed treatments and vaccine hesitancy.

Spending money on ineffective or harmful medicine is a waste of economic resources. SF medicines also lead to additional costs in the long term. Treatment of prolonged illness, adverse reactions, drug-resistant infections and infections resulting from failed prophylaxis strain the limited budget of health systems and health insurance companies. Especially in LMICs, where the share of „out-of-pocket" payments of the total current health expenditures is still high (37 %, compared to 14 % in high-income countries), this can lead to financial hardship for individuals and their families (WHO 2017c). Additional health interventions required due to treatment failure of SF antimalarials are estimated to cost between US$12.1 million and US$44.7 million annually (WHO 2017c). Lost productivity and income, lack of social mobility and increased poverty are among the socioeconomic impacts of SF medicines.

For legitimate manufacturers, counterfeit and falsified medicines mean lost sales and costs for brand protection and may lead to a loss of reputation. In the European Union, this results in an estimated €10 billion of lost sales annually (OECD and EUIPO 2020; EUIPO 2020).

Licit and illicit flows through complex supply chains

In 2020, two-thirds of the APIs used to manufacture generic medicines for the European market were produced in Asia (Progenerika 2020). APIs, excipients and packaging material are often produced in different countries and shipped to the place where the finished pharmaceutical product is produced, which may then be packaged in yet another country. Also, the subsequent supply chains are highly complex, and the medicines are often traded through several distributors situated in different continents and countries before they reach the health facility and patient (Hauk, Hagen and Heide 2021). Long and complicated routes and repeated repackaging by distributors and wholesalers make it easy for criminals to introduce substandard or falsified products into the legal supply chain. Especially wholesalers represent an entry point for falsifications, as licit and illicit flows can easily mix here, with or without intention by the wholesaler. This is exemplified by the Avastin® case described below. As a result, substandard and falsified medicines can be found in the legal supply chain, although their prevalence is higher on the black market (Buckley and Gostin 2013; Schäfermann et al. 2020).

Today, originator medicines (i.e. innovator products, usually protected by patents) represent only a minor part of the medications used, while the vast majority of patients is treated with generic medicines. In the US, only one out of ten prescriptions filled are for originator medicines, the rest are generics (FDA 2021). Many LMICs rely on imports of medical products. In some African countries, these account for more than 80 % of the medicines available in the country, and most of these are generics (Byaruhanga 2020). This is exemplified by a study on substandard and falsified medicines in Cameroon and the Democratic Republic of Congo: of the 502 samples investigated, 71 % were manufactured in Asia (mostly in India and China) and less than 3 % in the African country where the sample was collected. Only 6 % were originator medicines (Schäfermann et al. 2020).

Not only most of the legitimate medical products are manufactured in India and China, but also drug precursors and falsified products have been reported to come from these countries (UNODC 2010; INCB 2018). A total of 363 production places for falsified medicines were shut down by the Chinese government in 2008 (People's Daily Online 2009). Illegal distributors in Africa are often directly connected with criminal manufacturers in India or China. In these cases, illegal products, often containerised and falsely declared to avoid inspections, are shipped out through regular freight companies, but also through other distribution channels by specialised couriers (UNODC 2010).

Especially in LMICs, the supply chain is extremely fragmented and includes public, private and NGO distribution systems and specific donor-funded medicine procurement for HIV/AIDS, malaria, tuberculosis, vaccines and reproductive health programmes. These multiple parallel distribution systems and the lack of national coordination mechanisms make it difficult to control and plan procurement and distribution of medicines within a country (Yadav, Tata and Babaley 2011).

Trafficking of substandard and falsified medicines by informal networks, organised crime groups and terrorist organisations

As noticed by the UN Commission on Crime Prevention and Criminal Justice (CCPCJ), organised criminal groups (OCGs) are involved in all aspects of trafficking in SF medicines (UNODC 2011). But informal networks also play an important role, often centering around business partners, families or friends (Hall, Koenraadt and Antonopoulos 2017). According to INTERPOL, the size of the OCGs involved ranges from small clusters of three to ten persons up to larger groups that are well-established, hierarchical and sophisticated, often international (INTERPOL 2014). It is assumed that these OCGs as well as the informal networks use the same routes and techniques as they use for trafficking other illicit goods. They often operate in both licit and illicit circles, both globally and locally, and both online and offline. Especially the use of illicit online pharmacies has increased in recent years (INTERPOL 2021b, 2014). On the other hand, the use of legitimate companies that serve as a shield for criminal activities and allow OCGs and informal networks to expand their network and launder profits is also common (OECD and EUIPO 2020; INTERPOL 2014). Often, these OCGs and informal networks use new technologies and platforms such as the darknet for trafficking SF medicines and to avoid getting caught by law enforcement authorities (Hall, Koenraadt and Antonopoulos 2017; Europol 2021). In a pan-European operation supported by Europol in October 2019, six OCGs were disrupted and 48 suspects were arrested. During the operation, 34.5 million units of medicines and doping products worth €2.6 million were seized (Europol 2020).

Terrorist groups are also linked to trafficking SF medicines. One example is the Irish Republican Army (IRA), who falsified veterinary medicines (Ivomec® from Merck) to finance their activities in the 1990s. The falsified medicines were produced by IRA members in the US. They contained no API and were distributed through a subsidiary of a large distributor. The scam was discovered by Merck, who sued the distributor and the individuals involved (UNIFAB 2016; IRACM and Przyswa 2013).

The Lebanese Hezbollah is also frequently linked to the trade with SF medicines. In 2006, an international network with activities in Lebanon, Canada, China, Brazil, Paraguay and the US was busted by the US Terrorism Joint Force. The network had been involved in the trade of SF medicines for sexual disorders. According to documents found, some of the profits were used to fund Hezbollah (IRACM and Przyswa 2013).

Non-medical use of pharmaceuticals: the example of tramadol and Captagon® (fenetylline)

The non-medical (mis-)use of the painkiller tramadol has led to a veritable "tramadol crisis" in West Africa and the Middle East (Klein 2019; UNODC 2021a). The synthetic opioid tramadol is misused for its calming and euphoric effects and to overcome tiredness. With prolonged use, it may cause addiction, serious health damage and even death (UNODC 2021a). In countries influenced by Islamic laws and norms, alcohol and illegal drugs are often considered inacceptable, and consumption of substances with a medical appearance, such as tramadol, may offer a socially acceptable alternative (BBC 2018). Reportedly, in Egypt around 20 % of the male university students use tramadol and 60 % of these suffer from drug-related problems (Bassiony et al. 2018).

Tramadol is not under international control and therefore relatively easily available even in countries where it is on national control lists, such as Niger and Nigeria, as neighbouring states with lower levels of regulation can be used as entry points for illegal imports (UNODC 2021a). Internationally controlled substances are listed in the schedules annexed to the three UN Conventions of 1961, 1971 and 1988 on narcotic drugs and psychotropic substances and need an authorisation of the importing state to enter the country (UNODC 2021b). Governments have to estimate the quantities required for legitimate purposes beforehand to restrict the use and trade in such substances and to ensure adequate supply for medical and scientific purposes (UNODC 2021a; INCB and WHO 2012). The main source of misused tramadol tablets – often higher dosed than products which are legally available – is the illicit pharmaceutical market that is supplied by criminal networks. However, the legal and illegal sectors overlap at many points of the supply chain, and there are indications that large amounts of tramadol which had been legally produced and exported were diverted into illicit channels and smuggled across countries (UNODC 2021a). This problem afflicts many countries in Africa and the Middle East (INCB 2019). Most of the illicit tramadol is transported from South Asia via maritime routes to West African ports. For example, 87 % of the tramadol seized in Ghana in 2017 originated in India (UNODC 2021a). Both hierarchical and loose networks are involved in the trade (UNODC 2021a). According to INTERPOL, terrorist groups are also involved and may use this as a source of finance (INTERPOL 2020c).

In 2017, more than 92 tons of tramadol were seized in Nigeria (UNODC 2021a). To combat the illicit trafficking, India changed its legislation on tramadol in April 2018, placing the export of this substance under the regulations for controlled drugs. Indeed, the amount of tramadol seized in Nigeria decreased to about 22 tons in 2018, and its price on the informal market increased, demonstrating the effectiveness of India's intervention (UNODC 2021a). However, putting tramadol under international control, as requested e.g. by the Egyptian government, may impair the availability, accessibility and affordability of this essential analgesic for medical purposes, especially in LMICs and in humanitarian relief efforts (Klein 2019). Moreover, criminal networks may replace tramadol with other opioids, such as tapentadol, which is already being used by opioid addicts in India and West Africa (UNODC 2021a; Basu et al. 2020).

A connection between terrorist groups in the Middle East, terrorist attacks in Europe and the trade of the medical product Captagon® was suggested by several lay media reports. However, evidence is limited and further investigations, in particular forensic analysis, are necessary. In the 1960s, Captagon® with fenetylline, an amphetamine derivative, as the API was used e.g. for attention deficit disorder, mainly in Europe and the Middle East. After its declaration as a psychotropic substance by the UN Commission on Narcotic Drugs in 1986, the production and use of Captagon® was prohibited in most countries and legal manufacturing stopped worldwide in 2009. It is assumed that until the end of the 1990s genuine Captagon® tablets were diverted from European stocks for illicit sale, mainly in the Middle East and in some countries bordering the European Union. Subsequently, tablets bearing the distinctive Captagon® logo of two half-circles but containing different types and quantities of amphetamine derivatives and referred to as "Captagon", which were reportedly commonly used as a stimulant in these countries, emerged amongst the seizures. Although evidence is sparse, it is assumed that most of this falsified "Captagon" was illicitly produced in the Balkan region, with a shift to Middle Eastern production beginning in the mid-2000s (EMCDDA 2018).

Weak regulation favours trafficking of substandard and falsified medicines

Regulatory controls are strong, with corresponding high investment of resources, at the early stages of the medicine supply chain, which includes e.g. the regulation of clinical studies and the licencing of pharmaceutical products. Conversely, at the end of the supply chain, when the medicine reaches the patient, these controls are much weaker, and the resources invested are much more limited. The supply chain vulnerability increases thereby, and this is exacerbated by the increasing number of transactions and stakeholders involved (Fig. 2) (WHO 2017a).

Figure 2: Correlation between regulatory controls and supply chain vulnerability at different points of the supply chain. Modified from: WHO (2017a).

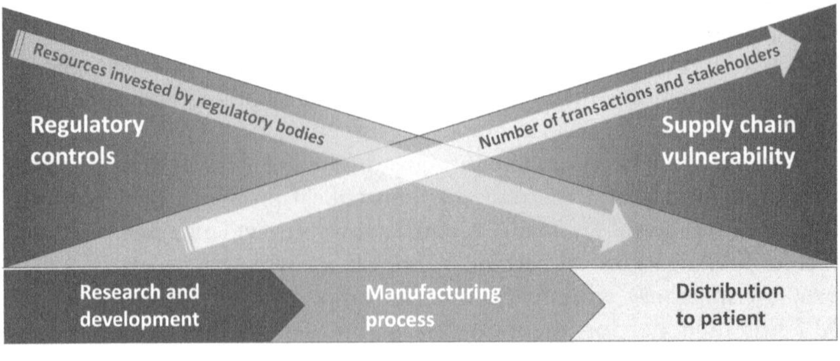

The quality of medical products made for export is often regulated much more poorly than that of those which are licensed for domestic marketing (Bate et al. 2014). The consequences of this poor regulation are aggravated by the fact that in many LMICs the NMRAs are weak and lack the capacity to thoroughly assess the quality of imported medicines before registration. Sometimes, it is even difficult to ensure that all imported medicines are indeed licensed. According to a WHO estimate, 74 % of the regulatory authorities of the 194 member states were classified as not "stable and well-functioning" in 2019 (WHO 2021a). Poor ethical practice due to corruption is a further problem. Once substandard or falsified medicines have entered the country, weak pharmacovigilance and post-marketing surveillance systems allow them to remain undetected and to cause harm to patients. Weak NMRAs, poor health supply chain systems and high prices of medicines from legal sources also foster flourishing black markets in LMICs: unavailability of essential medicines in the hospitals and health centers, as well as lack of appropriate health insurance, drive patients to black markets that are often well stocked and less expensive. On the black markets, however, substandard and falsified medicines are highly prevalent, and correct storage conditions are often not maintained, increasing the likelihood of product degradation (WHO 2017a).

High income countries, for example in Europe, are also affected by the problem of SF medicines, especially due to the popularity of e-commerce and online pharmacies. Medicines from unauthorised sources can easily enter this market, as the access barriers are low while the business model appears highly profitable (WHO 2017a; Dellasega and Vorrath 2020). The magnitude of this rapidly growing market for SF medicines is adumbrated by the amounts of seizures and arrests of INTERPOL's latest Operation Pangea (INTERPOL 2021b).

In Europe, the (legal) practice of parallel trading also represents a possible entry point for substandard or falsified medicines. Parallel trading takes advantage of price differences between markets in different countries, as well as differences in health care financing regimes and fluctuations of exchange rates: goods are bought in lower-priced markets, to be repackaged for resale in higher-priced markets. Often several distributors and traders are involved, increasing the opportunities for the entry of falsified products.

Examples of substandard and falsified medicines detected in high-income and in low- and middle-income countries

The following examples may illustrate how the complex global supply chains facilitate the entry of SF medicines and how the Global North is connected with the Global South in regard to this problem. They also stress the importance of reporting and communication between stakeholders in different world regions, e.g. via WHO, in order to detect SF medicines.

Falsified Avastin® in the United States: In 2012, falsified vials labeled as Avastin® (bevacizumab), a cancer drug costing about US$2,400 per vial, reached patients in the United States. They contained no API. At least 19 medical doctors had bought vials of this preparation from a distributor in Montana (US) under its Turkish brand name Altuzan®, at a price about US$500 lower than the US market price at that time. The US distributor had bought the medicine via the internet-based pharmacy of a wholesaler in the United Kingdom. This UK-based wholesaler had purchased the vials from a Danish company, which in turn had received them from a Swiss company who in turn had bought them from an Egyptian businessman. The Egyptian businessman had obtained the medicine from a Syrian dealer, apparently believing that it was the genuine product manufactured in Turkey (Keteyian 2012; WHO 2017a). This example shows the complexity of international supply chains, which can make it very difficult to trace the origin of a given medicine.

Falsified Herceptin® in Germany: In 2014, falsified Herceptin® (trastuzumab), an antibody against different types of cancer, was found in Germany (Streit 2017). The medicine showed different batch numbers on the primary and the secondary packaging, and some vials contained a liquid instead of a lyophilised powder. At least one vial contained the antibiotic ceftriaxone instead of trastuzumab (Streit 2017; Roche Pharma AG 2014). Apparently, the medicine had been stolen in Italy and had entered the legal supply chain via parallel trading. It was found not only in Germany but also in Finland, Austria, Sweden and the UK. The German parallel trader had obtained the medicine from two British distributors, who were supplied by an Italian distributor, who, however, had never been supplied by the manufacturing company, Roche. It turned out that further high-value medicines had also been stolen from hospitals in Italy, or from trucks delivering to these hospitals, and had then entered the legal supply chain in Germany and other European countries. It was suspected that Italian and East European mafia groups might be behind the thefts (Dugato, Riccardi and Polizzotti 2014).

Levomethorphan-containing cough syrups in Pakistan and Paraguay: In early 2012, 60 adults in two cities in Pakistan died (WHO 2013a, 2013b). As drug addicts, they had consumed large quantities of cough syrups. Investigations revealed that the two local manufacturers of these syrups had recently changed the source of the API, dextromethorphan, to a cheaper supplier from India. It was discovered that this material also contained the enantiomer of dextromethorphan, levomethorphan, which is a potent opioid analgesic, five times stronger than morphine (Wainer 1996). Few laboratories have reference samples of this strictly controlled drug substance, and it is difficult to distinguish it in chemical analysis from the cough suppressant dextromethorphan. In a separate event in September 2013, 44 children were admitted to a hospital in Paraguay after being treated for influenza-like symptoms with a cough syrup (WHO 2013b). An alert to the national authorities and to WHO allowed the similarity to the case in Pakistan to be recognised, and Paraguayan investigators found import records for the same dextromethorphan batch from India which had been supplied to the two manufacturers in Pakistan. The affected batches had been exported to several countries in Europe, North Africa, the Middle East and Latin America. In both Colombia and Peru, manufacturers had already used the contaminated batches to produce cough syrup fortunately, the products were recalled and never reached the patients in these countries (WHO 2017a).

Substandard misoprostol tablets in Malawi: In 2017, extremely substandard misoprostol tablets were found in the legal supply chain in Malawi (Hagen, Khuluza and Heide 2020). The tablets contained only 13 % of the declared content of misoprostol. Misoprostol is very instable, especially in humid conditions. Appropriate primary packaging such as double-sided aluminium blisters is therefore important to protect the misoprostol tablets from degradation (Hall and Tagontong 2016). In the substandard product, however, the tablets were only packed in plastic-aluminium blisters, which is insufficient to protect misoprostol from humidity. Chemical analysis revealed high amounts of the typical degradation products of misoprostol. Malawian authorities and WHO were informed about these findings, which led to a nationwide recall of the substandard product (Hagen, Khuluza and Heide 2020). The product had been distributed by a British distributor. Notably, this distributor was located at the same address and was apparently managed by the same family as a distributor company who had been reported to distribute substandard propofol, an anaesthetic, to the government of Zambia (Mumphansha et al. 2017). Through WHO, the British regulatory agency (MHRA) was informed. It initiated an investigation, and both distributor companies went into voluntary liquidation shortly thereafter (Hagen, Khuluza and Heide 2020). There is no information about any subsequent legal proceedings against the responsible persons. However, according to the UK company register Companies House, the same owner family still appears to run several pharmaceutical wholesale companies (Companies House 2021).

Substandard and falsified medicines and the COVID-19 pandemic

As a consequence of the COVID-19 pandemic, the supply chains for both raw materials and finished pharmaceutical products were frequently disrupted. For example, since the beginning of the COVID-19 pandemic, there was a global-level shortage of over 20 medicines, including four controlled substances according to WHO. In a joint statement, the International Narcotics Control Board (INCB), UNODC and WHO (2021) therefore called for facilitated access to (controlled) medicines in emergencies, such as climate-related disasters and the current COVID-19 pandemic. Supply bottlenecks in legal markets, the increasing demand for certain medical goods and suspended in-person inspections of pharmaceutical facilities by regulatory bodies due to COVID-19 are factors that facilitate the emergence of substandard and falsified medicines (Newton et al. 2020; Dellasega and Vorrath 2020). The COVID-19 pandemic provides examples of how quickly criminal manufacturers and traffickers of falsified medicines react to an increased demand for certain medicines. From February 2020, reports about a possible effectiveness of chloroquine and hydroxychloroquine against COVID-19 received massive media attention worldwide, and the demand for these two medicines skyrocketed (Newton et al. 2020). Only a few weeks later, falsified chloroquine tablets were detected in pharmacies and at informal vendors in Cameroon and the Democratic Republic of Congo (Fig. 3) (Gnegel et al. 2020; WHO 2020c). They contained little or no chloroquine. However, some of them contained small amounts of paracetamol and/or of the bitter-tasting antibiotic metronidazole, possibly to mimic the bitter taste of chloroquine. The labelling of the falsified samples contained mistakes and spelling errors – an indication that they were produced by criminals and not by established manufacturers. The dosage of metronidazole was subtherapeutic, which may lead to the emergence of antimicrobial resistance. These findings were amongst 14 reports of confirmed falsified chloroquine products from five different countries in Africa and Europe (WHO 2020c).

Figure 3: Falsified chloroquine tablets collected early in the COVID-19 pandemic in Cameroon and the Democratic Republic of Congo. The labels contain spelling errors (marked here with arrows), and the tablets of sample (A) are very poorly manufactured (Photo: Gesa Gnegel, Tübingen University, 2020).

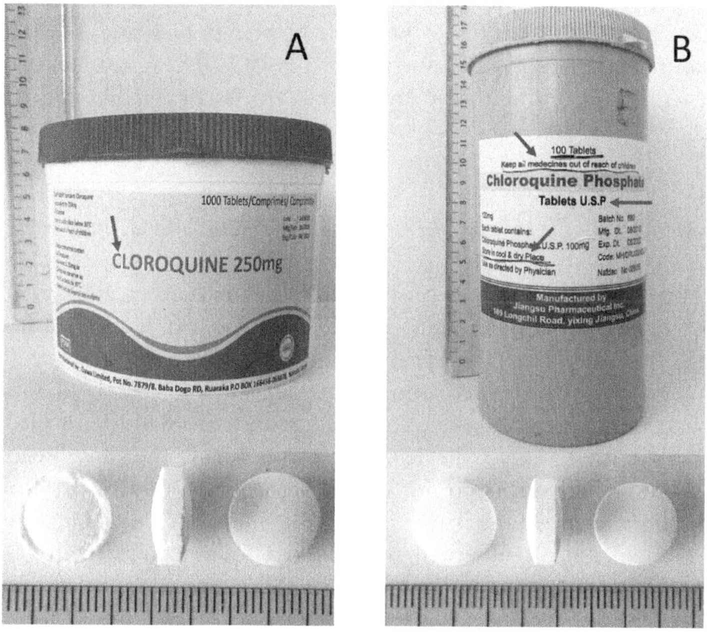

In March 2020, WHO published an alert about "Falsified medical products, including in vitro diagnostics, that claim to prevent, detect, treat or cure COVID-19" (WHO 2020b). In December 2020, INTERPOL issued an Orange Notice to warn about organised crime networks targeting COVID-19 vaccines (INTERPOL 2020b). Just a few weeks later, around 2,400 doses of fake COVID-19 vaccines were found in South Africa, as well as a large number of fake masks, leading to four arrests (INTERPOL 2021a). Also, in China, more than 3,000 doses of fake COVID-19 vaccines were seized, and 80 suspects were arrested (INTERPOL 2021a).

With the annual Operation Pangea, INTERPOL targets the illegal sale of medicines. In the 2020 Operation Pangea XIII, INTERPOL reported a 100 per cent increase in seizures of unauthorised chloroquine compared to the previous year (INTERPOL 2020a). The 2021 Operation Pangea XIV led to 277 arrests and seizures of potentially dangerous pharmaceuticals worth US$23 million. Additionally, 113,020 web links of fake online pharmacies and marketplaces were closed down or removed – the highest number so far since the first Operation Pangea in 2008. More than half of all medical devices seized were fake and unauthorised COVID-19 testing kits (INTERPOL 2021b).

The Medicine Quality Research Group at Oxford University, UK, monitors all reports in the public domain on substandard and falsified medical products related to COVID-19. Between 12 March 2020 and 31 May 2021, they found 123 reports of diverted or SF COVID-19 vaccines from 35 countries and/or online in the lay press (Van Assche, Caillet and Newton 2021b).

Recommendations for tackling the trade in substandard and falsified medicines

As summarised in the report on the WHO Global Surveillance and Monitoring System, the key elements in addressing the problem of substandard and falsified medicines are prevention, detection and response (WHO 2017a). To prevent SF medicines from entering the supply chains, it is crucial to improve availability, accessibility and affordability of medicines of good quality through the legal supply chain. If this is achieved, the demand for medicines from outside the legal supply chain will diminish, and the trade with SF medicines will become less attractive. Quality assurance in medicine procurement must be strengthened, following e.g. the "WHO quality assurance policy for the procurement of essential medicines and other health products" (WHO 2021e). The WHO Prequalification of Medicines Programme is a further very important contribution to this goal (WHO 2021c).

Track-and-trace systems such as the securPharm system, which commenced operation in Germany in 2019 in accordance with the EU Directive for the prevention of the entry into the legal supply chain of falsified medicinal products (Bergen and Hoferichter 2017), are very effective but costly. (Mobile) authentication applications are another, more affordable option, such as the Mobile Authentication Service (MAS), used by the National Agency for Food and Drug Administration and Control of Nigeria (NAFDAC) since 2010 (Oyetunde et al. 2019). WHO recently published a policy paper on traceability of medical products (WHO 2021b).

Field detection devices for rapid screening like the Minilab® of the Global Pharma Health Fund (GPHF 2021) or portable devices for infrared or Raman spectroscopy (Vickers et al. 2018) can help to detect substandard and falsified medicines which have entered into the supply chains and allow a more effective use of the costly resources of fully equipped medicine quality control laboratories. Recently, a chapter was added to the United States Pharmacopeia (USP) entitled "Evaluation of screening technologies for assessing medicine quality", acknowledging the benefits of such devices (USP 2020). The aim is to establish the capabilities and limitations of these devices.

To be able to respond appropriately to the problem of SF medicines, it is important to assess the scope of this problem in different geographical regions, in different parts of the health supply chain and for different types of medicines via systematic research, in accordance with current standards such as the WHO "Guidelines on the conduct of surveys of the quality of medicines" (WHO 2016) and the MEDQUARG guidelines (Newton et al. 2009).

A key aspect for mounting a response to SF medicines is strengthening the NMRAs – only with the right equipment and well-trained staff will these authorities be able to tackle the tasks required to assure the quality of medical products. Control mechanisms between and within authorities are necessary to fight corruption at all levels of the supply chain. In addition, stronger networking between health actors, regulatory authorities, law enforcement and customs leads to improvements in pharmaceutical surveillance (Vorrath and Voss 2019).

Communication between all stakeholders is important, as well as publicly sharing the data on SF medicines: if the precise problems are not known, precious resources are wasted in the response. The general public can be involved with awareness-raising campaigns, and civil society organisations may be important contributors in this regard. There are also initiatives to improve reporting and interventions by frontline healthcare professionals, specifically in regions with a high burden of SF medicines. For example, together with WHO the International Pharmaceutical Federation developed a compulsory education component on SF medicines that was introduced in five universities in Sub-Saharan Africa as part of a pilot project (FIP 2021). In this curriculum, pharmacy students learn how to avoid, detect and report SF medicines. Further, the United States Agency for International Development (USAID) and the USP collaborate with Nigerian universities in the course of their Promoting the Quality of Medicines (PQM) programme to strengthen the teaching on quality control in the curriculum of pharmacy students (PQM 2018).

A shared legal understanding between countries is necessary to respond appropriately to illicit trade of SF medicines. As long as penalties for the manufacture or trade of SF medicines are low, the benefits outweigh the risks for the criminals, and SF medicines will continue to be a global threat. UNODC (2019) has published a guide to good legislative practices to combat falsified medical product-related crime, and a model law on medicine crime has been suggested by Attaran (2015). Similarly, the MEDICRIME Convention of the Council of Europe provides countries with a model legal framework dealing with falsified medical products. The intention of this guide is to support states in enacting or strengthening domestic legislation regarding falsified product-related crime (Alarcón-Jiménez 2015). Specific laws for pharmaceutical crime, cross-border information sharing and cooperation in law enforcement as well as control mechanisms between and within relevant agencies are also needed to counter crime related to SF medicines (Dellasega and Vorrath 2020; Vorrath and Voss 2019). Effective joint law enforcement such as INTERPOL and custom controls have already led to some successes in the fight against SF medicines, for example with Operation Pangea, and they will also remain an important intervention to limit the extent of the trade with SF medicines.

SF medicines have a global impact – both in the Global North and in the Global South. The threat that is emerging from SF medicines for individuals, health systems, economies and states can therefore only be successfully addressed with the united, global participation of all parties involved. The authors of a Lancet comment rightly call for global interventions to ensure access to affordable, good quality medical products worldwide and stress that the world's population will depend on it as "[a]ll our fates are bound together" (Newton et al. 2020: e754).

References

Akuse, Rosamund Modupe/Eke, Felicia Uchezuba/Ademola, Adebowale Dele/Fajolu, Iretiola Bamikeolu/Gbelee, Henry Olusegun et al. (2012): "Diagnosing renal failure due to diethylene glycol in children in a resource-constrained setting". In: Pediatric Nephrology, 27, 6, pp. 1021–1028.

Alarcón-Jiménez, Oscar (2015): "The Medicrime Convention – Fighting against counterfeit medicine". In: Eurohealth International, 21, 4, pp. 24–27.

Almuzaini, Tariq/Choonara, Imti/Sammons, Helen (2013): "Substandard and counterfeit medicines. A systematic review of the literature". In: BMJ Open, 3, 8, e002923.

Attaran, Amir (2015): "Stopping murder by medicine. Introducing the Model Law on Medicine Crime". In: The American Journal of Tropical Medicine and Hygiene, 92, 6 Suppl, pp. 127–132.

Bassiony, Medhat M./Abdelghani, Mohamed/Salah El-Deen, Ghada M./Hassan, Mervat S./El-Gohari, Hayam/Youssef, Usama M. (2018): "Opioid use disorders attributed to tramadol among Egyptian university students". In: Journal of Addiction Medicine, 12, 2, pp. 150–155.

Basu, Debasish/Mahintamini, Tathagata/Ghosh, Abhishek/Roub, Fazle/Subodh, B. N./Mattoo, S. K./Avasthi, Ajit (2020): "Tapentadol, the new kid on the block in India. Is it time to worry?". In: Indian Journal of Psychiatry, 62, 6, pp. 697–702.

Bate, Roger/Jin, Ginger Zhe/Mathur, Aparna/Attaran, Amir (2014): "Poor quality drugs and global trade. A pilot study". National Bureau of Economic Research (NBER). At: http://www.nber.org/papers/w20469 (accessed 23 July 2021).

BBC (2018): "Nigeria's Tramadol crisis. The drug fuelling death, despair and Boko Haram". At: https://www.bbc.com/news/world-africa-44306086 (accessed 23 July 2021).

Bergen, Martin/Hoferichter, Reinhard (2017): "securPharm e. V. – der Schutzschild gegen gefälschte Arzneimittel". In: Bundesgesundheitsblatt – Gesundheitsforschung – Gesundheitsschutz, 60, 11, pp. 1255–1260.

Buckley, Gillian J./Gostin, Lawrence O. (eds.) (2013): Countering the problem of falsified and substandard drugs. Washington, D.C.: The National Academies Press. At: https://www.nap.edu/read/18272/chapter/1 (accessed 26 July 2021).

Byaruhanga, Janet (2020): "How Africa can manufacture to meet its own pharmaceutical needs". Africa Renewal. At: https://www.un.org/africarenewal/magazine/september-2020/how-africa-can-manufacture-meet-its-own-pharmaceutical-needs (accessed 15 July 2021).

Companies House (2021): "Companies House". At: https://www.gov.uk/government/organisations/companies-house (accessed 22 July 2021).

Dellasega, Maria/Vorrath, Judith (2020): "A gangster's paradise? Transnational organised crime in the Covid-19 pandemic". SWP Comment 2020/C 66. At: https://www.swp-berlin.org/en/publication/a-gangsters-paradise-transnational-organised-crime-in-the-covid-19-pandemic (accessed 26 January 2022).

Dugato, Marco/Riccardi, Michele/Polizzotti, Marcello (2014): "The theft of medicines from Italian hospitals". Transcrime – Joint Research Centre on Transnational Crime. At: https://www.researchgate.net/publication/260487710_The_Theft_of_Medicines_from_Italian_Hospitals (accessed 26 July 2021).

EMCDDA, European Monitoring Centre for Drugs and Drug Addiction (2018): "Captagon: understanding today's illicit market". EMCDDA Papers. Publications Office of the European Union, Luxembourg. At: https://www.emcdda.europa.eu/system/files/publications/9783/20184976_TDAU18002ENN_PDF.PDF (accessed 20 September 2021).

EUIPO, European Union Intellectual Property Office (2020): "2020 Status report in IPF infringement". At: https://www.opi.gr/images/various/2020_Status_Report_on_IPR_infringement_en.pdf (accessed 26 July 2021).

Europol (2020): "48 arrests and 6 organised crime groups dismantled in medicine-trafficking operation". At: https://www.europol.europa.eu/newsroom/news/48-arrests-and-6-organised-crime-groups-dismantled-in-medicine-trafficking-operation (accessed 26 July 2021).

Europol (2021): "European Union serious and organised crime threat assessment (SOCTA). A corrupting influence: the infiltration and undermining of Europe's economy and society by organised crime“. Publication Office of the European Union, Luxembourg. At: https://www.europol.europa.eu/sites/default/files/documents/socta2021_1.pdf (accessed 8 September 2021).

FDA, U.S. Food and Drug Administration (2021): "Generic Drugs". At: https://www.fda.gov/drugs/buying-using-medicine-safely/generic-drugs (accessed 22 July 2021).

FIP, International Pharmaceutical Federation (2021): "Curriculum for pharmacy students on substandard and falsified medicines. Curriculum guide and competency framework". At: https://www.fip.org/file/4917 (accessed 26 July 2021).

Gnegel, Gesa/Hauk, Cathrin/Neci, Richard/Mutombo, Georges/Nyaah, Fidelis/Wistuba, Dorothee/Häfele-Abah, Christina/Heide, Lutz (2020): "Identification of falsified chloroquine tablets in Africa at the time of the COVID-19 pandemic". In: The American Journal of Tropical Medicine and Hygiene, 103, 1, pp. 73–76.

GPHF, Global Pharma Health Fund e.V. (2021): "The GPHF-Minilab™ – protection against counterfeit medicines". At: https://www.gphf.org/en/minilab/ (accessed 19 July 2021).

Hagen, Nhomsai/Khuluza, Felix/Heide, Lutz (2020): "Quality, availability and storage conditions of oxytocin and misoprostol in Malawi". In: BMC Pregnancy and Childbirth, 20. No. 184.

Hall, Alexandra/Koenraadt, Rosa/Antonopoulos, Georgios A. (2017): "Illicit pharmaceutical networks in Europe. Organising the illicit medicine market in the United Kingdom and the Netherlands". In: Trends in Organized Crime, 20, 3, pp. 296–315.

Hall, Peter E./ Tagontong, Navaporn (2016): "Quality of medicines. Quality of misoprostol products". In: WHO Drug Information, 30, 1, pp. 35–39.

Hauk, Cathrin/Hagen, Nhomsai/Heide, Lutz (2021): "Identification of substandard and falsified medicines. Influence of different tolerance limits and use of authenticity inquiries". In: The American Journal of Tropical Medicine and Hygiene, 104, 5, pp. 1936–1945.

INCB, International Narcotics Control Board (2018): "Precursors and chemicals frequently used in the illicit manufacture of narcotic drugs and psychotropic substances“. United Nations Office at Vienna. At: https://www.incb.org/documents/PRECURSORS/TECHNICAL_REPORTS/2017/E_ebook_with_annexes.pdf (accessed 27 April 2022).

INCB, International Narcotics Control Board (2019): "Report of the International Narcotics Control Board for 2019“. United Nations Office at Vienna. At: https://www.incb.org/documents/Publications/AnnualReports/AR2019/Annual_Report_Chapters/English_ebook_AR2019.pdf (accessed 27 April 2022).

INCB and WHO (2012): "Guide on estimating requirements for substances under international control“. United Nations Office. At: https://www.incb.org/documents/Narcotic-Drugs/Guidelines/estimating_requirements/NAR_Guide_on_Estimating_EN_Ebook.pdf accessed 27 April 2022).

INCO, UNODC and WHO (2021): "INCB, UNODC and WHO Joint Statement on Access to Controlled Medicines in Emergencies". At: https://www.who.int/news/item/08-09-2021-incb-unodc-and-who-joint-statement-on-access-to-controlled-medicines-in-emergencies (accessed 16 September 2021).

INTERPOL (2014): "Pharmaceutical crime and organized criminal groups. An analysis of the involvement of organized criminal groups in pharmaceutical crime since 2008". At: https://www.republicoftogo.com/content/download/35515/742319/file/RAPPORT%20INTERPOL.pdf (accessed 22 July 2021).

INTERPOL (2020a): "Global operation sees a rise in fake medical products related to COVID-19". At: https://www.interpol.int/News-and-Events/News/2020/Global-operation-sees-a-rise-in-fake-medical-products-related-to-COVID-19 (accessed 22 July 2021).

INTERPOL (2020b): "INTERPOL warns of organized crime threat to COVID-19 vaccines". At: https://www.interpol.int/News-and-Events/News/2020/INTERPOL-warns-of-organized-crime-threat-to-COVID-19-vaccines (accessed 22 July 2021).

INTERPOL (2020c): "Operation in the Middle East and North Africa targets pharmaceutical crime". At: https://www.interpol.int/News-and-Events/News/2020/Operation-in-the-Middle-East-and-North-Africa-targets-pharmaceutical-crime (accessed 22 July 2021).

INTERPOL (2021a): "Fake COVID vaccine distribution network dismantled after INTERPOL alert". At: https://www.interpol.int/News-and-Events/News/2021/Fake-COVID-vaccine-distribution-network-dismantled-after-INTERPOL alert (accessed 22 July 2021).

INTERPOL (2021b): "Thousands of fake online pharmacies shut down in INTERPOL operation". At: https://www.interpol.int/News-and-Events/News/2021/Thousands-of-fake-online-pharmacies-shut-down-in-INTERPOL-operation (accessed 22 July 2021).

IRACM, Institute de Recherche Anti-Contrefaçon de Médicaments/Przyswa, Eric (2013): "Counterfeit medicine and criminal organizations". At: https://globalinitiative.net/wp-content/uploads/2017/12/IRACM-Counterfeit-Medicines-and-Criminal-Organizations-Oct-2013.pdf (accessed 26 July 2021).

Keteyian, Armen (2012): "How fake Avastin from overseas ends up in the U.S.". CBS News. At: https://www.cbsnews.com/news/how-fake-avastin-from-overseas-ends-up-in-us/ (accessed 22 July 2021).

Klein, Axel (2019): "Drug problem or medicrime? Distribution and use of falsified tramadol medication in Egypt and West Africa". In: Journal of Illicit Economies and Development, 1, 1, pp. 52–62.

McManus, Dominic/Naughton, Bernard David (2020): "A systematic review of substandard, falsified, unlicensed and unregistered medicine sampling studies. A focus on context, prevalence, and quality". In: BMJ Global Health, 5, 8.

Mumphansha, Hazel/Nickerson, Jason W./Attaran, Amir/Overton, Sean/Curtis, Sharon/Mayer, Paul/Bould, M Dylan (2017): "An analysis of substandard Propofol detected in use in Zambian anesthesia". In: Anesthesia & Analgesia, 125, 2, pp. 616–619.

Newton, Paul N./Bond, Katherine C./Adeyeye, Moji/Antignac, Marie/Ashenef, Ayenew et al. (2020): "COVID-19 and risks to the supply and quality of tests, drugs, and vaccines". In: The Lancet Global Health, 8, 6, pp. e754–e755.

Newton, Paul N./Lee, Sue J./Goodman, Catherine/Fernández, Facundo M./Yeung, Shunmay et al. (2009): "Guidelines for field surveys of the quality of medicines. A proposal". In: PLOS Medicine, 6, 3, e1000052.

OECD, Organization for Economic Co-operation and Development/EUIPO (2020): "Trade in counterfeit pharmaceutical products". Paris: OECD Publishing. At: https://www.oecd-ilibrary.org/content/publication/a7c7e054-en (accessed 26 July 2021).

Oyetunde, Olubukola O./Ogidan, Olayiwola/Akinyemi, Mary I./Ogunbameru, Adeteju A./Asaolu, Olubunmi F. (2019): "Mobile authentication service in Nigeria. An assessment of community pharmacists' acceptance and providers' views of successes and challenges of deployment". In: Pharmacy Practice, 17, 2, pp. 1449–1449.

Ozawa, Sachiko/Evans, Daniel R./Bessias, Sophia/Haynie, Deson G./Yemeke, Tatenda T./Laing, Sarah K. Laing/Herrington, James E. (2018): "Prevalence and estimated economic burden of substandard and falsified medicines in low- and middle-income countries. A systematic review and meta-analysis". In: JAMA Network Open, 1, 4, e181662.

Peyraud, Nicolas/Rafael, Florentina/Parker, Lucy Anne/Quere, Michel/Alcoba, Gabriel et al. (2017): "An epidemic of dystonic reactions in central Africa". In: The Lancet Global Health, 5, 2, pp. e137–e138.

People's Daily Online (2009): "China's ministries work together to bust online counterfeit drug dealers“. At: http://en.people.cn/90001/90776/90882/6659053.html (accessed 22 November 2021)

PQM, Promoting the Quality of Medicines (2018): "Promoting the Quality of Medicines Program annual performance report: Fiscal Year 2018, October 1, 2017–September 30, 2018“. U.S. Pharmacopeial Convention (USP). Rockville, MD: U.S. Agency for International Development by the Promoting the Quality of Medicines Program. At: https://www.usp-pqm.org/sites/default/files/pqms/2018-annual-report-pqm.pdf (accessed 26 July 2021).

Progenerika (2020): "Where do our active ingredients come from?". At: https://www.progenerika.de/studies/where-do-our-active-ingredients-come-from/?lang=en (accessed 26 July 2021).

Rahman, Mohammad S./Yoshida, Naoko/Tsuboi, Hirohito/Tomizu, Naoki/Endo, Jamie/Miyu, Onishi/Akimoto, Yoshio/Kimura, Kazuko (2018): "The health consequences of falsified medicines. A study of the published literature". In: Tropical Medicine & International Health, 23, 12, pp. 1294–1303.

Roche Pharma AG (2014): "Fälschungen des Arzneimittels Herceptin® 150 mg Pulver zur Herstellung eines Infusionslösungskonzentrats (Trastuzumab) – Verschiedene Chargen sind betroffen". Rote-Hand-Brief 22. April 2014. At: https://www.akdae.de/Arzneimittelsicherheit/RHB/Archiv/2014/20140422.pdf (accessed 26 July 2021).

Schäfermann, Simon/Hauk, Cathrin/Wemakor, Emmanuel/Neci, Richard/Mutombo, Georges et al. (2020): "Substandard and falsified antibiotics and medicines against noncommunicable diseases in Western Cameroon and Northeastern Democratic Republic of Congo". In: The American Journal of Tropical Medicine and Hygiene, 103, 2, pp. 894–908.

Streit, Renz (2017): "Der Herceptin®-Fall". In: Bundesgesundheitsblatt – Gesundheitsforschung – Gesundheitsschutz, 60, 11, pp. 1203–1207.

UNIFAB, Union des Fabricantes (2016): "Counterfeiting & Terrorism. Report 2016". At: https://euipo.europa.eu/ohimportal/documents/11370/71142/Counterfeiting+%26%20terrorism/7c4a4abf-05ee-4269-87eb-c828a5dbe3c6 (accessed 26 July 2021).

UNODC, United Nations Office on Drugs and Crimes (2010): "Counterfeit Products". In: The Globalization of Crime. A Transnational Organized crime Threat Assessment, pp. 173–190. At: https://www.unodc.org/documents/data-and-analysis/tocta/TOCTA_Report_2010_low_res.pdf (accessed 26 July 2021).

UNODC, United Nations Office on Drugs and Crimes (2011): "Resolution 20/6. Countering fraudulent medicines, in particular their trafficking". At: https://www.unodc.org/documents/commissions/CCPCJ/Crime_Resolutions/2010-2019/2011/CCPCJ/Resolution_20-6.pdf (accessed 23 July 2021).

UNODC, United Nations Office on Drugs and Crimes (2019): "Combating falsified medical product-related crime. A guide to good legislative practices". At: https://www.unodc.org/documents/treaties/publications/19-00741_Guide_Falsified_Medical_Products_ebook.pdf (accessed 26 July 2021).

UNODC, United Nations Office on Drugs and Crimes (2021a): "At the crossroad of licit and illicit. Tramadol and other pharmaceutical opioids trafficking in West Africa". At: https://www.unodc.org/documents/nigeria/Tramadol_Trafficking_in_West_Africa.pdf (accessed 22 July 2021).

UNODC, United Nations Office on Drugs and Crimes (2021b): "International Drug Control Conventions". At: https://www.unodc.org/unodc/en/commissions/CND/conventions.html (18 September 2021).

USP (2020): "<1850> Evaluation of Screening Technologies for Assessing Medicine Quality". In USP 43–NF 38. Rockville, MD: United States Pharmacopeial Convention.

Van Assche, Kerlijn/Caillet, Céline/Newton, Paul (2021a): "Medical Product Quality Report. COVID-19 Issues". Issue 10, May 2021. Medicine Quality Research Group, Centre of Tropical Medicine & Global Health, Nuffield Department of Medicine, University of Oxford. At: https://www.iddo.org/document/medical-product-quality-report-covid-19-issues-issue-10-march-2021-main-text-plus-annexes (accessed 26 July 2021).

Van Assche, Kerlijn/Caillet, Céline/Newton, Paul (2021b): "Medical Product Quality Report. COVID-19 vaccines". Issue 5, June 2021. Medicine Quality Research Group, Centre of Tropical Medicine & Global Health, Nuffield Department of Medicine, University of Oxford. At: https://www.iddo.org/sites/default/files/publication/2021-06/Medical%20Product%20Quality%20Report_COVID-19%20VACCINE%20issues_Up%20to%2031May2021.pdf (accessed 26 July 2021).

Vickers, Serena/Bernier, Matthew/Zambrzycki, Stephen/Fernández, Facundo M./Newton, Paul N./Caillet, Céline (2018): "Field detection devices for screening the quality of medicines. A systematic review". In: BMJ Global Health 3, 4, e000725.

Vorrath, Judith/Voss, Maike (2019): "The hidden dangers of falsified and substandard medicines." SWP Comment 2019/C 25. At: https://www.swp-berlin.org/publikation/the-hidden-dangers-of-falsified-and-substandard-medicines (accessed 27 January 2022).

Wainer, Irving (1996): "Toxicology through a looking glass. Stereochemical questions and some answers". In: Wong, Steven H. Y./Sunshine, Irving (eds.): Handbook of analytical therapeutic drug monitoring and toxicology. Boca Raton/New York: CRC Press, pp. 21–34.

WHO, World Health Organization (2013a): "Drug Alert No. 126. Contaminated Dextromethorpan active pharmaceutical ingredient". Information Exchange System. At: https://www.who.int/medicines/publications/drugalerts/Final_Alert_126_Information_on_Dextromethorphan.pdf?ua=1 (accessed 22 July 2021).

WHO, World Health Organization (2013b): "Drug Alert No. 129. Contaminated Dextromethorphan active pharmaceutical ingredient". Information Exchange System. At: https://www.who.int/medicines/publications/drugalerts/App_Drug_Alert_No_129_Paraguay_Dextro.pdf?ua=1 (accessed 22 July 2021).

WHO, World Health Organization (2016): "Annex 7: Guidelines on the conduct of surveys of the quality of medicines". WHO Expert Committee on Specifications for Pharmaceutical Preparations. Fifth report, pp. 227–261. WHO Technical Report Series No.996. At: https://www.who.int/medicines/publications/pharmprep/WHO_TRS_996_web.pdf?ua (accessed 22 July 2021).

WHO, World Health Organization (2017a): "WHO Global Surveillance and Monitoring System for substandard and falsified medical products" At: https://www.who.int/publications/i/item/9789241513425 (accessed 26 July 2021).

WHO, World Health Organization (2017b): "Member State mechanism on substandard/spurious/falsely labelled/falsified/counterfeit medical products". At: https://apps.who.int/gb/ebwha/pdf_files/WHA70/A70_23-en.pdf (accessed 22 July 2021).

WHO, World Health Organization (2017c): "A study on the public health and socioeconomic impact of substandard and falsified medical products". At: https://apps.who.int/iris/handle/10665/331690 (accessed July 2021).

WHO, World Health Organization (2020a): "Urgent health challenges for the next decade". At: https://www.who.int/news-room/photo-story/photo-story-detail/urgent-health-challenges-for-the-next-decade (accessed July 2021).

WHO, World Health Organization (2020b): "WHO Medical Product Alert N°3/2020". At: https://cdn.who.int/media/docs/default-source/essential-medicines/drug-alerts20/no3-2020-falsified-mp-forcovid-en.pdf?sfvrsn=cd866001_16 (accessed July 2021).

WHO, World Health Organization (2020c): "WHO Medical Product Alert N°4/2020". At: https://www.who.int/news/item/09-04-2020-medical-product-alert-n4-2020 (accessed 22 July 2021).

WHO, World Health Organization (2021a): "Evaluating and publicly designating regulatory authorities as WHO listed authorities: policy document". At: https://www.who.int/publications/i/item/9789240023444 (accessed 26 July 2021).

WHO, World Health Organization (2021b): "Policy paper on traceability of medical products". At: https://www.who.int/publications/i/item/policy-paper-on-traceability-of-medical-products (accessed 26 July 2021).

WHO, World Health Organization (2021c): "WHO – Prequalification of medical products (IVDs, medicines, vaccines and immunization devices, vector control)". At: https://extranet.who.int/pqweb/medicines (accessed 20 July 2021).

WHO, World Health Organization (2021d): "WHO global surveillance and monitoring system". At: https://www.who.int/who-global-surveillance-and-monitoring-system (accessed 22 July 2021).

WHO, World Health Organization (2021e): "WHO quality assurance policy for the procurement of essential medicines and other health products". At: https://www.who.int/publications/i/item/9789240023789 (accessed 23 July 2021).

Yadav, Prashant/Teta, Helen Lega/Babaley, Magalie (2011): "The world medicines situation 2011. Storage and supply chain management" Geneva: World Health Organization. At: https://www.asrames.org/wp-content/uploads/2016/07/THE-WORLD-MEDICINES-SITUATION-2011-STORAGE-AND-SUPPLY-CHAIN-MANAGEMENT.pdf (accessed 26 July 2021).

Illicit trade in cultural property: looted in the Global South, sold in Europe

Jan Schubert

1. *Trafficking in cultural property: as old as the pyramids*

Illicit trafficking in cultural property is not a new criminological phenomenon. History is full of trafficking and destruction of cultural heritage for various reasons: for ideological, political, religious reasons or fuelled by greed. For thousands of years, illicit trade and illicit flows of cultural goods have taken place in every civilisation. Even the ancient Egyptians tried to protect their pyramids and tombs against looters: by using traps, hidden doors and even spells and curses in order to secure their passage to the afterlife.

However, this crime field has never been as sophisticated and professional as it is today. Open borders and transnational trade liberalisation have opened up new opportunities to sell illegally acquired antiquities on the European market (BLKA 2021).

A UNESCO convention in 1970 marked the beginning of international attention to cultural property. By now, 141 countries in the world have ratified this convention and implemented it in national legislation to save cultural property (UNESCO n.d.). These laws are supposed to stop the drain of cultural goods to other countries and to respect foreign culture even in times of war.

The term "cultural property" in this context refers to mobile items which are of importance to a specific culture for various reasons (UNESCO 1970: Art. 1) and are of relevance to science as well. These items can be works of art, tools, religious objects and every piece of at least some value for scientific research. There are two relevant types of antiquities within the criminological definition of stolen or looted cultural property: those that are "known" and those that are "unknown". "Known" antiquities, which either have been previously excavated by archaeologists or have never been lost, are "comparatively easy to consider within normal conceptions of ownership and protection". They are documentable and possibly securable, and their restitution after a theft is facilitated by the fact that they have clear owners to claim them. The largest part is of course cultural property which has never been acknowledged by science because no one knew of its existence – the "unknown" antiquities (Mackenzie et al. 2019: 2).

2. *The European art market as a trading venue for cultural goods from the Global South: "looting in the South, selling in the North"*

International smuggling and trafficking of cultural property is on the rise. Decades ago, European centres of ancient cultures like Italy, Greece and Spain used to be the top source countries for looted artefacts. Due to political erosions caused by war and social tensions, case numbers of looted antiquities from the Global South, especially countries in the Middle East, Latin America and Southeast Asia are rapidly increasing (BLKA 2021).

The classic modus operandi and supply chain are as follows: first of all, looting takes place in regions of the Global South, maybe near historical sites, where authorities are simply not present or corrupt. The following definition of "looting" is a broad one: it could be the illegal but "professional" extraction of artefacts at an archaeological site or just the use of force in order to "dig up" antiquities in unofficial excavations. "Looting" here refers to every form of excavation outside of established norms (Mackenzie et al. 2019: 3). In cases of illicit trafficking, it does not matter whether cultural goods were illegally excavated or stolen in a museum.

The economic goals in this field of illicit trade are the same as on the legal art market: everyone along the supply chain wants to make money. It is a criminal billion-dollar business – and it is expanding. According to INTERPOL (2018), this "low-risk, high-profit business" achieves estimated profits of about US$10 to 12 billion per year. Due to a highly diverse mixture of artefacts, an allegedly enormous dark figure and very volatile market prices partially based on irrational parameters, it is extremely hard to estimate the amount of worldwide profits. Numbers of trafficked artefacts per year such as the number mentioned by INTERPOL should merely be regarded as a very conservative educated guess. The real figures may be at a much higher level; there may just not be any scientific evidence to prove this (LKA BW 2021).

As for every type of illicit flow, the supply chain forms the backbone of illicit trafficking in cultural property. The following chapter tries to outline the specific mechanism of this illicit transnational lifeline.

2.1. Criminal supply chain: from looters in the Global South to Europe's art markets

Figure 1: Illicit Flows: Trafficking in Cultural Objects

Stage 1: illegal acquisition

This first stage starts with any type of illegal acquisition of cultural goods. In most cases, it begins with looting in the Global South, which includes every form and every modus operandi conceivable: either with local looters being hired by an intermediary or with pieces that were accidentally found being bought – this is all it takes for the supply chain to begin (BLKA 2021). The range goes from unauthorised excavations as far as classic thefts. Corrupt and weak state authority as well as unstable economic conditions, accompanied by military conflicts and a lax legal framework unable to tackle the issue effectively, provide the necessary environment for systematic looting (Dietzler 2013: 331).

The local looters, mostly living under precarious conditions in countries of the Global South, receive only about 1 % of the overall profit (Dietzler 2013: 330). Often this means less than 1 US cent per item (Mackenzie et al. 2019: 6). As a consequence, there is often a gap of thousands of per cent regarding the amount of money looters and other kinds of thieves earn for their efforts in comparison to the profits ultimately being made on the

European art market (Groß 2018: 53). It is not very uncommon for rare cultural objects to be sold for a six-figure sum of euros or US dollars (LKA BW 2021).

In most cases, the looted goods have to leave the source countries of the Global South to reach potential buyers. In order to compensate the (financial) efforts along the supply chain and to generate the biggest possible profit, the value of the saleable piece has to be high enough (Polk 2009: 15).

After being professionally cleaned, the artefacts are provided with forged documents by counterfeiters or corrupt officials in order to be smuggled across borders as a "legalised" part of the international goods traffic (BLKA 2021).

Stage 2: transit

The second stage is usually transit. Sometimes, though, there are some further preparations before the illegal journey begins. These preparations consist of cleaning and freeing from soil, sand and other forms of dirt that could reveal the illicit origin. In addition, forged documents are necessary for every artefact being transported as a "legally excavated archaeological antiquity": provenance for a legal trade as well as valid export and import documents for the transit route to the destination country. Otherwise, the cultural goods have to be smuggled across international borders. If the export documents do not arouse any suspicion, receiving authentic import documents from national authorities in transit countries or destination countries will not be a problem at all. It is not necessary to counterfeit all the official permissions if artefacts are "laundered" with documents issued without justification. As a result, the required documents for the illicit transport are often authentic ones issued by corrupt officials. Cultural property transported via smuggling operations or with the support of corrupt officials simply needs a (moderately) plausible provenance for being legally sold in the destination country – depending on national regulations.

Based on illegally issued official certificates (provenance and export/import documents), cultural goods from the Global South find their way to (licit) European marketplaces.

As some artefacts are not small enough for efficient transport, they are reduced in size by force (Polk 2009: 15). This has the additional advantages that large transport containers – which are easier to detect – are not required and that the profit margin increases if larger objects are sold in parts. This may mean that initially intact archaeological finds, like reliefs or mosaics, are not only looted, but also often destroyed in their original form.

Law enforcement agencies have learned that there are no special transit routes exclusively for the illicit flow of cultural property (yet). However, the route is crucial for the transport of archaeological artefacts, especially for regions on UN embargo lists in the Middle East, like Syria and Iraq. The transport has to be cost-efficient but also safe enough to get the goods to their ultimate destination. Well-planned cooperation and organisation are needed to hand over the objects from one transport stage to the next. Many aspects have to be considered in this regard: logistics, contacts, corrupt officials, particular time windows, certain routes and so on. The illicit flow of cultural property uses the same routes as drug trafficking, illegal migration, human trafficking and other kinds of transnational crime. Trafficking in cultural goods highly benefits from the land route to (Western) Europe: the so-called "Balkan route". It has been the most practicable pathway from the Orient to Europe for hundreds of years. The "Balkan route" comprises three variations:

1. The classic route via Turkey, Bulgaria, North Macedonia, Kosovo, Serbia, Bosnia and Croatia
2. The northern route via Turkey, the Black Sea, Ukraine or Bulgaria, Romania, Hungary and finally to Austria
3. The southern route via Greece, North Macedonia and Albania to Italy (Krasniqi 2013: 597)

There is no other illicit transit route linking the Global South with Europe as prominent as the "Balkan route". Artefacts are transported via air, land and sea mixed with other types of illegal "goods" like arms, narcotic drugs and even smuggled or trafficked human beings.

Figure 2: Geographical overview for illicit flow of cultural goods

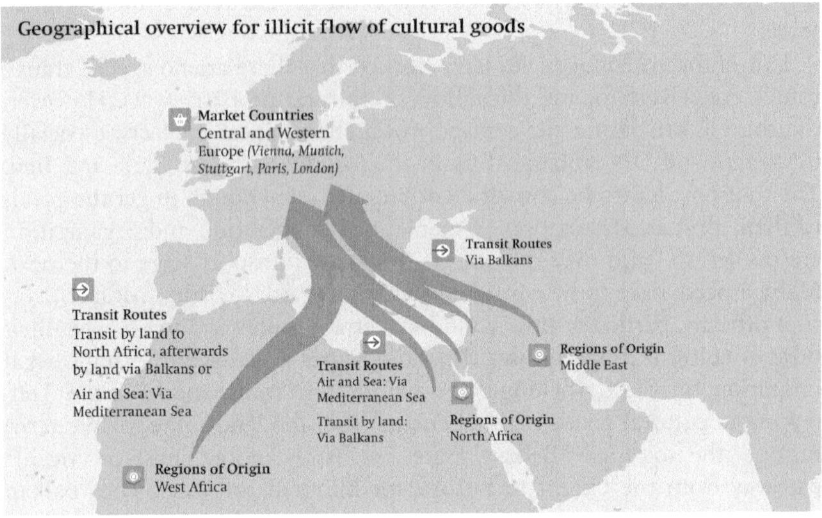

Stage 3: crime-as-a-service

Another prospering market exists besides the classic trade: the manufacturing and sale of fake artefacts and the provision of all kinds of illegal services ("crime-as-a-service") along the trade route. The latter could be forging export documents, offering escrow or "mixing services" to disguise virtual trades via cyber currencies and, of course, brokerage, i.e. connecting the sellers with interested customers. Adding fake antiquities can be compared to "extending" the quantity of illegal narcotic drugs: mixed-in fakes increase the profits by being sold either to unknowing buyers (hidden within originals) or to customers actually searching for fake artefacts. The sellers can broaden their product portfolio in both ways. Potential customers are defrauded, or they get what they are looking for.

Almost every form of "crime-as-a-service" can be pulled off in the context of illicit trafficking in cultural property. There is not much difference to other crime fields or illicit flows in this regard.

Stage 4: sale

The last stage is the European art market: this market includes every sort of commerce in the private sector for art and cultural goods, which can be executed in art galleries, art exhibitions, auction houses and even online auctions – ultimately, the only mandatory requirement is having an office in the market country (Roth 2015: 29).

In the majority of investigated cases, intermediaries, straw people or other contacts bring the cultural objects to auction houses in the different market countries. Achieving the desired effect, public auctions provide a "cloak of licitness" as the antiquities are sold on the legal art market (BLKA 2021).

Some artefacts have been found to be traded on the art market since the 1970s, steadily lengthening their chain of provenance – and thereby increasing their price above the average by passing through value-adding hands (LKA BW 2021).

In order to estimate the dark figure of illicit trafficking in cultural goods more precisely, the scientific study "ILLICID. Dark figure study on illegal trade of cultural goods from the Eastern Mediterranean region" (undisclosed study by GESIS – Leibniz-Institut für Sozialwissenschaften 2019) provided a critical glance behind the curtain of the European art market. In this context, the study showed a high rate of at least suspicious artefacts on the German art market in particular. The German market serves as an adequate model and microcosm of Europe's entire art market.

Between July 2015 and June 2017, 6,133 cultural objects were scientifically analysed (ILLICID 2019: 4). These 6,133 objects were sold for a final amount of €1,693,674. 39.9 % of these cultural goods had their presumed origin in Syria or Iraq. There is still an embargo for these countries on the sale of cultural property because of war or warlike conditions. By the current legal standards in Germany, 42.8 % of all monitored artefacts failed to provide evidence of a licit origin (missing or not verifiable provenance). But this provenance is a mandatory requirement for every cultural object in order to be legally traded on the German art market (ILLICID 2019: 7).

This scientific dark figure study is just one example that leads to the thesis (which cannot entirely be dismissed) that there must be a certain "culture of ignorance" (Dietzler 2013: 332) in the market countries: sellers, mostly auction houses, receive tempting commissions – usually between 12.5 and 20 % (Groß 2018: 54). What this exemplary study also shows is the grey nature of the art market. It has to be considered as a mixed portfolio of cultural objects with a licit, illicit, questionable or just unknown background (Mackenzie et al. 2019: 146). Not every seller or buyer necessarily acts in bad faith, nor deals in illicit goods. The destination market is where licit and illicit flows finally merge, as is the case with other markets as well.

Before reaching the ultimate buyer, intermediaries appear as profiteers in different forms and at different stages between the looting and the final sale: as intermediaries reaching out to local looters, as intermediate buyers for storing and cleaning or as the ones handling the final sales in direct contact with the buyers at antique fairs or auction houses at the last stage (Müller-Karpe and Laufer 2011: 16).

However, what increases the demand? Who are the buyers at the end of the supply chain?

2.2 Investors and speculators

Recent police investigation cases have shown that the final buyers are not always collectors, but are sometimes buying antiquities for investment reasons. Purchased cultural goods are intended to be resold in the near future in order to achieve higher prices. For example, investigators discovered several cases in which antiquities from the Global South were bought in Munich and afterwards sold to the United States with a huge surcharge via big auction houses in London – only to be delivered to auction houses in Europe again afterwards. It is even not unusual that the same antiquities are submitted once more by the same first sellers (BLKA 2021).

European and US investors and collectors are the main customers for cultural property. They regard cultural goods as enlargements to their own collection or as value-adding investments (Groß 2018: 53). Antiquities are regarded as a safe investment combined with an outstandingly increasing value (Müller-Karpe and Laufer 2011: 17).

Passionate collectors form another large group of customers for cultural property. "Collectomania is one of the main reasons for looting and destruction of culture" (Müller-Karpe and Laufer 2011: 17, own translation).

2.3 Museums and state collections

Museums and state collections have often received antiquities with a doubtful background – whether by active buying or by artefacts being donated (Müller-Karpe and Laufer 2011: 17). If acting in bad faith, this group of customers would be the most paradoxical one, as science is supposed to preserve cultural heritage.

3. Sale in cyberspace

Nowadays, not only in times of a worldwide pandemic, the virtual market is increasingly attractive for sellers and buyers likewise. Key players in international illicit markets for all kinds of goods reacted quickly to improve online trading in order to compensate for the restrictions on the conventional markets. Online auction trading is one good example of this more virtual approach. Due to this relocation of larger parts of the art market, COVID-19 has had almost no detectable impact on the illicit trade with cultural property (BLKA 2021).

As a matter of fact, this is not a new phenomenon caused by a pandemic: cyberspace with its (seemingly) unlimited possibilities has always been underestimated by international law enforcement. Thus, the power of criminals and their illegal markets has simply not been anticipated (Shelley 2018: 4). Like all other forms of trade, the internet and its hidden side called "darknet" or "deep web" provide manifold options for anonymously trafficking in cultural objects. Legal and illegal purchases are commonly processed via online auctions. In some cases, incriminated artefacts with false provenances are sold on the internet for all the world to see.

On the "darknet", different conditions prevail: drugs, arms, "crime-as-a-service" and other categories of an illegal portfolio are traded on the very same restricted website (Shelley 2018: 10). In 2017, Europol already declared illegal online commerce – including illegal trafficking in cultural property – a prioritised criminal phenomenon for the European Union in terms of internal security (Europol 2017a: 57).

Despite this development, the majority of expensive products like smuggled antiquities are still (virtually) traded in high-end stores or auction houses (Shelley 2018: 10).

4. Cultural property as a perfect asset for money laundering

Money laundering is primarily about protecting illicit money and illegal profits against being seized by law enforcement agencies – and of course about avoiding criminal prosecution (Barreto da Rosa and Diergarten 2015: 2). This is why dealing with art and cultural goods is an excellent option for potential money laundering. Very high prices are achieved, sometimes not completely based on rational reasons. These large amounts of transferred money, combined with cash payments, which are not uncommon, generate an almost perfect environment for money laundering: they provide attractive opportunities to legalise illegal earnings and to increase financial resources at the same time by investing in art.

There is a rise in customers from emerging countries considered as homelands for well-established organised crime, which appears to be connected with these opportunities for money laundering by trading in cultural objects on the art market. In this way, not only drug trafficking profits but also assets gained by corruption flow back into the legal financial market (Roth 2015: 14 f.). Such criminal operations are likely to be executed by organised crime groups, as a certain degree of sophisticated organisation and knowledge is necessary for successful and systematic money laundering.

5. Criminal participants: "different backgrounds, different motivations"

While it is mostly pursuit of profit that draws the offenders into this field of crime, it is also desperation and the will to survive. In countries devastated by war, political instability and poverty, this field offers criminal participants access to some of the few available resources (BLKA 2021). It is the exploitation of these regional and personal crises by internationally operating crime groups that gives these offences a new dimension of transnational crime.

In view of an artefact's journey with all the different stages to reach the destination country and the final customer, it is quite understandable that there are not many criminal protagonists working on their own: without the means and networks, single offenders are not able to participate in this kind of transnational "business" – without access to this criminal network, single players will sooner or later fail. On top of that, groups that are already operating will not tolerate competing rookies not protected by powerful organisations.

6. Playground for Organised Crime Groups

As illicit flows are extremely complex and profitable, organised crime controls most of the illicit flows, especially when it comes to cultural property.

Practicability is the key word: joint ventures, networks, logistics also used for other criminal operations, reliable routines and unused capacities open organised crime's portfolio to this kind of business.

From 2004 to 2009, the number of legal art sellers from the Middle East rose by about 400 %. During the same period, the prices in the top market segments increased very rapidly, which has been associated with a clandestine involvement of new organised crime groups in the art market (Roth 2015: 13).

Scientific studies that include countries of the Global South differ in their results regarding the linkage between the art market and organised crime.

In Latin America, for example, a significant role of criminal groups could not be observed in the field of illicit trafficking in cultural goods. Paradoxically, organised crime is in fact one of the biggest threats to the entire region of Latin America. Furthermore, many regions are rich in pre-Columbian artefacts, and organised crime could rely on existing effective trade routes and other forms of necessary infrastructure (Yates 2014: 31). While Latin America with its historical Mayan, Olmec, Inca and Aztec cultures is a source region, the exploitation and trafficking of the Latin American cultural heritage appears to be less "industrialised" to be considered organised crime (Mackenzie et al. 2019: 20).

In Cambodia, on the other hand, there is proof of organised groups operating in drug trafficking and in looting from historical sites, too (Schönleber 2010: 17). Jordanian law enforcement agencies detected that organised crime groups are operating in the Middle East, even in regions occupied by Islamist militias (BLKA 2021).

However, cultural goods as resources or required infrastructure being available is not decisive for organised crime to start dealing in antiquities. What works well on the "Balkan route" need not necessarily be profitable in other regions, too. In order to guarantee a lucrative trading route and a long-term market as well, all puzzle pieces have to interlock.

Police investigations show that well-organised crime groups are to be found at every stage of the supply chain (BLKA 2021). The annual operations "Actionweek Pandora" of INTERPOL and its partners are the most extensive international investigation efforts that prove the involvement of transnational organised crime (LKA BW 2021). Flexible forms of cooperation with criminal specialists such as looters, smugglers and counterfeiters are part of this illegal business, as well as classic Italian mobsters: "Organised Crime" (established hierarchical organisations) and "organised crime" (cooperation for short-term operations) (Hagan 2006: 134) participate in this criminal market at the same time (Tijhuis 2011: 89). The often one-dimensional image of small mafia families pulling strings from Sicily is just one piece of a large puzzle – if at all (Dietzler 2013: 334; 338). The major part allegedly consists of illegal syndicates seeking maximal profit and power over regional markets and trading routes. In this context, operating in criminal "joint ventures" based on a network of professionals with special skills is just one of the instruments – pulling strings from a management level is a different one. The transition between different stages of the supply chain is the most critical factor, as it requires a very high degree of professionalism, logistics and organisation (Dietzler 2013: 338).

Due to its complexity, illicit trafficking in cultural property is predestined to be a field of operation for organised crime groups. Criminal organisations decide whether or not to participate, based on various factors such as regional specificities, competitors, risk assessment, profit forecast and options to control the market. Generally speaking, the entire supply chain is not controlled by a single criminal organisation, but by different groups according to their regional competence (BLKA 2021).

7. *Terrorist organisations*

Terrorist groups like the Islamic State of Iraq and Syria (ISIS) exploit the indigenous cultural heritage of regions under their control to finance their terrorist activities. They follow an economic plan: gaining money by selling cultural items from the respective area, destroying its cultural identity and enslaving the region for financial and ideological reasons.

7.1 Islamic State of Iraq and Syria (ISIS)

In 2014, ISIS started its campaign to establish a caliphate in the Middle East, primarily focused on regions in Iraq and Syria. At its peak, ISIS commanded 30,000 to 40,000 jihadist fighters (Schwind 2016: 704 f.).

Terrorist organisations like ISIS draw value out of the territories they control. Using this powerful monopoly position, the local ruling terrorist organisation can generate high profits (Shelley 2014: 192) through trade in cultural property: in 2014, ISIS controlled more than 12,000 excavation sites on their territory and built facilities for strategic exploitation nearby (Aust/Malzahn 2014). Without being directly involved in the sales, ISIS raised taxes from 10 % to 30 % on each traded (cultural) good (Shelley

2018: 77). This taxation is justified as a contribution to Allah akin to the "fifth of the spoils of war" paid by defeated enemies (Charney 2016: 67). Illicit trafficking in cultural objects was just one financial source for ISIS: like a prospering multinational company, ISIS used a diversified portfolio consisting of gas and oil trading, abduction, banking, blackmailing as well as smuggling (Europol 2018: 43; Shelley 2018: 131; Schwind 2016: 706).

A special "department" was created in order to professionalise the trade in antiquities: "Diwan al-Rikaz", loosely translated: "department for precious archaeological finds". Its responsibilities primarily included the trade in oil and artefacts from occupied territories (Heing 2018: 38; Wessel 2015: 44). It is not possible to confirm the exact amount of profits ISIS generated from selling archaeological antiquities, but an estimate can be obtained: ISIS earned about US$36 million by looting artefacts in only a small region near Damascus in 2014 (Wessel 2015: 40).

On 15 May 2015, a high-ranking ISIS leader linked to the organisation's financial institutions was supposed to be arrested in Iraq by US special forces but was killed in this operation. Artefacts of great value like ancient coins made of precious metals, manuscripts in Aramaic and hundreds of other cultural objects were seized during the raid. In order to finance its terror regime, ISIS had looted regional museums, e.g. the prominent museum of Mosul. This was proven due to the fact that unique items from this museum were identified (US Department of State 2016). ISIS had not destroyed the artefacts (as it had claimed for propaganda reasons), but looted and sold at least some of the "heretical" cultural goods. ISIS not only profited by illegal excavations "on an industrial level" (FBI 2016), but also by using opportunities to loot museums and other kinds of state collections.

In 2016, international embargoes had a severe impact on ISIS' oil trades. Due to this, ISIS changed its business model and intensified its efforts regarding trafficking in antiquities (Groß 2018: 52). At this point, estimates differ widely: millions or even several billions of US dollars may have been made by systematic exploitation of the occupied regions (Heing 2018: 38).

Even after the military defeat of ISIS, it is very likely that remaining terrorist groups keep trafficking in cultural property in the Middle East, exploiting the power vacuum fostered by corruption and unstable political systems. However, this is also not a new phenomenon: the Taliban regime already looted ancient tombs in Afghanistan, looking for artefacts to finance its activities. These finds were shipped from Pakistan to Brussels, Paris and even the United States (Shelley 2014: 259).

7.2 Africa

Africa is a large continent with a great diversity of heritage resources. Nearly every region in Africa has reason to be concerned about losing this heritage (Abungu 2016: 33). The systematic looting clearly started with Europe's imperial ambitions (Abungu 2016: 36). The illicit traffic of cultural property in Africa is rooted in the North's self-righteous dominance over the Global South.

Due to having been neglected for a long time, at least some of the African regions have recently turned into new hotspots for international terrorism and looting. In the past decades, internal conflicts, poverty and re-emerging religious fundamentalism have led to appalling atrocities and have fostered the illicit trade in African cultural goods.

Unfortunately, many attempts to address this issue internationally in an adequate way have failed (Abungu 2016: 33). There are two main causes for an increase of looting in recent years: the political erosion following the "Arab Spring" in North African states like Egypt and Libya in 2011, with members of security agencies resigning from their duties (Abungu 2016: 34; Europol 2017b: 35; Europol 2018: 38 f.), and the rise of Islamist fundamentalism, especially in the Sahel region with its terrorist focal point in Mali (Abungu 2016: 35; Europol 2018: 40; Europol 2016: 33). In the meantime, Boko Haram is creating an unstable political situation in large parts of Nigeria, Cameroon, Chad and Niger. In 2015, the terrorist organisation swore allegiance to ISIS, which led to Nigeria being labelled as an ISIS province in West Africa (Europol 2016: 33). Boko Haram's transnational activities destabilise entire regions.

In Mali, with its rich cultural heritage, the trade in cultural objects ranks with the trade in arms and drugs as one of the three most serious illicit international trading activities (Abungu 2016: 35; 39). The looted artefacts find their way to Europe, allegedly using the same channels as African migrants and illegal narcotic drugs: through Libya (Abungu 2016: 38). Neither French military interventions, nor the UN peacekeeping mission MINUSMA are capable of combatting certain forms of serious crime effectively – they simply do not have the clear mandate and means they would need to be successful (Abungu 2016: 39; Europol 2018: 39). Stabilisation and counter-terrorism efforts are prioritised in Mali's extensive and inhospitable territory. Countermeasures against trafficking of antiquities with all its economic and cultural consequences for the region is clearly not one of the most pressing problems if it is not directly linked to terrorist financing.

Terrorist organisations such as Ansar Dine in Mali pursue a dual strategy: immovable cultural goods such as monumental buildings were destroyed to achieve a public effect or used as shields against air strikes. Movable cultural goods on the other hand were sold to finance further operations (Charney 2016: 66; Groß 2018: 50; Wessel 2015: 44). This meant the annihilation of the cultural heritage of entire regions, combined with ethnic cleansing of "inferior" minority groups. The (multiple) devastations of Palmyra in Syria and the levelling of the Assyrian city of Nimrud in Iraq with bulldozers are only two examples of terrorist groups destroying immovable cultural property (Wessel 2015: 37 ff.).

So far, only one terrorist leader has been convicted exclusively of "atrocities committed against cultural heritage" by the International Criminal Court in The Hague: in 2016, Ahmad al-Mahdi, member of an Islamist militia in Mali, was sentenced to nine years in prison for destroying the UNESCO world heritage site Timbuktu in Mali (Groß 2018: 57). The amount of movable cultural property looted from sites like these will remain unknown.

An ongoing process of slow decline is noted for the northern part of Africa: for hundreds of years now, the incredibly culturally rich African North has been struggling with a steady illicit drain of cultural property. The systematic plunder by Europeans started in colonial times and has never been easier than today. To give only a small example: in 2017, it was still possible for European citizens to avoid the security check at a big North African airport by paying a bribe of €3 in order to smuggle literally any artefact even by plane.

8. *How to respond?*

A blueprint for combatting this entire illicit flow is unlikely to be developed in the near future. All aspects of the supply chain, all types of protagonists, all different kinds of modi operandi and of course the economic profits as the main reason would have to be tackled at once (BLKA 2021).

Even though perpetrators are usually identified as already known to the police, building a criminal case including an unbroken chain of evidence from the art market back to the source country is quite rare. Most of the looted items originally come from unstable regions and countries of the Global South. On top of that, the international legal assistance process often appears to be very slow and bureaucratic and to undermine quick and effective law enforcement measures (BLKA 2021).

Against this background, it is necessary to improve existing international networks of law enforcement authorities to make them capable of tackling transnational forms of crime effectively. Authorities located all along the supply chain have to be connected: in source, transit and destination countries. Contacts to foreign lead investigators and decision makers are vital to handle cross-border cases professionally. Established supranational agencies like INTERPOL, Europol and Eurojust are able to provide support in coordinating and connecting the national actors or – if necessary – to provide law-enforcement-based capacity building as well as special trainings for prosecutors or investigators. By these means, more and more transnational investigations have lately become examples of successful collaborations (BLKA 2021). Furthermore, national liaison officers abroad are able to stay in continuous close contact with the different foreign investigation units – even without an ongoing specific case.

The following recent operational results are good examples of successful international cooperation in combatting this specific form of illicit flow:

> *Operations ATHENA and PANDORA II, inter alia by INTERPOL, Europol and the World Customs Organization (WCO) in 2017:*
> 53 persons were arrested and 41,000 artefacts were seized in global operations by law enforcement agencies from 81 different countries (Europol 2018b).

> *Operation DEMETRA, inter alia by the Italian Carabinieri Art Squad, the Spanish Guardia Civil and the State Criminal Police Office of Baden-Württemberg, coordinated by Europol in 2018:*
> After four years of international investigations, 23 perpetrators partially associated with Italian Organised Crime were arrested and 25,000 seized archaeological antiquities from Sicily were restituted to Italy (LKA BW 2021; Phillips and Huggler 2018).

> *Operations ATHENA II and PANDORA IV, initiated by INTERPOL, Europol and the WCO in 2020:*
> 101 individuals were arrested, and 19,000 stolen artefacts (inter alia coins, ceramics, historical weapons, paintings and fossils) were seized in worldwide raids by law enforcement agencies from 103 countries. 8,670 of the 19,000 seized objects were found to have been sold online. In the source country Afghanistan, customs authorities confiscated 971 items at the Kabul airport (INTERPOL 2020).

Bi- and multilateral projects between source and destination countries can also become a further pillar for achieving a lasting and strategic strengthening of international cooperation. One of several European projects on connecting source and destination countries is already in progress: the German Federal Criminal Police Office (BKA), the State Criminal Police Office of Baden-Württemberg and the Bavarian State Criminal Police Office (BLKA) are closely cooperating with Jordan to improve bilateral communication and coordinate law enforcement measures. In this way, strategic approaches can be efficiently coordinated and synergy effects can be achieved (BLKA 2021; LKA BW 2021).

Furthermore, issues associated with the illicit trade in cultural property must not be seen as isolated law enforcement problems. They are embedded in Western societies and linked to everyday life in the Global South as well. They have to be addressed by society in order to eventually be tackled politically. The first step has to be an awareness-raising process to shed some light on this rather neglected topic. Science has to play a major role within this process by providing objective information to raise public awareness. Thereafter, societal awareness will hopefully build pressure on relevant policy fields to address these issues properly.

The routine activities of the European art market have to be put under scrutiny without any prejudgement. The restitution of former stolen artefacts to source countries of the Global South is a necessary step in showing that destination countries actually care about the issue. These often complicated legal processes are also signs of respect for other cultures and counteract the image of the Western world as only being interested in its own heritage, as it has been for centuries, especially in regard to Europe's colonial history.

The absence of licit business segments in source countries fosters every kind of unrestrained illicit trade. The trafficking in cultural property is no exception. Sustainable economic support for source countries of the Global South means simultaneously reducing incentives for illicit looting and other forms of regional exploitation. Therefore, economic alternatives have to be provided.

9. *Conclusion*

The illicit trade in cultural property is one of the most underestimated transnational threats. Humankind is slowly but surely losing its cultural heritage and part of its identity. A looted tomb can be compared to an old book: if someone steals a page, the full content may not be understandable any more. The damage is not done with a specific missing artefact, but with the entire scientific context being lost. The original content may be lost forever – for science and for coming generations. An intact archaeological site on the other hand potentially tells an entire story of the past, not just a fragmentary chapter.

Trafficking in cultural goods has many reasons, such as poverty, greed, conflicts, weak legal frameworks or just ignorance. It should be viewed as a "by-product" (Mackenzie et al. 2019: 5) of social and economic disruption, often associated with (internal) conflicts. Root causes may quite readily be named, but all nations – source, transit and destination countries – have to fight this problem to protect the world's cultural heritage and to save our common history.

International threats like transnational organised crime and terrorism in all its forms cannot be defeated just by national approaches. They require a holistic international approach.

Great efforts combining law enforcement, politics, science and societal responsibility are needed to tackle the different components with various strategies: international cooperation of law enforcement agencies and international awareness raising for this worldwide issue from source countries in the Global South to destination countries in the Global North. Financial compensation in the form of strategies like "alternative development", already established in sustainable drug-policy projects, is also needed to provide licit solutions to people living in precarious circumstances.

Trafficking in cultural objects is not a crime without a victim: every looted tomb means a possible abuse of indigenous people in source countries, losing pieces of human history and strengthening crime and terror. Trafficking in cultural goods means dealing with cultural identity. Humankind deprives itself by selling its heritage for financial purposes.

References

Abungu, George (2016): "Illicit trafficking and destruction of cultural property in Africa. A continent at a crossroads". In: The Journal of Art Crime, 15, pp. 33–40.

Aust, Stefan/Malzahn, Claus Christian (2014): "Der islamische Staat im Zenit seiner Macht". At: https://www.welt.de/politik/ausland/article134379366/Der-Islamische-Staat-im-Zenit-seiner-Macht.html (accessed 9 February 2021).

Barreto da Rosa, Steffen/Diergarten, Achim (2015): Praxiswissen Geldwäscheprävention. Aktuelle Anforderungen und Umsetzung in der Praxis. Berlin: De Gruyter.

BLKA, Bavarian State Criminal Police Office (2021): Interview from 25 January 2021 with Detective Chief Inspector C. Klein, Special Investigations Unit, Munich (interview conducted in German).

Charney, Noah (2016): "Lessons from the history of art crime 'Saving artifacts from terrorists'". In: The Journal of Art Crime, 15, pp. 65–68.

Dietzler, Jessica (2013): "On 'Organized Crime' in the illicit antiquities trade. Moving beyond the definitional debate." In: Trends in Organized Crime, 16, pp. 329–342.

Europol (2016): "European Union Terrorism Situation and Trend Report 2016 (TE-SAT)". At: https://www.europol.europa.eu/publications-events/main-reports/european-union-terrorism-situation-and-trend-report-te-sat-2016 (accessed 11 May 2022).

Europol (2017a): "Serious and Organized Crime Threat Assessment (SOCTA). Crime in the age of technology". At: https://www.europol.europa.eu/sites/default/files/documents/socta2017_0.pdf (accessed 11 May 2022).

Europol (2017b): "European Union Terrorism Situation and Trend Report 2017 (TE-SAT)". At: https://www.europol.europa.eu/sites/default/files/documents/tesat2017.pdf (accessed 11 May 2022).

Europol (2018): "Over 41 000 artefacts seized in global operation targeting the illicit trafficking of cultural goods". At: https://www.europol.europa.eu/newsroom/news/over-41-000-artefacts-seized-in-global-operation-targeting-illicit-trafficking-of-cultural-goods (accessed 8 February 2021).

FBI, Federal Bureau of Investigation (2016): "ISIL antiquities trafficking". At: https://www.fbi.gov/file-repository/isil-art-psa-082516.pdf (accessed 8 February 2021).

GESIS – Leibniz-Institut für Sozialwissenschaften (2019): ILLICID. Dark Figure Study on Illegal Trade of Cultural Goods from the Eastern Mediterranean Region (2019): Final report (undisclosed, translated by the author)

Groß, Steffen W. (2018): "Can cultural property protection be an effective counter-terrorism instrument?". In: The Journal of Art Crime, 19, pp. 49–62.

Hagan, Frank E. (2006): "'Organized crime' and 'organized crime'. Indeterminate problems of definition." In: Trends in Organized Crime, 4, pp. 127–137.

Heing, Bridey (2018): Cultural destruction by ISIS (Crimes by ISIS). Berkeley Heights: Enslow Publishing.

INTERPOL (2018): "Protecting cultural heritage by disrupting the illicit trade". At: https://www.interpol.int/News-and-Events/News/2018/Protecting-cultural-heritage-by-disrupting-the-illicit-trade (accessed 5 August 2020).

INTERPOL (2020): "101 arrested and 19,000 stolen artefacts recovered in international crackdown on art trafficking". At: https://www.interpol.int/News-and-Events/news/2020/101-arrested-and-19-000-stolen-artefacts-recovered-in-international-crackdown-on-art-trafficking (accessed 8 February 2021).

Krasniqi, Kole (2013): „Entstehungsbedingungen und Herausforderungen der Organisierten Kriminalität auf dem Balkan". In: Kriminalistik, 10, pp. 11–14.

LKA BW, State Criminal Police Office of Baden-Wurttemberg (2021): Interview from 8th of February 2021 with Detective Chief Inspector S. Holz, Art Crime Unit, Stuttgart (interview conducted in German).

Mackenzie, Simon/Brodie, Neil/Yates, Donna/ Tsirogiannis, Christos (2019): Trafficking culture. New directions in researching the global market in illicit antiquities. London: Routledge.

Müller-Karpe, Michael/Laufer, Eckhard (2011): Kriminalarchäologie. Mainz: Verlag des Römisch-Germanischen Zentralmuseums.

Phillips, John/Huggler, Justin (2018): "Italian police smash £30m international ancient artefact smuggling ring". At: https://www.telegraph.co.uk/news/2018/07/04/italian-police-smash-40m-international-ancient-artefact-smuggling/ (accessed 8 February 2021).

Polk, Kenneth (2009): "Wither criminology in the study of the traffic in illicit antiquities?". In: Mackenzie, Simon/Green, Penny (eds.): Criminology and archaeology. Studies in looted antiquities. London: Bloomsbury Publishing, pp. 13–28.

Roth, Monika (2015): Wir betreten den Kunstmarkt. Geldwäscherei / Zollfreilager – ein zu diskretes Geschäft? / Interessenkonflikte, Manipulationen und Preisabsprachen. Zurich: Dike.

Schönleber, Wolfgang (2010): „Das Phänomen ‚Raubgräberei' – nationaler und internationaler Kulturgutschutz". In: Mitteleuropäische Polizeiakademie (mepa), 1, pp. 4–13.

Schwind, Hans-Dieter (2016): Kriminologie. Eine praxisorientierte Einführung mit Beispielen. Heidelberg: Kriminalistik Verlag.

Shelley, Louise (2014): Dirty entanglements. Corruption, crime and terrorism. Cambridge: University Press.

Shelley, Louise (2018): Dark commerce. How a new illicit economy is threatening our future. Princeton: University Press.

Tijhuis, A. J. G. (2011): "The trafficking problem. A criminological perspective". In: Chappell, Duncan/Manacorda, Stefano (eds.): Crime in the art and antiquities world. Illegal trafficking in cultural property. Berlin: Springer Verlag, pp. 87–97.

UNESCO (1970): Convention on the Means of Prohibiting and Preventing the Illicit Import, Export and Transfer of Ownership of Cultural Property. At: http://portal.unesco.org/en/ev.php-URL_ID=13039&URL_DO=DO_TOPIC&URL_SECTION=201.html (accessed 11 May 2022).

UNESCO (n.d.): "About 1970 Convention". At: https://en.unesco.org/fighttrafficking/1970 (accessed 10 November 2021).

US Department of State (2016): "ISIL leader's loot". At: https://eca.state.gov/files/bureau/isil_leader_loot.pdf (accessed 8 February 2021).

Wessel, Günther (2015): Das schmutzige Geschäft mit der Antike. Der globale Handel mit illegalen Kulturgütern. Berlin: Ch. Links Verlag.

Yates, Donna (2014): "Displacement, Deforestation, and Drugs: Antiquities Trafficking and the Narcotics Support Economies of Guatemala". In: Balcells, Marc/Kila, Joris (eds.): Cultural property crime. An overview and analysis of contemporary perspectives and trends. Leiden: Brill Academic Publishers, pp. 21–36.

Part IV:
The illicit in natural resource supply chains

Undercurrents: illegal fishing and European Union markets

Ina Tessnow-von Wysocki, Dyhia Belhabib and Philippe Le Billon

Introduction

Fish is currently the most widely traded food commodity on the planet. With a global capture fisheries production of 96.4 million tons in 2018, it is a crucial industry for exporters and a source of protein for importers (FAO 2020). The massive scale of this trade hides a deep crisis within capture marine fisheries which is notably characterised by illegal fishing practices undermining the sustainability of overexploited fish stocks and involves fraudulent and abusive practices ranging from tax evasion to slavery. There is a dire need to stop the flow of illegal, unreported and unregulated (IUU) wild-seafood products (fish and other marine life forms) within international markets. Despite numerous efforts to counter such activities, so far, limited progress has been made at the *global* level. Here, we look at the case of illegally caught fish reaching European markets, with a focus on fish originating from Ghana in West Africa.

Illegal fishing refers to fishing activities that violate existing laws, such as fishing in foreign waters without permission and activities that do not abide by regulations of the Regional Fisheries Management Organisations (RFMOs) that the state under which the vessel operates has to follow, or by other international or national legislation. Illegal fishing is often linked to other forms of 'fish crimes' (crimes related to the fishing sector, including labour abuses, document fraud, smuggling and money laundering, see Belhabib, Le Billon and Wrathall 2020; Belhabib and Le Billon 2020; INTERPOL 2020), though we caution against framing all illegal fishing activities as organised crime (Satizábal et al. 2021).

International strategies to reduce illegal fishing have been delayed so far for two main reasons. First, existing global and regional measures lack implementation and currently do not include comprehensive regulations to fight IUU fishing as a global problem, namely to disincentivise these activities, ensure transparency along the supply chain, detect violations and prosecute perpetuators, particularly beneficial vessel owners (i.e. the individuals who benefit from the ownership though the corporations may be under another name). A lack of international consensus, for example within the Food and Agriculture Organization (FAO) and the World Trade Organization (WTO), has so far had a negative impact on the emergence of global regulations, such as the obligation to provide detailed information on the origin of fish or a broad ban on fishing subsidies (Pramod and Pitcher 2019; Sumaila et al. 2021). Second, illegal fishing and its impacts on depleted stocks are in part the result of subsidies that increase fleet capacity (Arthur et al. 2019). Estimates of global fisheries subsidies identify China, the European Union (EU), the United States (US), South Korea and Japan as the largest subsidy providers (Sumaila et al. 2019). Despite Sustainable Development Goal (SDG) target 14.6 and the initial timeline of 2020 for WTO negotiations to end fisheries subsidies, progress was delayed (Koop and Aldred 2020) and an agreement only adopted recently (June 2022). Five countries account for about 90 % of the global Distant Water Fishing (DWF) effort, including China (38 %; note that its DWF fleet could be much larger than previously estimated, see Guttierez et al. 2020), Taiwan (21 %), Japan (10 %), South Korea (10 %) and Spain (10 %) (Yozell and Shaver 2019).

European markets play a major role in this international trade: while the DWF fleet from the EU is comparatively small, the EU's consumption market for *potentially* illegally caught fish is among the largest in the world (EUMOFA 2020). In 2008, the European Council passed a regulation to prevent, deter and eliminate IUU fishing (European Council 2008).[1] One pillar of the EU regulation introduced a 'carding system' to prevent illegally caught fish from entering EU markets and to incentivise exporting countries to improve their management of fisheries and ensure that their exports are legal. Countries exporting to the EU can be warned ('yellow card') to rapidly address identified shortcomings and be banned ('red card') if they fail to address them. At the time of writing, nine countries (Cameroon, Ecuador, Ghana, Liberia, Panama, Sierra Leone, St Kitts and Nevis, Trinidad and Tobago, Vietnam) have been yellow-carded and three

---

1 Council Regulation (EC) No 1005/2008 of 29 September 2008 establishing a Community system to prevent, deter and eliminate illegal, unreported and unregulated fishing (IUU Regulation) in conjunction with Commission Regulation (EC) No 1010/2009 of 22 October 2009 laying down detailed rules for the implementation of Council Regulation (EC) No 1005/2008 https://eur-lex.europa.eu/legal-content/EN/ALL/?uri=celex%3A32008R1005. This regulation, which entered into force on 1 January 2010, resembles other market-access based initiatives, such as the European Union's Forest Law Enforcement, Governance and Trade Action Plan (see Maryudi and Meyers 2018) or the Kimberley Process Certification Scheme for diamonds (Le Billon 2008). For US regulations, including the Seafood Import Monitoring Program (SIMP), see He (2018) and Fang and Asche (2021).

(Cambodia, Comoros, St Vincent and the Grenadines) red-carded. While this carding system can be regarded as a best-practice example in countering IUU fishing, it still has some shortcomings, including interests to avoid the yellow- or red-carding of countries with which the EU maintains broader trade relations, such as China (Okafor-Yarwood and Belhabib 2020), and differences in the thoroughness of inspections of catch landings and imports in the ports of different EU members, with some fishers landing illegal catches in selected EU countries rather than others in order to reduce the risk of penalties (Mundy 2018). Illegally caught fish entering EU markets remains a complex challenge that requires further regulations and cooperation on regional and international levels.

Following this introduction, the first section provides a brief overview of the global extent of IUU fishing and resulting environmental, social and economic impacts, the second examines the modi operandi of how illegal fish enters EU markets, focusing on the example of Ghana, the third describes existing efforts to curb these activities and current shortcomings, and the fourth discusses possible solutions to counter IUU fishing, followed by the conclusion.

1. The global problem of illegal fishing

Illegal fishing is a global problem prevalent in various geographical areas, including coastal waters and the high seas, and affects numerous target species (Liddick 2014; Sumaila, Alder and Keith 2006; Battista et al. 2018; Österblom and Bodin 2012). It is accompanied by fishing activities that lack reliable reporting or that are not regulated under existing law. In order to prevent impacts from illegal, unreported and unregulated (IUU) fishing, this complex problem has to be tackled with a holistic approach.

1.1 Defining IUU

Coined in the late 1990s, the term IUU covers three categories of fishing activities, as defined below according to the FAO (2001):

> **Illegal fishing**, i.e. fishing conducted a) by national or foreign vessels in waters under the jurisdiction of a state, without the permission of that state, or in contravention of its laws and regulations; b) by vessels flying the flag of states that are parties to a relevant Regional Fisheries Management Organisation (RFMO) but operate in contraven-

> tion of the conservation and management measures adopted by that organisation and by which the states are bound, or relevant provisions of the applicable international law; or c) in violation of national laws or international obligations, including those undertaken by cooperating states to a relevant RFMO.
>
> **Unreported fishing** concerns fishing activities that a) have not been reported or have been misreported to the relevant national authority, in contravention of national laws and regulations; or b) are undertaken in the area of competence of a relevant RFMO and have not been reported or have been misreported, in contravention of the reporting procedures of that organisation.
>
> **Unregulated fishing** refers to fishing a) in the area of application of a relevant RFMO that is conducted by vessels without nationality, or by those flying the flag of a state not party to that organisation, or by a fishing entity, in a manner that is not consistent with or contravenes the conservation and management measures of that organisation; or b) in areas or for fish stocks in relation to which there are no applicable conservation or management measures and where such fishing activities are conducted in a manner inconsistent with state responsibilities for the conservation of living marine resources under international law.

This chapter focuses on *illegal* fishing, though it also covers some other governance issues such as misreporting and unregulated practices. We stress that more thorough reporting and sound regulations beyond the EU are needed to address IUU fishing as a global problem. Some activities not (yet) considered illegal, such as the instrumental use of flags and ports of convenience, transshipment and '*post-fishing*', require greater regulatory attention, as discussed in Section 4.

1.2 Impacts of IUU fishing

IUU fishing has significant adverse effects on the marine environment and coastal communities. It is also often linked to crimes affecting national and regional security. This section discusses the various environmental, social and economic harms of IUU fishing (Liddick 2014).

Environmental harms include impacts on marine ecosystems (Metuzals et al. 2010; Liddick 2014; Petrossian 2015) through the destruction of marine habitats (Petrossian and Pezzella 2018) and the overexploitation and depletion of fish stocks beyond legal limits (Liddick 2014; Flothmann et al. 2010; Petrossian 2015). In addition, the use of destructive fishing methods, including blast bombing and cyanide fishing, and of prohibited gear further contributes to the problem of bycatch (the unintended capture of non-target species). For example, illegal longline fishing results in the annual loss of an estimated 100,000 albatross (Petrossian 2015) and contributes to dramatic losses of sharks (Pacoureau et al. 2021). Illegal fishing can negatively affect fish populations and the ecosystems supporting them, including through ignoring and undermining national and regional fisheries management and conservation measures (Flothmann et al. 2010).

IUU fishing also contributes to a number of social impacts, affecting millions of people who depend on fisheries for survival (Petrossian 2015; Petrossian and Pezzella 2018). Such activities also threaten regional and national stability, as they are often linked to major human rights violations and to organised crime (Soyer, Leloudas and Miller 2018). The social harms of illegal fishing are far-reaching, as it impacts society at present and in the future. IUU fishing exacerbates poverty, as it takes away catch opportunities from the most vulnerable, and often reduces food security and livelihood options of coastal populations (Liddick 2014; Petrossian and Pezzella 2018; Soyer, Leloudas and Miller 2018). This, in turn, can undermine the buffering effects of small-scale fishing crucial to the resilience of small-scale fishing-dependent coastal communities and countries, especially when these are affected by natural disasters or armed conflicts (Belhabib et al. 2018). In addition, illegal fishing often creates situations in which people are forced to take extreme measures, such as working on board vessels that are prone to human rights violations (Soyer, Leloudas and Miller 2018). Illegal fishing is often self-perpetuating: by reducing catch opportunities in vulnerable poverty-prone regions, it creates the need to seek alternative forms of livelihood such as illegal fishing (e.g. fishing using illegal gear or fishing in marine protected areas), illicit drug trade (Belhabib et al. 2020) or armed robbery and piracy – activities that are often linked to poverty and environmental crimes such as marine pollution (Okafor-Yarwood 2020).

Economic losses due to IUU fishing are significant. Estimates of illegal and unreported catch range from 11 to 16 million tons with a value of US$10–23.5 billion yearly (Agnew et al. 2009), accounting for at least 15 % of the total world catch (Liddick 2014). The cost to developing countries amounts to US$2–15 billion in economic losses annually (Liddick 2014). In the short run, illegal fishing takes away fish that can secure high prices on markets (e.g. tuna or sword fish) and hence economic prospects for coastal states. In the long run, illegal fishing threatens the commercial viability of targeted fish species by jeopardising conservation efforts and can undermine the sustainability of fish populations more generally, including through bycatch and damage to marine ecosystems (Metuzals et al. 2010). At the community level, illegal fishing takes away fishing opportunities, reducing income and resulting in increased poverty and reduced economic resilience and employment prospects (Belhabib, Sumaila and Pauly 2015).

1.3 Drivers of illegal fishing

Deterrence models argue that an individual commits a crime if the expected benefits from doing so exceed the benefits from engaging in legal activity (Sumaila, Alder and Keith 2006). Sumaila, Alder and Keith (2006) assume the following direct drivers and motivators for illegal fishing: (1) benefits that can be realised by engaging in the illegal activity; (2) the probability that the illegal activity is detected, depending on the level of enforcement and existing regulations; (3) the penalty the fisher faces if caught; (4) the cost to the fisher of engaging in avoidance activities; (5) the fisher's moral and social standing in society and how it is likely to be affected if the fisher engages in illegal fishing.

Beyond the concept of "opportunity makes the thief" quoted by Felson and Clarke (1998) and revisited by Sumaila, Alder and Keith (2006), the driver of *necessity* to engage in illegal activities (rather than greed) is often associated with a low threshold for resilience to crises and poverty and has not been sufficiently studied. In this case, the cost of being caught matters less than the cost of not engaging in such illicit activity, which – especially in the case of poor individual fishers – is associated with survival as opposed to profit (Belhabib, Le Billon and Bennett 2022). The fight against IUU fishing needs to take this into account if it is not to harm vulnerable small-scale fishing households and communities. Anti-IUU efforts can hurt small-scale fishers, notably when these efforts disregard the "diversity, legitimacy and sustainability of small-scale fisheries practices and their governing systems", unfairly burden small-scale fishers, favour large-scale fishers able to meet anti-IUU and certification requirements and result in violent crackdowns against small-scale fishing (Song et al. 2020: 831). It is thus crucial to differentiate between small-scale fishers, who are often themselves the "victims", when they engage in illegal activities due to poverty, and people benefiting from industrial-scale IUU fishing activities.

To date, IUU fishing has been a lucrative, low-risk and high-reward activity. IUU fishing is "positively related to the number of commercially significant species found within [a country's] territorial waters and its proximity to known ports of convenience" (Petrossian 2015). Such ports of convenience are strategically chosen by the actors undertaking the illicit activity, as regulations and standards of port inspections are lower there (Petrossian, Marteache and Viollaz 2015). IUU activities tend to occur in circumstances of low monitoring, control and surveillance (MCS) capacity, particularly in highly corrupt states (Petrossian 2015) and on the high seas – that is, beyond the limits of coastal states' Exclusive Economic Zones (EEZs), areas which are 200 nautical miles away from shore and for which the UN Convention on the Law of the Sea (UNCLOS) requires "measures for the conservation of the living resources of the high seas" (UNCLOS 1982: Part VII. Section 2. Art. 116–120), rather than national regulations (Österblom et al. 2016). A combination of economic incentives, a fragmented international governance framework and a lack of enforcement capacity results in the persistence of the problem (Widjaja et al. 2019). While low-income countries are particularly vulnerable to IUU fishing, due to limited monitoring and enforcement capacity (Agnew et al. 2009; Battista et al. 2018), the markets reached by illegally caught seafood are much more widespread, including in jurisdictions with elaborate regulations and ethical consumer concerns, including the European Union.

2. *IUU fishing and European Union markets*

The European Union is the largest fish importing market, before the US and Japan (EUMOFA 2021: 62). The EU's fish demand mainly relies on imports, particularly for the top five species consumed in the EU: tuna, salmon, cod, Alaska pollock and shrimps (EUMOFA 2021: 31). Table 1 gives an overview of seafood imports into the EU market (to which are added 17,000 tonnes of mostly salmonids from aquaculture), countries of origin and their associated IUU Fishing Index and port risk (i.e. risk of illegally caught fish entering ports), as well as the cards issued to them under the EU carding system.

Table 1: Import of seafood products into EU markets and associated IUU fishing risks and responses

Country of origin	**Percentage of imports (in value) (2020)**	**IUU Fishing Index (2021)**	**Port risk (2020)**	**Countries listed under the EU carding system (2012–2021)**
Norway	26.0 %	2.10	2.43	-
Faroes	UK 7.0 %	n.a. (UK 2.17)	n.a. (UK 2.65)	-
China	6.0 %	3.86	3.08	-
Ecuador	5.0 %	2.38	2.66	Yellow (since October 2019)
Morocco	5.0 %	2.28	2.45	-
Iceland	4.0 %	1.95	2.08	-
Greenland	3.0 %	n.a. (Denmark: 1.72)	n.a.	-
Vietnam	3.0 %	2.33	2.92	Yellow (since October 2017)
United States	3.0 %	2.51	2.26	-
India	3.0 %	2.36	2.57	-
Other 141 non-EU countries	35 %	n.a.	n.a.	n.a.

Sources: Percentage of imports: European Commission 2021; IUU Fishing Index: GI-TOC 2021[2]; port risk: Pew 2020: 10; carding: European Commission 2021[3], Mundy 2018.

2 IUU Fishing Index uses 40 indicators to assess the vulnerability to, prevalence of, and response to IUU fishing from 1–5.

3 Continuously updated list of pre-identified, revoked, identified, listed and de-listed third countries.

Given its nature and the broad scope of its definition, there is no precise and robust estimate of illegal catch. In 2007, EU market imports of illegal fishery products were estimated at 500,000 tons, amounting to about US$1.3 billion (Mundy 2018).[4] Illegally caught fish entering the EU are often high-value species. While it is difficult to trace value chains, certain trends after the yellow-carding of some countries illustrate trade anomalies in species such as tuna, swordfish and sharks and in surimi preparations, which have – despite new carding regulations – found ways into the EU, e.g. through the Netherlands from Ghana and Thailand and through France from Belize, the Philippines and Sri Lanka (Mundy 2018). The industrial sector is often the main sector involved in fish exports (apart from limited artisanal sea cucumber and shark fin fisheries, whose main market is not the EU).

2.1 Modus operandi of illegal fishing: major flows and actors

Illegal fishing activities are manifold and include fishing in prohibited areas (e.g. marine protected areas, zones reserved for artisanal fishers), fishing in contravention of the licence issued (e.g. species, above quota, out of season) and the use of prohibited gear (e.g. drifting nets) and illegal fishing techniques.

There are two main ways through which illegally caught seafood products reach EU markets.

> Illegal fishing by EU fleets: several countries within the EU have large fishing fleets, many of whose vessels operate under fishing access agreements, with an unknown number of them operating illegally. Despite operating under a legitimate fishing access agreement with a coastal state, vessels can infringe upon domestic regulations (by incursions into prohibited zones) (Belhabib et al. 2020) or upon EU regulations (e.g. Italian vessels shark finning off Sierra Leone where shark finning is not illegal, CFFA 2020). These vessels' products may not be seized by the coastal state and may be transshipped (i.e. transferred to another ship – generally a 'reefer' (refrigerated cargo ship) – at sea rather than at a port, thus increasing the risk of fraud), then traded within the EU market using EU ports. If the vessel is not caught, it is unlikely that the product is banned from EU markets.

4 Amounts were converted from euros to US dollars for the sake of comparison within the article (1 US dollar equals 0.83 euros).

Third-party vessels, sea food companies and trading entities, including individual exporters/importers: this is exemplified by cases where illegally caught seafood products from non-EU countries enter EU markets under international trade deals or through intermediaries, including organised-crime networks specialising in bringing illegally caught fish into EU markets and laundering financial gains.

To undertake illegal fishing activity, perpetrators are following a pattern of activities (modus operandi) (INTERPOL 2014) which are currently low-risk and high-gain (Long et al. 2020). Figure 1 shows the different pathways by which illegal fishing takes place and how the catch enters EU markets. Prior to fishing activity, companies need to register their vessels under the flag of a state (flag state) under which activities will be conducted and obtain fishing licences for the intended activity. In this step, abuses of vessel registries and licences serve as a pathway into IUU fishing. This includes not registering at all, registering several vessels under the same identity (sister ships) and using flags of convenience (FOCs) to take advantage of weak or non-existent regulations in certain flag states, leading to misrepresentation (e.g. false vessel identity), tax evasion and illegal domestication (i.e. re-registration of a foreign vessel as a domestic coastal state one), fuelled by corruption. FOCs are one of the many diversion strategies used by fishing vessels and illegally operating seafood companies to escape detection. The use of dual or false flags is a strategy to change some aspects of a vessel's identity, while registration in tax havens and the multiplication of subsidiaries and branches remain two of the best options to reduce illegal fishing sanctions through the domestic re-registration of a vessel (which results in a lower sanction based on laws directed towards domestic vessels, compared to foreign ones) or to avoid any sanctioning at all if the flag state has lax regulations.

Figure 1

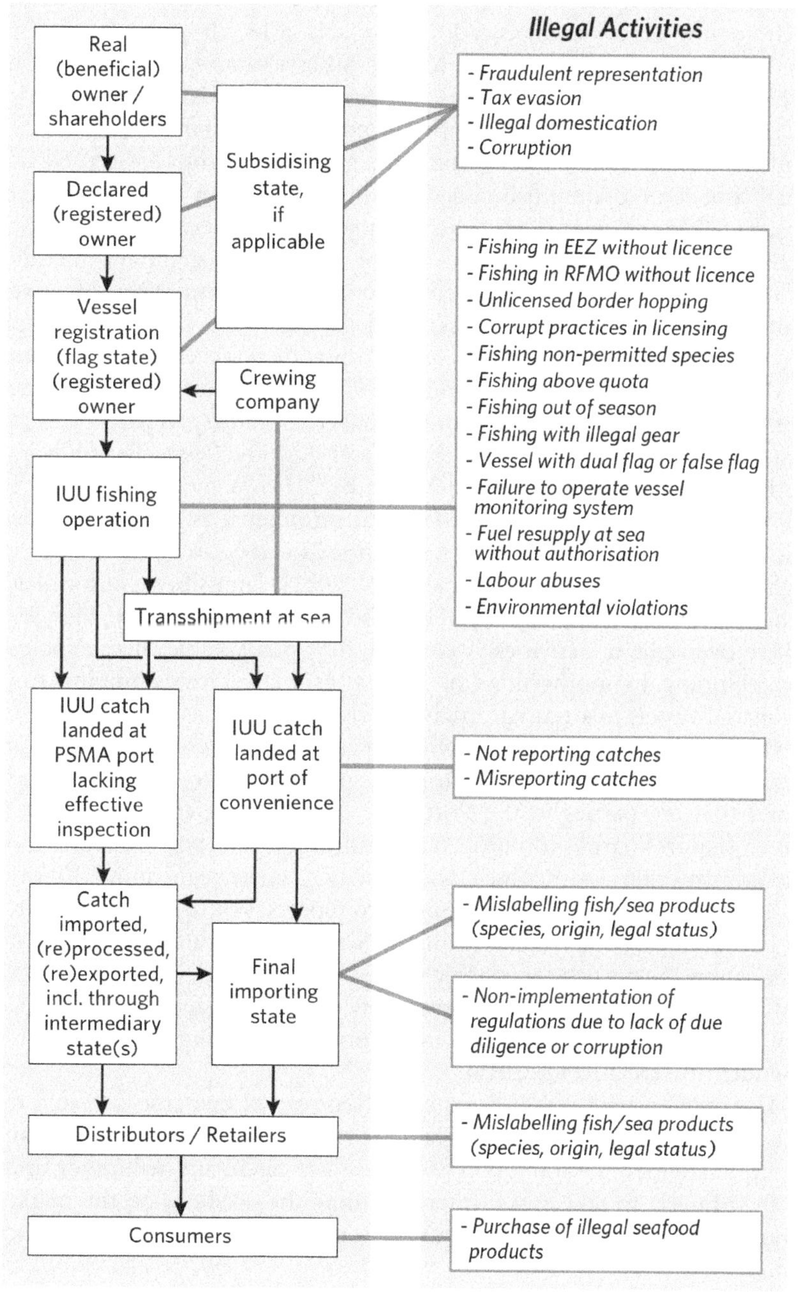
Real (beneficial) owner / shareholders
Declared (registered) owner
Vessel registration (flag state) (registered) owner
Subsidising state, if applicable
Crewing company
IUU fishing operation
Transshipment at sea
IUU catch landed at PSMA port lacking effective inspection
IUU catch landed at port of convenience
Catch imported, (re)processed, (re)exported, incl. through intermediary state(s)
Final importing state
Distributors / Retailers
Consumers
Illegal Activities
- Fraudulent representation
- Tax evasion
- Illegal domestication
- Corruption
- Fishing in EEZ without licence
- Fishing in RFMO without licence
- Unlicensed border hopping
- Corrupt practices in licensing
- Fishing non-permitted species
- Fishing above quota
- Fishing out of season
- Fishing with illegal gear
- Vessel with dual flag or false flag
- Failure to operate vessel monitoring system
- Fuel resupply at sea without authorisation
- Labour abuses
- Environmental violations
- Not reporting catches
- Misreporting catches
- Mislabelling fish/sea products (species, origin, legal status)
- Non-implementation of regulations due to lack of due diligence or corruption
- Mislabelling fish/sea products (species, origin, legal status)
- Purchase of illegal seafood products

A second significant modus operandi of illegal fishing is transshipment. Transshipment is the practice of transferring catches, supplies, crews, fuel from one vessel to another (Miller et al. 2018). It poses an extreme challenge to transparency when reliable observers are lacking and allows fishing vessels to stay out at sea for extended periods of time – up to several years – without ever visiting a port. Transshipment can serve to trade fish in defiance of regulations (e.g. getting fish from unlicensed artisanal fishers, unloading fish outside authorised ports or in the absence of observers). In this way, illegal catch is mixed with legal catch at sea, which makes it practically impossible to reliably document origin and methods of catch and to detect illegal activity during port inspection. However, transshipment goes beyond masking illegal catch and has been strongly linked to other fisheries crimes, such as human rights and labour abuses in various forms, as has been extensively documented in relation to human trafficking and forced labour within the fishing industry in parts of Southeast Asia and within some Distant Water Fishing fleets (Belhabib and Le Billon 2022; Vandergeest and Marschke 2021). A model developed by Global Fishing Watch has identified transshipments as mostly occurring with tuna longliners, with transshipments also co-occurring with human rights and labour abuses (McDonald et al. 2021). Transshipment for illegal activities is undertaken in port, near coastal harbours and on the high seas, where oversight of activities is currently not manageable. It can include transshipping to motherships or reefers, as well as transshipping from industrial vessels to artisanal vessels and vice versa.

Often, ports of convenience, where regulations for port inspections are low or completely lacking, are used by perpetrators to land their catch. States that are parties to the Port State Measures Agreement (PSMA) – which requires parties to put in place and implement port inspections on landed fish catch – sometimes lack capacity to enact regulations (Vince et al. 2021). This provides an opportunity to reprocess or re-export IUU catch to change seafood origin or to mislabel seafood products (size, volume, species) for the purpose of evading regulations or taxes.

Common modi operandi to avoid MCS include interfering with electronic monitoring systems and intentionally obscuring vessel markings and identity (INTERPOL 2014).

The previous pathways all require willing vessel operators to catch the fish illegally, unwilling or incapable state(s) to monitor, supervise and control activities, a willing port to receive the catch, and willing or uninformed buyers to take and further distribute the products on the market. Another willing actor is the subsidising state whose subsidies enable illegal fishing.

2.2 Illegally caught fish making its way into EU markets: the case of Ghana

Ghana has been associated with heavy fishing within prohibited zones in its waters by (domesticated) Chinese vessels and with illegal catch imports into EU markets (Belhabib, Sumaila and Le Billon 2019). Ghana is generally recognised as one of the most stable and best governed countries in West Africa but suffers from several of the problems affecting African fisheries (see Belhabib, Sumaila and Le Billon 2019). With about 539 km of coastline on the Gulf of Guinea and an EEZ of 225,000 km^2, Ghana controls major fishing grounds since it ratified UNCLOS in 1983. As a member of the International Commission for the Conservation of Atlantic Tunas (ICCAT), Ghana also has a voice and role in regional tuna stock management. Its waters are mostly patrolled by Ghana's navy, whose two primary missions are oil infrastructure protection and counter-narcotics. All fishing operations fall under the mandate of the Monitoring, Control, and Surveillance Division (MCSD) of the Fisheries Commission, which enforces fisheries regulations and manages satellite-gathered data on (foreign) fishing vessels (MFAD 2020). About 85 % in value of Ghana's fisheries exports are going to EU markets (EJF 2020). Mostly consisting of processed and unprocessed tuna products valued at about US$176 million, exports to the EU also include about US$15 million in cephalopods (squid, cuttlefish and octopus). More sea products from Ghana could also be transiting via China before ending up in EU markets (EJF 2020).

In 2021, Ghana had an IUU Fishing Index of 1.95 and a port risk of 2.35, compared to the worldwide medians of 2.25 and 2.36, respectively. Based on 2017 data, Pramod (2018) identified major weaknesses in the area of aerial patrols and onboard fisheries observers. This report also noted that Ghana has a poor inspection and sanctioning record despite the rampant use of illegal gear, particularly by Chinese-owned (Ghanaian-flagged) vessels. In addition, Belhabib et al. (2020) identified Ghana as a hotspot for fishing within prohibited zones.

Ghana received a yellow card in 2013, which was lifted in 2015 and recently reintroduced in June 2021. The European Commission's rationale for carding Ghana in 2013 included: Ghana's trawlers not yet having been fitted with vessel monitoring systems (VMS); ICCAT notifications of illegal transshipments between vessels flagged to Ghana; IUU fishing vessels being (re)registered in Ghana; Ghanaian-flagged vessels operating in neighbouring waters without fishing authorisations; and laundering of IUU-caught fish through Ghanaian (processing) companies (European Commission 2013). Even though the vessels are flagged to Ghana, most of the beneficial ownership is Chinese (EJF 2020). The opaque transactions behind this domestication seek to circumvent regulations against foreign involvement in the trawl sector, challenging efforts to determine who ultimately benefits from illegal fishing activities. Investigations by the Environmental Justice Foundation have found that trawlers with IUU fishing records "are linked to the same beneficial owners as tuna vessels authorised to export seafood to the EU" (EJF 2020: 5).

Industrial trawlers contribute to illegal fishing in four main ways (EJF 2020). First, by catching a species that they are legally authorised to fish (e.g. squid) but not to export to the EU market, which is instead exported to China before being re-exported (legally) as Chinese catch to the EU market. Second, by catching a species that they are not legally authorised to fish (e.g. sardinella, a key species for local food security), which is then illegally transshipped onto local Ghanaian canoes (artisanal fishing boats that are legally authorised to catch these species) to be brought to the Ghanaian market and then exported to the EU market. Third, trawlers illegally operating in prohibited areas, often reserved to the artisanal fleet. Ghanaian fishing by trawlers within prohibited areas constitutes 40 % of all fishing within prohibited areas of Africa (Belhabib, Sumaila and Le Billon 2019). Fourth, transshipping fish illegally to smaller boats for a fee. The smaller boats operating as "saiko" (i.e. laundering low-value fish illegally caught by industrial vessels through canoe operators) then land the fish in local ports and outcompete the genuine artisanal fishing sector by selling it as legal catch on local markets. In these cases, Chinese industrial trawlers fraudulently domesticated in Ghana use the Chinese and Ghanaian markets to traffic IUU fish into EU markets. Furthermore, imports of potential IUU-caught fish into EU markets seem to be selectively channelled according to the level of port inspections within the different EU jurisdictions. Out of 4,349 non-EU vessels that landed in EU ports in 2016 and 2017, EU member states inspected only 635 (European Commission 2020). An extensive study by a number of NGOs, including the Environmental Justice Foundation, Oceana, The Pew Charitable Trusts and WWF, found that within the context of the yellow-carding of Ghana in 2013, while indeed some species imports into EU markets – which are still allowed under a yellow card, as opposed to a red one – did decline, other fish imports into EU markets *shifted* from Spain and Germany to Italy and the Netherlands (Mundy 2018). In 2021, Ghana received a yellow card again, due to identified shortcomings including illegal transshipments at sea of large quantities of undersized juvenile pelagic fish between industrial trawl vessels and canoes in Ghanaian waters, deficiencies in the monitoring, control and surveillance of the fleet and a legal framework that is not aligned with the relevant international obligations Ghana had signed up to (EC 2021b). The EJF links illegal fishing activities in Ghanaian waters to human rights abuses (Alberts 2021). It is expected that Ghana ensures effective monitoring and control of fishing activities, the implementation of its enforcement and sanctioning system and sound fisheries management; otherwise it would be regarded as a "non-cooperating country" and be issued a red card, followed by sanctions such as a ban of fishery exports from Ghana to the EU market (EC 2021b).

3. *Efforts to curb illegal fishing and their shortcomings*

Efforts to reduce illegal fishing need to take place across many jurisdictions along the fishing supply chains to be globally effective (FAO 2001), including ensuring regional and international cooperation, the integration of various actors and holistic application of existing frameworks (Lindley and Techera 2017).

Fishing area jurisdiction: Within territorial waters and EEZs, coastal states have fishing area jurisdiction. Governance of the remaining parts of the world's ocean – comprising 64 % of the surface and nearly 95 % of its volume – is *beyond* the jurisdiction of any individual state and regulated under intergovernmental organisations. Within their mandates, RFMOs have fishing area jurisdiction in ABNJ, which, however, do not comprehensively cover all areas and species. Vulnerability to illegal fishing depends on the capacity and political will of the responsible state or RFMO to monitor, supervise and control the waters under its jurisdiction and the fleets operating therein and to enforce compliance;

Fishing fleet jurisdiction: On the high seas, flag states have exclusive jurisdiction over vessels; fishing activity is therefore subject to the flag state's treaty obligations (Ferrell 2005). The registration of fishing vessels is overseen by the flag state. Based on a vessel's history and intended fishing activity, certain flags of convenience and flag hopping practices are likely to be used to facilitate illegal activities. Authorisation for the vessel is given by the flag state – at this stage, conditions for adequate identification of the vessel, reliable reporting of catch and authorisation for transshipment, if applicable, are overseen. Moreover, the flag state has the responsibility to hold a record of its fishing fleet and report its catch.

Fish imports jurisdiction: The port state sets regulations and standards for port inspection. The port state's engagement in countering landing and port operations by vessels involved in IUU practices determines the port state's openness to illegal and poorly traceable fishing products and to serving vessels with known infractions. The PSMA intends to counter this risk factor, but efficient monitoring requires resources, which are often lacking despite a state's engagement within the framework of the PSMA. The port state is responsible for certification schemes and the transparency and documentation of catch imports.

Several efforts have been made to curb illegal fishing since IUU fishing emerged on national and international agendas in the mid-1990s (see Christensen 2016).

The European Union has been active in addressing the problem through a regulation to prevent, deter and eliminate IUU fishing, which includes three strategies: First, a catch certification scheme seeks to ensure that only marine fisheries products validated as legal by the competent flag state or exporting state can be imported into or exported from the EU. This, however, may be challenged by a lack of transparency from the flag states, as vessels can launder illegal catches through legitimate ports. Second, the European Commission instituted a carding system that incentivises exporting countries to reduce illegal fishing under their flag in order to maintain their access to the EU market and has led to improvements of measures in exporting countries (Sumaila 2019). This carding process includes issuing warnings to and eventually blacklisting states that do not take action against IUU activity. The regulation includes measures for blocking access to EU markets at EU ports for blacklisted vessels identified as involved in IUU fishing, or for vessels registered under countries that have a poor reputation for cooperating with international efforts to prevent, deter and eliminate IUU fishing (Soyer, Leloudas and Miller 2018). An EU list of IUU vessels is issued regularly, based on IUU vessels identified by RFMOs.[5] Since the introduction of the system, three formerly red-carded countries were removed from the list, and 13 countries had their yellow card removed. Third, substantial penalties for EU operators undertaking illegal fishing, proportional to the economic value of their catch, have deprived them of any – or at least some – of their profit (Petrossian and Pezzella 2018).

---

5 We note that while the EU uses RFMO lists, China has an additional independent blacklist for its own fleet, which often results in stricter measures against vessels and companies by the Chinese government (Shen and Huang 2021).

Despite the significance of these measures in improving seafood sourcing for EU members and fishing practices in exporting countries (Leroy, Galletti and Chaboud 2016; Wongrak et al. 2021), some IUU-caught fish is still being imported into the EU, in part due to shortcomings in the regulation and its implementation. For example, Okafor-Yarwood and Belhabib (2020) have shown that the EU failed to red-card countries with which it has major trade exchanges. In addition, diversion strategies still exist, notably relabelling the origin of fish caught in red-carded countries, relocating companies from the countries carded and transshipping fish on the high seas. Some recent examples show the inability of the EU to sanction its own DWF fleet when it operates illegally, as seen with an Italian vessel shark finning off Sierra Leone which went unpunished (CFFA 2020). Some exporters have learnt how to navigate the differing capacities and diligence among EU members (Mundy 2018). After the carding system was implemented, some exporters of suspected IUU-caught fish made use of differing port inspection standards within the EU (Mundy 2018). In terms of impacts on fishers and the countries where the fishing is taking place, Beyens, Failler and Asiedu (2018) observed "growing difficulty of institutions in adapting to more and more stringent EU regulations and developing new sets of domestic rules and […] lack of collaboration between key institutions, which does not allow the setting up of efficient food safety systems". This may have negative impacts on developing countries and small-scale fishers in particular.

On the international level, various additional frameworks exist to counter illegal fishing. The United Nations Fish Stocks Agreement (UNFSA) adopted in 1995 is an implementation agreement of UNCLOS regarding the conservation and sustainable use of fisheries (Metuzals et al. 2010; Rosello 2017). RFMOs are responsible for the management of fisheries within their respective geographical mandates. One measure adopted by RFMOs allows the blacklisting of vessels that have been engaging in some forms of illegal fishing (Metuzals et al. 2010). However, the resulting aggregated list contains less than 300 vessels combined and does not paint an accurate picture of the other thousands of vessels that engage in similar illegal activities but have not been suggested for blacklisting (Belhabib and Le Billon 2018).

The FAO has adopted soft law, including the 1995 Code of Conduct for Responsible Fisheries and the 2001 International Plan of Action to Prevent, Deter and Eliminate Illegal, Unreported and Unregulated Fishing, which have significantly contributed to solutions (Agnew et al. 2009; Metuzals et al. 2010; Rosello 2017). The FAO's Committee on Fisheries (COFI) has adopted a range of Voluntary Guidelines, including for Flag

State Performance clarifying state obligations (Ventura 2015), and for Catch Documentation Schemes (Hosch 2020). The 2005 PSMA, as an international legally binding agreement to reduce incentives of IUU vessels to operate while blocking IUU fish from reaching national and international markets (European Commission 2020), has been joined by 68 states to date (the EU is also party to the agreement). It describes the steps that should be taken by responsible port states and relevant RFMOs to ensure compliance at ports (Petrossian and Pezzella 2018; Soyer, Leloudas and Miller 2018). Through this measure, port states can take action by inspecting and/or detaining visiting vessels, and the access of IUU catches to markets can be blocked (Soyer, Leloudas and Miller 2018). However, varying implementation capacities result in a small number of ratifications and a lack of effective enforcement, preventing international standards of port inspections.

The Commission for the Conservation of Antarctic Marine Living Resources (CCAMLR) should also be mentioned (Metuzals et al. 2010), regarding its regulatory measures (including observation schemes), flag and port state measures (including documentation schemes and inspection standards) as well as various resolutions (Miller, Slicer and Sabourenkov 2010). Best-practice examples include CCAMLR's electronic documentation system, which resulted in more comprehensive and accurate catch reporting and real-time access to documents, enhancing enforcement and reducing misreporting, catch laundering and fraud; as well as public dissemination of CCAMLR's IUU Vessel Lists which, however, did not entirely eliminate the problem in the region (Miller, Slicer and Sabourenkov 2010).

Current MCS measures entail a number of activities, including: the tracking of vessel movements and monitoring of vessel activities based on their VMS and automatic identification systems (AIS); the deployment of surveillance assets such as vessels, planes and drones; as well as community co-surveillance operations (Soyer, Leloudas and Miller 2018). NGOs undertake data collection to reveal information to authorities and the public, assist with arrests and raise general awareness (Soyer, Leloudas and Miller 2018). This includes investigations into trade flows and ownership, the creation of spyglass.fish (which removes a layer of opacity from illegal fishing activities), the IUU Fishing Index (a joint project between a for-profit firm and a non-profit organisation to analyse states' vulnerability, exposure and responses to IUU fishing (Lycan & van Buskirk, 2021)) and policy advocacy at national, regional and international levels. We stress that the militarisation of surveillance of small-scale fisheries may result in the securitisation of the latter, to the benefit of an industrial sector that is much more harmful when it engages in illegal fishing (Okafor-Yarwood 2019). Hence, addressing illegal fishing within the small-scale sector requires understanding the drivers of illegal fishing within this sector and addressing them accordingly. Lastly, efforts of the private sector can discourage illegal fishing through the use of traceability and labelling schemes (Soyer, Leloudas and Miller 2018). Overall, measures have been taken on fishing area, fleet and port jurisdiction, but stronger regulations and oversight are necessary to close governance gaps to prevent, deter and eliminate IUU fishing as a global problem.

4. The way forward: possible solutions to reduce harm from IUU fishing

Despite the above-mentioned efforts to curb IUU fishing, the solution remains a global challenge. This section lays out how shortcomings of existing efforts can be bridged and environmental, social and economic harms from IUU fishing be reduced along the supply chain (see also Introduction in this volume).

4.1 Address flags of convenience and tax havens

Strategies to eliminate IUU fishing often focus explicitly on prosecuting the vessel and crew members that were actively involved in the activity but fail to address the problem at its source by identifying the networks and prosecuting the beneficial owners that stand behind the operations (Widjaja et al. 2019). Increased transparency in vessel registries and closure of flag of convenience (FOC) registries are needed to prevent IUU fishing. Holding flag of convenience states accountable and requiring full disclosure of a company's corporate network of fishing vessels will play a major role in reducing some of the IUU practices enabled by FOC-based evasion strategies.

Apart from identifying and sanctioning FOC IUU vessel owners, blacklisting and financial methods (Ferrell 2005), more recent suggestions include encouraging a) countries with open registries to close them to fishing vessels; b) coastal states and RFMOs to ban the use of FOCs by all fishing vessels authorised to fish within their fishing area jurisdictions; c) flag states, coastal states and RFMOs to make access agreements and lists of authorised vessels public; d) all countries to publicly register their entire fishing fleet (including foreign-flagged vessels owned by their nationals);

and e) all countries to adopt legislation similar to the EU legislation to prevent their nationals from engaging in, supporting or benefiting from the activities of identified IUU vessels (Petrossian et al. 2020).

4.2 Curtail economic gains from illegal fishing

Illegal fishing is currently still a low-risk and high-reward activity. Future efforts to curb illegal fishing therefore need to curtail economic gains from illegal activities and reward compliance with existing regulations.

Subsidised industrial fleets put local fleets at a disadvantage and contribute to illegal fishing (Arthur et al. 2019). Ending such subsidies has been encouraged by a number of NGOs, as well as formally proposed by the COFI members (FAO 2021). The WTO agreement reached in 2022 is a step towards ending such subsidies, provided that comprehensive implementation and continued dialogue on pending issues follow (Fitt 2022). Restrictions of access to insurance for those involved in IUU fishing could also increase the financial risks of IUU practices (Miller et al. 2016). Studies of how availability of liability insurance contributes to the problem of IUU fishing reveal that vessels suspected of involvement in illegal fishing have no serious difficulty in obtaining liability insurance, which facilitates illegal fishing. Companies can be financially disincentivised through trade sanctions, e.g. through the EU carding system (Rosello 2017). As discussed in this chapter, stricter sanctions by the EU (Okafor-Yarwood and Belhabib 2020) and additional sanctions by other main seafood markets, such as Japan and the US, (Sumaila 2019) would more comprehensively address global IUU fishing. Certification schemes encourage seafood companies to integrate greater transparency into the supply chain and point customers to the legal fish on the market. However, the practice of mislabelling seafood challenges this measure when MCS and enforcement measures are lacking (Helyar et al. 2014). Another way to stop illegal fishing of attractive species would be to further safeguard such species through additional trade bans and limitations (Petrossian 2015), e.g. under the Convention on International Trade in Endangered Species of Wild Fauna and Flora (CITES). Moreover, making non-compliance with existing fishing regulations public can damage an industry's image and could encourage further transparency in the supply chain on the part of the seafood producers.

4.3 Increase monitoring, control and surveillance by linking available data

Especially on the high seas, illicit activities often remain "unseen". MCS is a real challenge, particularly for low-income countries and in areas beyond national jurisdiction, as it is expensive and requires high technological standards. AIS data linked to the vessel's GPS can identify individual fishing vessels (IMO number, maritime mobile security information number, vessel name, call sign) and trace position, speed and course in real-time (Dunn et al. 2018) from the port of departure until the final destination. Through the real-time location of fishing vessels and their speed, fishing activity can be suspected and even predicted (Crespo et al. 2018), and thus conservation and sustainable use measures can be improved. For this to happen, however, a comprehensive coverage of the global fishing activity needs to be available.

Turning off AIS may imply suspicious activity but is not proof of an offence in contexts where AIS is not mandatory for fishing vessels. Currently, only vessels with gross tonnage over 300 have to carry AIS for safety purposes (IMO 2015), which translates to only 14 % of all vessels registered in the Consolidated List of Authorized Vessels for tuna, and in many cases individual country regulations are weaker or entirely lacking (Dunn et al. 2018).

Comprehensive coverage of activities at sea can be ensured through 1) mandatory use of AIS at all times; 2) registration of IMO numbers and 3) effective enforcement of regulations (Dunn et al. 2018). Sierra Leone, for instance, has made AIS mandatory on all industrial fishing vessels licensed to fish in the country's waters, and Russia sanctions its DWF vessels if they shut down the AIS.

The combination of AIS technology, data obtained using VMS and cameras on board the vessels is valuable to ensure traceability throughout the supply chain. Satellite technology can identify further crimes at sea, such as forced labour (McDonald et al. 2021). Having open access to and sharing information with authorities of flag and port states across jurisdictions and combining different data sources is crucial for comprehensive data analysis. Law enforcement on the high seas is challenged by the reliance on flag state responsibility, as well as governance gaps in areas beyond national jurisdiction and many states' lack of capacity for MCS activities (Cremers, Wright and Rochette 2020a). In this regard, the ongoing negotiations for a legally binding agreement on the conservation and sustainable use of marine biological diversity of areas beyond national jurisdiction offer an opportunity to strengthen MCS obligations on the high seas (Tessnow-von Wysocki and Vadrot 2020).

4.4 Enhance international cooperation and capacity building

The importance of regional and international cooperation to address the global problem of IUU fishing is undisputed. The EU is seen as a pioneer in adopting IUU regulations that combine transparent reporting (catch documentation scheme) and concrete sanctions (blacklisting of vessels). However, measures against (and sanctions for) serious infringements differ among member states, with rules being differently interpreted and enforced (European Commission 2020). A unified implementation of the IUU regulations needs to be found in order to tackle the problem holistically. Cooperation among different authorities within one country is as important as regional and international cooperation, as well as the integration of different stakeholders, including RFMOs, NGOs, the fisheries sector and authorities from the flag and port states along the supply chain. Best-practice examples include FISH-i Africa[6], Project Eyes on the Seas[7] and Global Fishing Watch[8] (Cremers, Wright and Rochette 2020b). Moreover, access to technologies, tools and training to collect, access and analyse data needs to be guaranteed for states that do not have these capacities to effectively engage in MCS and enforcement.

4.5 Eliminate transshipment, particularly on the high seas

While transshipment reduces logistical costs, it also challenges transparency in the supply chain, which is necessary to trace the fishing methods used and the origin of catch and to determine whether the fish was caught legally. A recent FAO report shows evidence that transshipment can be linked to severe crimes at sea and concludes that the "lack of sufficient ca-

---

6 FISH-i Africa is a partnership of eight East African countries – Comoros, Kenya, Madagascar, Mauritius, Mozambique, Seychelles, Somalia and Tanzania – that brings together national enforcement authorities, regional organisations and international technical and legal experts to combat large-scale illegal fishing in the Western Indian Ocean through information-sharing and regional cooperation. See https://fish-i-network.org/.

7 Project Eyes on the Seas is a partnership between The Pew Charitable Trusts and the UK Government's Satellite Applications Catapult to help governments detect suspicious fishing activity using AIS and VMS data, satellite imagery, vessel information databases and computer algorithms.

8 Global Fishing Watch is an independent NGO founded by Oceana, Google and SkyTruth that makes data on global commercial fishing activity more publicly available.

pacity in competent authorities makes it impossible to deter and prevent these activities systematically" (Quelch et al. 2020: 115). The South East Atlantic Fisheries Organisation (SEAFO) has prohibited all transshipment at sea by members operating within the convention area (Ewell et al. 2017), but transshipment regulations vary significantly among flag states and RFMOs (Miller et al. 2018). With regard to transshipment notifications and authorisations of RFMO secretariats, only 62.5 % of them reported having a requirement for the RFMO to be informed by the flag state contracting parties prior to/at the point of authorisation for at-sea transshipments, and 12.5 % reported having a mechanism to review and approve transshipment authorisations by flag states (Quelch et al. 2020). Scholars have suggested a moratorium on transshipment on the high seas to address both IUU fishing and human rights abuses (Ewell et al. 2017). Until transparent prior notification of intended transshipments and tonnages and MCS strategies are sufficiently developed to oversee transshipment operations, such activities need to be declared illegal to prevent greater harm.

The FAO has recognised the need for national and international guidelines for effective regulation, monitoring and control of transshipment (FAO 2020). Recently, COFI members were urged to develop global transshipment guidelines (Carreon 2021) to define transshipment, containerisation and landing; introduce transshipment authorisation requirements; require the submission by fishing vessels of standardised transshipment declarations to all relevant authorities; monitor measures; and standardise open-access information-sharing procedures among flag, coastal and port states and RFMO secretariats, which would mark a "major step towards establishing transparent transshipment processes that support a sustainable and verifiable seafood supply chain" (Borg Costanzi and Wozniak 2021).

4.6 Address ports of convenience through the PSMA

At sea, MCS is dangerous, costly and in most cases impossible to undertake. Having effective measures in place when the vessels get into port is therefore unavoidable. The Port State Measures Agreement has been an important milestone in this regard. However, all port states must ratify and implement the PSMA to ensure that IUU fishing perpetrators are not making use of ports of convenience (Widjaja et al. 2019). To date, many countries that are party to the PSMA do not have the capacity to implement it. Capacity translates into the ability to have qualified inspectors at ports at all times during vessel landings. Inspectors should be trained to inspect catches and detect multiple offences. Hence, international efforts should focus on capacity building in these countries, in terms of either personnel or resources directly allocated to these countries (without intermediaries).

4.7 Digitalise records of fish imports

Effective documentation of the catch is crucial for transparency. Catch documentation schemes (CDS) can address and eliminate several types of illegal fishing, including fishing without licence and (in combination with VMS) non-compliance with days-at-sea regulations as well as spatial and temporal fishing closures, among others (Hosch 2020). Existing examples of CDS include three multilateral schemes and one unilateral scheme, the latter being that of the EU, which covers all marine wild-caught fish traded by non-EU countries into the EU market. The FAO Voluntary Guidelines for CDS indicate a preference for electronic catch documentation (FAO 2017). While all schemes initially started as paper-based schemes, two have by now switched to electronic CDS, namely CCAMLR and ICCAT. The European Commission has suggested a switch to an electronic system (CATCH), which would facilitate information sharing between member states and increase efficiency of IUU controls and now awaits adoption and implementation. The adoption of the Fisheries Control System (European Parliament 2021) enables greater transparency through the introduction of on-board cameras and by tracing the origin of fishery and aquaculture products throughout the entire food chain. It is, however, equally important to ensure accurate reporting of the catch, as the increased margin of error in the reports could leave up to 40 % of seafood caught by the EU fleet unreported (EU Fisheries Control Coalition 2021).

4.8 Extend the concept of IUU to 'post-fishing' harm to marine life

So-called 'ghost fishing gear' is wreaking havoc on marine life long after fishing operations have ended. Every year, about 640,000 tonnes of 'ghost gear' are added to the ocean, adding not only to plastic pollution but also to deadly drifting nets, lines and hooks (Greenpeace 2019). This abandoned, lost or otherwise discarded fishing gear (ALDFG) should be seen as a form of IUU fishing since – intentionally or not – it kills fish in illegal ways. Research has pointed to this problem and suggested ways forward (Richardson, Hardesty and Wilcox 2019; Tessnow-von Wysocki and Le Billon 2019), and several initiatives seek to reduce and recover ALDFG, such as the Global Ghost Gear Initiative (an alliance of NGOs, private sector, fishing industry, academia and governments) and the FAO Voluntary Guidelines on the Marking of Fishing Gear (FAO 2019). Among the most promising initiatives is the reporting of fishing gear before and after fishing operations, so that vessels suspected of having generated ALDFG can be properly tracked and sanctioned, including through listing on the EU's IUU vessels lists in case of repeated ALDFG reports and suspicion of negligent practices. ALDFG recovery could also benefit from economic incentives, replacing cost-cutting with revenue generation incentives (e.g. Sea Shepherd's (2019) programme for the recovery of totoaba gillnets in vaquita habitats).

4.9 Going beyond IUU to look into fairness of fishing licence contracts

'Legally', fish may be caught under contracts that are unfair to coastal states and local fishing communities. There is a need for greater transparency and benchmarking in the contracts between foreign (or domesticated) fishing fleets and host authorities (Belhabib and Le Billon forthcoming). These contracts also need to consider impacts on local populations in terms of both food security and domestic fishing-related livelihoods. Ensuring such 'fair' fisheries is not only the next step after ensuring 'legal' ones, but one that needs to happen in parallel to prevent negative impacts on local fishing. Supply chain policies and instruments involving formalisation and legalisation can have counterproductive effects, such as increased inequalities among resource users (Le Billon and Spiegel 2021). Parallel efforts at a *global* level therefore need to be made in order to ensure a level playing field among DWFs from different countries. Disclosure of licensing contracts and regional transparency standards are required. Existing initiatives such as the Fisheries Transparency Initiative or the Extractive Industries Transparency Initiative could – despite their limitations – serve as a starting point (Rustad, Le Billon and Lujala 2017).

5. *Conclusion*

Illegal fishing is a severe environmental crime with adverse impacts on the environment on the one hand, but also with negative consequences for small-scale fishers, coastal populations and entire economies of low-income countries. Often linked to drug and human trafficking, as well as slavery, IUU fishing constitutes a complex challenge with a variety of actors involved within a global supply chain. In light of the overexploitation and depletion of fish stocks, it is a significant threat to the marine environment on which the natural system as well as current and future generations rely. In order to effectively curb IUU activities, solutions are required that go beyond the existing national, regional and international regulations, which were important steps in the fight to curb IUU fishing but have proven insufficient.

This chapter has introduced the global problem of IUU fishing with its significant impacts on different levels that go beyond economic losses and include severe environmental and social harms. It shows that while low-income countries in the Global South may be more prone to illegal and unreported fishing activities due to limited MCS measures, developed countries play an integral part in the supply chain by offering a consumer market. To prevent IUU fishing, several regulations have been put in place on national, regional and international levels. Ten years after the implementation of the EU's IUU fishing regulation, the Environmental Justice Foundation assessed the initiative as "a truly effective policy that has had a real, positive impact around the world, safeguarding marine ecosystems and the communities that rely on them" (Trent 2020). Many researchers point to the importance and challenges of spreading the adoption of this governance approach to other major fish markets across the world (Sumaila 2019; Fang and Asche 2021; Garcia, Barclay and Nicholls 2021; Rogers 2021). Yet, as this chapter suggests, there is still room for improvement. The supply chain of IUU fish is complex and requires extensive consideration of local, national and transnational dimensions, from the legality of the fishing activity, the implications of the implementation of anti-IUU reforms on small-scale fishers and the licence and operations of the fishing vessels to processes of transshipment, re-exportation and verification at landing ports and within European markets.

As a next step, the EU is encouraged to more strongly counter IUU activities, including with regard to unified implementation of IUU regulations among EU member states, its own fishing fleet and main foreign trade partners. Our case study of Ghana suggests that many backdoors to EU seafood markets exist, such as the illegal domestication of third-country vessels. This implies that the problem of IUU fishing cannot be solved regionally but requires a global approach. The identification of the different steps and actors within the supply chain can help to identify the motivations and connections behind illicit activities in order to develop more effective measures to prevent IUU fishing on a global level. Finally, this chapter briefly presented some of the options to curb IUU fishing, including i) addressing flags of convenience and tax havens; ii) curtailing economic gains; iii) increasing MCS; iv) enhancing international cooperation and capacity building; v) eliminating transshipment; vi) implementing the PSMA; vii) digitalising records of fish imports; and extending the concept of IUU fishing by viii) addressing 'post-fishing'; and ix) ensuring fairness of fishing licence contracts.

References

Agnew, David J./Pearce, John/Pramod, Ganapathiraju/Peatman, Tom/Watson, Reg/ Beddington, John R./Pitcher, Tony J. (2009): "Estimating the worldwide extent of illegal fishing". In: PLOS ONE, 4, 2, e4570.

Alberts, Elizabeth Claire (2021): "On board Ghana's trawlers, claims of human rights abuses and illegal fishing". At: https://news.mongabay.com/2021/08/on-board-ghanas-trawlers-claims-of-human-rights-abuses-and-illegal-fishing/ (accessed 16 May 2022).

Arthur, Robert/Heyworth, Stephanie/Pearce, John/Sharkey, William (2019): "The cost of harmful fishing subsidies". At: https://pubs.iied.org/16654iied (accessed 13 May 2022).

Battista, Willow/Romero-Canvas, Rainer/Smith, Sarah Lindley/Fraire, Jose/Effron, Micah/Larson-Konar, Dylan/Fujita, Rod (2018). "Behavior change interventions to reduce illegal fishing". In: Frontiers in Marine Science, 5.

Belhabib, Dyhia/Cheung, William W. L./Kroodsma, David/Lam, Vicky W.Y./Underwood, Philip J./Virdin, John (2020): "Catching industrial fishing incursions into inshore waters of Africa from space". In: Fish and Fisheries, 21, 2, pp. 379–92.

Belhabib, Dyhia/Dridi, Raouf/Padilla, Allan/Ang, Melanie/Le Billon, Philippe (2018): "Impacts of anthropogenic and natural 'extreme events' on global fisheries". In: Fish and Fisheries, 19, 6, pp. 1092–1109.

Belhabib, Dyhia/Le Billon, Philippe (2018): "Tax havens are the tip of the iceberg". In: Nature Ecology & Evolution, 2, 1679.

Belhabib, Dyhia/Le Billon, Philippe (2020): "Editorial: Illegal fishing as a trans-national crime". In: Frontiers in Marine Science, 7.

Belhabib, Dyhia/Le Billon, Philippe (2022): "Fish crimes in the global oceans". In: Science Advances, 8, 12, eabj1927.

Belhabib, Dyhia/Le Billon, Philippe (forthcoming): "Adjacency and vessels domestication as enablers of fish crimes". In: Frontiers in Marine Science.

Belhabib, Dyhia/Le Billon, Philippe/Bennett, Nathan (2022): "Ocean sustainability for all requires deeper behavioural research". In: Nature Human Behaviour, 6, pp. 6–8.

Belhabib, Dyhia/Le Billon, Philippe/Wrathall, David J. (2020): "Narco-Fish: Global fisheries and drug trafficking". In: Fish and Fisheries, 21, 5, pp. 992–1007.

Belhabib, Dyhia/Sumaila, U. Rashid/Le Billon, Philippe (2019): "The fisheries of Africa. Exploitation, policy, and maritime security trends". In: Marine Policy, 101, pp. 80–92.

Belhabib, Dyhia/ Sumaila, U. Rashid/Pauly, Daniel (2015): "Feeding the poor. Contribution of West African fisheries to employment and food security". In: Ocean & Coastal Management, 111, pp. 72–81.

Beyens, Yolaine/Failler, Pierre/Asiedu, Berchie (2018): "Institutional challenges and constraints for Ghana in exporting fishery products to the European Union". In: Food Reviews International, 34, pp. 265–89.

Borg Costanzi, Dawn/Wozniak, Esther (2021): "International guidelines would helps illegal activity tied to at-sea transfer of fish". At: https://www.pewtrusts.org/en/research-and-analysis/articles/2021/01/22/international-guidelines-would-help-stem-illegal-activity-tied-to-at-sea-transfer-of-fish (accessed 13 May 2022).

Carreon, Bernadette (2021): "FAO Committee on Fisheries members urged to adopt global transshipment guidelines by 2022". At: https://www.seafoodsource.com/news/environment-sustainability/fao-committee-on-fisheries-members-urged-to-adopt-global-transshipment-guidelines-by-2022 (accessed 13 May 2022).

CFFA, Coalition for Fair Fisheries Agreements (2020): "CSOs complaint about Italian vessels illegal activities in Sierra Leone. The European Commission is dragging its feet". At: https://www.cffacape.org/news-blog/csos-complaint-about-italian-vessels-activities-in-sierra-leone-the-european-commission-is-dragging-its-feet (accessed 13 May 2022).

Christensen, Joseph (2016): "Illegal, unreported and unregulated fishing in historical perspective". In: Poulsen, Bo/Schwerdtner Máñez, Kathleen (eds.): Perspectives on Oceans Past. A handbook on marine environmental history. Dordrecht: Springer, pp. 133–153.

Cremers, Klaudija/Wright, Glen/Rochette, Julien (2020a): "Strengthening monitoring, Control and surveillance in Areas Beyond National Jurisdiction". At: https://www.prog-ocean.org/wp-content/uploads/2020/01/Cremers-Wright-and-Rochette-2019.-Strengthening-Monitoring-Control-and-Surveillance-in-Areas-Beyond-National-Jurisdiction-1.pdf (accessed 13 May 2022).

Cremers, Klaudija/Wright, Glen/Rochette, Julien (2020b): "Strengthening monitoring, control and surveillance of human activities in marine areas beyond national jurisdiction: Challenges and opportunities for an international legally binding instrument". In: Marine Policy, 122, 103976.

Crespo, Guillermo Ortuño/Dunn, Daniel C./Reygondeau, Gabriel/Boerder, Kristina/Worm, Boris/Cheung, William/Tittensor, Derek P./Halpin, Patrick N. (2018): "The environmental niche of the global high seas pelagic longline fleet". In: Science Advances, 4, 8, eaat3681.

Dunn, Daniel C./Jablonicky, Caroline/Crespo, Guillermo O./McCauley, Douglas J./Kroodsma, David A./Boerder, Kristina/Gjerde, Kristina M./Halpin, Patrick N. (2018): "Empowering high seas governance with satellite vessel tracking data". In: Fish and Fisheries, 19, 4, pp. 729–739.

EC, European Commission (2013): "Commission Decision of 26 November 2013 on notifying the third countries that the Commission considers as possible of being identified as non-cooperating third countries pursuant to Council Regulation (EC) No 1005/2008 establishing a Community system to prevent, deter and eliminate illegal, unreported and unregulated fishing (2013/C 346/03)". In: Official Journal of the European Union, pp. C 346/26–C 346/49.

EC, European Commission (2020): "Report from the Commission to the European Parliament and the Council on the application of Council Regulation (EC) No 1005/2008 establishing a community system to prevent, deter and eliminate illegal, unreported and unregulated (IUU) fishing (the IUU Regulation)". At: https://eur-lex.europa.eu/legal-content/EN/TXT/?uri=CELEX:52020DC0772 (accessed 13 May 2022).

EC, European Commission (2021a): "Illegal fishing". At: https://ec.europa.eu/oceans-and-fisheries/fisheries/rules/illegal-fishing_en (accessed 31 May 2022).

EC, European Commission (2021b): "Fighting against illegal, unreported and unregulated fishing. Commission notifies the Republic of Ghana with a yellow card". At: https://ec.europa.eu/commission/presscorner/detail/en/ip_21_2745 (accessed 13 May 2022).

European Council (2008): "Council Regulation (EC) No 1005/2008 of 29 September 2008 establishing a Community system to prevent, deter and eliminate illegal, unreported and unregulated fishing". At: https://eur-lex.europa.eu/eli/reg/2008/1005/oj (accessed 13 May 2022).

EJF, European Justice Foundation (2020): "Europe – A market for illegal seafood from West Africa. The case of Ghana's industrial trawl sector". At: https://ejfoundation.org/reports/europe-a-market-for-illegal-seafood-from-west-africa-the-case-of-ghanas-industrial-trawl-sector (accessed 13 May 2022).

EU Fisheries Control Coalition (2021): "Two steps forward, one giant step back. European Parliament votes for modern and transparent fisheries, but opens grave loophole". At: http://www.transparentfisheries.org/2021/03/11/two-steps-forward-one-giant-step-back-european-parliament-votes-for-modern-and-transparent-fisheries-but-opens-grave-loophole/ (accessed 13 May 2022).

European Parliament (2021): "Fishing rules: Compulsory CCTV for certain vessels to counter infractions". At: https://www.europarl.europa.eu/news/en/press-room/20210304IPR99227/fishing-rules-compulsory-cctv-for-certain-vessels-to-counter-infractions (accessed 13 May 2022).

EUMOFA, European Market Observatory for Fisheries and Aquaculture Products (2020): "The EU Fish Market. 2020 Edition". At: https://www.eumofa.eu/documents/20178/415635/EN_The+EU+fish+market_2020.pdf/fe6285bb-5446-ac1a-e213-6fd6f64d0d85?t=1604671147068 (accessed 13 May 2022).

EUMOFA, European Market Observatory for Fisheries and Aquaculture Products (2021): "The EU Fish Market. 2021 Edition". At: https://www.eumofa.eu/documents/20178/477018/EN_The+EU+fish+market_2021.pdf/27a6d912-a758-6065-c973-c1146ac93d30?t=1636964632989 (accessed 16 May 2022).

Ewell, Christopher/Cullis-Suzuki, Sarika/Ediger, Mikaela/Hocevar, John/Miller, Dana/Jacquet, Jennifer (2017): "Potential ecological and social benefits of a moratorium on transshipment on the high seas". In: Marine Policy, 81, pp. 293–300.

Fang, Yingkai/Asche, Frank (2021): "Can U.S. import regulations reduce IUU fishing and improve production practices in aquaculture?". In: Ecological Economics, 187, 107084.

FAO, Food and Agriculture Organization of the United Nations (2001): "International Plan of Action to prevent, deter and eliminate illegal, unreported and unregulated fishing". At: http://www.fao.org/fishery/ipoa-iuu/en (accessed 06 October 2021).

FAO, Food and Agriculture Organization of the United Nations (2017): "Voluntary Guidelines for Catch Documentation Schemes". At: http://www.fao.org/iuu-fishing/resources/detail/en/c/1132200/ (accessed 16 May 2022).

FAO, Food and Agriculture Organization of the United Nations (2019): "Voluntary Guidelines on the Marking of Fishing Gear. Directives volontaires sur le marquage des engins de pêche. Directrices voluntarias sobre el marcado de las artes de pesca". At: http://www.fao.org/documents/card/en/c/CA3546T/ (accessed 16 May 2022).

FAO, Food and Agriculture Organization of the United Nations (2020): "The State of World Fisheries and Aquaculture 2020. Sustainability in action". At: http://www.fao.org/publications/sofia/2020/en/ (accessed 16 May 2022).

FAO, Food and Agriculture Organization of the United Nations (2021): "2021 COFI Declaration For Sustainable Fisheries and Aquaculture, Thirty-fourth Session, 1–5 February". At: http://www.fao.org/3/ne472en/ne472en.pdf (accessed 16 May 2022).

Hosch, Gilles (2020): "Catch documentation schemes". In: FAO, Food and Agriculture Organization of the United Nations/Hosch, Gilles: Catch Documentation Schemes for Deep-sea Fisheries in the ABNJ, pp. 17–43.

Felson, Marcus/Clarke, Ronald V. (1998): Opportunity makes the thief. Practical theory for crime prevention. London: Home Office Research, Development and Statistics Directorate.

Ferrell, Jessica K. (2005): "Controlling flags of convenience. One measure to stop overfishing of collapsing fish stocks". In: Environmental Law, 35, 2, pp. 323–390.

Fitt, Elizabeth (2022): "WTO finally nets deal curbing fisheries subsidies, but tables key bits for later". At: https://news.mongabay.com/2022/06/wto-finally-nets-deal-curbing-fisheries-subsidies-but-tables-key-bits-for-later/ (accessed 22 August 2022).

Flothmann, Stefan/Von Kistowski, Kristín/Dolan, Emily/Lee, Elsa/Meere, Frank/Album, Gunnar (2010): "Closing loopholes. Getting illegal fishing under control". In: Science, 328, 5983, pp. 1235–1236.

Garcia, Sonia Garcia/Barclay, Kate/Nicholls, Rob (2021): "Can anti-illegal, unreported, and unregulated (IUU) fishing trade measures spread internationally? Case study of Australia". In: Ocean & Coastal Management, 202, 105494.

GI-TOC, Global Initiative Against Transnational Organized Crime (2021): "IUU Fishing Index". At: https://iuufishingindex.net/ (accessed 31 May 2022).

Greenpeace (2019): "Ghost gear. The abandoned fishing nets haunting our oceans". At: https://www.greenpeace.org/aotearoa/publication/ghost-gear-the-abandoned-fishing-nets-haunting-our-oceans/ (accessed 16 May 2022).

Gutierrez, Miren/Daniels, Alfonso/Jobbins, Guy/Guttierez Almazor, Guillermo/Montenegro, Cesar (2020): "China's distantwater fishing fleet -Scale, impact and governance". At: https://cdn.odi.org/media/documents/chinesedistantwaterfishing_web.pdf (accessed 16 May 2022).

He, Juan (2018): "From country-of-origin labelling (COOL) to seafood import monitoring program (SIMP). How far can seafood traceability rules go?". In: Marine Policy, 96, pp. 163–174.

Helyar, Sarah J./Lloyd, Hywel Ap D./De Bruyn, Mark/Leake, Jonathan/Bennett, Niall/Carvalho, Gary R. (2014): "Fish product mislabelling. Failings of traceability in the production chain and implications for illegal, unreported and unregulated (IUU) fishing". In: PLOS ONE, 9, 6, pp. e98691.

IMO, International Maritime Organization (2015): "Resolution A.1106(29) Adopted on 2 December 2015 (Agenda item 10) Revised Guidelines for the Onboard Operational Use of Shipborne Automatic Identification Systems (AIS)". At: https://wwwcdn.imo.org/localresources/en/OurWork/Safety/Documents/AIS/Resolution%20A.1106(29).pdf (accessed 16 May 2022).

INTERPOL (2014): "Study on fisheries crime in the West African coastal region." In: INTERPOL Environmental Security Sub-Directorate (ENS).

INTERPOL (2020): "Fighting illegal, unreported and unregulated fishing". At: https://www.interpol.int/News-and-Events/News/2020/Fighting-illegal-unreported-and-unregulated-fishing (accessed 16 May 2022).

Koop, Fermin/Aldred, Jessica (2020): "WTO fails to meet fishing subsidies deadline". At: https://chinadialogueocean.net/15886-wto-fails-to-meet-fishing-subsidies-deadline/ (accessed 16 May 2022).

Le Billon, Philippe (2008): "Diamond wars? Conflict diamonds and geographies of resource wars". In: Annals of the Association of American Geographers, 98, 2, pp. 345–372.

Le Billon, Philippe/Spiegel, Samuel (2021): "Cleaning mineral supply chains? Political economies of exploitation and hidden costs of technical fixes." In: Review of International Political Economy.

Leroy, Antonia/Galletti, Florence/Chaboud, Christian (2016): "The EU restrictive trade measures against IUU fishing". In: Marine Policy, 64, pp. 82–90.

Liddick, Don (2014): "The dimensions of a transnational crime problem: the case of iuu fishing". In: Trends in Organized Crime, 17, pp. 290–312.

Lindley, Jade/Techera, Erika J. (2017): "Overcoming complexity in illegal, unregulated and unreported fishing to achieve effective regulatory pluralism". In: Marine Policy, 81, pp. 71–79.

Long, Tony/Widjaja, Sjarief/Wirajuda, Hassan/Juwana, Stephanie (2020): "Approaches to combatting illegal, unreported and unregulated fishing". In: Nature Food, 1, pp. 389–91.

Lycan, Tyler/Van Buskirk, Lexie 2021: "What we know about maritime environmental crime". At: http://www.safeseas.net/wp-content/uploads/2021/09/What_We_Know_About_Maritime_Environmental_Crime.pdf (accessed 16 May 2022).

Maryudi, Ahmad/Myers, Rodd (2018): "Renting legality. How FLEGT is reinforcing power relations in Indonesian furniture production networks". In: Geoforum, 97, pp. 46–53.

McDonald, Gavin G./Costello, Christopher/Bone, Jennifer/Cabral, Reniel B./Farabee, Valerie/Hochberg, Timothy/Kroodsma, David/Mangin, Tracey/Meng, Kyle C./Zahn, Oliver (2021): "Satellites can reveal global extent of forced labor in the world's fishing fleet". In: Proceedings of the National Academy of Sciences, 118. 3, e2016238117.

Metuzals, Kaija/Baird, Rachel/Pitcher, Tony/Sumaila, Rashid/Ganapathiraju, Pramŏd (2010): "One fish, two fish, IUU and no fish. Unreported fishing worldwide". In: Grafton, R. Quentin/Hilbron, Ray/Squires, Dale/Tait, Maree/Williams, Mery (eds.): Handbook of marine fisheries conservation and management. Oxford: Oxford University Press, pp. 165–181.

MFAD, Ministry of Fisheries and Aquaculture Development, Republic of Ghana (2020): "Monitoring, Control, and Surveillance Division". At: https://www.mofad.gov.gh/agencies/fisheries-commission/divisions-of-fisheries-commission/monitoring-control-and-surveillance-division/ (accessed 06 October 2021).

Miller, Dana D./Sumaila, U. Rashid/Copeland, Duncan/Zeller, Dirk/Soyer, Baris et al. (2016): "Cutting a lifeline to maritime crime. Marine insurance and IUU fishing". In: Frontiers in Ecology and the Environment, 14, 7, pp. 357–362.

Miller, Denzil G. M./Slicer, Natasha/Sabourenkov, Eugene N. (2010): "IUU fishing in Antarctic waters. CCAMLR actions and regulations." In: Vidas, Davor (ed.): Law, technology, and science for oceans in globalisation". Leiden: Brill Nijhoff, pp. 175–196.

Miller, Nathan A./Roan, Aaron/Hochberg, Timothy/Amos, John/Kroodsma, David A. (2018): "Identifying global patterns of transshipment behavior". In: Frontiers in Marine Science, 5.

Mundy, Victoria (2018): "The impact of the EU IUU Regulation on seafood trade flows. Identification of intra-EU shifts in import trends related to the catch certification scheme and third country carding process". At: http://www.iuuwatch.eu/wp-content/uploads/2018/02/TDA_report_IUUwatch_HQ.pdf (accessed 16 May 2022).

OECD, Organisation for Economic Co-operation and Development (2020): "Fighting illegal, unreported and unregulated fishing". In: OECD Review of Fisheries 2020. Paris: OECD iLibrary.

Okafor-Yarwood, Ifesinachi (2019): "Survival of the richest! Towards an understanding of the impacts of the securitisation of small-scale fisheries in West Africa". Edinburgh: European Conference on African Studies. At: https://nomadit.co.uk/conference/ecas2019/paper/48744 (accessed 16 May 2022).

Okafor-Yarwood, Ifesinachi (2020): "The cyclical nature of maritime security threats. Illegal, unreported, and unregulated fishing as a threat to human and national security in the Gulf of Guinea". In: African Security, 13, 2, pp. 116–46.

Okafor-Yarwood, Ifesinachi/Belhabib, Dyhia (2020): "The duplicity of the European Union Common Fisheries Policy in third countries. Evidence from the Gulf of Guinea". In: Ocean & Coastal Management, 184, 104953.

Österblom, Henrik/Bodin, Örjan (2012): "Global cooperation among diverse organizations to reduce illegal fishing in the Southern Ocean". In: Conservation Biology, 26, 4, pp. 638–648.

Österblom, Henrik/Bodin, Örjan/Press, Anthony J./Sumaila, U. Rashid (2016): "The high seas and IUU fishing". In: Smith, Hance D./Suárez de Vivero, Juan Luis/Agardy, Tundi S.: Routledge Handbook of Ocean Resources and Management. Abingdon, Oxon, UK: Routledge, pp. 232–240.

Pacoureau, Nathan/Rigby, Cassandra L./Kyne, Peter M./Sherley, Richard B./Winker, Henning et al. (2021): "Half a century of global decline in oceanic sharks and rays". In: Nature, 589, pp. 567–571.

Petrossian, Gohar A. (2015): "Preventing illegal, unreported and unregulated (IUU) fishing. A situational approach". In: Biological Conservation, 189, pp. 39–48.

Petrossian, Gohar A./Marteache, Nerea/Viollaz, Julie (2015): "Where do 'undocumented' fish land? An empirical assessment of port characteristics for IUU fishing". In: European Journal on Criminal Policy and Research, 21, 3, pp. 337–351.

Petrossian, Gohar A./Pezzella, Frank S. (2018): "IUU fishing and seafood fraud. Using crime script analysis to inform intervention". In: Annals of the American Academy of Political and Social Science, 679, 1, pp. 121–139.

Petrossian, Gohar A./Sosnowski, Monique/Miller, Dana/Rouzbahani, Diba (2020): "Flags for sale. An empirical assessment of flag of convenience desirability to foreign vessels". In: Marine Policy, 116, 103937.

PEW, The Pew Charitable Trusts (2020): "Port Risk: risk of illegally-caught fish passing through port". At: https://www.pewtrusts.org/en/research-and-analysis/data-visualizations/2020/port-activity-study-reveals-potential-for-illegal-fish-to-enter-markets (accessed 16 May 2022).

Pramod, Ganapathiraju (2018): "Ghana country report". In: IUU Risk Intelligence: Policing the open seas, global assessment of fisheries monitoring control and surveillance in 84 countries. Canada.

Pramod, Ganapathiraju/Pitcher, Tony J. (2019): "In defence of seafood import analysis. Credulity bamboozled by supply chain laundering". In: Marine Policy, 108, 103651.

Quelch, Glenn D./Von Kistowski, Kristin/Young, Mark/Carrara, Giuliano/Rey Aneiros, Adelaida et al. (2020): "Transshipment: a closer look. An in-depth study in support of the development of international guidelines". In: Moistero Cabanelas, Alicia (ed.): FAO Fisheries and Aquaculture Technical Papers, Series No. 661. Rome: Food and Agricultural Organization.

Richardson, Kelsey/Hardesty, Britta Denise/Wilcox, Chris (2019): "Estimates of fishing gear loss rates at a global scale. A literature review and meta-analysis". In: Fish and Fisheries, 20, 6, pp. 1218–1231.

Rogers, Kimberly (2021): Examining the impact of the European Union's carding scheme to combat Illegal, Unreported, and Unregulated fishing on the Republic of Panama's seafood trade. San Diego: Center for Marine Biodiversity and Conservation, UC San Diego.

Rosello, Mercedes (2017): "Cooperation and unregulated fishing. Interactions between customary international law, and the European Union IUU fishing regulation". In: Marine Policy, 84, pp. 306–312.

Rustad, Siri Aas/Le Billon, Philippe/Lujala, Päivi (2017): "Has the Extractive Industries Transparency Initiative been a success? Identifying and evaluating EITI goals". In: Resources Policy, 51, pp. 151–162.

Satizábal, Paula/Le Billon, Philippe/Belhabib, Dyhia/Saavedra-Díaz, Lina M./Figueroa, Isabela/Noriega, Gina/Bennett, Nathan J. (2021): "Ethical considerations for research on small-scale fisheries and blue crimes". In: Fish and Fisheries, 22, 6, pp. 1160–1166.

Sea Shepherd (2019): "Sea shepherd removes over 1000 pieces of illegal fishing gear from vaquita habitat". At: https://seashepherd.org/news/sea-shepherd-removes-over-1000-pieces-of-illegal-fishing-gear-from-vaquita-habitat/ (accessed 16 May 2022).

Shen, Huihui/Huang, Shuolin (2021): "China's policies and practice on combatting IUU in distant water fisheries". In: Aquaculture and Fisheries, 6, 1, pp. 27–34.

Song, Andrew M./Scholtens, Joeri/Barclay, Kate/Bush, Simon R./Fabinyi, Michael/Adhuri, Dedi A./Haughton, Milton (2020): "Collateral damage? Small-scale fisheries in the global fight against IUU fishing". In: Fish and Fisheries, 21, 4, pp. 831–843.

Soyer, Barış/Leloudas, George/Miller, Dana (2018): "Tackling IUU fishing. Developing a holistic legal response". In: Transnational Environmental Law, 7, 1, pp. 139–163.

Sumaila, Ussif Rashid/Alder, Jacqueline/Keith, Heather (2006): "Global scope and economics of illegal fishing". In: Marine Policy, 30, 6, pp. 696–703.

Sumaila, Ussif Rashid (2019): "A carding system as an approach to increasing the economic risk of engaging in IUU fishing?". In: Frontiers in Marine Science, 6.

Sumaila, Ussif Rashid/Ebrahim, Naazia/Schuhbauer, Anna/Skerritt, Daniel/Li, Yang et al. (2019): "Updated estimates and analysis of global fisheries subsidies". In: Marine Policy, 109, 103695.

Sumaila, Ussif Rashid/Skerritt, Daniel/Schubauer, Anna/Villasante, Sebastian/Cisneros-Montemayor, Andres M. et al. (2021): "The World Trade Organization must prohibit harmful fisheries subsidies". In: Science, 374, 6567, p. 544.

Tessnow-von Wysocki, Ina/Le Billon, Philippe (2019): "Plastics at sea. Treaty design for a global solution to marine plastic pollution". In: Environmental Science & Policy, 100, pp. 94–104.

Tessnow-von Wysocki, Ina/Vadrot, Alice B. M. (2020): "The voice of science on marine biodiversity negotiations. A systematic literature review". In: Frontiers in Marine Science, 7.

Trent, Steve (2020): "A decade of the EU's regulation on illegal fishing. Real-world progress". At: https://ejfoundation.org/news-media/a-decade-of-the-eus-regulation-on-illegal-fishing-real-world-progress (accessed 16 May 2022).

UNCLOS (1982): United Nations Convention on the Law of the Sea.

Vandergeest, Peter/Marschke, Melissa (2021): "Beyond slavery scandals. Explaining working conditions among fish workers in Taiwan and Thailand". In: Marine Policy, 132, 104685.

Ventura, Victor Alencar Mayer Feitosa (2015): "Tackling illegal, unregulated and unreported fishing. The ITLOS Advisory Opinion on Flag-state Responsibility for IUU fishing and the principle of due diligence". In: Revista de Direito Internacional, 12, 1, pp. 51–66.

Vince, Joanna/Hardesty, Britta Denise/Wilcox, Chris (2021): "Progress and challenges in eliminating illegal fishing". Fish and Fisheries, 22, 3, pp. 518–531.

Widjaja, Sjarief/Long, Tony/Wirajuda, Hassan/Van As, Hennie/Bergh, Per Eik et al. (2019): "Illegal, unreported and unregulated fishing and associated drivers". At: https://www.oceanpanel.org/blue-papers/illegal-unreported-and-unregulated-fishing-and-associated-drivers (accessed 16 May 2022).

Wongrak, Garnchanok/Hur, Nancy/Pyo, Insoo/Kim, Jungsuk (2021): "The Impact of the EU IUU regulation on the sustainability of the Thai fishing industry". In: Sustainability, 13, 12, 6814.

Yozell, Sally/Shaver, Amanda (2019): "Shining a light. The need for transparency across distant water fishing". At: https://www.stimson.org/2019/shining-light-need-transparency-across-distant-water-fishing/ (accessed 16 May 2022).

Illegal logging, timber laundering and the global illegal timber trade

Inga Carry and Günther Maihold

Introduction

Deforestation claims an estimated 10 million hectares each year (FAO 2020). Today's global demand for timber products[1] simply cannot be met by legal, sustainable forestry anymore. The competition for cheap wood products on the global timber market has become a major driver of illegal deforestation and the global illegal timber trade. This article focuses on activities related to the licensing, harvesting, processing and trading of timber products inconsistent with international, national or subnational law at any point in the supply chain.

Legal deforestation is regulated through national or local forestry legislation, often in the form of forest codes that include a system of logging concessions and permits. However, even where forestry legislation exists, the definition of what exactly constitutes legal, informal and illegal logging often remains ambiguous. Boekhout van Solinge et al. (2016) identify three different types of illegal logging: (1) informal logging, (2) illegal forest conversion and (3) criminal logging. Informal logging, also known as "chainsaw" or artisanal logging, is mostly carried out by forest communities that rely on subsistence logging as their regular income. This form of informal logging is often perceived by these communities "neither as a criminal nor a harmful activity" (Bisschop 2015: 115), and yet it contributes a significant share of the illegal production and export of timber from tropical countries (Kishor and Lescuyer 2012 and Wit et al. 2010, as cited in Gan et al. 2016: 39). Increasingly, illegal logging occurs in the form of forest conversion, mostly for commercial agricultural purposes, for instance by converting forest land into pasture or crop land. While this has become a major driver of illegal deforestation, it must be distinguished from criminal logging in the sense that the extraction of wood is not the primary motivation of this criminal activity. Rather, the timber cut

1 Timber products include round wood, paper and derivative products.

in this process is a by-product of forest clearing for other purposes. In contrast, criminal logging refers to the process of unauthorised large-scale deforestation or the selective cutting of (high-value) timber for the sole purpose of generating profits through the international trade and sale of illegally harvested timber.

Illegal timber trade is the commercial activity of illegally trading timber across one or more state borders without proper papers or authorisation. Most illegally extracted timber is consumed domestically and never actually enters the international market (Bisschop 2015: 106). The timber that does get traded on regional and international markets mostly comprises high-value species characterised by a large profit margin. The illegal trade in timber is almost always linked to other criminal offenses, including forgery, mislabelling, tax evasion, corruption, bribery and money laundering.

Both illegal logging and the associated illegal timber trade are thus not isolated crimes, but need to be seen as "a mosaic of interdependent criminal activities" (INTERPOL and World Bank 2010: 9). As such, they often exist in a grey area between the legal and the illegal, between clandestine and legitimate business activities, carried out by legal, informal and criminal actors and on multiple layers of timber markets (local, regional and international) (Nellemann and INTERPOL Environmental Crime Programme 2012). This interplay of legal and illegal actors can be observed throughout the entire supply chain – from producer to transit to consumer countries – and creates the central gateway for timber laundering, a process by which illegal timber is given a clean bill of health and integrated into the legal supply chain, from where it ends up as seemingly legitimate timber on our market shelves.

Global supply chains of tropical timber follow a trade pattern from producer countries in the Global South to consumer countries in the Global North. Practically all global timber supply chains include at least one transit country that forms the link between production sites in the Global South and buyers of timber products in the Global North. China has become the most important transit country for both legal and illegal timber products; other common transit countries include Brazil, Malaysia, Madagascar, Mozambique and several Central African states. On the purchasing end, the biggest importers of tropical wood products are China, the US, Japan, the EU (particularly Germany, Italy, the Netherlands and Belgium) and the UK.

The international character of timber supply chains not only adds to the difficulty of tracing the origin of the timber but also creates legal hurdles for addressing the problem of illegal logging and timber trade. Illegal logging constitutes a localised crime that is subject to national legislation. It becomes relevant to international law enforcement only when the timber is leaving the country in which it was cut. Whether the timber is legal or illegal thus depends on the legislation of its country of origin, not on the legality or illegality of the downstream process. Consequently, a piece of wood can originate from illegally logged timber and still be sold with complete legality in another country (INTERPOL and World Bank 2010: 16).

Environmental, social and economic implications of illegal logging

Illegal logging and its associated timber trade have enormous environmental, social and economic implications. Illegal deforestation threatens the unique composition of tropical rainforests and their ability to serve as a habitat for a vast variety of flora and fauna. With the loss of biodiversity also comes an ecological instability and degradation that may ultimately prove irreversible (Bisschop 2015: 108; Peck 2001: 17). Tropical rainforests also function as a carbon sink – the Amazon has played a significant role in absorbing up to a quarter of all fossil fuel emissions since 1960 (Carrington 2021). As deforestation continues, however, tropical forests are gradually losing their ability to act as a climate regulator. In fact, scientists confirmed in 2021 that the Amazon is now actually emitting more carbon dioxide than it is able to absorb (Gatti et al. 2021).

In terms of social impacts, illegal logging is often directly linked to the disempowerment and displacement of local and indigenous communities as well as a growing tendency for violence towards environmental activists. The year 2020 has been declared the deadliest year so far for land and environmental defenders, with more than 220 lethal attacks recorded, many of which were associated with forestry (Global Witness 2021). In some cases, the proceeds from illegal timber are also used to actively fuel and finance armed conflict, as has been the case in Liberia, Cambodia and the Democratic Republic of the Congo (DRC). Oftentimes, the timber supply chain is further linked to other crimes, such as the illegal trade of wildlife, drug trafficking and money laundering (Boekhout van Solinge 2008).

Seen from a financial angle, illegal logging and the global illegal timber trade bear economic consequences, including the distortion of market prices, a loss of state revenues and taxes and increasing income disparities (McElwee 2004; Sotirov et al. 2015; Kleinschmit, Leipold and Sotirov 2016). This causes an annual global market loss of up to US$10 billion, with governments losing an additional US$5 billion in assets and revenue

(World Bank 2008). At the same time, illegal logging is estimated to be the highest-value environmental crime, accumulating a global worth of $US 51–152 billion every year (Nellemann et al. 2020). The latest WWF report on the EU Forest Crime Initiative (2021) captures the situation as follows: "Forestry crime may involve the greatest mismatch of government and intergovernmental resources spent on combating them relative to the crime profits that they generate." (WWF 2021: 4 citing Nellemann et al. 2020)

And yet, with the exception of the Convention on International Trade in Endangered Species of Wild Fauna and Flora (CITES; also known as the Washington Convention) that aims at protecting endangered plants and animals, a formal overarching international treaty on illegal logging and related timber trade remains lacking. In the early 2000s, concerted efforts by governments, civil society and the private sector to improve forest management and law enforcement have led to a significant decline in illegal logging activity in many countries, including Brazil, Cameroon and Indonesia. However, these improvements are seen as mainly "procedural rather than substantive" (Kleinschmit, Leipold and Sotirov 2016: 15), mostly because they have since been offset by two major developments. First, while the US, Australia and the European Union have developed legal frameworks in order to prevent the placement of illegal timber on their markets, the illegal timber trade has gradually shifted towards non-sensitive markets (i.e. those with less strict regulations on legality). China in particular has emerged as the new timber trading hub, with the People's Republic now being a major importer, exporter and consumer of timber products. This geographic shift has rendered the policies of traditional consumer countries significantly less powerful and effective.

Second, the rising demand for agricultural products such as soy and beef as well as large-scale mining and infrastructure projects has led to massive conversions of forest land into areas used for agricultural or other industrial purposes. Around half of the tropical timber traded around the globe today stems from forest conversion, of which two thirds are deemed illegal. Brazil and Indonesia account for 75 per cent of the global tropical forest area that has been illegally converted for commercial agriculture between 2000 and 2012 (Lawson 2014: 2).

The issue of illegal deforestation has long been conceived solely from an environmental and climate protection angle. However, greater attention is increasingly being paid to the role of transnationally operating criminal networks associated with illegal logging and related timber trade. The spatial dimension in which illegal logging takes place – from the local to the regional up to the global level – as well as the sophistication with which the timber is harvested, laundered, transported and then traded indicate the involvement of well-equipped and organised criminal networks. As such, these groups possess the capacity and capital to provide heavy equipment, hire and coordinate workers and devise methods with which to pass off illegally harvested timber as legal products (Human Rights Watch 2019: 32). According to INTERPOL and UNEP, it is estimated that between 50 and 90 per cent of timber harvested in key tropical producer countries in Amazonia, Central Africa and Southeast Asia is illegal (Nellemann and INTERPOL Environmental Crime Programme 2012: 6). These groups often forge interlinkages with other networks of organised crime, such as drug syndicates, private militias, wildlife traffickers and illegal mining groups. Together, these transnationally organised crime groups act along the entire supply chain, exploiting institutional and legislative weaknesses and a lack of communication between law enforcement agencies both within and between countries (INTERPOL 2019: 2).

This chapter examines illegal logging and the global illegal timber trade as a form of transnational criminal activity. The chapter first presents a description of the structure and stages of illegal logging and timber flows. This will be followed by an analysis of two case studies, the Brazilian Amazon and the Southeast Asian region, to exemplify the characteristics of illegal logging and timber trade in two different contexts. This analysis will serve as a basis for identifying possible entry points at the local, regional and global levels to curb illegal logging and control the global illegal timber trade.

Three stages of illegal logging and timber trade

Before illegal timber enters the market of consumer countries in the Global North, it passes through a complex global supply chain involving multiple layers and types of markets as well as a wide network of actors, including tree owners, millers, intermediaries, traders and purchasers (Kishor and Lescuyer 2012: 258). Like money laundering, illegal logging and illegal timber trade follow a clear three-step process: extraction (placement), laundering (layering) and integration (integration).[2]

2 See the Financial Action Task Force (FATF) on the different stages of money laundering, https://www.fatf-gafi.org/faq/moneylaundering/.

Extraction

The use of forest codes or similar forestry legislation has become a standard tool for countries to improve their forest management by better monitoring, tracking and safeguarding of forest inventory and timber licenses. However, legal loopholes, a lack of resources and understaffing of responsible authorities as well as a high susceptibility to corruption have curtailed the effectiveness of many of these mechanisms. In general, there are four main forms of illegal timber harvesting.

Cutting outside of concessions and with fraudulent permits: One of the most commonly practised forms of illegal logging is cutting outside of or without concessions and permits. This includes overcutting beyond allocated quotas, using forged or expired permits or harvesting protected timber species without logging permits. For rare and/or protected timber species, logging concessions are limited, and their harvest is regulated by CITES (the Convention on International Trade in Endangered Species of Wild Fauna and Flora). The higher the value attributed to these timber species, the higher the incentive for criminal groups to illegally harvest and trade them for lucrative prices on the international market. Increased logging and trade, in turn, amplify the rarity of these species, intensifying their threatened status and even driving them to extinction (Gan et al. 2016: 38). A tactic of selective single-tree logging makes it more difficult for satellite imagery to detect the illegal loggers or their harvest under the dense tree cover. As Chimeli, Boyd and Adams (2012: 2) explain, "[a]lthough this method of selective logging in remote tropical forests may entail large opportunity costs, some species fetch high enough prices in international timber markets to justify the construction of logging feeder roads and other infrastructure for selective harvesting".

Overestimation of forest inventory: The allocation of cutting concessions is based on a forest inventory that catalogues existing tree species and their quantity within a certain forest area. Weaknesses in inventory systems offer an easy way for corrupt forest engineers to systematically accumulate fraudulent credits, for instance by way of misidentifying undesirable trees as valuable species, overestimating the volume of rare wood species or listing non-existent specimens (Greenpeace 2018: 6). By overestimating the legal amount of timber allowed for harvest, incorrect forest inventories create a gateway for illegal loggers and facilitate the legalisation of their indiscriminate harvest.

Land conversion: The illegal clearance of forest space is increasingly taking place under the pretext of land conversion for agricultural and other industrial purposes. Here, the primary motive is not the extraction of timber per se; rather, the timber becomes a by-product of the clearance of forest land for agricultural (e.g. cattle ranching, soy production or plantations) or other industrial purposes, such as mining and infrastructure projects. It is estimated that by now around half of all tropical timber derives from forest conversion.

Cutting in road corridors: Since many deforestation sites are concentrated dozens of kilometres away from main roads, forest aisles provide the necessary access to concession and plantation areas. These forest aisles then create incentives for illegal loggers to cut along existing road corridors or create extensive "fishbone" patterns of unauthorised secondary roads (Ungar 2018: 10).

Laundering

After timber is illegally cut, criminal groups use a variety of methods with which to conceal its illegal origin, a process known as timber laundering. Once extracted, the timber is transported from the cutting site to the sawmill as quickly as possible, often on the very same transport routes that are used for legal timber. Transport passes and timber labels ought to verify the legality of the timber in transit. However, the common practice of simply forging the necessary documents or issuing false labels has made this control system extremely fallible. Forgers typically provide incorrect information on the botanical identity of the wood (e.g. the species), its geographic origin or the product type itself (e.g. solid wood vs. particleboard) (Wiedenhoeft et al. 2019). Transport passes are also forged or simply used multiple times. This type of fraud and mislabelling can occur at all stages of the timber supply chain, beginning with the forestry permit system up to the transport pass at the international trade harbour. Investigators found that the large majority of wood traded on the regional or international market is falsely declared as legally sourced and traded (Nellemann et al. 2014).

Once at the sawmill, the illegal timber is processed, making it almost impossible to discern its origin and legality. Sawmill operators mix the illegal with the legal timber, giving it a "clean" origin statement. They do so either voluntarily as beneficiaries of the illegal timber business, or because of pressure and extortion by criminal groups. Fraudulent permits and inventory credits are used to "cook the books" of sawmills processing illegally harvested timber (Greenpeace 2018: 3).

To further disguise the origin of the timber, it is common practice to export illegal timber for further processing. Neighbouring countries are a particularly attractive market for illegal timber traders owing to their close geographic proximity, their potentially laxer timber regulations as well as the historical, economic, cultural and political ties among the region's countries and their markets (Schloenhardt 2008; Forest Trends 2010, as cited in Kleinschmit, Leipold and Sotirov 2016). The more processing stations and countries are involved, the more difficult and costly it becomes to monitor and trace the legality of the timber along the supply chain (Nellemann and INTERPOL Environmental Crime Programme 2012).

Figure 1: Intersections between the legal and the illegal timber supply chain.

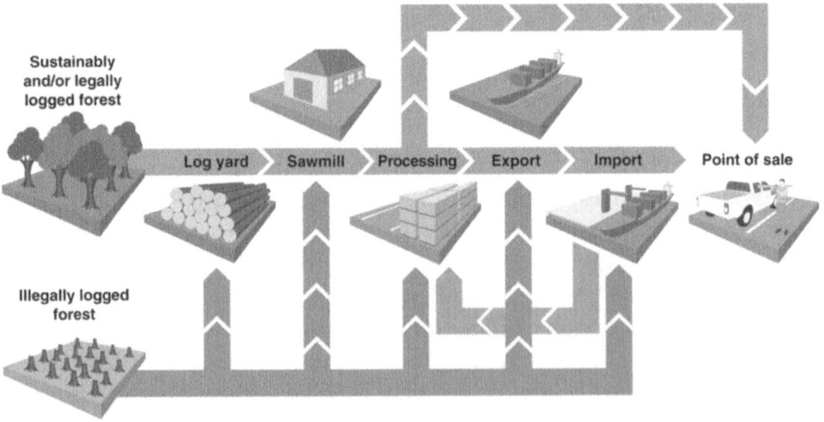

Source: Lowe et al. 2016

Integration

The large majority of tropical timber is consumed directly on domestic markets; only ten per cent of illegally produced wood products are traded on the international markets (Gan et al. 2016: 52). Due to the clandestine nature of the illegal timber trade, quantifications of the volume of illegally traded timber on the global market are mostly based on "guesstimates" (Bisschop 2012) rather than certainty. Comparing trade data can give a good indication; however, this method is not without errors. Trade discrepancies could simply be the result of shipment issues, incompatible and incoherent classification and measuring systems as well as time lags (Liu et al. 2020).

Even though the exact scope of illegal timber on the global timber market remains somewhat vague, there is extensive knowledge on the different methods used by criminal networks to introduce illegal timber into legal markets. As at the earlier two stages, forgery and corruption play a central role also at this stage of the supply chain.

Illegally logged timber can be integrated into the legal supply chain through different entry points along the supply chain (see Figure 1). Legally logged timber (dark arrows) passes from extraction sites over log yards and sawmills to (multiple) processing stations. Illegally logged timber (bright arrows) can potentially enter the legal supply chain at each of these stages; most often, however, it is integrated through sawmills (as described above) or through the practice of exporting the illegal timber to foreign processing stations and then reimporting it for further processing or trade.

Timber smuggling across state borders is a common practice used by criminal networks to circumvent export or import bans and disguise the origin of the illegally extracted timber. The majority of illegal timber supply chains involve at least one transit country before the timber reaches its final destination. Especially rare and high-value timber species are often shipped across the entire globe to conceal their true origin. This is confirmed by Bisschop (2015: 118) using the example of Afrormosia, a protected timber species from West Africa: "The seller and buyer [...] know that we know it comes from West Africa. Therefore it gets sent to Brazil, stays there for a few years, an edge is machined into it and then it is shipped to Europe. They know our alarms don't go off if this type of wood comes from Brazil."

Ports and international trade hubs are a key juncture in the process of mislabelling timber and integrating it into the global timber market. Hong Kong's free trade port in particular has been identified as a major smuggling hub for tropical timber species. The international shipping magazine SeaNews Turkey reported that 114 tonnes of high-value wood were smuggled into Hong Kong in the first half of 2018, marking a 170 per cent increase from the previous year (Papachristou 2018). The timber that reaches Hong Kong, often through brokers based in Singapore or Taiwan, is then exported to mainland China, where it is processed and passed on to third countries (Joy 2010: 4). According to INTERPOL, most of these import crimes remain undetected since less than two per cent of the cargo is actually inspected (INTERPOL and World Bank 2010: 12).

China, which has become the biggest importer, consumer and exporter of timber products, now plays a central role in the global timber market. As one of the biggest players in the timber business, China has also emerged as the primary destination for the illegal timber trade. Since 2016, China has successively imposed commercial logging bans to preserve its own natural forests. As an export-oriented economy, the country now depends on imported timber to produce secondary wood products for export (Zhang and Gan 2007). According to the Environmental Investigation Agency (EIA) (2012: 8), "[t]he gap between domestic timber supplies and the volume of timber used by the industry has in effect led to China exporting deforestation to a host of countries around the world". The organisation found that state-owned companies are directly involved in logging operations in countries with a high risk of illegality in the timber sector, including Indonesia, Mozambique and Myanmar.

National or regional policies to combat illegal logging have further been linked to a trade diversion towards China as a primary export market. During the negotiations between Indonesia and the European Union for a Voluntary Partnership Agreement (VPA), the value of Indonesia's sawnwood exports to China almost doubled, while its exports to the EU decreased by 40 per cent (Gan et al. 2016: 50). This trade diversion is indicative of a broader geographic shift that has taken place over the past decade and that suggests that timber traders choose regional and global markets with less stringent regulatory frameworks (such as China or India) since legality requirements set by other markets (such as the EU, Australia and the US) often come with extra costs for legality certificates and other required documentation (Giurca et al. 2013).

The who, the where and the how: criminal networks and market structures

The organisation and professionalisation of illegal logging and the associated timber trade are indicative of a shift from individual front-line timber criminals to conglomerates and organised crime groups. These criminal networks are typically involved not only in illegal logging but also in a multitude of other logging-related crimes, including violence, extortion, fraud and corruption. These "timber mafias", "criminal syndicates" or "timber gangs", as they are commonly referred to, use "an international network of quasi-legitimate businesses and corporate structures to hide their illegal activities" (WWF 2021: 6).

The more countries are involved in the processing, transport and trade of the illegal timber, the harder it is to retrace its origin, and the easier it is to take advantage of inconsistencies between different national legislations and international treaties (INTERPOL and World Bank 2010: 5). According to INTERPOL and the World Bank (2010), the illegal trade in timber has a business-like structure, with both provider and buyer companies. "It is driven by the economic principle of supply and demand: an increase in the demand for specific, often cheap wooden goods leads directly to an increase in the scale of illegal logging" (INTERPOL and World Bank 2010: 4).

Wyatt, Uhm and Nurse (2020: 351) distinguish three types of criminal networks: (1) organised crime groups, (2) corporate crime groups and (3) disorganised crime groups, each with a distinct set of actors, motives and modus operandi. In the context of illegal logging and timber trade, the boundaries between these types are often blurred, creating multiple intersections and "hybrid concepts" between corporate and state actors, organised criminal networks and disorganised groups. Thus, the concept of organised forestry crime might better be understood as a social system and social world "composed of relationships binding professional criminals, politicians, law enforcers, and various entrepreneurs" (Block 1983: vii, as cited in Boekhout van Solinge et al. 2016).

Interlinkages between illegal and legal actors are made possible through the involvement of so-called "facilitators of crime". These facilitators are brought in through bribery and corruption and can be found at every stage of the supply chain, from the origin through the transit up to the consumer station. Facilitators of crime include "security guards" hired by violent criminal groups to protect network members and illegal logging sites and transport routes (Boekhout van Solinge et al. 2016: 86). Other examples include members of law enforcement, political and military elites, corrupt officials from the forestry sector, money launderers and document forgers. The latter play a key role in falsifying logging and transport permits or timber certificates, sometimes even by hacking into government websites and forestry databases (Kleemans 2013; Lawson and MacFaul 2010).

For instance, Brazilian hackers once "legalised" 500,000 cubic metres of illegal timber by infiltrating the governmental digital timber control system. In investigating the case, the Federal Police also searched the houses of members of the Brazilian Institute of Environment and Renewable Natural Resources (IBAMA), whose responsibilities include monitoring and regulating national deforestation and logging activities. The involvement of government authorities and high-ranking personnel is by no means an exception. Several non-profit organisations have found a direct link between illegal logging groups and corrupt actors at the highest level of government, a form of cooperation known as "state-capture corruption" (Goncalves et al. 2012: 6). In Indonesia, illegal logging is often facilitated by high-ranking members of the government or military, and in African countries traditional chiefs and "custodians of the land" function as gatekeepers in this business. Owing to their connections and reputation, these actors are able to control and exert influence over the entire process of illegal logging and timber trade, for instance by granting forest concessions (INTERPOL and World Bank 2010: 7) or permits for the harvest, transport, processing and trade of illegal timber.

On the international level, such facilitators of crime include members of border authorities or shipping companies as well as personnel working at airports or trade harbours, where they can ensure that illegal cargo or certain people are not checked (Boekhout van Solinge et al. 2016: 86). In Indonesia, investigations by the EIA and Telapak found that in addition to members of the country's economic, political and military elites, businessmen, brokers and banks from Malaysia as well as international logging companies were involved as facilitators in the illegal transnational timber trade (EIA and Telapak 2004, 2005, 2006).

Finally, governments in the production, transit and consumer countries can play a facilitating, even perpetuating role by tolerating or even engaging in corruption and bribery and thus allowing the trade in illegal timber for the benefit of criminal actors.

As in other cases of transnationally organised illegal transactions, there is a starkly asymmetrical distribution of profits along the global timber supply chain. The greatest share of the financial benefit from the illegal timber trade goes to the intermediaries, i.e. processors, traders and financers, particularly in transit and processing countries, while (informal) loggers on the local level only receive a tiny fraction of the ultimate timber price. This means that the global illegal timber trade involves significant profits for intermediaries, with most of the money ending up in the hands of "elites" (Kishor and Lescuyer 2012). A study by the EIA and Telapak (2001) tracing the global supply chain of illegally extracted ramin found that the local logger in Indonesia received about US$2.2/cum, while the final product sold for close to US$1000/cum in the European and US markets. This not only shows that the production of illegal timber and its trade on international markets involve "a complex web of operators within and across countries, characterized by highly unequal political and market power and division of the 'spoils'", but further means that very little of the true market value of this high-value timber actually ends up in its original producer country (Kishor and Lescuyer 2012: 259–260).

Case studies

The bulk of illegal logging takes place in tropical forests such as the Amazon rainforest and the East Asia and Pacific region, where 50 to 90 per cent of all forestry is believed to be illegal. Brazil, which covers around 60 % of the Amazon basin, Indonesia, which contains the largest expanse of rainforest in all of Asia, and Malaysia, which is home to an equally rich rain forest, count as the world's leading exporters of tropical wood-based products. All three countries are vulnerable to and known for illegal logging and the export of illegally harvested timber. At the same time, their most lucrative destination markets for timber products are countries of the Global North, most notably the US, Italy, the Netherlands and Japan.

With a little help from the state: forest crime in Brazil

With over 670 million hectares, the Amazon basin is the largest rainforest in the world. Around 60 % of the Amazon rainforest lies in Brazil, making the country a major exporter of timber products. Brazil accounts for 70 to 80 per cent of all timber exported from the region, of which almost half goes to China and the US, with Italy and the Netherlands as top destination markets following closely behind. Over the past few years, Brazil's forestry sector generated more than US$3 billion in annual revenue and employed more than 200,000 people, although this number is likely to be significantly higher when informal employment in the forestry sector is included (see Lippe, Cui and Schweinle 2021).

Illegal logging continues to be a major issue in Brazil, where up to 70 per cent of the total forestry production is believed to be illegal (Perazzoni 2018: 24; Gan et al. 2016). Up until 2010, the Brazilian government had actually made significant progress in curbing (illegal) deforestation, with data showing that deforestation rates were down 70 per cent in 2013 compared to the average from 1996 to 2005, while greenhouse gas emissions resulting from deforestation had been cut by almost 70 per cent (Corrêa 2014). This drop was likely the result of a combination of a soy and beef moratorium and several private sector initiatives that sought to tackle illegal deforestation by establishing negative lists of properties and municipalities known to deforest illegally (Corrêa 2014; Azevedo et al. 2017). However the rate of deforestation in Brazil has been on an upward trajectory once more since 2012 and reached a 12-year high in 2020 (Phillips 2020). Data from Brazil's real-time Deforestation Detection System (DETER) and the Brazilian National Institute of Space Research

(INPE) show an 85 per cent increase in deforestation from 2018 to 2019, and another 34 per cent increase in deforestation in 2020 (Abdenur et al. 2020: 2; Escobar 2020). This latest uptick in deforestation has been encouraged by the policies of Brazil's current administration under President Jair Bolsonaro. Since coming to power in 2019, Bolsonaro has initiated major policy changes resulting in the weakening of environmental regulations, the dismantling of central governance structures and resource cuts for agencies tasked with monitoring and enforcing forest management. His positive attitude towards deforestation has further incentivised (illegal) land conversion for agricultural purposes and encroachment on indigenous lands. Meanwhile, the COVID-19 pandemic is believed to play a part as well, as criminal networks exploit "the lack of state attention and official discourses promoting land invasions in the Amazon" (Abdenur et al. 2020: 4 citing Kimbrough 2019; Butler 2020). According to the Instituto BVRio (2016: 8), Brazil has one of the most comprehensive and sophisticated timber control mechanisms, combining a federal system with two separate systems in Mato Grosso and Pará. However, "[w]idespread corruption and fraud [...] have rendered these systems unreliable and put Brazil at the top of the list of risky countries worldwide".

Organised criminal networks are increasingly believed to play a central role in the illegal logging business in Brazil. These networks include ranchers, loggers, miners and land grabbers and possess the logistical capacity to coordinate large-scale extraction, processing and sales of timber (Human Rights Watch 2019: 1). By extorting protection money, these criminal networks are able to force loggers and timber transporters into an alliance, granting them control over entire portions of the country. In fact, a study on environmental crime in the Amazon basin concludes that there are cities within the Brazilian state of Pará whose economies largely depend on revenue stemming from environmental crime, including illegal logging and timber trade (Abdenur et al. 2020: 5).

Criminal groups active in organised forest crime can rely on an extensive network of partners and facilitators that reaches up to the highest level of legitimate businesses, authorities and governments. In 2021, a group of researchers uncovered the close connections between the illegal timber business and drug trafficking. Investigative researchers found that there is a growing overlap in the infrastructure used by drug traffickers and illegal logging groups. Between 2017 and 2021, at least 16 major drug seizures revealed cocaine hidden within shipments of timber destined for export to Europe (Barros 2021).

In 2015, Brazil's Federal Police and Federal Prosecutor started an investigation into a large illegal logging and trade network that had used fraudulent timber credits and transport documents to pass off illegally harvested timber as legal. A large timber company that also owned several sawmills coordinated the illegal timber scheme, while several corrupt officials were found at the federal level (at the IBAMA and the National Institute for Colonisation and Agrarian Reform (INCRA)), at the state level in Pará as well as at the municipal level. This case of "state-capture corruption" was not the first one and was not going to be the last one, either. In mid-2021, high-ranking government officials once again became the focus of an investigation related to illegal logging and the timber trade. In the same year, Brazil's environment minister Ricardo Salles was forced to resign after facing an investigation into his involvement in alleged illegal timber exports. Several high-ranking environmental officials of IBAMA, including the head of the agency, were suspended after the Federal Police carried out raids on several ministry offices (Hanbury 2021). The investigation goes back to a decision by IBAMA's superintendent in 2019 to cancel a fine against Brazil's largest wood floor and deck exporter, which was suspected of illegal practices (Earthsight 2021). These cases exemplify the close-knit connection between (some) members of the administration and corporations involved in illegal logging and timber trade.

Illegal loggers in Brazil apply many of the methods for illegal timber harvesting laid out in the section above (cutting beyond or without concessions, selective logging, land conversion, etc.). However, even before the first tree is illegally cut, a flawed forest inventory system constitutes Brazil's first weak link in the chain of illegal logging. A study from 2018 analysing Brazil's licensing system found a strong overestimation bias towards high-value timber species and their assigned volumes in logging permits. This fraudulent surplus of licensed timber can then be used to launder and legalise the illegally harvested timber (Brancalion et al. 2018: 1). This method has become particularly attractive for rare and high-value species such as the ipê tree, a wood species known for its durability, which once processed can reach up to US$2,500 per cubic metre in export value (Greenpeace 2018: 8). Since the average population density of ipê trees is just one tree per ten hectares, loggers have to clear large swaths of forest in order to access the species and make the logging of ipê trees commercially viable (Schulze et al. 2008). This leads to a sprawl of illegal roads – the total length of unauthorised roads in Brazil has reached almost 170,000 km (Perazzoni 2018: 24) – encroaching on indigenous lands and protected areas and often resulting in violence between illegal loggers and local communities. Additionally, the selective logging of valuable timber has become a precursor for land grabbing and (illegal) land conversion. After the most valuable logs have been harvested, the rest of the forest is set on fire and turned into pasture land (Alessi 2021).

Once harvested, the timber is assigned a transport document and an associated identification number by IBAMA. However, the flawed inventory and credit system paired with corrupt state authorities and law enforcement agents as well as the widespread use of forged documents make these documents near useless for guaranteeing the legality of Brazilian timber. Effective oversight of logging activities and forest management is impeded by the vast physical dimensions and complex characteristics of the Brazilian rainforest. Environmental agencies are chronically understaffed, and with their offices located in major urban areas, land owners and environmental agents are rarely present in remote areas of the Amazon. Additionally, the decentralised system of Brazil's forest management and the coordination issues between federal and state agencies have created bureaucratic barriers and a lack of transparency (Hummel 2016: 3). If and when illegal logging activities are caught by the authorities, the perpetrators face very few consequences. In fact, during the first eight months of Jair Bolsonaro's presidency, the number of fines for offences related to deforestation fell by 38 per cent, reaching its lowest number in at least two decades. Meanwhile, NGOs promoting enforcement efforts have been limited in their capacity and even received threats against their members and local forest defenders (Human Rights Watch 2019: 9–10).

Most of the (illegal) timber harvested in Brazil is processed and sold domestically, with an overall export rate of timber products of around 44 per cent. According to data collected by Chatham House (n.d.-a) in 2014, about 2 per cent of Brazil's timber exports were deemed illegal, most of them pulp and paper product, while the export of ipê timber made up a large share, with the US, France, Portugal, Belgium and the Netherlands being the top destination countries (Greenpeace 2018: 12). Meanwhile, the steady rise in deforestation indicates that much of the timber harvested is a result of (illegal) land conversion mostly for agricultural products. In fact, both the opening of the Chinese market and the continuously high demand from the US and the EU have drastically increased the production of soybean and beef in Brazil, leading to a steady increase in the expansion of forest area lost to industrial agriculture (Forest Trends 2018). Even though illegal timber does not reach countries of the Global North through the direct trade of timber, roughly 20 per cent of soy exports and at least 17 per cent of beef exports from the Amazon and Cerrado to the EU may be contaminated with illegal deforestation (Rajão et al. 2020: 246). This share is expected to increase further in light of the possible implementation of the EU-Mercosur and US-China trade agreements, which are expected to lead to a growing EU demand for Brazilian products and to incentivise trade with lower tariffs (Rajão et al. 2020: 248).

The timber triangle: Indonesia, Malaysia and China

Indonesia is not only the world's top-selling palm oil producer but also one of the world's leading exporters of tropical timber. Indonesia ranks second to Brazil on tropical deforestation. Forest loss on the islands doubled between 2000 and 2012, mostly as a result of forest conversion for palm oil and timber plantations. Studies estimate that over 75 per cent of this forest conversion was illegal (Hoare and Wellesley 2014: 5). Even though longitudinal data suggest that illegal logging in Indonesia has decreased consistently since the 2000s, around 40 per cent of Indonesia's total timber production is still believed to stem from illegal sources (Hoare and Wellesley 2014: 5). Systematic illegal logging thus continues to be a widespread issue, with illegal activities occurring at the extraction, laundering and integration stages.

According to Hoare and Wellesley (2014), Indonesia's illegal logging issue is rooted in three major factors: a poorly functioning governance system, widespread corruption and a lack of transparency. As in Brazil, criminal groups involved in the illegal timber business have strong connections to other networks of organised crime, particularly those involved in the trade of narcotics. These networks use their influence to collude with law enforcement, judges and patrol officers, but also lawyers, banks and government officials who benefit from the profits gained through illegal logging activities (Joy 2010: 2). Using social network analysis, Baker (2020: 1) was able to characterise the landscape of forest criminals in Indonesia as "informal local networks of public and private actors" involving corrupt "forest field officials, timber entrepreneurs and brokers, army personnel, village and customary law leaders, and pioneer agriculturalists". The political elite plays a central role in this constellation, as illegal logging networks "reconfigured around the political authority of the regent", who, once elected, "appoints a cohort of corrupt administrators willing to manufacture licenses and permissions for campaign donors" (Baker 2020: 2).

Companies also play a central role in the illegal extraction of timber. In her analysis of one particular organised timber network, Baker identified members of the pulp industry as the largest occupational group involved in the network (41 %), followed by district and provincial forestry officials (28 %) (Baker 2020: 20). These companies cut beyond concessions and use "farmers' groups and indigenous communities as fronts for harvesting in areas that would otherwise be off-limits for commercial logging" (Jong 2019). Using boats and tugs, they transport the illegally cut wood along the rivers towards the sawmills, where it is processed and mixed in with legal timber (Joy 2010). The rising demand for timber products is putting pressure on poorer communities to collude with criminal groups for lucrative profits that far exceed the revenue they would otherwise get from legal logging activities. Meanwhile, plantation companies are known to systematically bypass fines and penalties associated with illegal land conversion and logging.

The extraction of high-value timber species has become a lucrative business for illegal logging groups. Rare and high-value timber species such as merbau and ramin are in high demand, particularly in China, where they are increasingly used for flooring, furniture and musical instruments. The high economic value of these timber species makes them an attractive target for illegal loggers and timber traders. Once extracted, the timber is smuggled across the border into Malaysia via the overland route. Even though Malaysia and several other countries, including China and Singapore, banned the import of timber from Indonesia in 2001, trade data between Malaysia and Indonesia revealed that cross-border timber trade continued illegally. For example, in 2003, the EIA uncovered a sophisticated network of ramin smugglers ferrying 4,500 cubic metres of illegal ramin from the Indonesian island of Sumatra to the neighbouring Malaysian port of Pasir Gudang every month. There, the wood was packed into containers, mislabelled as Malaysian and shipped to Shanghai and Hong Kong (EIA 2012: 10). Similarly, the EIA revealed the existence of an international criminal syndicate comprising government, police and military officials operating from Indonesia, Malaysian logging gangs, Singapore-based shipping companies and financiers as well as timber brokers in Hong Kong and mainland China, who were shipping large amounts of illegal merbau logs from Papua, Indonesia, to China.

This practice of declaring timber as Malaysian to disguise its origin and legality and then transferring it to neighbouring countries has become common among timber networks in this region. Ports in particular have become a hotspot for the illegal timber business. Since Hong Kong does not have a forestry crime policy, Indonesian illegal logging activities are not considered foreign indictable offences in Hong Kong (Joy 2010: 4). This provides a safe haven for criminal networks for timber trafficking and money laundering. Shipments to Singapore often contain illegal timber hidden beneath legal logs or equipped with forged documents and transport permits. From these initial destinations, the illegal timber is either shipped back to Indonesia, where it is considered imported wood, or exported on to China. Trade data show significant discrepancies between Chinese and Indonesian trade records, as China reports much higher import volumes of timber than Indonesia's export records show, indicating that fraud and smuggling remain frequent practices between the two countries (Hoare and Wellesley 2014: 26).

Illegal logging has long been a problem in Indonesia, which has not only put stress on the country's forestry sector but has also led to international pressure on Indonesia as a major timber exporter to address the issue. As a response, in 2009, Indonesia engaged in a multi-stakeholder process to refine the legal framework for wood extraction and develop a timber verification system, the SVLK (Sistem Verifikasi Legalitas Kayu). The system allows for third-party auditing to verify the legality of the operations of certificate holders and for independent monitoring by civil society groups while requiring licensed timber companies and concessionaires to obtain official SVLK certificates (Pohnan, Stone and Cashore 2014: 246). Since the introduction of the system, observers have criticised its weak enforcement and several loopholes that curb the effectiveness of the SVLK in tackling illegal logging. One example is the lack of what is known as "chain of custody verification", which means that certified sawmills are not required to source their timber from likewise certified logging concessionaries (Hoare and Wellesley 2014; Jong 2019). Nonetheless, in 2014, Indonesia and the EU ratified a VPA within the framework of the EU's Forest Law Enforcement, Governance and Trade (FLEGT) Action Plan, and the EU has since imported timber from Indonesia on the basis of its SVLK system. This was the first such agreement struck between the EU and a major Asian timber exporter and has been considered a cornerstone of the EU's efforts to curb illegal logging.

Yet, several major problems remain. Recent confiscations of shipping containers have revealed a large volume of illegally harvested timber, of which some could be traced back to companies certified under the SVLK system. Moreover, although Indonesia is the EU's biggest FLEGT VPA trading partner, the country exports only a minor share of its total timber volume to the European Union. In fact, trade data show that Indonesia's exports to sensitive markets such as the EU have continuously fallen, while its exports to non-sensitive markets, particularly China, have more than doubled over the years. At almost 30 per cent of its timber export volume, China has become Indonesia's top trading partner for timber products[3], followed by Japan (11 per cent) and the US (7 per cent) (United Nations

3 Comprising timber products HS 44, 47 and 48.

n.d.). Chatham House (n.d.-b) estimates that 70 per cent of Indonesia's timber exports to China come from illegal sources, meaning that a significant portion of Indonesian timber reaching the European Union via China and often declared as of Chinese origin must be considered illegal as well.

International regulation

There exist a number of loosely connected international instruments that focus on forest governance in the form of binding or non-binding multilateral treaty regimes and agreements, transnational governance frameworks, public-private partnerships or other types of non-binding norms, pacts, principles or coalitions (see Sotirov et al. 2020, as cited in Abdenur 2022: 11). CITES is arguably the most important mechanism to fight illegal logging and the illegal trade of timber, as it requires states to criminalise the illegal trade of timber species protected under the convention. However, its limited applicability to only certain timber species leaves room for illegal deforestation of non-listed species. Moreover, CITES does not contain an international enforcement mechanism and has thus far failed to implement a consistent verification procedure that addresses the multiple levels involved in the illegal timber trade (Kaphengst, Umpfenbach and Bräuer 2008: 8; Goncalves et al. 2012: 25; Bisschop 2015: 125–126).

This has led to a number of other policy measures being developed on the national, regional and international levels. Some of these are market-based incentives such as the Forest Stewardship Council (FSC) certification scheme; others are regulatory enforcement mechanisms, including the 2008 US Lacey Act; and yet others, such as the EU's Forest Law Enforcement, Governance and Trade (FLEGT), include both market and enforcement instruments. The FLEGT combines producer country-based instruments in the form of bilateral trade agreements (VPAs) as a way to curb illegal timber harvest and trade at the beginning of the supply chain with consumer country-based mechanisms in the form of the 2013 EU Timber Regulation (EUTR) that prohibits operators at the other end of the supply chain from placing illegally sourced timber on the European market. The two instruments are thought to reinforce one another by covering both ends of the supply chain. However, certain provisions within this mechanism have led to a number of loopholes and have thus reduced its effectiveness. The EUTR applies only to first-time operators, i.e. companies that place wood on the EU market for the very first time. All other downstream actors are only required to maintain records of purchases and sales for a period of five years, which they need to make available only upon request (EIA 2018).

Another weakness of the EUTR is its limited scope, which is significantly narrower than that of the US Lacey Act and the Australian Illegal Logging Prohibition Act. A study by WWF has found that only around a third of products that contain wood are covered by the EUTR (Drewe and Barker 2016). Raw materials typically have a higher coverage ratio, while finished or processed wood products are less likely to be covered. At the same time, timber and wood-based products originating from Southeast Asian countries are among those that are most often not covered by the EUTR (Weimar, Janzen and Dieter 2015).

Lastly, implementation of the EUTR varies considerably among member states, with many state authorities lacking the necessary resources to fully apply the regulation. A study by WWF (2021: 10) examining six European timber-consuming countries exposed the apparent lack of "capacity of relevant authorities to fight forestry crime [...] at certain or at all levels, showing a discrepancy between mission/intention and reality on the ground". Examining the implementation of the EUTR using Ukraine and Romania as two case studies, Davidescu and Buzogány (2021) confirm that the implementation of the EUTR is at best limited and uneven among consumer countries, and at worst impeded by state-supported illegal activities, corruption and mafia-like structures to the benefit of EU-based timber companies.

A 2018 study on the enforcement of the EUTR showed that Germany, which has the largest number of operators placing imported timber on the EU market, carried out the highest number of checks on companies (103 in total) and found that almost two thirds of those companies had not fully complied with the regulation. In contrast, Belgium, the biggest importer of tropical timber, conducted only two checks in the period under study. This stark disparity creates a loophole that encourages companies to trade with countries in which they expect no or only minimal checks (Blackman 2018). Additionally, many timber-consuming countries lack the necessary national legislation to criminalise transports of illegal timber. Therefore, to determine whether timber was logged, processed and transported legally or illegally, law enforcement agencies in importer countries rely on the national and local laws of the timber producing countries (Bisschop 2015: 126).

Responding to illegal logging and the global illegal timber trade

Regulatory mechanisms such as the US Lacey Act, the EU's FLEGT and third-party certification systems such as the FSC have certainly contributed to reducing the rate of illegal timber harvest and trade by bringing together business and civil society to develop common understandings and strategies for fighting (illegal) timber flows and increasing awareness of the problem. Yet, suffering from issues of inconsistency and transparency themselves,[4] these initiatives have proven inadequate to tackle the underlying structures of illegal logging and the global illegal timber trade. One reason for this is their inability to respond and adapt to the geographically shifting nature of the illegal timber industry. This applies both to the geographic shift of illegal timber markets, i.e. moving from highly regulated to loosely regulated environments, and to the trend away from large-scale illegal logging towards selective cutting and illegal land conversion.

The second reason is the absence of a comprehensive, integrated criminal justice strategy that combines the mechanisms for tackling illegal logging with strategies to counter corruption, organised criminal networks and financial crime. Such an integrated criminal justice strategy faces problems of coordinating the efforts of the different levels of governments and must include measures at each stage of the timber supply chain (from extraction to laundering to integration) and each level of the timber market (local, regional and global). But the stakes are high: the EU can provide certain incentives, support or exert pressure through conditionality at various points, but it must be aware that corresponding regulations can be quickly circumvented or undermined.

Extraction

At the local level, the focus should lie on preventing the illegal extraction of timber. To this end, strengthening national capacities to monitor and enforce forest law is key. In the Brazilian Trairão National Park, two forest officers are responsible for monitoring 257,000 hectares of forest; in the Riozinho do Anfrísio Park, the same number of staff looks after 736,000 hectares (WFB 2011). An effective response to forestry crime must allocate

4 For instance, Greenpeace revoked its membership in the Forest Stewardship Council in 2018, citing doubts about the effectiveness of the FSC to guarantee the protection of forests.

appropriate resources to forestry officers as much as to anti-corruption agencies, law enforcement and auditing and financial oversight institutions. Forestry and criminal justice personnel should not only have access to specialised investigative training but also to appropriate equipment needed to effectively monitor forest areas (e.g. helicopters, drones, satellite imagery). The strategic use of technological equipment especially for vast and remote forest areas plays a pivotal role in this. Some governments co-operate with local forest communities in using GPS satellite technology to collect evidence on illegal logging and timber trafficking routes (Boekhout van Solinge et al. 2016: 91). Additionally, deep learning and AI could soon be used as auxiliary tools for better monitoring and tracking logging activities (Abdenur 2020).

At the same time, governments must establish structures for greater intersectoral and interagency cooperation, for example by establishing specific interagency committees or task forces, such as a National Environmental Security Task Force (NEST) as proposed by INTERPOL. (Illegal) deforestation is not exclusive to forestry, but rather constitutes a cross-cutting issue also spanning the agricultural, mining, rural development and energy sectors. While actors involved in illegal logging and timber laundering are increasingly interlinked, the responsibility and competency to combat forestry crime is dispersed along the supply chain across different institutions at the local, regional and federal level, making it harder to develop an integrated strategy (Schönenberg 2002: 25).

Central to making domestic interagency cooperation more effective is to recognise that illegal logging and timber laundering are perpetuated by systemic corruption that reaches the highest levels of governments and corporations. This demands a change in strategy from reactive to proactive engagement: rather than going after the smaller and more visible offenders (i.e. (informal) loggers, millers, etc.), law enforcement should focus on the "big fish", those higher up in the pyramid of organised networks. A 2019 report by INTERPOL revealed that of all actors arrested for forestry crime, only ten per cent were company owners and managers and only two per cent were identified as heads of criminal groups, although they are the ones pulling the strings and driving the business of the illegal timber trade.[5]

---

5 The report revealed that between 2012 and 2017, 48 per cent of actors arrested for illegal logging or timber trade activities were loggers and truck drivers, 40 per cent were intermediaries, 10 per cent were company owners and managers, while only 2 per cent were identified as heads of criminal groups (INTERPOL 2019: 7); see also Goncalves et al. 2012: 7.

In parallel with responding better to the sophisticated nature of these networks, law enforcement must also end the common practice of foregoing prosecutions and issuing non-dissuasive penalties. One study found that the probability of a forestry crime being penalised in Brazil lies at just about 0.082 per cent; in Papua, Indonesia, that rate is even lower (Gonclaves 2012: 5). Even if offenders are prosecuted, the imposed penalties hardly affect the business conduct of the actors involved. After all, informal loggers can easily be replaced and seizures of timber transports do little damage to the established networks. The first steps for law enforcement would therefore be to make use of effective deterrence mechanisms such as appropriate dissuasive penalties and to include other related criminal offenses such as tax fraud, forgery, or bribery in the prosecution.

Laundering

Regulative frameworks that address illegal logging and the global illegal timber trade should be augmented to ensure a more tightly knit system of traceability and responsibility. This includes attributing more responsibility to timber processors and traders to conduct due diligence not only on their immediate suppliers but also further down the supply chain, including sawmills, shipment companies and operators of trade hubs. The central gateway for introducing illegal timber into the legal supply chain is at the point of processing, predominantly at the sawmill. Efforts to prevent the mixing and mislabelling of timber products must therefore concentrate on increasing transparency at the sawmills as well as both upstream and downstream along the supply chain.

Additionally, multi-agency and cross-border cooperation between border and customs agencies must be strengthened in order to curb the systematic smuggling of timber. When preventive measures have failed to prevent the illegal timber harvest, border checkpoints become a crucial point at which to break the link between supply and demand of illegal timber (UNODC 2013: 8). Ports and transit countries play a central role in this process, as they create and facilitate regional trade routes and trafficking hubs. VPAs can be an effective tool to promote legality verification schemes and curb illegal timber harvesting, but their effectiveness is diminished if they do not take into account major regional players such as Singapore and China. The European Union should therefore work towards extending its VPAs to third-party processing countries, most notably China, in order to close this loophole.

One way of addressing the issue of facilitating transit countries is to make anti-money laundering (AML) and confiscation laws central elements of the anti-logging and illegal timber trade strategies. According to Kishor and Lescuyer (2012: 265), the traditional "follow-the-log" approach must be complemented by a "follow-the-money" strategy to effectively trace back the proceeds from illegal timber trades that flow through third countries and trafficking hubs. Employing AML laws would enable authorities to prosecute agents involved in the illegal timber trade even in areas with no forestry crime policies, such as Hong Kong. It would also allow them to monitor financial institutions that take part in financing and enabling large-scale timber extraction in countries such as Indonesia and to mandate them to exercise enhanced due diligence for high-risk customers (Goncalves et al. 2012: 39; Reboredo 2013).

Integration

An integrated criminal justice strategy on the international level must embrace anti-logging and border control measures taken on the local, national, and regional levels while making use of tools of cooperation in the area of organised crime and corruption on the global level. Such tools include extradition and mutual legal assistance in criminal matters, a form of cooperation between countries for collecting and exchanging information. International police and justice cooperation should prioritise the prevention and detection of what Boekhout van Solinge et al. (2016) call "opportunity structures" or "illegal windows of opportunity". This involves the above-mentioned shift from reactive to proactive engagement and a focus on facilitators of crime, "some of whom are found at or near the interface of the legal and illegal" (Beokhout van Solinge et al. 2016: 92). Existing regional networks as well as financial intelligence units (FIU) can serve as an effective operating base for these forms of international cooperation.

Forensic tools analysing the chemical and genetic properties of timber have also become an established tool for verifying the geographic origin of timber. They can help identify and expose international timber trafficking routes and increase supply chain transparency. However, in order to do so, they rely on a large reference database. The creation of large and transnationally accessible databases would further enable states and organisations to better analyse and identify key actors, trade routes as well as direct and indirect risks along the supply chain. The use of big data analysis appears as a promising tool. By combining the outputs of a wide range of approaches (e.g. GPS tracking, DNA analysis, bar codes, radio frequency identifiers, mass spectrometry (Lowe et al. 2016)), analysis based on big data is able to more accurately determine the origin and legality of timber (Instituto BVRio 2016).

Additionally, policies on illegal logging and timber trade should focus as much on identifying and breaking the criminal networks and beneficiaries of forestry crime as on the direct and indirect drivers that perpetuate the business of illegal logging. Illegal deforestation is largely incentivised by the continuously high demand for wood products from consumer countries in the Global North and the correspondingly high profit margin that can be achieved with illegal timber on the global timber market. Additionally, the demand for agricultural products such as palm oil, meat, soy and maize needs to be recognised as another indirect driver of illegal deforestation. The focus of any policy aiming to tackle illegal logging and the global illegal timber trade should lie on identifying and reducing these direct and indirect drivers of illegal deforestation. This is particularly important from an environmental and climate protection angle: once the tree is cut, it is no longer able to absorb greenhouse gases and reduce the global carbon footprint. Reforestation initiatives, while certainly important, are laborious and take a long time before the tree's maximum storage capacity is reached. The European Union's initiatives for deforestation-free supply chains and comprehensive mandatory due diligence are positive signals in this regard.[6] Finally, international efforts should be directed at harmonizing the existing heterogeneity of certification schemes, labels and sustainability standards to create more transparency for consumers and ensure consistent legality verification along the entire supply chain.

6 In November 2021, the European Commission unveiled its proposal for a regulation to minimize EU-driven deforestation and forest degradation. The Regulation sets mandatory due diligence rules for operators who place specific commodities on the EU market that are associated with deforestation and forest degradation -soy, beef, palm oil, wood, cocoa and coffee as well as some derived products, such as leather, chocolate and furniture. Its purpose is to ensure that only deforestation-free and legal products (according to the laws of the country of origin) are allowed on the EU market. Each member state will be responsible for implementing the regulation. At the time of writing, the draft legislation has yet to be approved by the EU member states and the European Parliament.

References

Abdenur, Adriana (2020): "How can artificial intelligence help curb deforestation in the Amazon?". At: https://theglobalobservatory.org/2020/11/how-can-artificial-intelligence-help-curb-deforestation-amazon/ (accessed 2 June 2022).

Abdenur, Adriana (2022): What Can Global Governance do for Forests? Cooperation and Sovereignty in the Amazon. United Nations University, Centre for Policy Research.

Abdenur, Adriana/Ferguson, Brodie/de Carvalho, Ilona Szabo/Risso, Melina/Muggah, Robert (2020): "Environmental Crime in the Amazon Basin. A Typology for Research, Policy and Action". At: https://igarape.org.br/wp-content/uploads/2020/08/2020-08-19-AE-47_Environmental-Crime-Typology.pdf (accessed 2 June 2022).

Alessi, Gil (2021): "The Amazon rainforest under Bolsonaro. A story of fire and violence in Brazil". At: https://english.elpais.com/usa/2021-09-16/the-amazon-rainforest-under-bolsonaro-a-story-of-fire-and-violence-in-brazil.html (accessed 2 June 2022).

Azevedo, Andrea/Rajão, Raoni/Costa, Marcelo/Stabile, Marcelo/Macedo, Marcia et al. (2017): "Limits of Brazil's Forest Code as a means to end illegal deforestation". In: Proceedings of the National Academy of Sciences of the United States of America, 114, 29, pp. 7653–7658.

Baker, Jacqui (2020):" Corrupt networks in the Indonesian forestry sector. Politics and pulp in Pelalawan, Riau". At: https://www.u4.no/publications/corrupt-networks-in-the-indonesian-forestry-sector.pdf (accessed 2 June 2022).

Barros, Ciro (2021): "The intimate relationship between cocaine and illegal timber in Brazil's Amazon". At: https://insightcrime.org/news/intimate-relationship-between-cocaine-illegal-timber-brazil-amazon/ (accessed 2 June 2022).

Bisschop, Lieselot (2012): "Out of the woods. The illegal trade in tropical timber and a European trade hub". In: Global Crime, 13, 3, pp. 191–212.

Bisschop, Lieselot (2015): Governance of the illegal trade in e-waste and tropical timber. Case studies on transnational environmental crime. Farnham: Ashgate.

Blackman, Jo (2018): "EU ban on illegal timber. Uneven enforcement lets companies off the hook". At: https://www.globalwitness.org/en/blog/eu-ban-illegal-timber-uneven-enforcement-lets-companies-hook/ (accessed 21 December 2021).

Block, Alan (1983): East Side-West Side. Organizing Crime in New York, 1930–1950. New Brunswick: Transaction Books.

Boekhout van Solinge, Tim (2008): "Eco-Crime. The tropical timber trade". In: Siegel, Dina/Nelen, Hans (eds.): Organized crime. Culture, markets and policies. New York, NY: Springer Science/ Business Media LLC, pp. 97–111.

Boekhout van Solinge, Tim/Zuidema, Pieter/Vlam, Mart/Cerutti, Paolo/Yemelin, Valentin (2016): "Organized forest crime. A criminological analysis with suggestions from timber forensics". In: Kleinschmit, Daniela/Mansourian, Stephanie/ Wildburger, Christoph/Purret, Andre (eds.): Illegal logging and related timber trade. Dimensions, drivers, impacts and response. A global scientific rapid response assessment report. Vienna: IUFRO, pp. 82–97.

Brancalion, Pedro/Almeida, Danilo de/Vidal, Edson/Molin, Paulo/Sontag, Vanessa/Souza, Saulo/Schulze, Mark (2018): "Fake Legal Logging in the Brazilian Amazon". In: Science Advances, 4, 8.

Butler, Rhett A. (2020): "Despite COVID, Amazon deforestation races higher". Mongabay. At: https://news.mongabay.com/2020/04/despite-covid-amazon-deforestation-races-higher/ (accessed 2 June 2022).

Carrington, Damien (2021): "Amazon rainforest now emitting more CO2 than it absorbs". At: https://www.theguardian.com/environment/2021/jul/14/amazon-rainforest-now-emitting-more-co2-than-it-absorbs (accessed 21 December 2021).

Cashore, Benjamin/Leipold, Sina/Cerutti, Paolo Omar/Bueno, Gabriela/Carodenuto Sophia et al. (2016): "Global governance approaches to addressing illegal logging. Uptake and lessons learnt". In: Kleinschmit, Daniela/Mansourian, Stephanie/Wildburger, Christoph/Purret, Andre (eds.): Illegal logging and related timber trade. Dimensions, drivers, impacts and responses. A global scientific rapid response assessment report. Vienna: IUFRO, pp. 120–131.

Chatham House (n.d.-a): "Forest Governance and Legality. Brazil". At: https://forestgovernance.chathamhouse.org/countries/brazil (accessed 21 December 2021).

Chatham House (n.d.-b): "Forest governance and legality. Indonesia". At: https://forestgovernance.chathamhouse.org/countries/indonesia (accessed 21 December 2021).

Chimeli, Ariaster/Boyd, Roy/Adams, Darius (2012): "International timber markets and tropical deforestation. The evidence from prices". In: Applied Economics, 44, 10, pp. 1303–1314.

Corrêa, Alessandra 2014): "Brasil é exemplo de sucesso na redução do desmatamento, diz relatório". At: https://www.bbc.com/portuguese/noticias/2014/06/140604_desmatamento_relatorio_ac_hb (accessed 21 December 2021).

Davidescu, Simona/Buzogány, Aron (2021): "Cutting deals. Transnational advocacy networks and the European Union Timber Regulation at the eastern border". In: The International Spectator, 56, 3, pp. 105–118.

Drewe, Charles/Barker, Tim (2016): Analysis of potential European Union Timber Regulation product scope changes. WWF – World Wide Fund for Nature.

Earthsight (2021): "Untamed timber. The Brazilian flooring giant let off the hook by Bolsonaro's government and now thriving across the US and EU". At: https://www.earthsight.org.uk/news/investigations-brazil-untamed-timber (accessed 21 December 2021).

EIA, Environmental Investigation Agency (2012): Appetite for destruction. China's trade in illegal timber. Environmental Investigation Agency (EIA).

EIA, Environmental Investigation Agency (2018): A tale of two laws. Using existing EU and US laws to strengthen action on illegal timber trade. Environmental Investigation Agency (EIA).

EIA, Environmental Investigation Agency/Telapak (2001): Timber trafficking. Illegal logging in Indonesia, South East Asia and international consumption of illegally sourced timber. Environmental Investigation Agency (EIA)/Telapak.

EIA, Environmental Investigation Agency/Telapak (2004): Profiting from plunder. How Malaysia smuggled endangered wood. Environmental Investigation Agency (EIA)/Telapak.

EIA, Environmental Investigation Agency/Telapak (2005). The last frontier. Illegal logging in Papua and China's massive timber theft. Environmental Investigation Agency (EIA)/Telapak.

EIA, Environmental Investigation Agency/Telapak (2006): Behind the veneer. How Indonesia's last rainforests are being gelled for flooring. Environmental Investigation Agency (EIA)/Telakap.

Escobar, Herton (2020): "Deforestation in the Brazilian Amazon is still rising sharply". In: Science, 369, 6504, p. 613.

European Commission (2021): "Questions and Answers on new rules for deforestation-free products". At: https://ec.europa.eu/commission/presscorner/detail/en/qanda_21_5919 (accessed 2 June 2022).

FAO, Food and Agricultural Organization of the United Nations (2020): The state of the world's forests 2020. Forests, Biodiversity and People: FAO and United Nations Environment Programme (UNEP).

Forest Trends (2010): Timber markets and trade between Laos and Vietnam. A commodity chain analysis of Vietnamese-driven timber flows. Forest Trends.

Forest Trends (2018): The economic impacts of illegal agro-conversion on tropical forest countries. A new framework supports national and global cost estimates. Forest Trends.

Gan, Jianbang/Cerutti, Paolo/Masiero, Mauro/Pettenella, Davide/Andrighetto, Nicola/Dawson, Tim (2016): "Quantifying illegal logging and related timber trade". In: Kleinschmit, Daniela/Mansourian, Stephanie/Wildburger, Christoph/Purret, Andre (eds.): Illegal logging and related timber trade. Dimensions, drivers, impacts and responses. A global scientific rapid response assessment report. Vienna: IUFRO, pp. 38–59.

Gatti, Luciana/Basso, Luana/Miller, John/Gloor, Manuel/Gatti Domingues, Lucas et al. (2021): "Amazonia as a carbon source linked to deforestation and climate change". In: Nature, 595, 7867, pp. 388–393.

Giurca, Alexandru/Jonsson, Ragnar/Rinaldi, Francesca/Priyadi, Hari (2013): "Ambiguity in timber trade regarding efforts to combat illegal logging. Potential impacts on trade between South-East Asia and Europe". In: Forests, 4, 4, pp. 730–750.

Global Witness (2021): "Last line of defence. The industries causing the climate crisis and attacks against land and environmental defenders". At: https://www.globalwitness.org/en/campaigns/environmental-activists/last-line-defence/ (accessed 2 June 2022).

Goncalves, Marilyne/Panjer, Melissa/Greenberg, Theodore/Magrath, William (2012): Justice for forests. Improving criminal justice efforts to combat illegal logging. Washington, D.C: World Bank.

Greenpeace (2018): "Imaginary trees, real destruction. How licensing fraud and illegal logging of Ipe trees are causing irreversible damage to the Amazon rainforest". At: https://www.greenpeace.de/publikationen/20180301-greenpeace_report_imaginary_trees_real_destruction.pdf (accessed 2 June 2022).

Hanbury, Shanna (2021): "Brazil's environment minister faces second probe linked to illegal timber". At: https://news.mongabay.com/2021/06/brazils-environment-minister-faces-second-probe-linked-to-illegal-timber/ (accessed 21 December 2021).

Hoare, Alison/Wellesley, Laura (2014): "Illegal logging and related trade. The response in Indonesia. A Chatham House Assessment". At: https://chathamhouse.soutron.net/Portal/DownloadImageFile.ashx?fieldValueId=4153 (accessed 2 June 2022).

Human Rights Watch (2019): "Rainforest mafias. How violence and impunity fuel deforestation in Brazil's Amazon". At: https://www.hrw.org/report/2019/09/17/rainforest-mafias/how-violence-and-impunity-fuel-deforestation-brazils-amazon (accessed 2 June 2022).

Hummel, Antônio (2016): "Deforestation in the Amazon: What is illegal and what is not?". In: Elementa: Science of the Anthropocene, 4.

Instituto BVRio (2016): "Using big data to detect illegality in the tropical timber sector. A case study of BVRio Due Diligence and Risk Assessment System". At: https://www.bvrio.org/publicacao/160/using-big-data-to-detect-illegality-int-the-tropical-timber-sector.pdf (accessed 2 June 2022).

INTERPOL (2019): Global forestry enforcement. Strengthening law enforcement cooperation against forestry crime. INTERPOL.

INTERPOL/World Bank (2010): Chainsaw Project. An INTERPOL perspective on law enforcement in illegal logging.

Jong, Hans (2019): "In Indonesia, a flawed certification scheme lets illegal loggers raze away". At: https://news.mongabay.com/2019/05/in-indonesia-a-flawed-certification-scheme-lets-illegal-loggers-raze-away/ (accessed 21 December 2021).

Joy, Ajit (2010): Following the money trail. The challenges in illegal logging investigations. United Nations Office on Drugs and Crime (UNODC).

Kaphengst, Timo/Umpfenbach, Katharina/Bräuer, Ingo (2008): Ökonomische Folgen illegaler Holzimporte für die deutsche Holzwirtschaft. Greenpace / Ecologic – Institut für Internationale und Europäische Umweltpolitik.

Kimbrough, Liz (2019): "Experts blame Bolsonaro for surge in deforestation, warn of worse to come". At: https://news.mongabay.com/2019/11/experts-blame-bolsonaro-for-surge-in-deforestation-warn-of-worse-to-come/ (accessed 2 June 2022).

Kishor, Nalin/Lescuyer, Guillaume (2012): "Controlling illegal logging in domestic and international markets by harnessing multi-level governance opportunities". In: International Journal of the Commons, 6, 2, pp. 255–270.

Kleemans, Edward (2013): "Theoretical perspectives on organized crime". In: Paoli, Letizia (ed.): Oxford handbook on organized crime. Oxford: Oxford University Press.

Kleinschmit, Daniela/Leipold, Sina/Sotirov, Metodi (2016): "Introduction. Understanding the complexities of illegal logging and associated timber trade". In: Kleinschmit, Daniela/Mansourian, Stephanie/Wildburger, Christoph/Purret, Andre (eds.): Illegal logging and related timber trade. Dimensions, drivers, impacts and responses. A global scientific rapid response assessment report. Vienna: IUFRO, pp. 14–20.

Lawson, Sam (2014): Consumer goods and deforestation. An analysis of the extent and nature of illegality in forest conversion for agriculture and timber plantation. Forest Trends.

Lawson, Sam/MacFaul, Larry (2010): Illegal logging and related trade. Indicators of the global response. The Royal Institute of International Affairs/Chatham House.

Lippe, Rattiya/Cui, Shannon/Schweinle, Jörg (2021): "Estimating global forest-based employment". In: Forests, 12, 9, 1219.

Liu, Fei/Wheiler, Kent/Ganguly, Indroneil/Hu, Mingxing (2020): "Sustainable timber trade. A study on discrepancies in Chinese logs and lumber trade statistics". In: Forests, 11, 2, 205.

Lowe, Andrew/Dormontt, Eleanor/Bowie, Matthew/Degen, Bernd/Gardner, Shelley et al. (2016): "Opportunities for improved transparency in the timber trade through scientific verification". In: BioScience, 66, 11, pp. 990–998.

McElwee, Pamela (2004): "You say illegal, I say legal". In: Journal of Sustainable Forestry, 19, 1–3, pp. 97–135.

Nellemann, Christian/INTERPOL Environmental Crime Programme (2012): "Green carbon, black trade. Illegal logging, tax fraud and laundering in the world's tropical forests. A rapid response assessment". At: https://www.grida.no/publications/126 (accessed 2 June 2022).

Nellemann, Christian/Henriksen, Rune/Pravettoni, Riccardo/Jesperson, Sasha (2020): "Forestry crimes and our planet". In: Nikolakis, William/Innes, John L. (eds.): The wicked problem of forest policy. A multidisciplinary approach to sustainability in forest landscapes. Cambridge: Cambridge University Press, pp. 197–230.

Nellemann, Christian/Henriksen, Rune/Raxter, Patricia/Ash, Neville/Mrema, Elizabeth (2014): The environmental crime crisis. Threats to sustainable development from illegal exploitation and trade in wildlife and forest resources. United Na tions Environment Programme (UNEP)/Interpol.

Papachristou, Lucy (2018): "Hong Kong woman sentenced in Rosewood trafficking case". At: https://www.occrp.org/en/daily/8569-hong-kong-woman-sentence d-in-rosewood-trafficking-case (accessed 21 December 2021).

Peck, Tim (2001): The international timber trade. Cambridge: Woodhead Publishing/Elsevier Science.

Perazzoni, Franco (2018): "Amazonia, organized crime and illegal deforestation. Best practices for the protection of the Brazilian Amazon". In: Ungar, Mark (ed.): The 21st century fight for the Amazon. Environmental enforcement in the world's biggest rainforest. Cham: Palgrave Macmillan, pp. 21–55.

Phillips, Tom (2020): "Amazon deforestation surges to 12-year high under Bolsonaro". At: https://www.theguardian.com/environment/2020/dec/01/amazon-deforestation-surges-to-12-year-high-under-bolsonaro (accessed 18 May 2022).

Pohnan, Erica/Stone, Michael/Cashore, Benjamin (2014): "Global forest governance to address illegal logging. The rise of timber legality verification to rescue Indonesia's forests". In: Katila, Pia/Galloway, Glenn/Jong, Wil de/Pacheco, Pablo/Mery, Gerardo (eds.): Forest under pressure. Local responses to global issues. Vienna: International Union of Forest Research Organizations (IUFRO), pp. 241–254.

Rajão, Raoni/Soares-Filho, Britaldo/Nunes, Felipe/Börner, Jan/Machado, Lilian et al. (2020): "The rotten apples of Brazil's agribusiness". In: Science, 369, 6501, pp. 246–248.

Reboredo, Fernando (2013): "Socio-economic, environmental, and governance impacts of illegal logging". In: Environment Systems and Decisions, 33, 2, pp. 295–304.

Schloenhardt, Andreas (2008): The illegal trade in timber and timber products in the Asia-Pacific region. Canberra: Australian Institute of Criminology.

Schönenberg, Regine (2002): Die Kriminalisierung gesellschaftlicher Transformationsprozesse. Der Fall des brasilianischen Amazonasgebiets. Hessische Stiftung für Friedens- und Konfliktforschung.

Schulze, Mark/Grogan, James/Uhl, Chris/Lentini, Marco/Vidal, Edson (2008): "Evaluating Ipê (Tabebuia, Bignoniaceae) logging in Amazonia. Sustainable management or catalyst for forest degradation?". In: Biological Conservation, 141, 8, pp. 2071–2085.

Sotirov, Metodi/Pokorny, Benno/Kleinschmit, Daniela/Kanowski, Peter (2020): "international forest governance and policy. Institutional architecture and pathways of influence in global sustainability". In: Sustainability, 12, 17, 7010.

Sotirov, Metodi/Storch, Sabine/Aggestam, Filip/Giurca, Alex/Selter, Andy et al. (2015): Forest policy integration in Europe. Lessons learnt, challenges ahead, and strategies to support sustainable forest management and multifunctional forestry in the future. INTEGRAL EU Policy Paper.

Ungar, Mark (2018): "Introduction. The evolution of environmental enforcement". In: Ungar, Mark (ed.): the 21st century fight for the Amazon. Environmental enforcement in the world's biggest rainforest. Cham: Palgrave Macmillan.

United Nations (n.d.): "UN Comtrade Database. Indonesia's Export Partners for HS 44, 47, 48 (2019)". At: http://comtrade.un.org/ (accessed 10 November 2021).

UNODC, United Nations Office on Drugs and Crime (2013): criminal justice responses to the illegal trade in timber in Vietnam. At: https://www.unodc.org/documents/southeastasiaandpacific/Publications/wildlife/CJS_Response_-_VIETNAM_01_13_Dec_201.pdf (accessed 2 June 2022).

Weimar, Holger/Janzen, Niels/Dieter, Matthias (2015): Market coverage of wood imports by the EU Timber Regulation. Thünen Working Paper Nr. 45, Johann Heinrich von Thünen-Institut.

Wiedenhoeft, Alex/Simeone, John/Smith, Amy/Parker-Forney, Meaghan/Soares, Richard/Fishman, Akiva (2019): "Fraud and misrepresentation in retail forest products exceeds U.S. forensic wood science capacity". In: PloS one, 14, 7.

Wit, Marieke/van Dam, Jinke/Cerutti, Paolo Omar/Lescuyer, Guillaume/Kerret, Rohini/McKeown, James Parker (2010): "Chainsaw milling: supplier to local markets. A synthesis". In: European Tropical Forest Research Network (ETFRN) News 52, pp. 7–12.

Wood Floor Business (WFB) (2011): "Brazil notches big victory against illegal loggers". At: https://www.woodfloorbusiness.com/news/article/15126422/brazil-notches-big-victory-against-illegal-loggers (accessed 21 December 2021).

World Bank (2008): Forests sourcebook. Practical guidance for sustaining forests in development cooperation. Washington, D.C: The International Bank for Reconstruction and Development/The World Bank.

WWF, World Wide Fund for Nature (2021): "EU forest crime initiative. EU summary of the gap analysis. Project countries: Belgium, Bulgaria, France, Romania, Slovakia and Ukraine". At: https://www.wwf.de/fileadmin/fm-wwf/Publikationen-PDF/EU-Forest-Crime-Initiative-EU-GAP-Analysis.pdf (accessed 2 June 2022).

Wyatt, Tanya/van Uhm, Daan/Nurse, Angus (2020): "Differentiating criminal networks in the illegal wildlife trade. Organized, corporate and disorganized crime". In: Trends in Organized Crime, 23, 4, pp. 350–366.

Zhang, Jian/Gan, Jianbang (2007): "Who will meet China's import demand for forest products?". In: World Development, 35, 12, pp. 2150–2160.

The smuggling of fuel from Libya to Europe

Lorenzo Bagnoli

Since 2011, with the end of the Gaddafi era, instability has been reigning in Libya. The vacuum was filled by armed groups and militias, sometimes supported also with international funds and military supplies. The poor internal economy pushed at least one group, the Nasr Brigade, to go transnational. This militia has become stronger in a context of the Global South: the endless Libyan civil war. Its local relevance has increased thanks to its connections to the Global North (Italy and Malta). The fragmentation of the context suggests following an actor-based approach in order to depict the rise of a local group through its transnational connections. Until at least the end of 2018, the group's main sources of income included fuel smuggling. This illicit economy stole the scarce resources of the Libyan state. It is one of the sources of permanent instability in Libya because it channels state revenues to non-state actors who are fighting against the central state which is highly contested in its authority. At the time of writing, in January 2022, it is still uncertain whether and when elections in Libya will take place. The Government of National Unity (GNU) is a weak entity, but it is arguable whether the possible vote will elect a stable government. The most powerful actors currently shaping the power structure in Libya are the militias, including the Nasr Brigade. An analysis of the actors involved in this smuggling ring from Libya to Italy shows how it relied on the transnational actors involved in the illicit economy to increase its power locally. The Nasr Brigade cooperated with two Maltese businessmen in contact with oil traders and shipping companies all over Europe, legal companies keen to buy cheap fuel with forged bills of lading. These criminal actors could rely on a lack of laws in Libya, lax regulation in Malta and allegedly the complicity of some top officials in both countries.

The phenomenon subsided due to the law enforcement response in Libya and abroad, and COVID-19 reduced all the fuel flows, both legal and illegal. Still, the problem is that smuggling in Libya is among the main sources of income. The present article begins with a description of the Libyan state capture. The country is contested between factions and militias. Despite the promise of elections in the near future, stability still seems far off in Tripoli. Libya is a strategically important country because of its geographical location and its resources, such as oil and gas. The Libyan economy still depends on crude oil and oil products. Local consumption has been subsidised by the central government in order to make fuel affordable for the local population. This subsidised fuel has turned into one of the main products on the Libyan black market. This illicitly traded commodity is also lucrative for oil companies and traders in the northern part of the Mediterranean because it is tax-free. The article investigates the functioning of the Nasr Brigade in Zawiya in Western Libya. This militia represents an interesting case study because of its mafia-like structure and its international connections, especially to Malta. This island state in the centre of the Mediterranean Sea is a natural bridge between North Africa (and the Global South) and Southern Europe (and the Global North). The Maltese intermediaries set up a network to trade illicit fuel in Europe.

This criminal network has been investigated in several operations led by Italian prosecutors. The first and main one, in October 2017, was dubbed Dirty Oil. The trial is still ongoing, and it is the most important investigation into transnational fuel smuggling across the Mediterranean Sea. The UN Panel of Experts on Libya contributed extensively to revealing the existence of this parallel black market, but the United Nations are still struggling with the bigger goal of stabilising Libya. Without stability in Libya, there are still many opportunities for criminal networks to team up with international criminal groups to smuggle Libyan commodities elsewhere.

Libya, a crossroads for smuggling

The corridor of the Central Mediterranean is a crossroads for smuggled goods. Along this sea route, Libya has emerged as the main hub for transnational trafficking towards Europe, in particular human smuggling and trafficking. Since Muammar Gaddafi's fall in 2011, Libya has split into two main factions: the UN-backed government in Western Libya and the rival Libyan National Army (LNA) led by Marshal Khalifa Haftar in Cyrenaica, the eastern region of Libya. The chaotic situation has been the main driver of forced migration and a perfect environment for the rise of organised crime groups / militias.

"The fall of [Gaddafi's] regime brought open competition to the control of smuggling routes, as decades-old concessions no longer held sway and previous understandings among groups over the division of territory were re-contested. Competition over smuggling routes has contributed to the outbreak of localised conflict across the country. Individuals, networks and communities – ethnic, tribal and city-based – all compete for primacy in Libya's dynamic illicit marketplace." (Eaton 2018)

Among the different kinds of illicit flows from Libya towards Europe, human smuggling raised the most concerns in Europe because of the immediate social and political consequences, such as human rights violations and the rise of far-right movements on the continent. To tackle it, in 2017 the Italian Ministry of the Interior signed a controversial Memorandum of Understanding with the UN-backed government (led by Fayez al-Sarraj until 2021) in Tripoli, the capital of Libya (Libyan Government of National Accord and Government of Italy 2017). The main aim was to provide training and new naval assets to the Libyan Coast Guard in order to curb migration (El Zaidy 2017).[1] As we will see, among the alleged beneficiaries there are also criminal groups in Tripolitania in Western Libya. Known to the European public for their role in human smuggling, they were actually involved in various kinds of smuggling, including fuel smuggling.

The smuggled goods which affect the Libyan economy by far the most are the oil products, crude and its derivatives: "The practice of smuggling heavily subsidised fuel from Libya (fuel there costs as little as US$0.02c/0.03c per litre) is costing the country an estimated US$750 million a year" (Micallef 2018). "[S]ome of the same criminal actors and/or networks involved in the smuggling of people or fuel have also been able to use the criminal infrastructure they built to become involved in drug trafficking", according to Micallef (2019). Fuel smuggling is among the main sources of income that economically support their power structure, which is very strong in Western Libya. Several militias are involved in the business, and their activities were investigated by the UN Panel of Experts on Libya in the period between 2016 and 2018. These militias were allied with the UN-backed government in Tripoli at the time, the Government of National Accord, in its fight against Marshal Khalifa Haftar's Libyan National Army over control of the country. Among these militias, this paper will focus on the Nasr Brigade of Zawiya, which was investigated in Italy for its international connections. As argued by Mark Micallef (2019: 29):

> "[E]ven when there is no direct convergence of actors or networks, there is a symbiotic relationship between different smuggling trades.

---

1 Among the weaknesses of the memorandum, El Zaidy (2017: 5) mentions that it is "rather superficial" and "not transparent", "reflects short-term thinking" and lacks "legitimacy".

> The withdrawal of militias from human and fuel smuggling activities in coastal areas has been linked to the involvement of a growing number of actors in the import and export of drugs."

In the same report, Micallef (2019: 11) explains: "Pressure on both migration and fuel smuggling increased in 2015 and 2016, with a turning point coming in 2017", when the Memorandum of Understanding was completely implemented. Regardless of the implications for human rights abuses, from a merely political perspective the backlash of this measure was the political and financial recognition obtained by some of the militia groups, including the ones involved in fuel smuggling from Western Libya.

Since 2014, the main institution deeply engaged in tackling fuel smuggling has been the Libyan National Oil Corporation (NOC). The NOC succeeded in obtaining support from the UN for three years, through the Panel of Experts reports and proposed regulations. Further pressure on smugglers in the Mediterranean Sea came from the European Union law enforcement agencies and military operations such as Operation IRINI. The effort to "tackle migration", as the EU institutions say, from the southern side to Europe has been massive compared to the little effort made to stop fuel smuggling, but still there was at least one operation that was a game changer: Operation Dirty Oil.

In any case, since July 2017, the departure of migrants from Libya suddenly dropped by around 80 %, while seaborne fuel smuggling decreased considerably on account of commercial fuel tankers ceasing to operate in Libya between 2016 and 2017 (Micallef 2019). Given the instability in Libya, these dynamics change very quickly; for instance, the number of arrivals on the Central Mediterranean route started to increase again in 2020 (35,600) (EASO 2021: 44), and the trend is the same for 2021, when according to Frontex (2022) the arrivals from January to December reached 65,362. The main promoter of the Memorandum of Understanding and the other above migration policies in Libya was the Italian government because of its direct interest in preventing migration towards the Italian island of Lampedusa (Varvelli and Villa 2019). On the Italian side, different governments have always backed and supported the fight against irregular migration.

The dependence on the oil industry

Libya's per capita income is among the highest in Africa thanks to high oil revenues, which remain Libya's main source of income and are split among a small number of people (Libya has less than 7 million inhabitants). According to OPEC, the oil and gas sector accounts for about 60 per cent of the country's total GDP (OPEC n.d.), despite the 2020 drop due to the COVID-19 crisis. The zenith in the fight on fuel smuggling was in 2016, according to Tim Eaton (2018) of Chatham House. Despite the fact that Libya is an oil-rich country, it has structural deficits in processing oil products and in its internal demand calculation (Eaton 2019). There are just a few refineries in the country:

"The country's 120,000 b/d Zawiya oil refinery restarted operations on Oct. 20, according to state-owned National Oil Corporation. The two smaller refineries in the East – the 20,000 b/d Tobruk and 10,000 b/d Sarir -- also restarted recently, sources at NOC subsidiary Arabian Gulf Oil Company said. The 220,000 b/d Ras Lanuf remained offline without any timeline for restart. The refinery has been closed since 2013 due to an arbitration dispute." (Turner 2021)

Especially since the beginning of the COVID-19 crisis, by far the largest part of the Libyan sources of revenue is crude oil and its export. According to the figures released by the NOC (2016), the state-owned Libyan entity which controls the oil and gas sector, the petroleum products sold by the state company only account for 4 % of the October 2020 oil revenues. Still, the domestic market is dominated by petroleum products, often sold on the black market by individuals across the Libyan-Tunisian border.[2] The pandemic has certainly contributed to exacerbating the ongoing economic crises, but it is not clear what impact this has had on black market activities.

Despite the EU member states and the European Union strengthening their presence in the coastal cities – which are highly populated and have more connections abroad – since the eruption of the Libyan civil war in 2011, the plague of fuel smuggling has become more pervasive. In the Global North, the transnational aspect of this illicit activity has been the main focus. This biased view doesn't take into account the Global South dimension of this phenomenon. Coastal networks are one among other actors. The result is a shortage of fuel with severe impact, "forcing citizens

2 In November 2020 there were media reports of the reopening of the borders after seven months of shutdown (Arab News 2021).

to turn to the same black market and pay well above the official subsidised rate for fuel", as argued by Mark Micallef (2019: 11). Still, the interest shown by the international community is restricted to the transnational and not the internal dynamics.

International responses to illicit trade

With its Resolution 2509 (2020),[3] approved in a 5-minute meeting with 14 votes in favour and one abstention by Russia (United Nations 2020), the UN Security Council expressed its concern that "the illicit export of petroleum, including crude oil and refined petroleum products, from Libya undermines the Government of National Accord (GNA) and National Oil Corporation and poses a threat to the peace, security and stability of Libya" and noted with concern "the reports of the illicit import of petroleum, including crude oil and refined petroleum products to Libya" (UN Security Council 2020: 1). The export of oil and fuel threatens the stability in the country because it provides "support for armed groups or criminal networks" (UN Security Council 2020: 1). The resolution grants member states authority to inspect vessels suspected of exporting illicit oil goods in international waters. The resolution remained in force until 30 April 2021, with the UN Panel of Experts providing its report on 8 March 2021 (UN Panel of Experts 2021).

In the Mediterranean Sea, starting from October 2015 (Italian Ministry of Defense n.d.), the European Council approved a joint naval operation named IRINI from March 2020.[4] Its top priorities are to strengthen the arms embargo and to intercept and dismantle vessels carrying smuggled oil products. The mission has been criticised as biased, flawed and equipped with a limited mandate since its launch (Pietz 2020).

In its activity report from August, IRINI states (EEAS 2021):

> "Since its launch, Operation EUNAVFOR MED IRINI has boarded and inspected 18 suspect vessels. One vessel out of 18 was diverted to a port of an EU Member State where its cargo was seized."

---

3 The first resolution applying to this issue was Resolution 2146 in 2014, modified in 2018 by Resolution 2441.

4 The operation takes up the baton from Operation Sophia, which was labelled as a failure by the United Kingdom (a participating country) in a report published by the House of Lords in July 2017 (UK Parliament – European Union Committee 2017).

On several occasions, the inspected vessels were flying a Turkish flag. At least in six occasions, Turkey denied the consent to board and inspect suspect vessels. The report states that 3,789 vessels were inspected.

The report continues:

> "Furthermore, EUNAVFOR MED IRINI investigated 574 suspect flights, 25 airports and 16 ports, and provided 28 special reports to the UN Panel of Expert [sic] on Libya, 23 of which referred to violations or possible violations of the arms embargo and oil smuggling activities in the West and in the East of the Country. Finally, through the embedded Crime Information Cell, the operation issued to the relevant Law Enforcement agencies 41 recommendations of inspection of suspect vessels in EU Member States' ports, 32 of which were conducted."

These figures do not explain the impact of the mission on the criminal activities. No data are presented to assess whether criminal groups have been dismantled due to the investigative support of IRINI. The extent of the activities suggests that IRINI is fulfilling its mandate, compared to past missions, but it does not provide more substantial arguments to assess the impact.

This evaluation is crucial not just from an EU perspective but also from a Libyan one. The country is expected to elect a government, but it is not clear when. IRINI is not intervening in the Libyan national waters (EEAS 2022), but it is still an external actor operating with the Libyan navy and coastguards.

Despite the efforts, there are several signs of the difficulties to be overcome by the international presence in Libya. On 5 February 2021, the UN-led Libyan Political Dialogue Forum selected Abdul Hamid Mohammed Dbeibah as prime minister *ad interim*, until the election. The new prime minister is tasked to appoint members of the government from the three regions of Libya – Tripolitania, Cyreaica and Fezzan – with the purpose to have only one central body (UN News 2021). Currently, Western Libya is under the influence of Turkey while Eastern Libya is under the control of the Wagner Group, a military group from Russia (Barabanov and Ibrahim 2021). As reported by La Repubblica, between the end of 2020 and January 2021 Russian mercenaries built a fortified trench in the proximity of Sirte to defend Cyrenaica from the Turkish influence (Di Feo 2021). On top of these external influences, there is the fragmented political landscape, as reported by Al Jazeera (2021): "Libya's eastern-based parliament has passed a no-confidence vote in the country's unity government in a new blow to UN-backed peace efforts, but said the administration would continue to operate in a caretaker role". The withdrawal of confidence from the interim prime minister Abdul Hamid Dbeibah received 89 out of 113 votes.

The mechanism of the subsidies and the dynamic of the market flows

After the COVID-19 contraction of the oil production and 10 years of civil war, the economy in Libya is in increasing peril. As reported by Tim Eaton in May 2020: "Until now, the Interim Government has fused revenues from an annual budget settlement with Tripoli with the issuance of over 32 billion dinars (roughly $23 billion) of debt in the form of bonds to pay salaries and finance its spending. The bonds were initially sold directly to three banks headquartered in the eastern region" (Eaton 2020).

Given the situation, the central government and the National Oil Corporation of Libya are supposed to provide the citizens with subsidised fuel. This economic measure is meant to provide affordable energy to the population. Since October 2019, the GNU, led by the prime minister Abdul Hamid Dbeibeh and formed in March 2021, has been reducing the subsidies, particularly on fuel (Coface n.d.), because they are one of the main drivers of the local and regional illicit economy. Indeed, subsidised fuel from Libya is sold by smugglers at a higher price in neighbouring countries such as Tunisia and Egypt. The size of the illicit market is a threat to the future stability of the country. According to the latest estimates, "up to one-third [of fuel] goes missing from official supply chains each year, fuelling a black market that ultimately steals from state coffers at the expense of the population" (Eaton 2019).

The price of subsidised fuel is officially US$0.11 per litre (The Global Economy n.d.). The price Libyan citizens pay is often quite different, depending on the area where they fill their tank. According to research by Chatham House in August 2019, prices in cities such as Tripoli, Sebha or Ubari can vary from US$4.50 to US$53 to fill the same tank (Eaton 2019). This discrepancy implies that even internally the Libyan fuel market is very volatile: it depends on the capacity of the UN-backed government in Tripoli to impose the price. In early 2020, petrol stations beyond the coastal area from east to west went dry (Westcott 2020).

The country is constantly short of fuel because Libya only has few refineries and the oil-rich region known as the Oil Crescent – always unstable – only has petroleum facilities at risk of being locked down by militias,[5] and no refinery capacity. This has led to the paradox that Libya has to import roughly three-quarters of the fuel consumed domestically despite having massive crude oil resources in the country. The Libyan economy depends on the export of oil, but at the same time the energy demand depends on fuel imports. These two opposite forces inflate the black market for fuel. Given the higher profit margins for the export, black market products – including fuel – are often also sold abroad. The land borders with Tunisia and Egypt are the main gateways of this smuggling. These countries have a high demand for fuel. The other borders are in a desert area, which makes smuggling harder. The results of the UN Panel of Experts on Libya suggest that Europe became a market for fuel smugglers in Libya only when a local criminal network met a foreign one in need of the commodity (Rubino, Anesi and Bagnoli 2018).

The Petroleum Facility Guard of Zawiya: the local criminal network

Several analysts (e.g., Martín 2020) regard some of the Libyan criminal groups as something in between traditional militias and the Italian mafia groups in terms of internal structures. The main reasons are their familial ties (in Libya it is more accurate to call them clan-based/ethnic ties) and their capacity to blackmail local politicians, to control local councils and to provide social services with the aim of replacing the central state. Among them, the most noticeable in terms of the transnational connection is the Nasr Brigade (Nasr Martyrs Brigade) based in Zawiya, a coastal city where the Amazigh tribe is in the majority. This Libyan organised crime group is based at the Az Zawiya Oil Refinery, where some compounds are used either as prisons or as detention centres for migrants (Malakooti 2019). Their familial ties and their political scope are reminiscent of the Italian mafia. Some of the main pillars of a mafia clan are: the oath which binds the affiliates to the mafia family; violence as a tool to increase business and power; the command of silence; the hierarchical structure aimed to control both the politics and the economy; and a political agenda aimed at expanding the political influence of the criminal group, locally and nationally. All of the features but the first one, the oath, also characterise the Nasr Brigade (Bagnoli 2020). This group

5 The latest episode occurred in early 2020, before the peace conference of Berlin (Middle East Eye 2020). The oil blockade constitutes political leverage for militias.

is not the only one structured in this way, but it is the most prominent because of its transnational connections.

The group's involvement in the fuel smuggling industry was exposed by both the UN Panel of Experts and the public prosecutor's office of Catania. The operation which disrupted the smuggling network took place in October 2017 and was led by the Guardia di Finanza of Catania, an Italian law enforcement agency that deals with economic crime. The code-name was Dirty Oil. The investigation started in Italy because of the international protocol of collaboration in the framework of the larger Libeccio International operation in the Mediterranean Sea and because the Sicilian shore was the final destination of the smuggled fuel. However, the core of the crime occurred on the high seas, close to Maltese territorial waters. The alleged smugglers came from Libya and Malta, while the buyers were mainly Italians (Tribunale di Catania 2017). The smuggled product was bunkered using improvised bunkering facilities set up in the small port of Abu Kammash, 100 kilometres from Zawiya. "The area of Zuwarah and Abu Kammash has been the main launch pad for illicit exports of refined petroleum products (principally, marine gasoil 0.1 per cent sulphur (ISO 8217)) by sea", the UN Panel of Experts on Libya noted in a 2018 report (UN Panel of Experts 2018: 42).

The members of the group have been exposed not just in the Italian operation but also in several reports issued by the UN Panel of Experts on Libya. They have been placed on sanctions lists by the European Council, the US Department of State and the British Office of Financial Sanctions Implementation. The NOC also claimed that the group was dedicated to fuel smuggling. Like the entire city of Zawiya, the refinery is under the control of the Nasr Brigade, an armed group formed in 2011 and rebranded as a PFG unit in 2014. "PFG" stands for Petroleum Facility Guards, the militia-style security body of the oil plants in Libya (Eaton 2019). The PFG are divided into several "chapters", each with a leader. In Zawiya, the leader is Mohammed Kachlaf, a.k.a. al-Qasab, code LYi.025 on the UN sanctions list. Born in 1985, he is described as "the head of the Nasr brigade in Zawiya, Western Libya. His militia controls the Zawiya refinery, a central hub of migrant smuggling operations. Kachlaf also controls detention centres, including the Nasr detention centre – nominally under the control of the DCIM. As documented in various sources, the network of Kachlaf is one of the most dominant in the field of migrant smuggling and the exploitation of migrants in Libya. Kachlaf has extensive links with the head of the local unit of the coast guard of Zawiya, [Abd] al-Rahman al-Milad, whose unit intercepts boats with migrants, often of rivalling migrant smuggling networks.[6] Migrants are then brought to detention facilities under the control of the Al Nasr militia, where they are reportedly held in critical conditions. The Panel of Experts for Libya collected evidence of migrants that were frequently beaten, while others, notably women from Sub-Saharan countries and Morocco, were sold on the local market as 'sex slaves'. The Panel has also found that Kachlaf collaborates with other armed groups and has been involved in repeated violent clashes in 2016 and 2017" (UN Security Council 2018). The Kachlaf brothers are still popular in Zawiya, and al-Milad still holds a high position in the chain of command of the local coast guard (Scavo 2021). The Kachlaf militia "has been accused of using its control of the refinery to divert fuel to the black market and has frustrated the NOC's attempts to push it out", Tim Eaton (2019) reports.

The Petroleum Facility Guards are reported by NOC chairman Mustafa Sanalla to have been responsible on several occasions for fuel smuggling and oil blockades. Historically, since 2011, the different "chapters" have been organised as militias, with different affiliations with the GNA or the LNA. More recently, the oil facilities mainly came under the control of Marshal Haftar and consequently the PFG. Zawiya remains an exception, always allied to the GNA. On 16 November 2020, the acting Special Representative of the Secretary-General for Libya, Stephanie Williams, together with NOC chairman Mustafa Sanalla launched a reunification process to merge all the different chapters into a new petroleum facility force (UNSMIL 2020a). The aim of the process is to disarm the PFGs, which turned into militias during the conflict, and to reunify the body in charge of the security of Libya's most vulnerable and most profitable asset. Oil production was blocked for almost a year, with severe economic consequences. The control of the Libyan oil facilities is leverage in the hands of warlords and militias and is undoubtedly one of the major sources of instability in the country (International Crisis Group 2018). The roadmap of the peace process was established at the Berlin conference in January 2020 and envisaged shutting down the illicit market for fuel. Without these revenues – given the drop in the human smuggling profits with the decrease in the voyages towards Europe – militia groups are underfinanced and unable to maintain their territorial dominance. With the approaching promised elections and the renewed increase in migration from Libya to Europe ("The number of illegal border crossings at Europe's external borders in the first

6 To get an idea of the patrol boats used by smugglers in the Zuwarah and Abu Kammash area, see UN Panel of Experts 2018: Annex 52.

seven months of 2021 reached over 82 000, 59 % more than the total from a year ago, according to preliminary calculations" (Frontex 2021)), since late August new clashes have been reported in the country, mainly in Tripoli and Zawiya (Il Fatto Quotidiano 2021).

In early January 2021, all across Libya the PFG chapters started threatening an oil blockade if the government failed to pay their salaries. Protests were reported in both Eastern Libya (Ras Lanuf, Marsa el-Hariga and Es Sider) (Hellenic Shipping News Worldwide 2021) and Western Libya (Zawiya) (ANSA 2021). "The feud between the state-owned National Oil Corporation and the Central Bank of Libya on the distribution of oil revenues has resulted in a delay of oil payments. NOC has refused to release its oil revenues to the Central Bank, which are currently deposited with a foreign bank, until a unity government is formed", Hellenic Shipping News (2021) reported.

The importance of the intermediaries

The smuggling of fuel requires that the commodity is smuggled illegally from the legitimate producer to the legitimate consumer. Why illegally? Because the earnings from trade are higher for both counterparts when the trade is tax-free. The money saved in taxes is the origin of the crime.

The intermediation between supply and demand is brokered by professionals, who charge their own fees. These professionals are the brokers of the illicit activity. They bridge the needs of the sellers and the buyers. This role is typical in every kind of smuggling. The professional is the facilitator of the trade, a link in the chain which makes the connection possible. As on the legal market, the broker is the figure the counterparts rely on. In the illicit economy, specific trade channels exist only because of the brokers. The drug market shows that it takes time for big brokers to be substituted when they are arrested. Already from a geographical point of view, Malta is the natural bridge between the Global South and the Global North in the Mediterranean region. The histories of Libya and Malta are intertwined: Malta became independent from the United Kingdom in 1964 (and became a Republic in 1974) (Encyclopedia Britannica n.d.-b), while the Libyan revolution led by Muammar Gaddafi started in 1969 (Encyclopedia Britannica n.d.-a). When the British Royal Air Force left the island, the first cargo plane to land came from Libya with "44 men in civilian clothes who were lugging 4-ft.-long wooden crates. Government spokesmen insisted that the Libyans were 'technicians' who had come to operate Luqa when British air-traffic controllers leave; their crates merely contained technical gear", TIME reported in 1972. The Libyan leader Gaddafi also loaned millions of dollars to support the newborn government, which had to overcome the lack of income from the British.

The relationship between the two countries has remained close ever since. There is a vital and large Libyan community in Malta, some of the Libyan financial authorities are based or have branches in Malta, and the Maltese public bank Bank of Valletta (BOV) is currently under scrutiny by the local financial authority because of loans granted to Libyan citizens without due diligence and because it hid money diverted from Libya by the Gaddafi family (ANSAmed 2021). This long and solid relationship between the two countries was reported after the Libyan revolution of 2011.

When the Maltese came in: who are the intermediaries who made the smuggling between Libya and Europe possible

It is not clear exactly when the former Maltese football player Darren Debono met the Libyan kingpin Fahmi Slim Ben Khalifa, alias Malem (Arabic for "boss"), but certainly between 2015 and 2016 their business flourished.

The business opportunity in Libya came along with the chaos in Western Libya and the emerging power of the Nasr Brigade in the area. At the same time, Darren Debono seemed to be looking for a new opportunity for business. He was joined by another Maltese oil trader interested in expanding his business network in Libya: Gordon Debono (not a relative of Darren).

Ben Khalifa was reportedly "affiliated"[7] to the Kachlaf crime group. His criminal record is long: he fled a prison in 2011, during the Libyan uprising against Gaddafi. He was convicted for drug trafficking at the time. He was nicknamed the King of Zuwarah, which at the time was one of the main hotspots of the human trafficking between Libya and Italy. According to business records, he also owned shipping companies

7 The term would fit more accurately for a mafia clan rather than a Libyan crime group. Yet, as mentioned before, this Libyan group has similarities with the mafia-style groups in Italy. Ben Khalifa was prominently connected to the Kachlaf clan by ethnic ties.

in Tunisia and Libya at the time of his business association with Darren Debono.[8]

In Libya, Ben Khalifa succeeded in providing the bunkering facilities used in the smuggling ring at Abu Kammash, Sidi Ali and his pumping station at Marsa Tiboda, the harbour where the Italian navy docked its warships in the war against the local population back in 1912 (La Confédéré 1912).

The UN Panel of Experts (2018: 42) described these smuggling facilities[9]:

> "The gasoil comes from the Zawiya refinery along a route parallel to the coastal road [...]. The fuel is usually delivered to illegal fuel depots, of which there are about 40 in the area. From those facilities, the fuel is transferred in smaller tanker trucks to the port of Zuwarah, where it is loaded into small tanker ships or fishing boats with modified tanks. They then supply larger ships smuggling the fuel out of Libya. About 70 boats, either small tankers or fishing trawlers, were dedicated solely to this activity. The trucks also transport the fuel to one of three pumping stations located on the coast between Zuwarah and Abu Kammash. These are Marsa Tiboda, Sidi Ali and the Abu Kammash Chemical Factory [...]. From the pumping stations, smugglers use dedicated pipes to load the fuel into ships waiting between 1 and 2 nautical miles offshore. It is, however, not clear how many of those pumping stations are currently functioning."

---

8 Indictment based on Operation Dirty Oil: "Indice del coinvolgimento di BEN KHALIFA nel traffico illecito in esame è dato innanzitutto dalla sua partecipazione nella società maltese ADJ TRADING Ltd., unitamente a Darren DEBONO e al cittadino egiziano Ahmed Ibrahim Hassan Ahmed ARAFA, oggetto già alla fine del 2015 di attenzione mediatica e nel mese di marzo del 2016 del rapporto degli esperti nominati dal Consiglio di Sicurezza dell'ONU in quanto ritenuto al centro dei traffici illeciti di combustibili nel Mediterraneo." (Tribunale di Catania 2017: 24) – Own translation: "BEN KHALIFA's involvement in the illicit trafficking was revealed above all by his participation as a shareholder in the Maltese company ADJ TRADING Ltd., together with Darren DEBONO and the Egyptian citizen Ahmed Ibrahim Hassan Ahmed ARAFA, already exposed in the media at the end of 2015 and in March 2016 mentioned in the report by the UN Security Council as he was considered to be at the centre of illicit fuel trafficking in the Mediterranean."

9 For satellite pictures of the smuggling facilities, see UN Panel of Experts 2018, Annex 51, pg. 215.

In 2017, the criminal fuel smuggling industry comprised 500 people employed in around 20 criminal networks, but they were predominantly focused on the local market, except for the Nasr Brigade, which was also providing sea patrolling for the groups allied with it.

Darren Debono was relatively new in the oil business. After his football career, he managed a small fleet of fishing boats and a fancy restaurant, Scoglitti. In ADJ Trading Ltd., the first company of their entire network, Darren Debono and Ben Khalifa were associated with an Egyptian businessman already involved in different kinds of smuggling. Ben Khalifa also had a tanker at his disposal due to his role as a board member of the Libyan company Tiuboda Oil and Gas (Frattini 2016).

According to the Italian police, even if formally the PFG in Zawiya had been dissolved in January 2017, the fuel smuggling business was carried on by Ben Khalifa and his brothers: Nabil, Hafiz, Hakim and Fatimi. According to a leaked UN interim report from 2017, they were still operating at the time.

The duo wasn't able to go beyond Libya at that time. The addition of a proper oil broker, who is still in the business, was a game changer, according to the investigators. Gordon Debono gave the group the capacity to export Libyan fuel with forged certifications to circumvent the lack of national authorisation, according to the findings of the Guardia di Finanza. Moreover, the size of the ships at his disposal and his commercial network brought the group to the next level.

Fahmi Slim was arrested in August 2017, before the warrant issued in the course of Operation Dirty Oil, and is still in jail. According to confidential sources close to the investigation, his network dried out. Darren and Gordon Debono were arrested, but they are still operating. Darren Debono was granted bail in another case of money laundering in April 2021 (Agius 2021), while Gordon Debono was charged in another case of money laundering in November 2020 (Martin 2020) and is claiming in Malta that he is not a business associate of Darren Debono (Brincat 2021). Now they are waiting for the final trial in Italy. These three persons are still under sanctions by the US, the UK, the EU and the UN.

The modus operandi: faking the bill of lading[10]

The criminal network used the Maltese-Libyan Chamber of Commerce, the entity tasked with promoting business between the two countries, to label the fuel as Saudi. The camouflage allowed them to sell a product with a supposed higher quality (and price) and circumvent the export licence system. According to the Dirty Oil indictment, the Maltese network worked with the help of notaries and employees at the Maltese Ministry of Foreign Affairs.

The gasoline with the forged certificates[11] was bunkered in both Malta and Italy. The provider of the Italian customers was Darren Debono, who knew Nicola Orazio Romeo, a Sicilian fishing businessman indicted in Dirty Oil. According to the Italian investigators, Romeo controlled part of the Acireale fish markets, which were deeply infiltrated by the Sicilian mafia, the *cosa nostra*. He was connected to the clan of the Santapaolas of Catania as well. According to the investigators' hypothesis, the possibility to introduce Darren Debono to the Italian oil traders mentioned in Dirty Oil was provided by Romeo. According to the investigation, the price of the product was very competitive.

The Swiss NGO TRIAL International investigated a Swiss oil trading company which received over 50,000 metric tons of gasoil from the Zawiya refinery in Libya from spring 2014 to summer 2015. According to bank statements collected by the NGO, "[the company] transferred over USD 11 million to the small Maltese company Oceano Blu Trading Ltd from 18 June to 22 July 2015. At the time, the company was managed by Darren Debono" (TRIAL International 2020) and owned by Nicola Orazio Romeo.

When stored in legitimate companies, the illicit products entered the legitimate market. The ongoing trial for Operation Dirty Oil will have to establish whether the oil companies involved were aware of the origin of the fuel, as alleged in the Guardia di Finanza findings.

10 The following section is based on Rubino, Anesi and Bagnoli (2018)

11 For an example of such a forged certificate, see "Are the papers in order?" in Public Eye/TRIAL International (2020).

The case of the Temeteron

The disruption of the Debonos' network began with an event: the interception by the Libyan coastguard of Zawiya of a vessel called Temeteron, which occurred in June 2016. At that time, the equilibrium among the group broke down. Gordon Debono, the professional broker, wanted to take control of part of Darren's fleet. According to some wiretaps collected by the Guardia di Finanza of Catania, Gordon Debono had plans to expand the smuggling ring into Eastern Libya. There is no evidence that it had connections on the ground, nor evidence of the existence of a crime group dedicated to fuel smuggling in Eastern Libya. In any case, he succeeded in organising the bunkering of smuggled fuel through one of the most frequently used vessels of the group, the Temeteron.

This is one of the 70 vessels exposed by the UN for their role in the smuggling ring. Both Dirty Oil and the UN Panel of Experts investigations established the connection between the ship and Gordon Debono. However, the role played by the intermediary chartering company based in Greece is still not clear. The structure of the shipping industry and the extensive use of charters made assessing the level of complicity among different actors of the network more complex than in other sectors.

In each of its reports, the UN Panel of Experts on Libya updates a list of vessels spotted smuggling different goods, from weapons to fuel. The Temeteron was first named by the panel in the report S/2017/466. Many of these vessels are subsequently included in sanctions lists all around the world. Litigation for unpaid salaries or about the responsibility for incidents that occurred at sea is frequent. As a result, it is impossible to assess the actual involvement of the shipping companies in the fuel smuggling ring from Zawiya.

In June 2016, the Temeteron was heading to Zuwarah to load oil products. In an area near the Maltese territorial waters known as Hurd's Bank, the products were meant to be transshipped to other vessels and stored in either Italy or Malta. The chief operations officer on board, Sergey Samaylov, told IrpiMedia what he experienced on board the Temeteron when the ship was intercepted by the Libyan Coast Guard and later assaulted. As is usual, he was not aware of the kinds of products the ship was supposed to carry. He remembered that the first journey to Libya, with an associate of Darren Debono on board, went smoothly while a second one, a few days later, without anyone from Darren's network on board, caused the intervention of the Libyan Coast Guard. Sergey Samaylov provided evidence of the assault of the Libyan Coast Guard on the ship and the beating of the crew. After disembarking, the crew were imprisoned first at the Nasr Brigade compound close to the Zawiya refinery and later in the Mitiga prison of Tripoli, where they spent three years before their release. The trial against the crew of the Temeteron in Tripoli ended up with a conviction for conspiracy, illegal migration and fuel smuggling.

The head of the negotiations to release the (mainly Russian) crew was Lev Dengov, entrepreneur, chairman of the board of the Russian-Libyan Trade House and a close associate of Chechen leader Ramzan Kadyrov. In 2015, when the number of Russian seafarers arrested in Libya became significant, Dengov was appointed special advisor to the Ministry of Foreign Affairs in Russia. He also led the initial interactions with Khalifa Haftar, whose main foreign sponsor Russia later became, along with the UAE. Dengov failed to secure the release of the Temeteron's crew, and his replacement corresponded with a change in the Russian diplomatic strategy on Libya. The Ministry of Defence became Russia's main representative in Libya. Despite a public denial by the Kremlin, several investigations showed that the Russian military contractor Wagner Group, already used by Russia in other conflicts, had boots on the ground. At that point, the Russian diplomatic dialogue with the western part of Libya was over, and Eastern Libya and Haftar became the main ally.

The most notorious of the smugglers: Abd Al-Rahman Milad, a.k.a. al-Bija

As Sergey Samaylov recalls, the Temeteron was boarded by Abd Al-Rahman Milad, a.k.a. al-Bija (UNSMIL 2020b), a member of the Libyan Coast Guard affiliated with the Nasr Brigade. He became notorious in Italy thanks to several investigations on his abuses against migrants (Mannocchi 2017; Porsia 2017). As reported by Nello Scavo in the Italian newspaper Avvenire in a series of articles (Scavo 2019), al-Bija was also invited to visit a migrant facility in Mineo, Sicily, by the Italian government in May 2017. The event and his training in Italy were in line with what was established in the Memorandum of Understanding between Libya and Italy. As noted by the UN Panel of Experts and many other analysts, al-Bija was at the same time the guard and the felon beating people. According to the Dirty Oil investigation, al-Bija intervened to stop the Temeteron in response to a call by Darren Debono. This event shows the synergy between the Maltese and the Libyan smugglers and the role played by the Libyan Coast Guard of Zawiya in this context.

On 15 October 2020, al-Bija was arrested by the RADA Special Deterrence Forces, the armed group who brought the Temeteron crew from the Nasr Brigade prison to Mitiga in Tripoli. According to a UNSMIL (2020b) press report, al-Bija was "subject to a special bulletin of the International Criminal Police Organization (INTERPOL) and an arrest warrant issued in April 2019 by the Tripoli Public Prosecution Office on charges of human trafficking and fuel smuggling", in addition to the UN, UK, US and EU sanctions lists where he appears. This is the latest available report about him. It is not clear why he lost the support which allowed him to work with the Nasr Brigade as chief of the Libyan Coast Guard in Zawiya.

Conclusions

In Libya, the local militias are gaining power locally through their transnational networks. The instability of the country is fuelled by sanctioned businessmen and companies also operating in the European Union. On the side of the Global South, there are militias and criminal groups who are among the producers of instability in the country. Yet, Libya is an important oil and gas producer and a strategically important country to partner with for the European powers, so it is important to stay in dialogue and negotiations with the different factions, from the European perspective. The problem is that this dialogue legitimised actors who work on the black market, often in contact with transnational groups of criminals and alleged criminals with a background in fuel smuggling. On the side of the Global North, there are companies and businessmen eager to participate in a tax-free fuel trade, taking advantage of lax regulations and the lack of controls in the international waters outside Libya. Between these two poles, there are the brokers, the intermediaries who make smuggling rings possible. The external actors are the international powers who are supporting different factions, including the smugglers, in the Libyan civil war.

The Libyan turmoil is a perfect environment for the growth of organised crime groups. The chess game about the stabilisation of Libya between international actors such as Turkey, Russia, Egypt, the United Arab Emirates and the European Union – and the resulting split of its resources – has so far been another factor of instability. In this context, the main concern of the European Union has been to tackle human smuggling, perceived as the major crime occurring in Libya. Despite the intentions to disrupt other smuggling networks, the sea patrolling missions coordinated by the European Council failed to obtain the expected results in every sector. The consequences are a booming black market and a suffering legal economy. The unification of the country at this stage still seems a dream. Without a discernible diplomatic result, any fight against the group of smugglers will be useless. In the Balkanised situation that currently exists, smuggling is often a way to survive. Especially between 2014 and 2016, some of the groups more keen to expand their power found new allies in Europe, such as Gordon and Darren Debono in Malta. Strong coordination among more law enforcement agencies at the EU level made it possible to tackle that specific group. Still, in terms of the legal consequences it is not clear what will be the outcome of the investigations, due to the ongoing trial in Catania. The petroleum sector is under scrutiny because of its environmental impact. Countries such as Libya where the petroleum sector has a very high impact on the GDP will suffer the worst consequences. It is likely that the black market for oil derivatives will survive longer in Libya. It is not realistic to imagine any sort of transition from oil into renewable energies in a country where the central state is not able to govern. Rather than targeting local criminal actors, who sometimes smuggle to survive, the international community should sanction legal actors in the Global North and in the Global South who trade with smuggling networks. This strategy at least creates a deterrent for the companies who are buying smuggled fuel, even if the success of the sanctions also in other regions such as Iran or North Korea is still debatable (O'Sullivan 2010). The UN should keep its dominant role for the sanctions and the stabilisation of Libya to succeed. The UN should focus on how to dismantle the illegal structure providing earnings to economic actors who are stealing resources from Libya. The UN Panel of Experts has already collected much evidence of how the looting works; now it is time to determine the countermeasures, along with a Libyan government. Without a stable and elected parliament, every effort could harm the sovereignty of Libya. This is one of the reasons why the elections are a potential game changer in this context.

References

Agius, Matthew (2021): "Former gootballers Darren Debono and Jeffrey Chetcuti granted bail on money laundering charges". At: https://www.maltatoday.com.mt/news/court_and_police/108801/former_footballers_darren_debono_and_jeffrey_chetcuti_granted_bail_on_money_laundering_charges#.YVCmTUZBw4h (accessed 19 October 2021).

Al Jazeera (2021): "Libya's parliament passes no-confidence vote in Unity Government". At: https://www.aljazeera.com/news/2021/9/21/libya-parliament-withdraws-confidence-from-unity-government (accessed 1 November 2021).

ANSA (2021): "Libia: vertenze Guardie petrolifere, minacciano blocco pozzi". At: https://www.ansa.it/canale_ambiente/notizie/energia/2021/01/30/libia-vertenze-guardie-petrolifere-minacciano-blocco-pozzi_31916175-1d8e-4eec-9e5b-de4c4a1daa03.html (accessed 19 October 2021).

ANSAmed (2021): "Malta: pressure from Libya to recover Gheddafi assets". At: https://www.ansamed.info/ansamed/en/news/sections/generalnews/2021/05/12/malta-pressure-from-libya-to-recover-gheddafi-assets_e0b0e67d-49db-4559-ad5e-bf974d55e653.html (accessed 19 October 2021).

Bagnoli, Lorenzo (2020): "La mafia di Zawiya". At: https://irpimedia.irpi.eu/mediterraneocentrale-mafia-zawiya/ (accessed 19 October 2021).

Barabanov, Ilya/Ibrahim, Nader (2021): "Wagner: scale of Russian mercenary mission in Libya exposed". At: https://www.bbc.com/news/world-africa-58009514 (accesssed 11 May 2022).

Brincat, Edwina (2021): "Fuel trader Gordon Debono 'never partnered' with former footballer Darren Debono". At: https://timesofmalta.com/articles/view/fuel-trader-gordon-debono-never-partnered-with-former-footballer.861343 (accessed 1 November 2021).

Coface (n.d.): "Libya. Major macro economic indicators". At: https://www.coface.com/Economic-Studies-and-Country-Risks/Libya (accessed 28 February 2021).

Di Feo, Gianluca : "Il vallo di Putin e le fortezze turche. La nuova Libia ha due soli padroni". At: https://www.repubblica.it/esteri/2021/02/14/news/la_partita_a_scacchi_tra_lo_zar_e_il_sultano_cosi_russia_e_turchia_si_stanno_spartendo_la_libia-287591757/ (accessed 19 October 2021).

Eaton, Tim (2018): "Libya's war economy. Predation, profiteering and state weakness". At: https://www.chathamhouse.org/2018/04/libyas-war-economy-predation-profiteering-and-state-weakness (accessed 12 October 2021).

Eaton, Tim (2019): "Libya. Rich in oil, leaking fuel". At: https://chathamhouse.shorthandstories.com/libya-rich-in-oil-leaking-fuel/index.html (accessed 28 February 2021).

Eaton, Tim (2020): "As conflict escalates in Libya, the economy veers toward crisis". At: https://warontherocks.com/2020/05/as-conflict-escalates-in-libya-the-economy-veers-toward-crisis/ (accessed 1 November 2021).

EEAS, European External Action Service (2021): "Operation EUNAVFOR MED IRINI – Results Report – August 2021". At: https://eeas.europa.eu/headquarters/headquarters-homepage/103630/operation-eunavfor-med-irini-results-report-august-2021_en (accessed 19 October 2021).

EEAS, European Union External Action Service (2022): "Operation EUNAVFOR MED IRINI – Results Report / December 2021". At: https://www.eeas.europa.eu/eeas/operation-eunavfor-med-irini-results-report-december-2021_en (accessed 5 May 2022).

El Zaidy, Zakariya (2017): "EU migration policy towards Libya. The Memorandum of Understanding between Italy and Libya, analysed from a Libyan perspective". At: https://library.fes.de/pdf-files/bueros/tunesien/13752.pdf (accessed 12 October 2021).

Encyclopedia Britannica (n.d.-a): "History of Libya". At: https://www.britannica.com/place/Libya/History (accessed 19 October 2021).

Encyclopedia Britannica (n.d.-b): "Malta". At: https://www.britannica.com/place/Malta (accessed 19 October 2021).

EASO, European Asylum Support Office (2021): "EASO Asylum Report 2021. Annual report of the situation of asylum in the European Union". At: https://easo.europa.eu/asylum-report-2021 (accessed 12 October 2021).

Frattini, Davide (2016): "Quelle petroliere fantasma dalla Libia all'Italia. I traffici nel Mediterraneo (e i Big Data per tracciarli". At: http://www.corriere.it/reportage/esteri/2016/quelle-petroliere-fantasma-dalla-libia-allitalia-i-traffici-nel-mediterraneo-e-i-big-data-per-tracciarli/?refresh_ce-cp (accessed 11 May 2022).

Frontex (2021): "July: increase in the central Med and Western Balkans". At: https://frontex.europa.eu/media-centre/news/news-release/july-increase-in-the-central-med-and-western-balkans-IOsJpO (accessed 19 October 2021).

Frontex (2022): "EU external borders in 2021: arrivals above pre-pandemic levels". At: https://frontex.europa.eu/media-centre/news/news-release/eu-external-borders-in-2021-arrivals-above-pre-pandemic-levels-CxVMNN (accessed 11 May 2022).

Hellenic Shipping News Worldwide (2021): "Fresh blow for Libya's oil revival, as militia threatens to stop crude exports at three ports". At: https://www.hellenicshippingnews.com/fresh-blow-for-libyas-oil-revival-as-militia-threatens-to-stop-crude-exports-at-three-ports/ (accessed 19 October 2021).

Il Fatto Quotidiano (2021): "Libia, liberato il trafficante di esseri umani 'Bija'. l'ex capo dei guardacoste di Zawiya era in carcere da ottobre". At: https://www.ilfattoquotidiano.it/2021/04/12/libia-liberato-il-trafficante-di-esseri-umani-bija-lex-capo-dei-guardacoste-di-zawiya-era-in-carcere-da-ottobre/6162694/ (accessed 19 October 2021).

International Crisis Group (2018): "After the showdown in Libya's oil crescent". At: https://www.crisisgroup.org/middle-east-north-africa/north-africa/libya/189-after-showdown-libyas-oil-crescent (accessed 19 October 2021).

Italian Ministry of Defense (n.d.): "EUNAVFOR MED Operation Sophia (conclusa il 31 marzo 2020)". At: https://www.difesa.it/OperazioniMilitari/op_intern_corso/eunavfor_med/Pagine/default.aspx (accessed 13 February 2021).

La Confédéré (1912): "La guerre italo-turque", 10 August 1912, pg. 3. At: http://doc.rero.ch/record/124855/files/1912-08-10.pdf (accessed 11 May 2022).

Libyan Government of National Accord/Government of Italy (2017): "Memorandum of Understanding on Cooperation in the Fields of Development, the Fight against Illegal Immigration, Human Trafficking and Fuel Smuggling and on Reinforcing the Security of Borders between the State of Libya and the Italian Republic". At: http://eumigrationlawblog.eu/wp-content/uploads/2017/10/MEMORANDUM_translation_finalversion.doc.pdf (accessed 12 October 2021).

Malakooti, Arezo (2019): "The political economy of migrant detention in Libya. Understanding the players and the business models". At: https://globalinitiative.net/wp-content/uploads/2019/11/Final-Report-Detention-Libya.pdf (accessed 19 October 2021).

Mannocchi, Francesca (2017): "Italy accused of bribing Libyan militias to stop migrants reaching Europe". At: https://www.middleeasteye.net/news/italy-accused-bribing-libyan-militias-stop-migrants-reaching-europe (accessed 11 May 2022).

Martin, Ivan (2020): "Fuel trader Gordon Debono charged in anti-smuggling bust". At: https://timesofmalta.com/articles/view/fuel-trader-gordon-debono-charged-in-anti-smuggling-bust.834445 (accessed 19 October 2021).

Martín, Javier (2020): "Lybia: the first totally privatized war in nodern history". At: https://www.novact.org/thelibyancrossroad/uploads/pdf/Libya-The-first-totally-privatized-war-in-modern-history.pdf (accessed 19 October 2021).

Micallef, Mark (2018): "Europe should help get fuel off Libya's fire". At: https://issafrica.org/iss-today/europe-should-help-get-fuel-off-libyas-fire (accessed 12 October 2021).

Micallef, Mark (2019): "Shifting sands – Libya's changing drug trafficking dynamics on the coastal and desert borders. Background paper commissioned by European Monitoring Centre for Drugs and Drug Addiction (EMCDDA) for the EU Drug Markets Report (EDMR) 2019". At: https://www.emcdda.europa.eu/drugs-library/shifting-sands-%E2%80%94-libya%E2%80%99s-changing-drug-trafficking-dynamics-coastal-and-desert-borders_en (accessed 12 October 2021).

Middle East Eye (2020): "Haftar forces block Libya oil exports, raising stakes for Sunday's Berlin Peace Summit". At: https://www.middleeasteye.net/news/haftar-forces-block-libya-oil-exports-raising-stakes-berlin-peace-summit (accessed 19 October 2021).

NOC, National Oil Corporation (2016): "The National Oil Corporation announces revenues from exports of oil and its derivatives for the months of September and October 2020". At: https://noc.ly/index.php/en/new-4/6201-the-national-oil-corporation-announces-revenues-from-exports-of-oil-and-its-derivatives-for-the-months-of-september-and-october-2020 (accessed 18 October 2021).

NOVA.news (2021): "Libia: ecco la bozza della legge per le elezioni presidenziali". At: https://www.nova.news/esclusiva-libia-ecco-la-bozza-della-legge-per-le-elezioni-presidenziali/ (accessed 19 October 2021).

OPEC, Organisation of Oil Exporting Countries (n.d.): "Libya facts and figures". At: https://www.opec.org/opec_web/en/about_us/166.htm (accessed 26 February 2021).

O'Sullivan, Meghan (2010): "Iran and the Great Sanctions Debate". In: The Washington Quarterly, 33, 4, pp. 7–21.

Pietz, Tobias (2020): "Operation Irini is wrong, for Libya and for sea rescues". At: https://euobserver.com/opinion/148307 (accessed 19 October 2021).

Porsia, Nancy (2017): "The kingpin of Libya's human trafficking mafia". At: https://www.trtworld.com/magazine/libya-human-trafficking-mafia-in-zawiya-301505 (accessed 11 May 2022).

Public Eye/TRIAL International (2020): "Libyan fuel smuggling. A Swiss trader sailing through troubled waters". At: http://stories.publiceye.ch/dirtyoil-libya/ (accessed 19 October 2021).

Rubino, Giulio/Anesi, Cecilia/Bagnoli, Lorenzo (2018): "Death in a smugglers' paradise". At: https://www.occrp.org/en/thedaphneproject/death-in-a-smugglers-paradise (accessed 19 October 2021).

Scavo, Nello (2019): "La trattativa nascosta. Dalla Libia a Mineo, il negoziato tra l'Italia e il boss". At: https://www.avvenire.it/attualita/pagine/dalla-libia-al-mineo-negoziato-boss-libico (accessed 19 October 2021).

Scavo, Nello (2021): "Libia. E ora Bija, sospetto trafficante, seleziona e addestra i futuri guardacoste". At: https://www.avvenire.it/attualita/pagine/ora-bija-seleziona-e-addestra-i-nuovi-guardacoste (accessed 13 May 2022).

The Global Economy (n.d.): "Libya: gasoline prices". At: https://www.theglobaleconomy.com/Libya/gasoline_prices/ (accessed 28 February 2021).

Time (1972): "MALTA: Gaddafi to the rescue". At: http://content.time.com/time/subscriber/article/0,33009,877632,00.html (accessed 10 May 2022).

TRIAL International (2020): "Smuggling Libyan gasoil: a Swiss trader navigates through troubled waters". At: https://trialinternational.org/latest-post/smuggling-libyan-gasoil-a-swiss-trader-navigates-through-troubled-waters/ (accessed 11 May 2022).

Tribunale di Catania, Sezione del Giudice per le Indagini Preliminari (2017): Ordinanza di custodia cautelare. Il Giudice per le Indagini Perliminari dott. Carlo Cannella, N. 113543/15 R.G.G.I.P.; N. 19269/14 R.G.N.R.

Turner, Ezla (2021): "Some of Libya's refineries resume, Ras Lanuf remains offline". At: https://www.spglobal.com/platts/en/market-insights/latest-news/oil/110520-refinery-news-roundup-some-of-libyas-refineries-resume-ras-lanuf-remains-offline (accessed 28 February 2021).

UK Parliament – European Union Committee (2017): "Operation Sophia: a failed mission". At: https://publications.parliament.uk/pa/ld201719/ldselect/ldeucom/5/502.htm (accessed 19 October 2021).

UN News (2021): "Libya: 'historic moment' as UN-led forum selects new interim leadership". At: https://news.un.org/en/story/2021/02/1084022 (accessed 19 October 2021).

UN Panel of Experts (2018): "Letter dated 5 September 2018 from the Panel of Experts on Libya Established Pursuant to Resolution 1973 (2011) addressed to the President of the Security Council". At: https://www.securitycouncilreport.org/atf/cf/%7B65BFCF9B-6D27-4E9C-8CD3-CF6E4FF96FF9%7D/s_2018_812.pdf (accessed 19 October 2021).

UN Panel of Experts (2021): "Letter dated 8 March 2021 from the Panel of Experts on Libya Established Pursuant to Resolution 1973 (2011) addressed to the President of the Security Council". At: https://digitallibrary.un.org/record/3905159?ln=en#record-files-collapse-header (accessed 19 October 2021).

UN Security Council (2018): "Sanctions list. Narrative summaries of reasons for listing: Mohammed Kachlaf". At: https://www.un.org/securitycouncil/sanctions/1970/materials/summaries/individual/mohammed-kachlaf (accessed 19 October 2021).

UN Security Council (2020): “Resolution 2509 (2020). Adopted by the Security Council at its 8719th Meeting, on 11 February 2020”. At: https://undocs.org/en/S/RES/2509(2020) (accessed 1 November 2021).

United Nations (2020): “Security Council extends measures against illicit export of petroleum from Libya, adopting Resolution 2509 (2020)”. At: https://www.un.org/press/en/2020/sc14105.doc.htmhttps://www.un.org/press/en/2020/sc14105.doc.htm (accessed 19 October 2021).

UNSMIL, United Nations Support Mission in Libya (2020a): “ASRSG Stephanie Williams attends the first meeting between NOC and the PFG commanders of eastern and western regions, hosted by Breiga’s Sirte Oil Company”. At: https://unsmil.unmissions.org/asrsg-stephanie-williams-attends-first-meeting-between-noc-and-pfg-commanders-eastern-and-western (accessed 11 May 2022).

UNSMIL, United Nations Support Mission in Libya (2020b): “UNSMIL welcomes arrest as a major step towards accountability, rule of law and dismantling criminal networks”. At: https://unsmil.unmissions.org/unsmil-welcomes-arrest-major-step-towards-accountability-rule-law-and-dismantling-criminal-networks (accessed 19 October 2021).

Varvelli, Arturo/Villa, Matteo (2019): “Italy’s Libyan conundrum. The risks of short-term thinking”. At: https://ecfr.eu/article/commentary_italys_libyan_conundrum_the_risks_of_short_term_thinking/ (accessed 18 October 2021).

Vella, Matthew (2015): “Battle of Libyan sovereign funds spills over into Maltese courts”. At: https://www.maltatoday.com.mt/business/business_news/52797/battle_of_libyan_sovereign_funds_spills_over_into_maltese_courts#.YVCgokZBw4g (accessed 19 October 2021).

Westcott, Tom (2020): “Running on empty. Oil-rich Libya hit by extreme fuel shortages”. At: https://www.middleeasteye.net/news/extreme-fuel-shortages-hit-oil-rich-libya (accessed 19 October 2021).

Part V:
Mineral supply chains and illicit flows

Following the supply chain of "illegal" gold from South Africa

Melanie Müller

Introduction

Artisanal extraction of gold is considered to have enormous potential for development. In many countries of the world, informal artisanal mining ensures the survival of workers and their families. But failures of policies to formalise artisanal mining prevent the realisation of socio-economic potential and push many artisanal miners into illegality, as informal activities are criminalised and therefore gold becomes "illegal". High commodity prices not only offer an incentive for people to work in the artisanal mining sector despite the risks involved. They have also attracted legal and illegal actors who want a piece of the pie.

Gold is not an illegal good, but its extraction can be illegal. Gold trade is also not illegal per se, but the trade of illegally extracted or brokered gold is. Therefore, at a certain point of the supply chain, gold from criminalised mining usually enters the legal market in order to become profitable. Traders of illegal gold have to find an entry point in order to "legalise" the resource. In many countries of the world, networks of legally and illegally operating actors have emerged around artisanal mining to help facilitate the smuggling of artisanal gold and the laundering of the associated profits. This makes the supply chain of gold particularly interesting. Since many different actors are involved, there are clearly legal and clearly illegal practices, but also shades of grey that could better be labelled "illicit".

South Africa is an interesting case to investigate the illicit nature of artisanal gold mining. It is one of the most important gold producers on the African continent and an important international trading partner for the European Union (EU), but has not succeeded in formalising artisanal mining in the country. The current regulations do not provide a coherent framework for artisanal miners, and certain activities are criminalised. This leads to a dual situation in South Africa: industrial mining is legally and formally recognised and encouraged, while the status of artisanal mining has not been clarified – it is an illicit activity, in many instances also illegal.

The focus of this article is to investigate the supply chain of artisanal gold from South Africa and to answer the following questions: At which points in the supply chain of gold do licit and illicit, legal and illegal practices intersect? Which networks and actors are involved at certain stages of the supply chain? Is it possible that gold from artisanal extraction in South Africa also enters the European market?

Although local conflicts and massive violent clashes over artisanal gold mining in South Africa have increased in the past years, its vulnerability to conflict has been overlooked. The South African case has not received much attention in recent debates about gold extraction, neither in the discussion on the formalisation of artisanal gold mining in Africa nor in the discussion on the implementation of the EU Conflict Minerals Regulation, because conflict areas in South Africa – compared to other examples like the Democratic Republic of the Congo (DRC) – remain below the threshold of civil war and are not considered high-risk areas. The gold supply chain from South Africa to Europe is of particular interest because South Africa is an important trading partner of the EU. The EU Conflict Minerals Regulation introduces responsibilities for European traders of gold from conflict-affected and high-risk areas (see Bauchowitz & von Carlowitz in this volume). The EU defines such areas as "[a]reas in a state of armed conflict, fragile post-conflict areas, as well as areas witnessing weak or non-existing governance and security, such as failed states, and widespread and systematic violations of international law, including human rights abuses" (Responsible Minerals Initiative n.d.). It provides European importers of gold with an indicative, non-exhaustive list of areas in different countries. Even though South Africa does not appear on the list, which includes 30 states all over the world (as of March 2022), it is indirectly affected. The implementation of the Regulation has increased the awareness of many European countries and companies about the risk of non-formalised artisanal gold entering the legal market. Reputational risks have driven many companies to adopt voluntary – and in many cases very extensive – standards. This also increases pressure on mining states worldwide to drive forward the mining regulations and to improve conditions in the artisanal mining sector. In addition, the European Commission has presented a proposal for a "Directive on corporate sustainability due diligence" which aims at fostering social and environmental standards in global value chains and ensuring compliance with human rights (European Commission 2022). The expected adoption of the Directive will increase the responsibilities of European companies when they import resources into the European market.

Supply chains of artisanal gold: illicit, informal and illegal elements

Gold ranks among the most precious metals in the world. In 2018, approximately 3.300 tonnes of gold was extracted all over the world. 27 % of worldwide gold production took place in Asia, followed by Africa with 18 % and Latin America and North America with 17 % each. 11 % of primary production took place in Oceania, followed by Europe with 10 % (Refinitiv 2020). The supply chain of gold can be divided into three stages. At the first stage of the supply chain, extraction of gold takes place in either the artisanal or the industrial form. After the raw material is extracted, gold is further refined in smelters or refineries. Smelters and refineries are considered the bottleneck in the supply chain of minerals and metals: once raw materials from different sources are melted together, it is more difficult to trace their origin later in the process (Young, Fernandes and Wood 2019). This means that actors who buy refined gold have to rely on transparent and reliable information from refineries about the origin of the material. Gold is often associated with jewellery, but this is not the only sector where the material plays a role. It is also used for investments, industrial demand or electronics (Refinitiv 2020).

Especially at the first stage of the supply chain of gold, different practices overlap – from legal through illicit to illegal. (For a distinction between illicit and illegal see also Shaw & Goodwin in this volume.) Gold extraction can happen in several ways. The most important and relevant distinction, between industrial mining and artisanal mining, refers to the method of extraction. There are various definitions of artisanal mining. The OECD refers to this practice as "artisanal and small-scale mining (ASM)" and defines it as follows: "formal or informal mining operations with predominantly simplified forms of exploration, extraction, processing, and transformation. ASM is normally low capital intensive and uses high labour intensive technology. 'ASM' can include men and women working on an individual basis as well as those working in family groups, in partnership, or as members of cooperatives or other types of legal associations and enterprises involving hundreds or even thousands of miners" (OECD 2016). This contrasts with industrial mining, which is carried out by – mainly large and international – mining companies in highly technologised operations. Industrial mining requires huge financial investments and in most countries of the world a comprehensive process of approval. Artisanal mining on the other hand can be carried out comparatively easily. Workers only need simple tools to begin with the artisanal extraction of gold. This explains why artisanal gold mining attracts unemployed or underemployed people in developing countries – and can therefore be regarded as an important activity of subsistence economies. In some cases, financial gain from artisanal gold mining for survival is tolerated up to a certain point. The legislation either leaves certain loopholes or does not criminalise the activity up to a certain income, and it can then be regarded as an informal practice (Engels 2019).

In other examples, the case is clearer. A number of African countries – among them Ghana and Zimbabwe – have advanced the formalisation of artisanal mining over the past twenty years (Hilson 2020). By applying for a licence and meeting certain requirements, artisanal miners can legalise their operations, allowing them to legally sell gold to traders and declare their taxes. Hilson and Maconachie argue that formalising and supporting ASM could also help governments to achieve their SDGs (Hilson and Maconachie 2020). But in practice, many countries have set the threshold for applying for a licence very high, which makes it difficult for artisanal miners to obtain a licence. As a result, even in many countries where artisanal gold mining has been formalised, workers continue to operate without a licence, making the activity de facto illegal (Hilson et al. 2021).

In addition, there are a number of countries – including the case of South Africa examined here – where the formalisation of artisanal mining is stagnating and has not yet made much progress. Up until now, the mining legislation does theoretically allow miners to apply for licences, but since it does not specifically mention the term "artisanal mining" and only distinguishes between small-scale and large-scale mining, processes are not adapted to the conditions of individual miners, which makes it impossible to obtain a licence (Interview Nel 2022; Martin 2019a; Roberts, Dixon and Merkle 2016).

In many cases around the world, artisanal gold mining has been linked to conflicts or their economies. The financing of armed conflicts in the Democratic Republic of the Congo has received particular attention (see also Bauchowitz & von Carlowitz in this volume). Moreover, social and political conflicts over artisanal mining also occurred in non-conflict areas, which can – among other reasons – be traced back to the unclear formalisation status of artisanal mining in many countries. Various studies have investigated conflicts between industrial and artisanal mining over access to land below the threshold of civil wars (Engels 2016; Engels und Dietz 2017) and – as a consequence – over access to the extraction of gold (Prause 2014; Wan 2014; Engels 2017; Crawford, Agyeyomah and Mba 2017). While industrial mining is technology-intensive and capital-intensive, small-scale miners can continue to search for raw materials in shafts of former industrial mines that can no longer be profitably operated by machines in the industrial process. This could be an opportunity to combine both techniques, but in many cases it leads to conflicts over access to former industrial mining sites, as labour protections on these sites are expensive and companies want to avoid liability (Hilson, Sauerwein and Owen 2020). Conflicts over artisanal mining on a community level are a second important aspect. In many mining communities, conflicts arise over the influx of workers and resulting social problems (lack of infrastructure, conflicts over jobs) (Medina Bernal et al. 2019) because toxic by-products from artisanal mining contaminate water and soil (Shandro, Veiga and Chouinard 2009; Durand 2012; Lusilao-Makiese et al. 2013) or because of the involvement of criminal actors that affects the security of mining communities (Hunter 2019; Wagner and Hunter 2020).

Gold mining in South Africa

South Africa is an interesting case to investigate the illicit nature of artisanal gold mining. Despite being one of the most important gold producers on the African continent, South Africa has not started to formalise artisanal mining. Currently, the most important mining regulation, the South African Mineral and Petroleum Development Resource Act (MPRDA), does not provide a coherent legal framework for artisanal mining, despite the Department of Mineral Resources and Energy (DMRE) indicating that the MPRDA could provide permits for artisanal workers. The Department has issued mining licences to artisanal miners only in a few cases in the diamond sector in the mining town of Kimberley. So far, the case of Kimberley is the exception, but it encourages artisanal miners from other regions to advocate for further formalisation of mining (Interview Lethoko 2022). Obtaining a licence for individuals is almost impossible: miners have to adapt to the requirements for small-scale mining, which set a high threshold for artisanal miners (Interview Nel 2022). This leads to a dual situation in South Africa: industrial mining is legally and formally recognised and encouraged, while the status of artisanal mining has not been clarified.

At the beginning of democracy in South Africa in 1994, artisanal small-scale mining was technically legalised, but when the MPRDA was introduced in 2002, it did not introduce a coherent framework for artisanal mining and well-defined criteria for this activity. Operating without a licence is a criminal activity in South Africa: artisanal miners without a licence operate as illegal miners and may face charges (Minerals Council South Africa n.d.). South Africa is currently debating a draft on artisanal and small-scale mining policy which is supposed to introduce specific requirements for artisanal miners (DMRE 2021). The policy is meant to clarify the status of artisanal and small-scale mining in the country and facilitate the application process for individuals, but many questions remain open (see last section) (Interview Nel 2022).

In general, the mining sector in South Africa is a highly conflictive environment. The South African government has not succeeded in resolving a wide range of conflicts over the extraction of the raw material, despite high human rights standards (Martin 2019a). The implementation of the far-reaching legislation fails in practice because the state's priority is economic profit. South Africa benefits from high commodity prices, which generate not only massive revenues for the sector but also fiscal gains for the state (PwC 2021). Ten years ago, a tragic incident occurred in this environment, known as the "Marikana massacre". In the mining town of Marikana, in the North West Province of the country, a wildcat strike in a platinum mine of Lonmin, an international mining company based in London, led to a confrontation between workers and the police at the mining site. The police opened fire and killed 34 mineworkers. Many more striking workers were injured. In the following years, academic articles critically investigated the events that led to the escalation in the mine, with a special emphasis on the difficult relationship between unions and the state, but focusing also on the relationship between workers and unions (Alexander 2013; Alexander et al. 2013). The focus on the platinum sector also led to deeper investigations into the impact of mining on local development and local communities, and scholars also started investigating the social and environmental impact of other minerals, for example gold (Cairncross and Kisting 2016).

In recent years, reports over violent conflicts in the gold mining sector in South Africa drew attention to the working conditions of artisanal miners in South Africa, conflicts over the extraction of resources in gold mining communities and the role of criminal networks, corruption and their links to formal institutions such as traditional authorities or the police (Thornton 2014; Nhlengetwa and Hein 2015). Especially non-governmental organisations, but also the South African Human Rights Commission, have focused more and more on the illicit and illegal nature of gold mining. This article draws on many of their findings by placing a focus on the broader supply chain of gold, particularly looking at the European market as a possible buyer of illegally extracted gold from South Africa.

Following illegal gold from South Africa to Europe

In the following chapters, the intention is to trace the activities of legal and illegal actors at different stages of the supply chain of gold from South Africa to Europe. Supply chains of metallic raw materials such as gold are particularly complex because there are various intermediate steps before the metal reaches the end consumer. After the extraction of the mineral, further processing of gold takes place in specialised gold smelters. After the smelting process, during which metals from different sources are melted together, it is almost impossible for buyers to trace the origin of the material. At the same time, the trade of illegal or illicit gold also plays a significant role, through which it is also possible to disguise its origin. Various studies suggest that the supply chain of artisanal gold from South Africa to the EU spans several countries. In addition to South Africa's neighbouring countries, key players are the United Arab Emirates – especially Dubai – and Switzerland.

Artisanal miners: driven by necessity or criminal activity?

As mentioned above, gold extraction in South Africa is not per se illegal, neither in the industrial nor in the artisanal form. But the Minerals Council South Africa estimates that most artisanal mining in the country is carried out without a licence and is considered an illegal activity.

With an estimated output of around 14 billion rand annually and more than 30,000 people working in the artisanal mining sector, South Africa is one of the biggest sources of artisanal gold on the African continent (Minerals Council South Africa 2019). Artisanal mining can be regarded as a means to survive for many people in South Africa who struggle because of the dire socioeconomic conditions many South Africans live in.

South Africa ranks among the countries with the highest inequality rates worldwide. A World Bank report from 2018 revealed that the lack of employment opportunities is the main driver for inequality, especially for people from rural areas who are disadvantaged in the labour market because they lack employment opportunities in their immediate surroundings. High costs for public transport set an additional threshold. Apart from that, the situation of the age cohort 15 to 34 years – around 12 million people – is particularly concerning. More than 40 percent of this age cohort were neither in work nor in any form of education (World Bank 2018). This explains why South Africans are looking for ways to make a living and are therefore attracted to jobs in informal economies.

In recent years, several violent clashes between security forces and artisanal miners, as well as conflicts between artisanal miners and communities, have drawn the attention of South African media to the difficult circumstances in the sector, and an intense debate has flared up about the responsibility and the role of the artisanal miners. Frequently, the media reports mainly on misconduct, which paints a negative picture of artisanal miners. This overlooks the fact that there are very different groups of actors. Many artisanal miners practice artisanal mining primarily as a subsistence economy. For these actors, formalisation would have positive consequences, because their activities have so far mainly been criminalised. More and more, they reject the designation "Zama Zama" – a Zulu expression which means "keep on trying" or "to gamble" – because this term has negative connotations (Interview Lethoko 2022). Many of the South African nationals working in artisanal mining were previously employed in bigger mining companies. But since the decline of gold mining in South Africa, these workers lost their jobs and were forced to work in the informal sector (Martin 2019b). Because it is not recognised as a formal economy, it can only be estimated how many people are involved in artisanal mining in South Africa (UNICRI 2016: 33). This also leads to contradicting statements about the involvement of foreign nationals. Zimbabwe and Mozambique are also in a difficult economic situation: both countries are highly indebted, suffer from massive economic crises and are also confronted with high levels of unemployment, especially youth unemployment. According to some estimates, 70 % of artisanal miners in South Africa are undocumented foreigners (Hunter et al. 2019). These miners often face double discrimination: first of all they are vulnerable because of their illegal – or at least illicit – status in the country, and secondly they are at risk because of the nature of their activity. Criminal networks exploit this situation. In some cases, workers were specifically recruited abroad without knowing that this would cause them to slip into an illegal status. This makes them particularly dependent on the criminal networks associated with artisanal mining in South Africa, which make this relationship a deliberate dependency – artisanal mining is often linked to other forms of criminal activities, sometimes organised crime (UNICRI 2016: 33). The National Association of Artisanal Miners (NAAM) – an organisation which was formed in 2019 to advocate for the legal recognition of artisanal mining – contradicts these estimates, stating that according to their research with Wits University in Johannesburg, "by far the majority are South African Citizens" (NAAM 2019). This also illustrates that criminalising artisanal mining – which is nevertheless an important economic activity – obscures important information about the relevance of the sector.

Many mining activities take place in abandoned mining sites which were used by industrial mining companies (Martin 2019a). According to South African legislation, a company has to obtain a closing certificate after it completes the industrial mining process. The company is then obliged to start a rehabilitation process. A key challenge in South Africa, however, is the implementation of the laws (Marais et al. 2021). One problem is that many mining sites were already abandoned before the end of Apartheid, so that it is almost impossible to trace their owners. Apart from that, governmental institutions in South Africa lack capacities to enforce the law, even if they know the company responsible. This explains why South Africa has more than 6.000 abandoned mines, which create an attractive venue for artisanal miners (Luthango 2022). While industrial exploitation of the material might not be profitable anymore, artisanal miners can still exploit smaller quantities of gold in the artisanal process and therefore enter old shafts or search for gold in mine tailings, which are very often located next to former industrial mining sites. At the same time, this unregulated activity puts many workers at risk. This is because old and abandoned shafts can collapse; moreover, toxic waste can still be found in narrow shafts, endangering workers' health in the short and medium term (Mhlongo et al. 2019). In some cases, this problem has led to conflicts between actors from the artisanal mining sector and from the industrial mining sector: artisanal miners were evicted after trespassing because companies fear legal consequences in case of an accident.

The lack of formalisation of the sector leads to an unfortunate situation because gold resources on former industrial mining sites will not get exploited and as a consequence are lost. There is untapped potential for combined approaches to unite both types of mining and thus exploit the full potential of gold mining. A recent World Bank report also argues that small-scale mining has a high potential for economic development in many countries worldwide and should not only be seen as a complement to industrial mining, but rather as an activity with high economic potential. Hilson et al. note that the rapid growth of artisanal mining is forcing more and more states and donors in Sub-Saharan Africa to consider far-reaching strategies to formalise artisanal mining (Hilson et al. 2021). While some African countries have passed legislation to formalise artisanal mining and have implemented programmes to reform the sector, South Africa has been more reluctant to try such combined models.

Illegal actors: the role of (criminal) networks in the context of artisanal gold mining

Successfully organising artisanal mining in South Africa would hardly be possible without the strong role of criminal networks. While the South African police have targeted illegal artisanal miners in the past, evidence also shows that other police actors are part of criminal networks engaged in artisanal mining (Clark 2019; Interview Nhlengetwa 2022; Parliamentary Monitoring Group 2017). Some experts have called for a stronger focus on those actors that facilitate the formation of criminal networks around artisanal mining and gold laundering (Hunter et al. 2019). In the South African case, criminal gangs but also legal actors – such as local security forces and the police – are involved in the organisation of small-scale mining. Ultimately, a network develops around artisanal mining in which not only the workers and criminal gangs, but in many cases also security forces and other members of communities indirectly benefit from the formation of artisanal gold mining (Martin 2019b).

With high profit rates for gold on international markets, South Africa's gold mining sector seems to have attracted national and international organised crime syndicates. In a 2017 meeting with the South African parliament, the Department of Mineral Resources stated that these syndicates were "highly organized, dangerous, well-financed and complex" and "use proceeds for furtherance of other crimes". In the same meeting, a representative of the Directorate for Priority Crime Investigation (DPCI) revealed that organised crime in the mining sector has "inter-linkages with other organized crime which include human smuggling and trafficking, money laundering, illegal weapons and explosives, violent crime, environmental degradation, the illicit economy, transnational organized crime, customs offences and tax evasion" (Parliamentary Monitoring Group 2017). Further research (e.g. Martin 2019a, see section below) indicates that in the South African case a network of legal and illegal actors is involved in the illegal extraction of gold and benefits from it – not a hierarchically organised criminal organisation. So far, the South African authorities have not succeeded in dismantling the organised crime networks in the mining sector. One of the main reasons is the involvement of local police forces that prevents the South African state from taking action against the trade in illegally mined gold. In some cases, police forces cooperate with networks of artisanal miners by "ignoring" illegal activities and benefiting economically in exchange (Martin 2019b).[1] In other cases, police officers do not declare confiscated gold as evidence, sell it to traders and as a consequence become an active pillar in the illegal trade of gold. According to the Environmental Justice Atlas (2021), "the zama zamas are also regular victims of cartels often working in tandem with police to rob the miners at gunpoint or coerce them into working for them" (Environmental Justice Atlas 2020). So far, the only measure taken by the South African state has been to increase the presence of the security sector in many regions, which – at the same time – increases insecurity because of escalating conflicts at mining sites.

There is insufficient evidence of the extent to which local community representatives or traditional elites are involved in illicit activities and/or cooperate with cartels or are even part of them. The unregulated nature of artisanal gold mining has negative impacts on local communities and in many cases jeopardises the rights to health, to a clean environment and to water, which are enshrined in the South African Constitution (Carry and Müller forthcoming). In addition to these severe violations of human rights, conflicts repeatedly arise over the mining of artisanal gold, which often escalate violently. Often, conflicts arise over access to particularly profitable mining sites. Such conflicts also affect residents in the immediate surroundings of mining operations, leaving affected communities particularly vulnerable because of a very tense environment. At the same time, artisanal miners are also victims of hostility, assault and violence. Their reputation is very low because they are blamed for violence exerted by gangs and mining bosses operating in communities. Communities, but especially the media, often make no distinction between ordinary workers who are looking for gold in search of economic prospects and those who are involved in the often violent illegal trade (Thornton 2014). The negative perception of artisanal miners can also be traced back to xenophobic attitudes in certain communities, which have been frequently reported in South Africa in recent years (Human Rights Watch 2020).

This escalation of conflicts around artisanal gold mining in South Africa explains the changing nature of reported causes of deaths of artisanal miners. In 2012, 92 per cent of fatalities were due to unsafe working conditions (rockfall or tunnel collapse), 8 per cent due to turf war and murder. Within three years, the situation changed completely. In 2015, 67 per cent of fatalities were due to turf war and murder, 1 per cent due to police or security battles and 32 per cent due to working conditions

---

1 See also: Directorate for Priority Crime Investigation (2017).

(Johnson 2016). The representativeness of these figures must be viewed with caution, as most accidents and assaults don't get reported because of the criminalisation of artisanal mining. But these figures do suggest that violence in mining communities continues to increase.

In South African media and politics, attention to the violent conflicts in the artisanal mining sector has increased in recent years. So far, however, no comprehensive efforts of the South African government to systematically address the problem are apparent. The discussion on the formalisation of artisanal mining is a step in the right direction but progresses much too slowly to change the situation immediately. Approaches such as more intensively policing communities and artisanal miners do not seem to solve the problem because they rather shift the blame to workers and do not necessarily address underlying causes as well as the role of criminal networks. In 2019, researcher and artisanal gold specialist Alan Martin presented an in-depth study for the Institute for Security Studies (ISS) in Johannesburg, which also reveals the role of networks involved in the trade of artisanal (and illegal) gold (Martin 2019a; Martin 2019b).

South Africa will have to address these challenges in the artisanal mining sector soon. This is because the socioeconomic impact of the COVID-19 pandemic is driving many people – in South Africa, but also in other countries in Southern Africa – to look for economic alternatives. Since the beginning of the pandemic in South Africa in the first quarter of 2020, the unemployment rate has risen from 29 percent to around 35 percent (Müller 2021; Statistics South Africa 2020: 1; Statistics South Africa 2021: 6). This dire economic situation has left many people with no other option than to take advantage of opportunities that arise to make money, even if they are short-term and often not legal, especially during the strict lockdown which the South African government imposed. At the beginning of the pandemic, gold production decreased as a consequence of strict lockdowns many countries worldwide imposed (Muthuri et al. 2021). But at later stages of the pandemic, increasing prices for commodities have provided an additional incentive for people to search for gold. It is therefore not surprising that South African media reported in March 2021 on a case of 100 gold miners who continued to work despite a strict lockdown and hid from the police in a shaft for fear of consequences (Harrisberg 2020). This shows that illegal gold mining remains financially lucrative as long as the material finds its way into the market.

"Legalising" artisanal gold

The question remains: what happens after the illegal extraction of gold in South Africa? When and how does gold from illegal artisanal mining enter the legal supply chain? The process of legalising illegal gold is called "gold laundering": "*Gold laundering is the process whereby illegally obtained gold is melted and recast into another form. The recasting is performed to obscure or conceal the true origin of the gold. The recast gold is then sold, thus laundering it into cash.*" *(Williams 2019)* South Africa is an exceptional case because – compared to many other African countries – it can be assumed that a large part of the gold laundering takes place in the country and the gold is transferred either to the legal market in South Africa or to the legal market in other countries.

Gold laundering in South Africa (and its neighbouring countries)

In his study, Alan Martin identified a "five-tier crime syndicate hierarchy" of "1) individual criminal miners; 2) gangs and illegal mining bosses; 3) bulk buyers at national/regional levels in the form of licensed or registered entities; 4) front company exporters; and 5) international intermediary companies and buyers." (Martin 2019b: 4–5). According to his research, the laundering of gold from illegal sources takes place at level 3. Actors with occupations in which it is legal to possess and process gold – such as licensed scrap-metal dealers, pawnshop owners or jewellers – are key players: "It is they who launder the illicit gold into the legal supply chain by converting the lower-grade doré bars (doré is a semi-pure alloy of gold and silver). Prior to delivering the gold to the refineries, the Level 3s often mix and melt down the doré with alloys to make it consistent with jewellery. As with the laundering of any product, the more stages it goes through to disguise its origins, the harder is it for police to connect it to its illicit source." (Martin 2019b)

Normally, every seller is legally required to document this process, but in the South African case, this requirement is regularly circumvented, e.g. by issuing fake certificates. After the laundering of illicit gold into the legal market, the product is either sold there or leaves the country as a legal product. Because actors at level 4 and level 5 "frequently operate from outside South Africa", the last possible access point for South African law enforcement is level 3 – which is the crucial step in the hierarchy. By selling gold as scrap metal, sellers disguise the poorer quality of artisanal gold that would normally give buyers an indication of its origin from non-industrial mining with lower quality. In South Africa, gold is already laundered in one of the many local refineries and leaves the South African market as an officially recognised "legal product" (Martin 2019b), thus making it even more complicated for gold importers to trace the origin of the metal. Illegal traders are taking advantage of the bottleneck in supply chains at the smelters. Although there are technical means to ensure traceability in the form of analytical fingerprints, these reach their limits, for example when many components are mixed together or only small proportions of gold of poorer quality are added. Larger smelters – Martin cites Rand Refinery as a positive example – are aware of the fact that artisanal gold is very often sold as scrap metal and are now checking provenance more closely (Martin 2019b). But it cannot be assumed that all smelters in South Africa are handling these processes responsibly. With more than 100 smelters in the Gauteng region alone, it has been almost impossible for the state to trace these activities (Martin 2019b: 5). In some cases, illegal gold is smuggled across the country's border and transferred to the legal market in the same way as in South Africa because smelters in neighbouring countries are used to launder gold from illegal sources (ibid: 7).

The role of international trading hubs

A number of other studies have highlighted the role of countries that are central to the illicit trade in commodities (The Sentry 2018; Lezhnev 2021). For the African region, the United Arab Emirates (UAE) are crucial actors. In recent years, several reports and studies have investigated the central role of the UAE in the global trade of gold, and the city of Dubai plays a particularly important role. Dubai's limited regulation of trade in commodities and inadequate implementation of existing regulatory approaches has created an attractive market for artisanal and small-scale gold traders. In the UAE, lack of money laundering regulation provides a favourable environment for illicit trade in commodities, according to "The Sentry": "Dubai's limited regulations and lax enforcement attract traders of artisanal and small-scale gold, and The Sentry has identified four main money laundering risk factors for gold in the UAE: large cash transactions for gold continue to take place, customs checks and controls for hand-carried gold are weak and do not require proof of payment, oversight of the Dubai gold souk is inadequate, and numerous large refiners are not subject to independent audits." (Lezhnev 2021: 7) Research points to the UAE as a gateway for the import of gold from conflict regions, whose origin is thus concealed (Grynberg and Singogo 2021a, 2021c). From the UAE, artisanal gold from various sources in Africa finds its way into the legal market, and very likely to Europe. Switzerland is one of the entry points for gold from other regions to enter the European market. In a recent study, the NGO SWISSAID revealed that Swiss gold smelters also source their raw materials from the UAE. It is thus likely that illegal gold – from South Africa but also from other African countries – enters the European market via this route, but so far there is no evidence that this connection exists (SWISSAID 2020).

The lack of an international scheme to measure and quantify illicit financial flows and to address trade misinvoicing and money laundering makes it even more difficult to prove connections, as this can lead to inaccurate and contradictory conclusions. In 2016, the UN Conference on Trade and Development (UNCTAD) released a report which investigated trade misinvoicing by comparing two decades of declared commodity exports from different developing countries with declared commodity imports into other countries (see also Fabricius in this volume). The report indicated that two-thirds of South Africa's gold exports were under-invoiced, which would amount to 78.2 billion dollars (UNCTAD 2016). Following UNCTAD's publication, the South African government commissioned an agency to get to the bottom of the findings, as it doubted the study's results. The agency concluded that the large discrepancies between exports and imports were not due to underinvoicing, but that the different methodologies used to record the origin of raw materials were the main reason for the mismatch. The agency compared figures from different South African databases and was able to narrow down the gap to US$19.5 billion: "We have now determined that most of the USD 19.5 billion discrepancy can very likely be attributed to errors in the reported gold imports of South Africa's trading partners, not in South Africa's reported gold exports. This likely occurs through the fact that SA refines large amounts of gold for certain African (e.g. Ghana or Mali) gold producing countries (currently standing at approximately 50 percent of total refined gold), which is reported as South African gold, instead of from its real origin.“ (Eunomix 2016) Although the information provided by the South African government led to the correction of the UNCTAD report, this example illustrates that the international regulatory framework is not sufficient to ensure adequate traceability of licit and illicit financial flows. Grynberg and Singogo (2021b) therefore argue that the use of trade data alone is not sufficient to estimate misinvoicing and illicit financial flows in the mining sector, but that other techniques – forensic techniques and accounting techniques – need to be included.

A transnational approach to the illicit trade of gold

The analysis of artisanal gold mining in South Africa shows that a complex network of legal and illegal actors facilitates the process of gold laundering in South Africa, from where the product finds its way to the legal market. After the smelting process is completed, it is almost impossible for international buyers to trace the origin of the metal. As a consequence, they rely on smelters to source their materials responsibly, but also on international traders to transparently report the origin of metals. While the analysis of the different stages of the supply chain can reveal (possible) linkages between actors in different countries, it also highlights the research gaps in the field of transnational supply chains. While individual stages of the gold supply chain have been investigated, hardly any analyses look at transnational linkages or at the role of actors who enable cross-border trade and smuggling. Such analyses are challenging and require investigative research approaches because the very goal of illegal traffickers and smugglers is to remain in the dark.

While conflicts over gold mining in South Africa remain below the threshold of a civil war, the chapter has shown that South Africa faces serious local conflict over artisanal mining, with negative impacts on human rights. The formalisation of artisanal mining in South Africa could help to address some of the serious questions the country is currently facing. First of all, it could release economic potential and create an opportunity for those who are already trying to make a living by working in the sector – but not in a legal environment. The state would also benefit from this because of tax revenues on legal artisanal mining. Supporting artisanal miners by applying for licences could be combined with educational programmes on safety and sustainability, which would increase safety both for workers and for surrounding communities. The state would be able to distinguish more clearly between actual criminal structures and artisanal mining activities that aim at making a living. The introduction of the draft policy on artisanal and small-scale mining in South Africa in 2021 (DMRE 2021) is a step in the right direction, but so far questions remain about the concrete design of the policy. Many points have not been clarified, such as legal questions about equal access to land, but also the question of whether foreign workers should also receive permits (Wet 2021). The draft policy proposes to issue licences only to South Africans, which has met with resistance from various actors from civil society, e.g. NAAM and mining-affected communities (Macua & Wamua 2021; NAAM 2019), and is also expected to be rejected by the South African constitutional court.

At the end of the supply chain, since the beginning of 2021 European companies must exercise special due diligence when importing tin, tantalum, tungsten or gold, especially if they import these raw materials from conflict-affected and high-risk areas. To date, South Africa has not been the focus of stakeholders concerned with the implementation of the EU Conflict Minerals Regulation, but the introduction of the Regulation has increased awareness of the risks associated with artisanal mining, especially in an informal environment. The possible introduction of a European directive on due diligence will increase the awareness of European companies even further. Therefore, South Africa could and should take the introduction of stronger European legislation as an opportunity to clarify the legal status of artisanal mining in the country and improve the human rights situation in the mining sector, which has been subject to critical investigations.

The chapter has shown that it is possible that illegally extracted artisanal gold from South Africa enters the European market as a legal product. After the laundering of gold in South Africa or its neighbouring countries, it becomes almost impossible to trace the origin of the product. It then enters the legal market and can be traded as a legal good. Trading hubs such as the UAE enable sellers to disguise the origin. Overall, the analysis highlights the importance of illicit trade as a precondition for making the extraction of artisanal gold lucrative. At various points in the supply chain of illegally mined artisanal gold, a network of actors is involved that benefits from the extraction. As the case of South Africa illustrates, these are not only illegal actors, but also legal ones that profit from gold laundering. These include security forces such as the police as well as traders and refineries. On a global scale, states such as the UAE have developed a lucrative business model because they benefit from their position in the international economy as a hub which facilitates smuggling of gold from illicit sources – not only from South Africa but also from war zones. This highlights that national approaches to tackling illicit trafficking in commodities are not sufficient. In order to understand the transnational interconnectedness of these actors, more research is needed to better understand the interrelationships and make policy recommendations to address these problems.

References

Alexander, Peter (2013): "Marikana, turning point in South African history". In: Review of African Political Economy, 40, 138, pp. 605–619.

Alexander, Peter/Sinwell, Luke/Lekgowa, Thapelo/Mmope, Botsang/Xezwi, Bongani (2013): Marikana. A view from the mountain and a case to answer. Johannesburg: Jacana.

Carry, Inga/Müller, Melanie (forthcoming): "Addressing environmental injustices in South African artisanal gold mining". In: Nalule, Victoria R./Okoi, Obasesam/ Okafor Yarwood, Ife (eds.): Natural resource governance and sustainable peace in Africa. Environmental justice and conflict resolution. London: Routledge.

Cairncross, E./Kisting, S. (2016): "Platinum and gold mining in South Africa. The context of the Marikana massacre". In: New Solutions, 25, 4, pp. 513–534.

Clark, Christopher (2019): "'There's a lot of money down there'. The deadly cities of gold beneath Johannesburg". At: https://www.theguardian.com/cities/2019/oct/24/theres-a-lot-of-money-down-there-the-deadly-cities-of-gold-beneath-johannesburg (accessed 8 June 2022).

Crawford, Gordon/Agyeyomah, Coleman/Mba, Atinga (2017): "Ghana – Big Man, Big Envelope, Finish. Chinese corporate exploitation in small-scale mining". In: Engels, Bettina/Dietz, Kristina (eds.): Contested extractivism, society and the state. Struggles over mining and land. London: Palgrave Macmillan, pp. 69–99.

Directorate for Priority Crime Investigation (2017): "Briefing session: Portfolio Committee on Police. Tackling illicit mining activities impacting South Africa. Presentation Lieutenant General Matakata". At: https://static.pmg.org.za/171114Illicit_Mining.pdf (accessed 1 June 2022).

DMRE, Department of Mineral Resources and Energy (2021): "Discussion document. Artisanal and Small-Scale Mining Policy. Second draft, V2". At: https://cer.org.za/wp-content/uploads/2021/09/Draft-Small-Scale-and-Artisanal-Mining-Policy-5-May-2021.pdf (accessed 1 March 2022).

Durand, Francois (2012): "The impact of gold mining on the Witwatersrand on the rivers and karst system of Gauteng and North West Province, South Africa". In: Journal of African Earth Sciences, 68, pp. 24–43.

Engels, Bettina (2016): "Mining conflicts in sub-Saharan Africa. Actors and repertoires of contention". In: GLOCON Working Paper Series, 2.

Engels, Bettina (2017): "Not all glitter is gold. Mining conflicts in Burkina Faso". In: Engels, Bettina/Dietz, Kristina (eds.): Contested extractivism, society and the state. Struggles over mining and land. London: Palgrave Macmillan, pp. 149–170.

Engels, Bettina (2019): "Handwerklicher Bergbau". In: Brunner, Jan/Dobelmann, Anna/Kirst, Sarah/Prause, Louisa (eds.): Wörterbuch Land- und Rohstoffkonflikte. Bielefeld: transcript Verlag, pp. 135–140.

Engels, Bettina/Dietz, Kristina (2017): Contested extractivism, society and the state. Struggles over mining and land. London: Palgrave Macmillan.

Environmental Justice Atlas (2021): "Zama zama gold mining in Durban Deep, Gauteng, South Africa". At: https://ejatlas.org/conflict/zama-zama-gold-mining-in-durban-deep-south-africa (accessed 1 June 2022).

Eunomix (2016): "A review of the UNCTAD report on trade misinvoicing, with a focus on South Africa's gold export". At: https://www.mineralscouncil.org.za/industry-news/media-releases/2017/send/29-2017/471-independent-review-of-the-unctad-report-final (accessed 1 March 2022).

European Commission (2022): "Just and sustainable economy. Commission lays down rules for companies to respect human rights and environment in global value chains". At: https://ec.europa.eu/commission/presscorner/detail/en/ip_22_1145 (accessed 1 March 2022).

Grynberg, Roman/Singogo, Fwasa (2021a): "Dubai: Conflict gold, money laundering and illicit global trade". In: Grynberg, Roman/Singogo, Fwasa K. (eds.): African gold. Cham: Springer International Publishing, pp. 315–355.

Grynberg, Roman/Singogo, Fwasa (2021b): "Taxation and illicit financial flows in the gold mining sector". In: Grynberg, Roman/Singogo, Fwasa K. (eds.): African gold. Cham: Springer International Publishing, pp. 443–469.

Grynberg, Roman/Singogo, Fwasa (2021c): "Trade and the smuggling of gold from West Africa to the UAE". In: Grynberg, Roman/Singogo, Fwasa K. (eds.): African gold. Cham: Springer International Publishing, pp. 217–245.

Harrisberg, Kim (2020): "Exclusive: Fears rise for illegal South African miners hiding underground in virus lockdown". At: https://www.reuters.com/article/us-health-coronavirus-safrica-exclusive-idUSKBN22B1F9 (accessed 10 February 2022).

Hilson, Gavin (2020): "'Formalization bubbles': A blueprint for sustainable artisanal and small-scale mining (ASM) in sub-Saharan Africa". In: The Extractive Industries and Society, 7, 4, pp. 1624–1638.

Hilson, Gavin/Maconachie, Roy (2020): "Artisanal and small-scale mining and the Sustainable Development Goals: Opportunities and new directions for sub-Saharan Africa". In: Geoforum, 111, pp. 125–141.

Hilson, Gavin/Mondlane, Salvador/Hilson, Abigail/Arnall, Alex/Laing, Tim (2021): "Formalizing artisanal and small-scale mining in Mozambique. Concerns, priorities and challenges". In: Resources Policy, 71.

Hilson, Gavin/Sauerwein, Titus/Owen, John (2020): "Large and artisanal scale mine development. The case for autonomous co-existence". In: World Development, 130.

Human Rights Watch (2020): "'They have robbed me of my life'". At: https://www.hrw.org/report/2020/09/17/they-have-robbed-me-my-life/xenophobic-violence-against-non-nationals-south (accessed 10 February 2022).

Hunter, Marcena (2019): "Combating criminal consortia in the African artisanal and small-scale gold mining and trade sector". At: https://enact-africa.s3.amazonaws.com/site/uploads/2019-04-24-pulling-the-golden-webs-research-paper.pdf (accessed 15 April 2021).

Hunter, Marcena/Sibanda, Mukasiri/Opala, Ken/Kaka, Julius/Modi, Lucy (2019): "Illicit gold markets in East and Southern Africa". At: https://globalinitiative.net/wp-content/uploads/2021/05/Illicit-gold-markets-in-East-and-Southern-Africa-GITOC-.pdf (accessed 10 February 2022).

Interview with Lethoko, Shawn, NAAM, online, 3 March 2022.

Interview with Nel, Lauren, Legal Resource Centre, Johannesburg, 4 March 2022.

Interview with Nhlengetwa, Kgothatso, researcher, online, 1 April 2022.

Johnson, Cecilia (2016): "Lethal toll of informal gold mining". At: https://www.groundup.org.za/article/lethal-toll-informal-gold-mining/ (accessed 10 June 2022).

Lezhnev, Sasha (2021): "Conflict gold to responsible gold. A roadmap for companies and governments". At: https://cdn.thesentry.org/wp-content/uploads/2021/02/ConflictGoldResponsibleGold-TheSentry-Feb2021.pdf (accessed 1 March 2022).

Lusilao-Makiese, Julien/Cukrowska, Ewa/Tessier, Emmanuel/Amouroux, David/Weiersbye, Isabel (2013): "The impact of post gold mining on mercury pollution in the West Rand region, Gauteng, South Africa". In: Journal of Geochemical Exploration, 134, pp. 111–119.

Luthango, Sikho (2022): "Extraterritorial obligations in the governance gap. South Africa's mine closures and the utility of binding international legal frameworks". At: https://www.rosalux.de/en/publication/id/46314/extraterritorial-obligations-in-the-governance-gap (accessed 1 June 2022).

Macua & Wamua (2021): "Submissions on the Draft Artisanal and Small-Scale Mining Policy 2021". At: https://macua.org.za/wp-content/uploads/2021/06/MACUA-WAMUA-Submission-On-ASM-Policy-June-21.pdf (accessed 1 March 2022).

Marais, Lochner/Nel, Verna/Rani, Kholisa/van Rooyen, Deidré/Sesele, Kentse/van der Watt, Phia/Du Plessis, Lyndon (2021): "Economic transitions in South Africa's secondary cities. Governing mine closures". In: Politics and Governance, 9, 2, pp. 381–392.

Martin, Alan (2019a): "Solving South Africa's Violent and Costly Zama Zama Problem". At: https://issafrica.org/iss-today/solving-south-africas-violent-and-costly-zama-zama-problem (accessed 1 March 2022).

Martin, Alan (2019b): "Uncovered. The dark world of the Zama Zamas". At: https://globalinitiative.net/wp-content/uploads/2019/04/ENACT-Policy-Brief-008-Zama-Zama-24Apr1115-WEB.pdf (accessed 1 March 2022).

Medina Bernal, Javier/Cuenca Castelblanco, Tatiana/Serrano Pérez, Catalina/Carrillo González, Lorena (2019): "Gold Mining and local communities in Southern Córdoba in Colombia, the case of El Alacrán mine". At: https://www.tecnologialibredeconflicto.org/wp-content/uploads/documentos/ALBOAN-MineriaColombia-en.pdf (accessed 15 April 2021).

Mhlongo, Sphiwe E./Amponsah-Dacosta, Francis/Muzerengi, Confidence/Gitari, Wilson M./Momoh, Abuh (2019): "The impact of artisanal mining on rehabilitation efforts of abandoned mine shafts in Sutherland goldfield, South Africa". In: Jamba: Journal of Disaster Risk Studies, 11, 2.

Minerals Council South Africa (n.d.): "Illegal Mining". At: https://www.mineralscouncil.org.za/work/illegal-mining (accessed 1 March 2022).

Minerals Council South Africa (2019): Facts and figures. Pocketbook 2019.

Müller, Melanie (2021): „South Africa's social and political challenges. Covid exacerbates socioeconomic inequalities amid ANC infighting". At: https://www.swp-berlin.org/publikation/south-africas-social-and-political-challenges (accessed 1 June 2022).

Muthuri, Judy/Jain, Aditya/Ndegwa, Arthur/Mwagandi, Shadrack/Tagoe, Naa (2021): "The impact of Covid-19 on gold and gemstone artisanal and small-scale mining in sub-Saharan Africa. The case of Ghana and Kenya". In: Africa Journal of Management, 7, 1, pp. 121–147.

NAAM, National Association of Artisanal Miners (2019): "Media Statement: 04 September 2019". At: https://macua.org.za/2019/10/27/national-association-of-artisanal-miners-media-statement-04-september-2019/ (accessed 1 March 2022).

Nhlengetwa, Kgothatso/Hein, Kim (2015): "Zama-Zama mining in the Durban Deep/Roodepoort area of Johannesburg, South Africa. An invasive or alternative livelihood?". In: The Extractive Industries and Society, 2, 1, pp. 1–3.

OECD, Organisation for Economic Co-operation and Development (2016): "OECD Due Diligence Guidance for Responsible Supply Chains of Minerals from Conflict-Affected and High-Risk Areas". At: https://www.oecd.org/daf/inv/mne/OECD-Due-Diligence-Guidance-Minerals-Edition3.pdf (accessed 14 December 2021).

Parliamentary Monitoring Group (2017): "Illegal Mining: Hawks & Department of Mineral Resources briefing". At: https://pmg.org.za/committee-meeting/24894/ (accessed 1 June 2022).

Prause, Louisa (2014): "If you put a catfish next to a caiman. Truning the local into global: resistance against land grabbing in Senegal". At: https://www.rosalux.de/fileadmin/rls_uploads/pdfs/Standpunkte/policy_paper/PolicyPaper_05-2014.pdf (accessed 1 March 2022).

PwC (2021): "SA Mine 2021. Harvest season, call to action". At: https://cer.org.za/wp-content/uploads/2021/09/Draft-Small-Scale-and-Artisanal-Mining-Policy-5-May-2021.pdf (accessed 1 March 2022).

Refinitiv (2020): "GFMS Gold Survey. H2 2019 Update & Outlook". At: https://images.marketing.refinitiv.com/Web/ThomsonReutersFinancialRisk/%7B08b444af-7357-485a-a6fc-4b2047c237f0%7D_GS19_H2_Update_for_Eikon_compressed.pdf?elqTrackId=105e8a3c0fa648ed9ce9def3e17653e6&elqaid=8538&elqat=2 (accessed 10 June 2022).

Responsible Minerals Initiative (n.d.): "Conflict Affected and High-Risk Areas (CAHRAs)". At: https://www.responsiblemineralsinitiative.org/minerals-due-diligence/risk-management/conflict-affected-and-high-risk-areas/ (accessed 1 March 2022).

Roberts, Richard James/Dixon, Roger/Merkle, Roland (2016): "Distinguishing between legally and illegally produced gold in South Africa". In: Journal of Forensic Sciences, 61, pp. 230–236.

Shandro, Janis/Veiga, Marcello/Chouinard, Rebecca (2009): "Reducing mercury pollution from artisanal gold mining in Munhena, Mozambique". In: Journal of Cleaner Production, 17, 5, pp. 525–532.

Statistics South Africa (2020): "Quarterly Labour Force Survey. Quarter 4: 2019". At: https://www.statssa.gov.za/publications/P0211/P02114thQuarter2019.pdf (accessed 7 June 2022).

Statistics South Africa (2020): "Quarterly Labour Force Survey. Quarter 4: 2019". At: https://www.statssa.gov.za/publications/P0211/P02114thQuarter2021.pdf (accessed 7 June 2022).

SWISSAID (2020): "Golden Detour. The hidden face of the gold trade between the United Arab Emirates and Switzerland". At: https://swissaid.kinsta.cloud/wp-content/uploads/2020/07/SWISSAID-Goldstudie-EN_final-web.pdf (accessed 10 February 2022).

The Sentry (2018): "The Golden Laundromat. The conflict gold trade from Eastern Congo to the United States and Europe". At: https://cdn.thesentry.org/wp-content/uploads/2018/10/GoldenLaundromat_Sentry_Oct2018-final.pdf (accessed 15 April 2021).

Thornton, Robert (2014): "Zamazama, 'illegal' artisanal miners, misrepresented by the South African Press and Government". In: The Extractive Industries and Society, 1, 2, pp. 127–129.

UNCTAD, United Nations Conference on Trade and Development (2016): "Trade Misinvoicing in Primary Commodities in Developing Countries. The cases of Chile, Côte d'Ivoir, Nigeria, South Africa and Zambia". At: https://unctad.org/system/files/official-document/suc2016d2_en.pdf (accessed 10 February 2022).

UNICRI, United Nations Interregional Crime and Justice Research Institute (2016): "Strengthening the security and integrity of the precious metals supply chain. Technical report". At: https://www.mineralscouncil.org.za/component/jdownloads/send/25-downloads/342-unicri-repor (accessed 1 March 2023).

Wagner, Livia/Hunter, Marcena (2020): "Links between artisanal and small-scale gold mining and organized crime in Latin America and Africa". In: Zabyelina, Yuliya/van Uhm, Daan (eds.): Illegal mining. Cham: Springer International Publishing, pp. 77–104.

Wan, Pei (2014): "Environmental justices and injustices of large-scale gold mining in Ghana. A study of three communities near Obuasi". In: The Extractive Industries and Society, 1, 1, pp. 38–47.

Wet, Phillip de (2021): "Illegal miners will get licences and help under a new govt plan – if they're South African". At: https://www.businessinsider.co.za/illegal-mining-formalisation-is-part-of-the-artisanal-and-small-scale-mining-draft-government-plan-2021-5 (accessed 1 March 2022).

Williams, Lee (2019): "Gold laudering: The new alchemy". At: https://www.minespider.com/blog/gold-laundering-the-new-alchemy (accessed 10 February 2022).

World Bank (2018): Overcoming poverty and inequality in South Africa. Washington, DC: World Bank.

Young, Steven/Fernandes, Shannon/Wood, Michael (2019): "Jumping the Chain. How Downstream Manufacturers Engage with Deep Suppliers of Conflict Minerals". In: Resources, 8, 1.

The hybrid global gold regime: a perspective from the Peruvian ASGM sector

Gerardo Damonte and Bettina Schorr[1]

1. Introduction: the global gold chain as a hybrid regime

Gold mining in Peru has a long tradition and grew significantly during the latest global commodity boom in the 2000s. About one third of the gold mined in Peru is artisanal and produced on a small scale by individual miners or small companies washing the mineral out of superficial sediments (referred to in the literature as Artisanal Small-Scale Gold Mining, henceforth ASGM). The bulk of ASGM production takes place in the Amazon basin, in the department of Madre de Dios, located in the Peruvian south.

The Peruvian state currently classifies small-scale gold mining in Madre de Dios into three types (Wieland 2020): formal or legal gold mining[2], which refers to mining activities that comply with the legal provisions established by the state; illegal gold mining, which refers to mining activities in places where mining is officially forbidden (in so-called "no-go zones"); and informal gold mining carried out by miners who operate without the required legal permits in places where mining is not forbidden. Many miners who have been working for decades in areas closed off for mining are only recently invoking what they consider their consuetudinary right to mine and see themselves as informal and not illegal miners. In some cases, the Peruvian government has accepted this claim.

This complex scenario, which includes the coexistence of different categories of gold mining in one and the same region, is the result of different policy responses to the sector that have varied over time: small-scale gold mining in Peru was not regulated by the state for most of the time since extraction started in the 19th century, hence it was neither legal nor illegal. Only recently, in 2012, Peruvian governments started to require miners to formalise their activities and to prohibit gold production in several

1 We greatly appreciate the support of Adriana Foronda Barrionuevo and Frauke Berg in the preparation of this chapter.

2 In this chapter we use the terms "formal" and "legal" interchangeably.

environmentally sensitive areas. At the same time, a transition period was established during which those miners operating in zones where mining is legally allowed are supposed to become legal miners. They are asked to "formalise" their businesses by registering their mining activities with public agencies and obtaining the public concession to operate. This transition period has been extended several times amid miners' protests and is currently in place until the end of 2021. So far, only few miners have complied with this formal process; they thus remain informal, neither legal nor illegal.

While this categorisation into formally, illegally and informally mined gold seems straightforward, we argue in this chapter that in practice the formal, illegal and informal activities related to the production and commercialisation of artisanally mined gold in Madre de Dios intermingle. Moreover, the intersection of formal, illegal and informal activities is not limited to the local level of the production site but applies to the entire global chain that connects the gold produced in Madre de Dios with consumers around the globe. Thus, we characterise the global gold chain as a hybrid regime that features formal, illegal and informal actors and actions that aim at converting informally or illegally mined gold into a legal commodity suitable for sale on the formal markets.

Conceptually and theoretically, the chapter draws on the literature on institutional hybridisation which has studied different governance schemes, e.g. in the environmental and natural resource sectors (Lemos and Agrawal 2006; Sindzingre 2006; Olivier de Sardan 2015). Hybridisation is defined as a process where state and non-state actors as well as formal, illegal and informal institutions converge, generating mixed forms of resource governance that are neither completely legal nor informal or illegal but combine all of these attributes (Sindzingre 2006; Damonte 2018, 2021). Institutional hybridity results from actor constellations where no actor commands enough power or political will to completely impose their own institutional vision.

Processes of institutional hybridisation tend to take place in weak states where territories exist that are not completely subject to state control or where the state is only marginally represented (Damonte 2018, 2021). Hybridisation may also occur when non-state groups are strong enough to contest the imposition of state regulation (Dargent et al. 2017). Often, the lack of citizens' trust in state actors promotes and reinforces hybrid modes of governance.

Historically, cycles of territorial expansion related to the exploitation of natural resources have provided the context for the emergence of hybrid modes of governance. During these periods, states tend to make inroads into new territories where natural resources are located, often at the margin of their control, and often against the resistance of established populations or powerful groups that settled there previously. With the state lacking the power to dominate these local groups, institutional hybridisation follows: the establishment of a sector that includes (at least partly) the new formal rules promoted by the state, the institutionalisation of informal or illegalised local practices as well as the local appropriation and reinterpretation of new formal rules promoted by the state or also by corporations.

Due to the complex entanglements among formal, illegal and informal activities, hybrid regimes are difficult to control. In addition, once these regimes are established, states tend to face even more difficulties in expanding the rule of formal law. In fact, with no actor strong enough to impose its will, hybrid sectors tend to be resistant to change. This does not mean that hybrid constellations are static. They rather have a fluid nature depending on the evolution of the balance of power and actors' capacities for adaptation to technological, political and social change. As a consequence, hybrid regimes are characterised by constant negotiations between state and corporate actors, with local powers aiming to legitimate their presence and often previously established economic activities, such as the extraction of natural resources.

The concept of hybridisation also provides a useful lens through which to understand the entire global gold chain and the problems regarding its regulation. Adopting this perspective, we conceptualise the global gold chain as a hybrid regime in which rules intended to govern and regulate a given area coexist with informal or illegal practices that cause the opposite outcomes to the ones envisioned by the formal rules.[3] Thus, the informal or illegal practices bend or circumvent the formal rules. The hybrid character not only implies that illegal actors participate in the chain. It is also hybrid in the sense that legal actors engage in informal or illegal activities or informal and illegal actors use legal means to reach their aims. In addition, the hybrid global regime is dynamic in nature: different actors can not only enter or exit but also move between the formal, illegal and informal subsectors: informal transactions can be legalised or be outlawed in the context of state formalisation plans (as in the case of small-scale gold mining in Madre de Dios) or new international regulations, while

3 We borrow the term "regime" from international relations theory, where it is defined as a set of "implicit or explicit principles, norms, rules, and decision-making procedures around which actors' expectations converge in a given area of international relations" (Krasner 1983).

new informal or illegal practices for producing or trading gold may be developed, depending on the domestic and international regulatory powers and market opportunities.

The hybrid character of the global gold chain is consequential for the opportunities of national and international control and enforcement bodies to monitor and police it. The close coexistence of formal, illegal and informal activities which combine to form a complex and sometimes confusing fabric requires actors in charge of policing to observe not only outright illegal groups but also the actions of legal actors able to occasionally or permanently expand their legal businesses by illegal means. These latter are much more difficult to detect, trace and verify, and formal actors may shift much more dynamically and flexibly between legal and illegal techniques than illegal actors. Thus, the concept of hybrid regimes helps to understand the difficulties regulators face in controlling and governing the global gold chain from the local producing areas through the different national and international intermediaries to the global consumer markets.

The consequences of these difficulties for regulation and control are significant, particularly in the producing areas in Peru and elsewhere. As a result of the growing global demand and the underregulated production and trade, people in the Peruvian Amazon, especially indigenous groups, have experienced ever-growing levels of environmental damage, health risks, violence and crime. The situation in the gold-producing areas can thus be characterised as a case of global interdependent inequalities in the sense that extra-local actors from different parts of the globe cause or reinforce social inequalities in specific localities (Jelin et al. 2018).

How to understand the global gold chain as a hybrid regime? In this chapter, we trace the hybrid character of the global gold chain starting in the Peruvian ASGM region in Madre de Dios and following the different stages and levels of the chain through which Peruvian artisanally mined gold travels until reaching the end consumers around the globe. We aim at identifying the causes that account for hybridity in the producing region in Madre de Dios and the ways formal, illegal and informal actions and actors intersect all along the chain to build a hybrid regime.

The chapter draws on a literature review which considered different sources: academic papers and books, grey literature as well as newspapers and journal reports. It also includes personal notes from the authors' fieldwork, collected using qualitative ethnographic methods such as non-participant observation of mining camps and activities. Fieldwork visits were conducted from 2012 to 2018. Informal interviews and structured interviews as well as field observation were undertaken during these visits.

This chapter is divided into four sections. The second section describes the evolution of gold mining in Peru in general and the ASGM sector in Madre de Dios in particular. It discusses the factors that have led to the hybrid constitution of that sector and describes a set of important recent developments. The third section analyses the global gold chain in which the gold from Madre de Dios participates. It emphasises the hybrid character of the chain by identifying how formal, illegal and informal activities intersect all along the chain. The fourth section summarises the main argument of the chapter about the global gold chain as a hybrid regime and explores the social and environmental consequences of the growing ASGM sector in Peru. It closes with a brief discussion of the international responses that aim at a more effective regulation of the global gold trade, which would be as important as the efforts in the production areas to reduce the negative consequences ASGM entails particularly for the local population.

2. *Small-scale gold mining in Peru*

The history of gold mining in the Central Andes dates back to as early as 1200 BCE, and minerals have dominated the economies of both the former Spanish colonies and the later independent republics of Bolivia, Ecuador and Peru. Since becoming a republic, Peru has experienced several gold rushes. The first one occurred between 1930 and 1960 and caused the first wave of migration into the Amazon rainforest, where enormous reserves of alluvial gold have accumulated in the riverbeds. The most recent one started in the mid-1990s under completely different conditions, in particular under the imperative of the global markets and with new technology available (Bebbington and Bury 2013). Driven mostly by Asian (Chinese) demand, prices for minerals increased significantly in the 2000s, with the gold price rising by 308 per cent to reach US$1,669 an ounce from 2004 to 2012 (Poveda 2015). Even after the price peaked and dropped, it remained high by historical standards. In Peru, the rising global gold price led to a period of massive growth in gold mining. While previously insignificant, currently the country ranges among the ten largest global producers (number six as of 2019 after China, Russia, Australia, the US and Canada) (World Gold Council n.d.). The volume of exports increased from 4294.4 thousand tr. oz. in 2001 to 6563 thousand tr. oz. in 2017.[4]

The gold sector in Peru is divided into large-scale and small-scale production. Large-scale mining is characterised by the presence of large companies operating with a considerable workforce, using heavy machinery and often sophisticated technology. It occurs in specific, officially circumscribed areas licensed by the state and involves the payment of taxes and royalties by companies. The latter makes large-scale mining attractive for governments, and indeed, since the 1990s, large-scale mining has been actively promoted in Peru (Bebbington et al. 2008; Humphreys Bebbington and Bebbington 2010; Salas 2008). Nowadays, the Peruvian Andes host some of the biggest gold mines in the world, in particular in the department of Cajamarca, where the Yanacocha mine operates. Before the formal large-scale gold sector was established, most gold production in Peru was small-scale and took place mainly in three departments: Madre de Dios, La Libertad and Puno (Echave 2016). Small-scale mining is carried out by individuals or small mining cooperatives instead of large companies. This sector is characterised by the use of rather rudimentary technology, if any. Since small-scale mining tends to be informal, the contribution to the public sector in terms of taxes is generally low.

The Peruvian ASGM sector also witnessed an enormous growth in terms of production and territory between 2003 and 2010. Given its partly informal and partly illegal character, the sector is difficult to quantify. However, official export statistics back the upward trend in a rather simple measure: until 2002, the volume of production and the volume of export of gold matched. Since 2003, Peru has been exporting more gold than it officially produces. This gap is explained by part of the production stemming from informal and illegal small-scale gold mining that takes place outside of public control. According to estimates, between 2003 and 2014, 19 out of 100 tons of gold were produced by the illegal and informal subsectors, and between 2010 and 2013, at the peak of the boom, they accounted for one quarter of the production (Torres Cuzcano 2015: 32). In terms of value, the illegal and informal subsectors are assumed to have produced gold worth US$15.777 billion between 2003 and 2014 (Torres Cuzcano 2015: 34), in some years exceeding the value of cocaine exports, the most important illegal commodity in the region (Global Initiative against Transnational Organized Crime 2016).

4 Data from: Banco Central de Reserva del Perú: https://estadisticas.bcrp.gob.pe/estadisticas/series/.

In territorial terms, 21 of 25 Peruvian departments currently register small-scale gold mining. A small part of the production takes place in the surroundings of large-scale projects in the Andean highlands. The bulk of small-scale gold production is located in the Amazon region. Within it, the Madre de Dios river basin is the centre for small-scale gold mining, providing ca. 70 % of Peruvian artisanal mining (Valdés, Basombrío and Vera 2019).

Figure 1: Annual gold production in Madre de Dios (in tons)

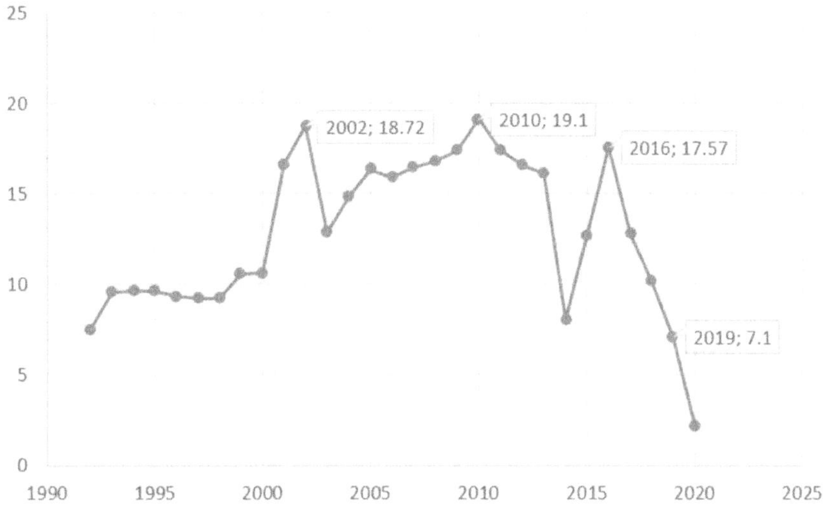

Source: own elaboration with data from the Peruvian Ministry of Energy and Mines (MINEM)

Attracted by the rising gold price, thousands of people have migrated from the country's poor highlands to the Amazon lowlands since the early 2000s to build livelihoods based on the production of gold. The number of miners in Madre de Dios increased from 9,500 to 15,000 between 2001 and 2009 (Pachas 2011a). According to MINEM, the Peruvian Ministry for Energy and Mining, gold production in Madre de Dios steadily grew from 7.5 tons in 1992 until reaching 10.3 tons in late 2019 (see Figure 1). Currently, in Madre de Dios small-scale mining is the most important economic activity, and miners are the most important economic and political group in the region (Mosquera 2009; Pachas 2011b).

Small-scale mining in Peru has historically been informal, which means that the state had not adopted any regulation concerning the activity, neither in an affirmative nor in a prohibitive way. A myriad of small producers operates the sector, and to different degrees also native communities, farmers and loggers are involved in the production of gold.[5] In fact, small-scale mining in Madre de Dios is no longer a mere subsistence activity. Many miners have achieved significant profits and enhanced their business by employing workers and mechanising their operations (Cortés-McPherson 2019).

The different Peruvian governments treated the sector in an ambivalent way subject to changes over time. After first fluctuating between promoting and ignoring the sector, which both ultimately caused it to grow, more recently the state has aimed at formalising it (i.e. putting it under the rule of law) and reducing it.

State presence has always been scarce in the Amazon region. While it was almost non-existent to the Peruvian state before, starting in the 19th century Madre de Dios was perceived as a frontier region – a quasi-mythical resource-rich territory to be conquered.[6] Against this background, the Amazonian rubber boom took place from 1879 to 1912, driving rubber companies, loggers and immigrants into the rainforest. The Peruvian government actively promoted the sector and tacitly backed numerous atrocities committed by the rubber companies that captured and enslaved local indigenous communities for labour and to gain access to their territories (Taussig 1986). When the rubber boom ended because Asian countries (such as former Ceylon and India) provided cheaper rubber to the world market, the Amazon region effectively 'disappeared' from the state's radar for decades. It was during the 1960s and 1970s that the Peruvian government again decided to promote small-scale mineral extraction in the entire country. This time, state sponsorship ended in the 1990s when structural reforms reduced state intervention in economic affairs to a minimum (Pachas 2011b; Valencia 2014).

In the following years, global demand put small-scale mining on a further growth path that caused severe social and ecological damage. Responding to both domestic business pressures to open up the Amazon region for large-scale operations and international pressures to preserve the important and sensitive Amazonian ecosystem, in the early 2000s the state

5 In total, there are 29 native communities in the region, with the Harakmbut being the main ethnic group living in the mining zones of Madre de Dios. While most communities practice agriculture, hunting and gathering, for many native people artisanal mining is a typical part of their livelihood (Gray 1986; CONAP 2007).

6 Regarding the concept of "frontier", see Peluso and Lund 2011 and De Jong et al. 2017.

turned its attention to small-scale gold production again, this time with a strategy to regulate (formalise) and, ultimately, reduce it. Starting in 2001, a series of laws were enacted that officially recognised small-scale gold mining (Law No. 27651), adopted a plan for Economic and Ecological Zoning (EEZ) in Madre de Dios (Huamán 2005) that allocated only 10.14 per cent of the territory to small-scale mining activities (Fernández 2010) and, in 2010, further reduced the territory available for small-scale mining to the so-called "mining corridor".

These new regulations proved largely ineffective. Spurred by the construction of the Interoceanic Highway connecting Peru and Brazil, illegal mining continued to expand into the buffer zones of natural reserves such as La Pampa in Madre de Dios. In response, the Peruvian state switched to a strategy of "mano dura" (firm hand), a concept well known from the anti-drug campaigns in the region. Under pressure from the international community (Cortés-McPherson 2019), a new formalisation plan was launched in 2012 (Legislative Decree No. 1102) which declared all mining activities not authorised by the state as illegal. The strategy to legalise small-scale gold mining was two-pronged, aiming on the one hand at formalising informal mining in the legal mining corridor and on the other hand at eradicating illegal mining outside this area. In addition to defining a process for formalisation (Wieland 2020), a system was put into place to trace gold production from extraction through processing to trade. It required all actors involved in the production (i.e. contractors, informal miners, suppliers of machinery and feedstock) and trade (i.e. buyers, traders, exporters) of gold to register and periodically report their operations to the Ministry of Energy and Mines. Buyers and traders were also required by law to verify the legal origin of the gold they buy lest they face criminal charges (León Pacheco 2020).

It was thus only in 2012 that small-scale gold mining in Madre de Dios became differentiated into formal, illegal and informal gold mining. Four years later, illegal mining was criminalised and classified as a type of organised crime subject to up to 15 years of prison (Legislative Decree No. 1244). As a consequence, the second component of the current strategy involves the military and includes the systematic use of force. As in the past in the context of anti-drug campaigns, the government declared a "war against illegal mining" (Pachas 2011a; Valencia 2014; Cortés-McPherson 2019). The General Directorate of Captaincies and Coastguards (DICAPI) was established as a branch of the Peruvian Navy and put in charge of decommissioning and dismantling unauthorised machinery in zones where mining is prohibited. In 2019, a series of spectacular military raids (*Operación Mercurio*) destroyed illegal mining camps and evicted miners, destroying millions of dollars in wildcat mining equipment (Saffon 2020a). By the end of 2020, almost two years after the beginning of *Operación Mercurio*, more than 25,000 miners and people linked to illegal mining were expelled from the Amazon region (Fiestas 2021).

Strengthening law enforcement included not only military operations in the production areas but also enhanced interdiction efforts regarding smuggling or illegal financial transactions, which broke up several illegal companies and networks of smugglers (Cortés-McPherson 2019). Notwithstanding these accomplishments, the illegal business reacted in a manner well known from other illegal commodities, particularly from the coca/cocaine sector, the number one illegal sector of the region (Colombia, Bolivia and Peru are the main producers of the coca leaf, the raw material for cocaine, see Zevallos 2017): a "balloon effect" occurred (Schorr 2013). Many illegal economies can be thought of as a big latex balloon. If control efforts "squeeze" it at one point, the air inside does not disappear but moves into another area of less resistance. With the Peruvian state ramping up law enforcement, small-scale gold mining has migrated further into the Amazon rainforest to areas not easily accessible to law enforcers. Gold mining operations have spread almost unchecked into previously unaffected areas, such as along the Napo and Nanay rivers in the department of Loreto (Saffon 2020b; see also Fiestas 2021). Moreover, a part of the illegal gold production has shifted to other countries in the region. In neighbouring Bolivia and Colombia, illegal gold mining has been on the rise in recent years, at least in the case of the former with far weaker political restrictions for the sector (Amengual and Dargent 2020). In fact, after the US company NTR was convicted of illegally buying Peruvian gold, its imports from Ecuador and Bolivia rose by US$485 million (Goi 2017).[7]

While the militarisation of Madre de Dios managed to reduce small-scale gold mining in the region, the COVID-19 pandemic caused it to increase again through a combination of global and domestic factors. First, with the COVID-19 pandemic the gold price soared on the international

7 Regionalisation can also be observed with regard to mercury smuggling. Several studies claim that since Peru no longer mines mercury as a result of the country's adherence to the Minamata Convention, the Peruvian ASGM sector has been supplied with mercury imported illegally from Bolivia (Campanini 2020; Montoya 2018). Bolivia is the second largest importer of mercury globally and buys mercury from Mexico and Russia, among others, to smuggle it to Peru. There is also evidence that some of the mercury crosses Peru to be sold in Ecuador (Montoya 2018).

markets. In May 2020, the price was US$1.764,55 per ounce – reaching the price level of 2012 during the peak of the last boom (Dupraz-Dobias 2020). Second, the pandemic interrupted the global gold chain, and formal large-scale gold mining had to adhere – temporarily – to the lockdown measures declared by the Peruvian government. As a consequence, the large-scale production of gold dropped, and legal mining exports from Peru decreased by 65 per cent in April 2020. Small-scale gold miners filled the gap (Saffon 2020a).

Another factor that contributed to the renewed growth of small-scale gold mining in the region was the interruption of the military campaign. While a minor military presence was maintained, the bulk of the troops were recalled in order to be employed in measures to contain the COVID-19 pandemic (Sierra Praeli 2020). Finally, as a result of miners' mobilisations and lobbyism, the state was forced to adapt the formalisation campaign in 2019 (Law No. 31007) by extending the period to register for formalisation until December 2021. All of these factors combined to offset the results obtained by the military campaign of the past years and put the sector back on a growth path. As a consequence, in 2020, Peruvian gold exports registered a surplus of 1500 tons in excess of the reported official production (Montaño Pastrana 2020).

3. *Madre de Dios in the hybrid global gold chain*

The gold mined in Peru travels through a global chain until reaching the customers across the globe. This global chain comprises different stages, sectors, countries and actors (Verbrugge and Geenen 2020). Five stages can be distinguished: mining, processing, refining, trade and consumption. Mining, processing and in some cases also small-scale refining take place in the localities and the countries where gold is being extracted. More often, large-scale refineries located in Switzerland, the US or China refine crude gold from all over the globe. According to the World Gold Council, 90 % of global trading takes place in three trading hubs: the London Bullion market, the US COMEX market and the Shanghai Gold Exchange (SGE) (World Gold Council n.d.). These are complemented by smaller market centres around the world, which include Dubai, India, Japan, Singapore and Hong Kong. The world's biggest gold importers (as of 2019), with over 10 % of market share, are the United Kingdom (US$70.8 billion, 23.1 % of total gold imports), Switzerland ($60.7 billion, 19.8 %), China ($43.9 billion, 14.3 %) and India ($32.2 billion, 10.5 %). Also, the share of the UEA is rapidly growing (Workman n.d.).

The miners in Madre de Dios sell their gold to different buyers. Generally, one part of the production is sold to specialised collectors or provisioners of input (such as machinery, fuel or chemicals) who run their businesses in the production area. Another part goes to bigger collectors who operate offices in the cities of Cuzco or Juliaca, or in the Peruvian capital Lima (Valdés, Basombrío and Vera 2019). These trading companies arrange the export to the global markets. Peruvian gold is mainly taken to refineries in the US, Switzerland and Italy. India is the largest purchaser of Peruvian gold with a 30 % share (SIICEX 2019).

The global gold chain from production to consumption can be conceptualised as a "hybrid regime" in which formal, illegal and informal activities intersect, turning it into what has been called in the literature a "grey market" (Hartnett and Dawdy 2013). Formally, illegally and informally mined gold is treated by formal, illegal and informal actors in order to reach the formal markets in Europe, the US and Asia.

The hybridisation can be observed at the very beginning of the gold chain. The inputs needed to extract gold in Madre de Dios, mostly machinery and chemicals, are supplied by legal companies, whereas fuel, required to operate machinery, is sometimes acquired through illegal channels (i.e. contraband; Damonte 2018). Illegally produced gold is laundered and smuggled into the global market through a myriad of intermediaries (Cortés-McPherson 2020). It is commercialised through formal and illegal channels (by contraband) by formal companies and illegal actors and ends up in formal refineries abroad. From there, Peruvian gold produced informally or illegally is sold as a completely legal commodity to the end customer around the world.

The laundering of informal or illegal gold takes place in different ways and involves different levels. During these processes, generally a lower price than the official market price is paid. At the production site, legal companies and processing plants buy informal or illegal gold and certify that it is of legal origin. At times, ghost companies operate to buy and formalise illegally produced gold. Sometimes the legal processing plants and the trading houses issue fictitious sales receipts to bring informal or illegal gold into the formal market (Wiener 2019; Valdés, Basombrío and Vera 2019). Also, other concession holders buy informal or illegal gold to raise their purported production level to the limit legally allowed. A third option for converting informal or illegal gold into legal gold involves regional networks. Increasingly, informally or illegally mined Peruvian gold is transported to neighbouring countries, particularly to Bolivia, where it is laundered and exported (Valdés, Basombrío and Vera 2019; Cawley 2014).

*Figure 2: Hybrid (formal-illegal-informal) global gold chain**

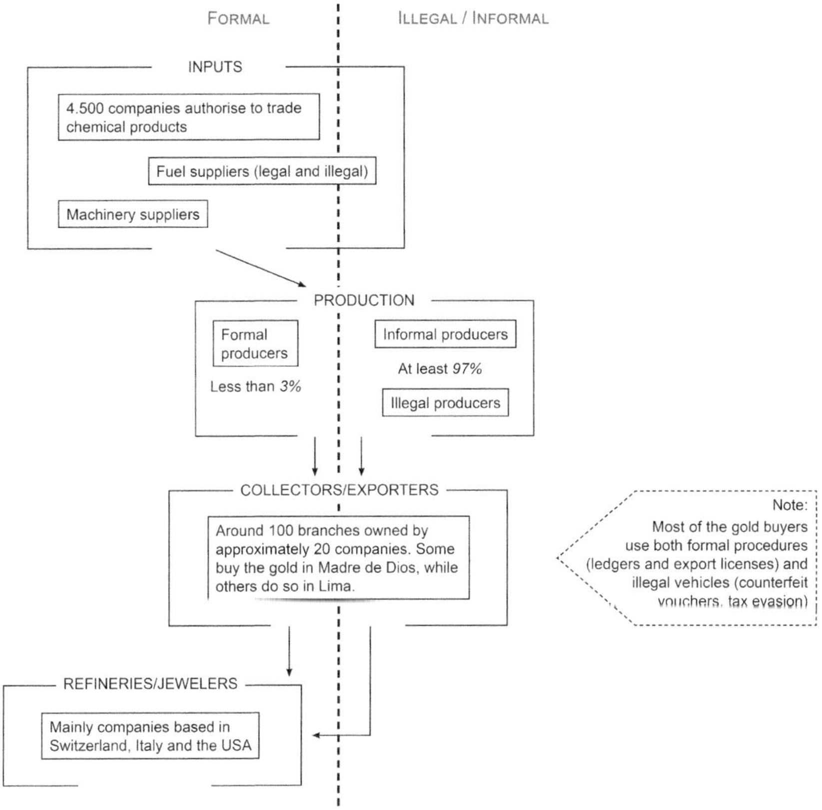

Source: own elaboration; adapted from Damonte (2018)

* In this figure we have integrated the informal and illegal subsectors. This was done in order to visualise the fact that there is no clear cut between illegal and informal production and to highlight the hybrid as well as fluid character of the global gold chain.

On the next level in the chain, informally and illegally mined gold can be exported in different ways. One way is through formal companies. There are legal companies based in Lima that purchase gold from different collectors and export it to the global markets. As mentioned, a lot of gold laundering also takes place in Bolivia. According to official Bolivian reports, gold exports have tripled since 2005, reaching US$331 million in 2013, without a corresponding increase in local production (Valdés, Basombrío and Vera 2019). Illegal gold is also smuggled by individuals on commercial flights departing from the airport in Lima (Cortés-McPherson 2020). Often, gold is stored by shell companies at the airport, waiting to be taken abroad by "mules". In fact, the trade in artisanal gold is facilitated by the material properties of gold as a small product that can be smuggled across borders with relative ease (Cortés-McPherson 2020). The tax authority of Peru estimates that 35 tons of illegal contraband gold worth over US$1 billion were shipped via Lima to the US and Switzerland between February and October of 2014 (Global Initiative against Transnational Organized Crime 2016).

Another way of converting informal or illegal gold into a formal commodity, which connects the second and third stages in the commercialisation chain, involves the large-scale international refineries in the US and Europe. In recent years, various investigations carried out by the Peruvian public prosecutor's office on money laundering have implicated international refineries in the London Bullion Market Association. For instance, an illegal Peruvian gold trader has been found guilty of exporting more than 13 tons of illegally mined gold worth more than $637 million to several companies in the US between April 2012 and May 2014. In particular, the cases of the North Texas Refinery (NTR) and of Kaloti Metals & Logistics are extensively documented (Society for Threatened Peoples 2016; Bargent 2015). According to a US Homeland Security investigation, between 2012 and 2015, NTR bought US$3.6 billion worth of gold in Latin America. The US-based refinery started to buy Peruvian gold in 2012 and had imported US$980 million worth of Peruvian ASGM gold a year later. In December 2013, Peruvian authorities seized 508 kg of gold destined for six foreign refineries, one of which was NTR. In 2017, the NTR refinery pleaded guilty to having purchased illegal gold from Peruvian sources; three of its executives were sentenced to prison.

Also, European refineries have been found to acquire illegal or informal gold from Peru. The most important cases involved the Swiss company Metalor (a subsidiary of a Japanese group), one of the most important refineries in the world (Cruz 2019), and the Geneva-based group MKS – Produits Artistiques Métaux Précieux (PAMP). In both cases, the public prosecutor's office in Peru initiated investigations after the confiscation of a gold shipment of unknown origin addressed to the Swiss companies (Castilla 2018). Another European case implicated the Italian company Italpreziosi in a case of money laundering with illegal gold (Society for Threatened Peoples 2016).

To sum up, this overview of the global gold chain in which the gold produced in Madre de Dios participates shows that informality and illegality are not only present at the extraction site but also in the commercialisation activities from local collectors to transnational companies in the US and Europe. In addition, this overview demonstrates how the intersections of formal, illegal and informal activities imprint a hybrid character on the entire global gold chain.

4. *Concluding remarks: the hybrid global gold regime and its consequences*

In parallel to the growth of global demand, the extraction and export of gold has increased significantly in Peru since the early 2000s. Within a couple of years, Peru has become a major player in the global gold chain which connects the states extracting gold from their subsoils with the end consumers on the world markets. One third of the gold mined in Peru is artisanally produced, and most of its production takes place in the Amazon region of Madre de Dios. Gold mined in this region corresponds to three different categories: a small part is formal, which means that miners have fulfilled the legal conditions as stipulated by the Peruvian government. Some gold is illegal because it is extracted from regions where mining is prohibited, and most is still informal because the majority of miners have not formalised their businesses and operate without restrictions due to the transition period established by the Peruvian government. The coexistence of these different types in one and the same region results from different policy approaches towards the sector that have varied over time.

This chapter argues that the global gold chain constitutes a hybrid regime since it encompasses formal, illegal and informal actors and activities. These not only coexist separately but intersect in the different stages and levels of the global chain, from production to commercialisation. As presented in Section 3, until gold reaches the consumers around the globe, a series of formal, illegal and informal actors perform formal, illegal and informal actions: for instance, informal or illegal gold is sold to formal companies or illegal collectors in Madre de Dios or legal international companies buy gold from illegal traders or informal or illegal producers.

The global gold chain is only one example of a hybrid regime among others. In the Andean region, the coca/cocaine chain constitutes another case of a hybrid regime. The coca plant is a traditional plant used for different medicinal and recreational purposes, which can be legally produced in parts of Peru and Bolivia. However, as raw material for the production of the illegal drug cocaine, a part of the legal production is diverted into the illegal business, and legal activities are mixed with illegal and informal ones all along the production and commercialisation stages of the global cocaine chain.

As stated in the introduction, an important characteristic of hybrid regimes is that they are difficult to govern and control. In Peru, the lack of regulation and control of the sector has motivated a steady growth that came at a high price, particularly for the people living in the gold-producing areas. Indeed, small-scale miners in Madre de Dios and customer around the globe are not only connected by the gold ingots travelling from the Amazon riverbeds to the world markets, changing form and value in the process. There is a flip side to the global gold chain: while gold leaves the region, a series of important problems for the local people and the environment are "imported". These include growing deforestation of the Amazon rainforest (Amazon Conservation Association 2014; Caballero et al. 2018; Valdés, Basombrío and Vera 2019; Asner and Tupayachi 2016), contamination of the soil and water resources by mining activities, particularly by the widespread use of mercury in the production process (UN Environment 2019), and a critical loss of biodiversity in a region with one of the highest levels of biodiversity on earth (Markham and Sangermano 2018).

In addition to the environmental problems, the extraordinary growth of small-scale gold mining in Madre de Dios has also produced important social problems, including an increase in criminal violence, human trafficking (Novak and Namihas 2009) and forced prostitution (Arriarán and Chávez 2017; Cortés-McPherson 2019; Salazar and Castro 2018; Valdés, Basombrío and Vera 2019; Steele 2013; Cortés-McPherson 2019). Human rights violations occur frequently in the gold camps, for instance the permanent exposure of workers to toxic substances known to cause serious illness (such as mercury), extended and exhausting working days and physical violence as well as child labour. Also, the region saw a dramatic increase of violence against environmental leaders, and there is a constant tension between miners and environmental groups that advocate for the eradication of illegal mining in prohibited areas and the constitution of new zones closed to mining (Actualidad Ambiental 2020). In 2020 alone, during the pandemic, five murders of environmental and indigenous leaders were registered, and several leaders reported death threats.

Regulating the sector and effectively curbing the problems arising from extended ASGM would be very important not only for the local people but also for the planet, given the important role of the Amazon rainforest for the regulation of the global ecosystem. However, as discussed above, it is the hybrid character of the chain that hinders the attempts at regulation and limitation on the local, national and global levels. The presence of formal channels provides a confusing abundance of opportunities to evade regulation by means of whitewashing and money laundering. In this process, illegal or informal gold associated with environmental destruction and human suffering is transformed into a formal commodity difficult to trace back to its origin.

The focus on the hybrid character of the global gold chain has some implications in terms of policy recommendations. First, this perspective allows for a better understanding of the complex situation in the gold-producing areas. In particular, it provides an explanation for the coexistence of the different types of gold by stressing the role of politics and of power relations and puts the states' opportunities for regulating the sector into perspective. The formalisation of ASGM would be a very important step in order to curb the uncontrolled growth of the sector. Small-scale gold mining is an important economic activity for many people in Peru and elsewhere, particularly due to the lack of other economic opportunities in these countries. In order to ensure a long-term effect, formalisation should be carried out considering local practices and needs and in cooperation with the (powerful) local miners. Besides enabling a more sustainable gold production, governments and international donors should provide stable economic alternatives to gold extraction instead of relying exclusively on military strategies and criminalisation. Also, the establishment of more market-based incentives, like the certification of eco-gold, could be of help. So far, these market incentives are rare in Peru and of limited effect.

On the other hand, the perspective on the hybridity of the global gold regime stresses the need to focus much more on the actions of legal actors and their illegal activities at all levels and stages of the global chain. In Peru, this applies to both formal miners and trading companies. Further up the chain, international trading companies and large-scale smelters should be subjected to closer scrutiny. While formalisation and law enforcement within Peru will take time to develop their teeth because of the structural restrictions on state capacity and the diversity and dynamism of local actors and transaction lines, more efforts in regulating the international intermediaries and markets would be an efficient step to reduce the negative impact of gold production on the ground.

How to govern a hybrid regime? The problems related to illegal and informal mining have motivated bilateral and multilateral activism. Several international conventions and national laws have been enacted in order to render global supply chains more transparent and less damaging (amongst them the US Dodd-Frank Act, the Palermo Convention, the Minamata Convention etc.). With regard to mining, a series of transnational networks have formed that promote transparency in supply chains, with some focusing on private corporations and others concentrating on political actors (Bebbington et al. 2016). They are led by international organisations (as in the case of the Global Reporting Initiative (founded in 1997), the Mining and Metals Sector Supplement (2003) and the UN's Global Compact (founded in 2000)), non-governmental organisations (for instance in case of the Publish What You Pay campaign and the Global Alliance for Tax Justice) and industry groups (in the case of the International Council on Mining and Metals (ICMM, founded in 2001)). The Extractive Industries Transparency Initiative (EITI) was launched in 2007 to bring together corporate, civil and governmental actors. Since these initiatives only involve voluntary mechanisms and lack effective tools for monitoring and sanctioning, their impact has been limited so far.

The European Union has also taken on the subject of "conflict minerals" in general and, more recently, human rights violations in the context of mining. It promotes a "raw materials diplomacy" which entails dialogues with several countries, among them Peru, Ecuador and Colombia. In addition, the EU Conflict Minerals Regulation was issued in 2017 and entered into force in 2021. This regulation targets risks such as child labour, forced labour, forced prostitution and the financing of armed groups in the context of extraction and trade of four minerals (tantalum, tungsten, tin and gold).

While without doubt an important step, the EU Regulation has been criticised for several flaws: first, the EU Regulation defines risk on the basis of a reduced canon of phenomena viewed as converting minerals into actual "conflict minerals". Many of the risks and negative impacts occurring widely at mineral extraction sites are not addressed. These include several of the mining-induced consequences observed in the Peruvian Amazon, such as environmental consequences, violent displacements, social conflicts, corruption and the presence of illegal groups. Given their highly adverse effects, these phenomena should be factored into the definition of "conflict minerals".

Related is, secondly, the fact that several countries suffering from the negative side effects of gold production do not fall under the EU Conflict Minerals Regulation. The Regulation is backed by a list of conflict-affected and high-risk areas (the CAHRA list) produced by an external contractor, which is supposed to guide companies with regard to high risks of illegal trade and/or possible conflicts over the exploitation of minerals.[8] Neither

8 See https://www.cahraslist.net/cahras; the contractor in charge is the UK-based RAND Corporation Europe.

Peru nor other countries in South America increasingly affected by illegal ASGM such as Bolivia, Ecuador or Brazil figure on the list. Exceptions are Colombia, where mineral extraction is in some places connected to armed conflict, and Venezuela, mostly for the same phenomena that also occur in Peru and neighbouring countries. The country selection appears inconsistent and should be extended accordingly.

Lastly, many critics claim that the establishment of due diligence for the process is still lacking, which hinders the proper implementation of the Regulation (Betancur 2019). Regarding the governance of the sector in general, experts still complain that the mineral-importing countries are not doing enough to oblige stakeholders and their subcontractors to comply with both international and domestic standards regarding human and labour rights and environmental protection. Also, law enforcement against companies that import and sell illegally mined gold is still weak.

As we have argued in this chapter, the gold chain is a hybrid global regime. All countries involved in the different stages of production, commercialisation and consumption must enforce rules to reduce in particular the destructive local side effects of the sector. Law enforcement should address not only illegal actions or actors but also legal ones and take into consideration the complexities of informality in the production areas, in Peru and other ASGM sectors elsewhere on the globe.

References

Actualidad Ambiental (2020): "Relator de la ONU recoge demandas de defensores de derechos humanos en Madre de Dios". At: https://www.actualidadambiental.pe/relator-de-ddhh-de-la-onu-recoge-demandas-de-comunidades-nativas-en-madre-de-dios/ (accessed 27 April 2022).

Amazon Conservation Association (2014): "Fact Sheet: Illegal Gold Mining in Madre De Dios, Peru". At: www.amazonconservation.org/pdf/gold (accessed 25 February 2015).

Amengual, Matthew/Dargent, Eduardo (2020): "The social determinants of enforcement". In: Brinks, Daniel M./Levitsky, Steven/Murillo, Maria V. (eds.): The politics of institutional weakness in Latin America. Cambridge: Cambridge University Press, pp. 161–182.

Arriarán, Gabriel/Chávez, Susana (2017): "Espacios de frontera y excepción. Encuentros entre los servicios y necesidades de salud de las mujeres en La Pampa". PROMSEX. At: http://promsex.org/publicaciones/espacios-de-frontera-y-excepcion/ (accessed 28 January 2022).

Asner, Gregory/Tupayachi, Raul (2016): "Accelerated losses of protected forests from gold mining in the Peruvian Amazon". In: Environmental Research Letters, 12, 9, pp. 94004.

Bargent, James (2015): "A seizure, a lawsuit and illegal gold from Peru". At: https://insightcrime.org/news/analysis/seizure-a-lawsuit-and-illegal-gold-from-peru/ (accessed 28 January 2022).

Bebbington, Anthony/Elisa, Arond/Dammert, Juan Luis (2016): Scalar politics and transnational governance innovations. A political settlements lens on the Extractive Industries Transparency Initiative in the Andes. Manchester: Effective States and Inclusive Development Research Centre (ESID), The University of Manchester.

Bebbington, Anthony/Bury, Jeffrey (2013): Subterranean struggles. New dynamics of mining, oil, and gas in Latin America. Austin: University of Texas Press.

Bebbington, Anthony/Humphreys Bebbington, Denise/Bury, Jeffrey/Lingan, Jeannet/Muñoz, Juan/Scurrah, Martin (2008): "Mining and social movements. Struggles over livelihood and rural territorial development in the Andes". In: World Development, 36, 12, pp. 2888–2905.

Betancur, María Soledad (2019): "Producción minera, territorio y conflicto en Colombia. Retos globales y locales para la protección de los derechos humanos y el medio ambiente". At: https://www.germanwatch.org/sites/germanwatch.org/files/Studie%20MINER%C3%8DA%20DEL%20ORO%2C%20TERRITORIO%20Y%20CONFLICTO%C2%A0EN%20COLOMBIA%2C%202019.pdf (accessed 28 January 2022).

Caballero Espejo, Jorge/Messinger, Max/Román-Dañobeytia, Francisco/Ascorra, Cesar/Fernandez, Luis/Silman, Miles (2018): "Deforestation and forest degradation due to gold mining in the Peruvian Amazon: a 34-year perspective". In: Remote Sensing, 10, 12, pp. 1903.

Campanini, Oscar (2020): „El negocio del mercurio en Bolivia. Estudio sobre la comercialización para la minería aurifera en Bolivia". At: https://www.iucn.nl/app/uploads/2021/03/regional_mercury_report_bolivia.pdf (accessed 28 January 2022).

Castilla, Óscar (2018): "Perú: investigan lavandería de oro de la minería ilegal". At: https://ojo-publico.com/764/peru-investigan-lavanderia-de-oro-de-la-mineria-ilegal (accessed 28 January 2022).

Cawley, Marguerite (2014): "Peru's illegal miners trafficking gold to Bolivia". At: https://insightcrime.org/news/brief/peru-illegal-miners-trafficking-gold-to-bolivia/ (accessed 28 January 2022).

CONAP, Confederación de Nacionalidades Amazónicas del Perú (2007): Explotación minera a pequeña escala entre los Harakmbut y Awajun de la Amazonía Peruana. Lima: CONAP.

Cortés-McPherson/Dolores (2019): "Labor trafficking of men in the artisanal and small-scale gold mining camps of Madre de Dios. A reflection from the "diaspora networks" perspective". In: Winterdyk, John A./Jones, Jackie (eds.): The Palgrave International Handbook of human trafficking. Cham: Springer International Publishing, pp. 1785–1802.

Cortés-McPherson, Dolores (2020): “Peru: Curtailing smuggling, regionalizing trade”. In: Verbrugge, Boris/Geenen, Sara (eds.): Global gold production touching ground. Cham: Springer International Publishing, pp. 135–149.

Cruz, Rodrigo (2019): "Perú es el principal exportador de oro ilegal a Suiza, el centro mundial de la refinería". At: https://elcomercio.pe/mundo/actualidad/peru-principal-exportador-oro-ilegal-suiza-noticia-ecpm-648272-noticia/ (accessed 28 January 2022).

Damonte, Gerardo Hector (2018): “Mining formalization at the margins of the state. Small-scale miners and state governance in the Peruvian Amazon”. In: Development and Change, 49, 5, pp. 1314–1335.

Damonte, Gerardo Hector (2021): “Limited state governance and institutional hybridization in ASGM in Peru”. In: Resources Policy, 72, pp. 102118.

Dargent, Eduardo/Feldmann, Andreas/Luna, Juan (2017): “Greater state capacity, lesser stateness”. In: Politics & Society, 45, 1, pp. 3–34.

De Jong, Edwin/Knippenberg, Luuk/Bakker, Laurens (2017): “New frontiers. An enriched perspective on extraction frontiers in Indonesia”. In: Critical Asian Studies, 49, 3, pp. 330–348.

Dupraz-Dobias, Paula (2020): “High gold prices spur more illegal mining in Peru”. At: https://www.swissinfo.ch/eng/gold-finds-favour-in-the-pandemic-but-at-what-cost-/45987080 (accessed 28 January 2022).

Echave, José de (2016): “La minería ilegal en Perú. Entre la informalidad y el delito”. NUSO 263. At: https://nuso.org/articulo/la-mineria-ilegal-en-peru-entre-la-informalidad-y-el-delito/ (accessed 28 January 2022).

Fernández Felipe-Morales, Lourdes (2010): Desarrollo territorial en Madre de Dios. Los impactos socioambientales de la carretera Interoceánica Sur. Lima: Pronaturaleza Fundacíon Peruana para la Conservación de la Naturaleza.

Fiestas, Fiorella (2021): “#Elecciones2021: Minería ilegal en Madre de Dios y la tarea del próximo gobierno”. At: https://www.actualidadambiental.pe/cual-es-el-panorama-de-la-lucha-contra-la-mineria-ilegal-en-madre-de-dios/ (accessed 27 April 2022).

Global Initiative against Transnational Organized Crime (2016): “Organized crime and illegally mined gold in Latin America”. At: https://globalinitiative.net/wp-content/uploads/2016/03/Organized-Crime-and-Illegally-Mined-Gold-in-Latin-America.pdf (accessed 28 January 2022).

Gray, Andrew (1986): And after the gold rush…? Human rights and self-development among the Amarakaeri of southeastern Peru. Copenhagen: IWGIA.

Hartnett, Alexandra/Dawdy, Shannon Lee (2013): “The archaeology of illegal and illicit economies”. In: Annual Review of Anthropology, 42, 1, pp. 37–51.

Humphreys Bebbington, Denise/Bebbington, Anthony (2010): “Anatomy of a regional conflict. Tarija and resource grievances in Morales's Bolivia”. In: Latin American Perspectives, 37, 4, pp. 140–160.

Goi, Leonardo (2017): “Peru-US gold case shows how importer shifted gears”. At: https://insightcrime.org/news/analysis/peru-us-gold-case-shows-how-importer-shifted-gears/ (accessed 28 January 2022).

Jelin, Elizabeth/Motta, Renata/Costa, Sérgio (eds.) (2018): Global entangled inequalities. Conceptual debates and evidence from Latin America. London, New York: Routledge.

Krasner, Steven (1983): International Regimes. Ithaca/New York: Cornell University Press.

Lemos, Maria/Agrawal, Arun (2006): "Environmental Governance". In: Annual Review of Environment and Resources, 31, 1, pp. 297–325. https://doi.org/10.1146/annurev.energy.31.042605.135621.

León Pacheco, Lucía (2020): "Minería artesanal y a pequeña escala en el Perú. La formalización que nunca llega". Lima: Derecho, Ambiente y Recursos Naturales (DAR). At: https://dar.org.pe/mineria-artesanal-y-a-pequena-escala-en-el-peru-la-formalizacion-que-nunca-llega/ (accessed 28 January 2022).

Markham, Kate/Sangermano, Florencia (2018): "Evaluating wildlife vulnerability to mercury pollution from artisanal and small-scale gold mining in Madre de Dios, Peru". In: Tropical Conservation Science, 11, pp. 194008291879432.

Montaño Pastrana, Fiorella (2020): "Más de 1500 toneladas de oro se exportaron desde el Perú sin que se sepa quién las extrajo" At: https://convoca.pe/investigacion/mas-de-1500-toneladas-de-oro-se-exportaron-desde-el-peru-sin-que-se-sepa-quien-las (accessed 28 January 2022).

Montoya, Percy (2018): Estudio de la cadena de abastecimiento, comercialización y distribución de mercurio en la MAPE en el Perú. Artisanal Gold Council.

Mosquera, César (2009): Estudio diagnóstico de la actividad minera artesanal en Madre de Dios. Lima: Fundación Conservación Internacional.

Novak, Fabián/Namihas, Sandra (2009): La trata de personas con fines de explotación laboral. El caso de la minería aurífera y la tala ilegal de madera en Madre de Dios. Lima: Organización Internacional para las Migraciones, Oficina Regional para los Países Andinos.

Olivier de Sardan, Jean Pierre (2015): "Practical norms. Informal regulations within public bureaucracies (in Africa and beyond)". In: De Herdt, Tom/Olivier de Sardan, Jean Pierre (eds.): Real governance and practical norms in Sub-Saharan Africa. The game of rules. London: Routledge, pp. 20–62.

Pachas, Víctor Hugo (2011a): A propósito del Plan Nacional para la Formalización de la Minería Artesanal en el Perú. Lima.

Pachas, Víctor Hugo (2011b): Historia de una incertidumbre. Habitat, conflicto y poder en la minería artesanal de oro de Perú. Lima: Earth First SAC. At: https://www.gomiam.org/wp-content/uploads/2014/11/pachas-historia-de-una-incertidumbre.pdf (accessed 28 January 2022).

Peluso, Nancy/Lund, Christian (2011): "New frontiers of land control: introduction". In: Journal of Peasant Studies, 38, 4, pp. 667–681.

Poveda, Pablo (2015): El oro en la economía internacional. In: Poveda Ávila, Pablo/Nogales, Neyer/Calla Ortega, Ricardo (eds.): "El oro en Bolivia. Mercado, producción y medio ambiente". La Paz: CEDLA, Centro de Estudios para el Desarrollo Laboral y Agrario (CEDLA), pp. 1–69.

Saffon, Sergio (2020a): "Soaring gold prices during pandemic fuel Peru's illegal mining". At: https://insightcrime.org/news/brief/peru-coronavirus-illegal-mining/ (accessed 28 January 2022).

Saffon, Sergio (2020b): "Satellite images show evolution of illegal gold mining in Peru". At: https://insightcrime.org/news/brief/satellite-images-gold-mining-peru/ (accessed 28 January 2022).

Salas, Guillermo (2008): Dinámica social y minería. Familias pastoras de puna y la presencia del proyecto Antamina (1997 – 2002). Lima: Instituto de Estudios Peruanos (IEP).

Salazar, Elisabeth/Castro, Jonathan (2018): "Los cuadernos de la esclavitud en Madre de Dios". At: http://ojo-publico.com/596/los-cuadernos-de-la-esclavitud-en-madre-de-dios (accessed 28 January 2022).

Schorr, Bettina (2013): "From business to war. Causes of transitional violence by the Mexican drug cartels". In: Behemoth, 6, 1, pp. 55–73.

Sierra Praeli, Yvette (2020): "Perú: asesinan a líder indígena y mafias siguen operando durante emergencia por COVID-19". At: https://es.mongabay.com/2020/04/peru-crimen-lider-indigena-y-actividades-ilegales/ (accessed 27 April 2022).

SIICEX, Sistema Integrado de Información de Comercio Exterior (2019): "Comercio De Oro. Partidas Arancelarias Del Producto Exportadas En Los Ultimos Años". At: https://www.siicex.gob.pe/siicex/portal5ES.asp%3f_page_%3d172.17100%26_portletid_%3dsfichaproductoinit%26scriptdo%3dcc_fp_init%26pproducto%3d%2024%20%26pnomproducto%3d%20Anillo%20de%20Oro (accessed 3 May 2021).

Sindzingre, Alice (2006): "The relevance of the concepts of formality and informality. A theoretical appraisal". In: Guha-Khasnobis, Basudeb/Kanbur, Ravi/Ostrom, Elinor (eds.): Linking the formal and informal economy: Concepts and policies. Oxford: Oxford University Press, pp. 58–73.

Society for Threatened Peoples (2016): "Dealings in illegal gold. Swiss, US and Italian refineries under suspicion. STP report – summary in English". At: https://www.gfbv.ch/wp-content/uploads/summary_englishgold_report_march16-1.pdf (accessed 28 January 2022).

Steele, Sarah (2013): "Human trafficking, labor brokering, and mining in Southern Africa. Responding to a decentralized and hidden public health disaster". In: International Journal of Health Services, 43, 4, pp. 665–680.

Taussig, Michael (1986): Shamanism, colonialism, and the wild man. A study in terror and healing. Chicago: University of Chicago Press.

Torres Cuzcano, Víctor (2015): "Minería ilegal e informal en el Perú. Impacto socioeconómico". Lima: CooperAcción. At: http://cooperaccion.org.pe/wp-content/uploads/2015/10/Libro_Mineria_Ilegal,%20Victor%20Torres%20Cuzcano.pdf (accessed 28 January 2022).

UN Environment (2019): "Global mercury assessment 2018". At: https://www.unep.org/resources/publication/global-mercury-assessment-2018 (accessed 28 January 2022).

Valdés, Ricardo/Basombrío, Carlos/Vera, Dante (2019): Minería no formal en el Perú. Realidades, tendencias y ¿soluciones?. Lima: KAS.

Valencia, Lenin (2014): Madre de Dios: ¿Podemos evitar la tragedia? Políticas de ordenamiento de la minería aurífera. Lima: Sociedad Peruana de Derecho Ambiental (SPDA). At: http://www.actualidadambiental.pe/wp-content/uploads/2014/07/Madre-de-Dios-Podemos-evitar-la-tragedia-SPDA.pdf (accessed 28 January 2022).

Verbrugge, Boris/Geenen, Sara (eds.) (2020): Global gold production touching ground. Cham: Springer International Publishing.

Wieland, Patrick (2020): "Hernando de Soto, the lone prospector and the formalization of artisanal and small-scale mining. A case study from La Rinconada, Peru". In: Environment, Law and Policy Journal, 43, 1, pp. 1–66.

Wiener, Leonidas (2019): La gobernanza de la minería en pequeña escala en el Perú. Lima: CooperAcción. At: http://cooperaccion.org.pe/wp-content/uploads/2019/06/La-Gobernanza-de-la-Miner%C3%ADa.pdf (accessed 28 January 2022).

Workman, Daniel (n.d.): "Gold imports by country". At: https://www.worldstopexports.com/international-markets-for-imported-gold-by-country/ (accessed November 11, 2020).

World Gold Council (n.d.): "Major global trading hubs". At: https://www.gold.org/gold-market-structure/global-gold-market (accessed 27 April 2022).

Zevallos, Nicolás (2017): "Dinámicas locales en torno al cultivo de hoja de coca. Elementos para el estudio desde el mercado ilegal de la cocaína". In: Revista de Ciencia Política y Gobierno, 4, 7, pp. 9–29.

A decade of due diligence: an emerging regulatory regime to fight the trade in conflict minerals

Stefan Bauchowitz and Leopold von Carlowitz[1]

Introduction

The extractive industries – and especially artisanal and small-scale mining – are a considerable source of illicit revenue flows. The trade in tin, tungsten, tantalum and gold (3TG) in Eastern Democratic Republic of the Congo (DRC) has been singled out as a driver of the intractable conflicts in the region, earning them the moniker "conflict minerals". Armed groups operating in the region, so the story goes, finance their activities through the control or extralegal taxation of artisanal mining activities. If these actors were cut off from the proceeds of mineral trade, they would lose their financial means to wage war. Despite the numerous initiatives and an incipient regulatory regime aiming to tackle the issue of conflict minerals, the illicit trade of minerals in the region continues to a considerable extent.

The promotion of responsible supply chains has become a prominent goal of governments, advocacy groups, development cooperation and increasingly the private sector. One of the early efforts to promote supply chain sustainability – besides the movement on fair trade of agricultural products and textiles – is the creation of initiatives, the drafting of codes and ultimately the adoption of legislation to curb the illicit trade in conflict minerals. The issue was initially taken up by international civil society organisations, whose advocacy efforts resulted in the adoption of various sustainability initiatives and laws. Amongst the latest of these efforts is the EU Conflict Minerals Regulation, which – together with the equally notable conflict minerals provision of the Dodd-Frank Act in the US – bookends a decade of due diligence regulation.

Unlike the trafficking of drugs or humans, the flows of these minerals are illicit due not to the product itself but to the conditions under which it is produced. Related regulatory efforts are mostly initiated by and ad-

1 The article reflects exclusively the opinions of the authors and not those of the Federal Ministry of Economic Cooperation and Development (BMZ) or GIZ GmbH.

dressed to actors in the Global North, whereas they aim to tackle problems in the Global South where the harm occurs at the beginning of the supply chain. At the same time, Northern activists and policymakers have at least initially paid insufficient attention to the complexities of the conflicts they sought to resolve (Cuvelier, Vlassenroot and Olin 2014).

Regulatory activities aimed at curbing the illicit trade in conflict minerals are a result of a process of norm diffusion. The lessons learnt from various consecutive and complementary, sometimes superimposed approaches to achieve responsible mineral supply chains led to more sophisticated, inclusive means of regulation. There is an increasing interplay between different governance instruments, including binding laws, self-imposed codes of conduct and voluntary initiatives. Regulation is becoming more versatile. Traditional state-based approaches are being complemented by "civil regulation" and "smart mixes" intended to overcome the regulatory gaps resulting from global but fragmented supply chains. Numerous forms of regulation exist, running the gamut from norms, customs and loose codes of conduct to formal legislation adopted by home or host governments and implemented by a combination of these and business and civil society actors.

Minerals and conflict in Eastern DRC

Eastern DRC is rich in deposits of tin, tungsten and tantalum, which in addition to gold are essential for the production of modern electronic devices. In the region, most of these minerals are mined artisanally. This means that they are extracted using simple, labour-intensive methods. Artisanal and small-scale mining (ASM) is a predominantly informal activity, and basic standards regarding health, safety or the environment are mostly not adhered to. These shortcomings alone would warrant a drive towards more sustainable practices, particularly as the sector is an important source of income for large parts of the rural population. However, the ASM sector has gained prominence for another reason, namely for fuelling the war economy through the extraction and sale of conflict minerals.

The so-called resource curse, according to which countries abundant in natural resources suffer from bad governance, slow growth, authoritarianism and conflict, has long been a concern of academics, policymakers and civil society organisations. Natural resources are said to have played a role in starting, prolonging or financing violent conflict. On the one hand, natural resource wealth increases the potential benefits of and hence competition for the control of resource-rich territories. On the other hand, grievances that result from the extraction of natural resources can cause conflict. The causes for the onset of civil conflict may be found in resource abundance directly as well as – indirectly – in economic underdevelopment or state weakness. Natural resources have also been linked to civil war more directly: rent-seeking arguments such as those made by Collier and Hoeffler (2004) look at natural resources as providing an incentive to initiate violent conflict or to finance fighting. The extraction of valuable minerals such as gold and diamonds has been blamed for the incidence, intensity or duration of violent conflict (Ross 2004a, 2004b; Le Billon 2000). The relative ease of extraction and low technological barriers, the high value and the remoteness of the deposits have contributed to financing violence in many parts of the world. Especially in the 1990s and 2000s, artisanally mined diamonds became notorious as "blood diamonds" in Angola, Sierra Leone and Liberia, but other minerals, including ores containing tin, tantalum or tungsten, as well as gold, also carry the label of conflict minerals.

Much to the chagrin of those researching conflicts in the DRC, the illegal extraction and trade of minerals often serve as a dominant explanation for violence in the DRC. Violence has been explained with fighting over the control of mine sites, the financing of the war effort through the proceeds from the exploitation of these resources and widespread violence against the civilian population, mainly to gain access to mineral-rich areas (Autesserre 2010: 65). Scholars of the region (e.g. Autesserre 2010; Cuvelier et al. 2014; Seay 2015) tend to argue, however, that the picture is more complex and conflicts in Eastern DRC are not solely determined by the presence of and the trade with 3TG minerals. The focus on natural resources rather than ethnic cleavages or grievances suffers, they claim, from reductionism and determinism. It does not do justice to the complex interplay of different actors, their motives and the levels at which they engage in violence (Ballentine and Sherman 2003).

The term conflict minerals is somewhat of a misnomer: while conflict is occurring in a mineral-rich region and minerals play a role in the conflict economy in Eastern DRC, it is an oversimplification to reduce the cause of conflict solely or predominantly to mineral wealth and related greed (Autesserre 2012; Seay 2015: 130). Autesserre highlights a few competing narratives about the conflicts in that region: they relate to the presence of (foreign) militias and armed groups, local tensions over land or disputes over charcoal and cattle. She notes that only about 8 percent of conflicts are over natural resources (Autesserre 2012: 211). Armed groups have considerable alternative sources of revenue. Besides mineral exploitation and trade, they acquire funding inter alia by setting up checkpoints, extralegal taxation and protection rackets (Hoffmann, Vlassenroot and Marchais 2016) or by involvement in the timber or charcoal trade. While mineral resources do play a role in the violence, it should not be expected that those motivated by inequalities or other grievances simply lay down their arms if revenues are cut off. To reduce the conflicts in Eastern DRC to violence and human rights abuses resulting from mineral trade betrays a deterministic view of the situation (Radley and Vogel 2015). However, at least initially, this was precisely the narrative and approach chosen to promote a regulatory regime to curb the trade in conflict minerals.

Norm emergence and the power of activism

Legislation to promote "conflict-free" minerals and/or responsible supply chains did not emerge out of a vacuum. Rather, it is the result of a process of norm diffusion following three stages: norm emergence, a norm cascade which occurs after a critical mass of states has embraced the new norm and drives others to follow suit, and finally norm internalisation, i.e. the stage at which a norm is taken for granted (Finnemore and Sikkink 1998).

While it was up to states or international organisations to adopt legislation (albeit with the twist of elevating guidelines to law, see below), civil society acted as a "norm entrepreneur" (Finnemore and Sikkink 1998: 893). Civil society played a crucial role in the emergence of norms and the subsequent passage of regulation addressing the link between natural resources and conflict. The path towards the creation of the EU Conflict Minerals Regulation serves as an example of norm diffusion and was initiated by civil society: NGOs such as Global Witness documented the links between conflict and natural resource extraction in Eastern DRC (Global Witness 2009, 2010). The Enough Project, founded in 2007 by human rights advocate John Prendergast to support more robust peace processes in central Africa, served as an organisational platform and was instrumental in garnering attention for the issue amongst US policymakers and the public. In 2009, the project published a paper entitled "Can You Hear Congo Now? Cell Phones, Conflict Minerals, and the Worst Sexual Violence in the World" (Prendergast 2009), which established a narrative link between Western consumption on the one hand and mineral extraction and conflict including sexual violence in the Kivu Provinces on the other. It drew considerable attention to the issue, and lawmakers in the US addressed the matter in broader measures aimed at financial market reforms. Eventually, the idea to curb the illegal trade of conflict minerals by means of supply chain due diligence spread globally and led to the adoption of the EU Regulation on conflict minerals.

While civil society actors are unable to impose norms, they inform and persuade others. They are the "socialising agents" of norms, providing information and documentation on what they perceive to be the most salient issues (Finnemore and Sikkink 1998: 895; 900; 902). In addition to pressuring companies from the outside, international NGOs such as Global Witness possess a considerable amount of expertise and credibility. Governments, international organisations and even companies often rely on their input to shape and implement strategies to improve governance in the extractive industries. NGOs aim at "changing consciousness and creating mechanisms of accountability" (Newell 2001a: 105). They work towards holding corporations accountable by creating awareness not just among the public but within relevant regulatory authorities directly. Florini and Simmons (2000: 11) point out that "civil society tries to shape [...] norms in two ways: directly, by persuading policy makers and business leaders to change their minds [...] or indirectly, by altering the public's perception of what governments and businesses should be doing". Thus, NGOs create accountability either by proxy – through shaping states' and publics' demand for accountability or directly in collaborating with businesses in order to shape and oversee their policies and actions (Oliviero and Simmons 2002). While NGOs and other non-state actors generally command a softer and more indirect form of power than that of states, they were nevertheless able to draw international attention to the issue by linking it to electronic consumer products. They were thereby paving the way for consumer pressure on manufacturers leading to changes in the perceptions of law- and policymakers. In general, activist pressure is most likely to yield results if the salience of the issue addressed resonates with the wider public and if the "brand value" and the company's reputation are at stake (Haufler 2001: 23). Meanwhile, NGOs and companies are increasingly cooperating in fostering responsible supply chains rather than resorting to naming and shaming, the NGOs' classical mode of exerting pressure.

Norms on natural resource governance were already in existence or themselves in the process of emerging in the early 2000s. The issues of better governance and transparency in the extractive industries (Gillies 2010), be it the pursuit of transparency or greater respect for the environment and human rights, had also been gaining international attention prior to the fight against conflict minerals. There were also international initiatives specifically related to the link between natural resources and conflict that helped pave the way for conflict minerals regulation and due diligence. These are the Kimberley Process, which aims to reduce the trade of so-called "blood diamonds" (Haufler 2009), and the OECD Guidelines for Multinational Enterprises (OECD 2011), which aim to promote responsible business conduct (see below). So while the campaign to curb the trade in conflict minerals resulted in the showcase pieces of legislation of the Dodd-Frank Act and the EU Conflict Minerals Regulation, they do not stand alone. Though they may be amongst the first instances of hard law on conflict minerals (with the exception of the Kimberley Process) they are not the first regulatory efforts in a broad sense of the term. The norm entrepreneurs were able to use existing initiatives as a vehicle onto which the issue of combating the illicit trade in the DRC's minerals could be "grafted" (Price 2003: 584).

Approaches to conflict minerals regulation – towards a smart mix

There are many governance gaps in the extractive industries. States and international organisations largely fail to regulate multinational enterprises and global supply chains, and corporate social responsibility alone is inadequate to address the externalities associated with global supply chains. At first, states did not take the initiative in regulating the extractive industries. It was "civil regulation" in which civil society actors, alongside states (and private sector actors) promoted or implemented regulation (Newell 2001b: 908). For over a decade, governments, international organisations, the private sector and civil society organisations have been trying to master the challenge of complex conflicts in resource-rich regions. The rise to prominence of the issue of conflict minerals in the Global North led to a proliferation of regulation of the issue. The engagement of multiple actors with different interests, roles and preferences in the rulemaking process resulted in a patchwork of different regulations and initiatives.

In the extractive sector, which often operates in zones of weak governance, regulation often targets companies to limit corrupt practices or human rights abuses. Challenges of regulation tend to arise from the multinational character of large companies operating outside the jurisdiction of their headquarters in areas where the capacities of host governments are limited. In fragmented or long global supply chains, as in the case of 3TG in Eastern DRC, regulation is fraught with problems, as the minerals are produced in the largely informal ASM sector. Undesirable practices are common, and minerals pass through numerous hands before finding their way into consumer products. Regulation does not seek to address the question of whether minerals are extracted "sustainably" but rather focuses on the illicit trade in those minerals that are said to fuel conflict.

Regulation is becoming more sophisticated and inclusive. Conventional regulation by individual states or international organisations and groups of states through mandatory rules often does not fit the physical realities of global supply chains. Newer types of regulation include different types of actors, such as private sector actors, their associations or civil society groups. They either establish and enforce regulatory schemes themselves or collaborate with states and international organisations to do so. Firms also collaborate with, and are regulated by, intergovernmental organisations, which cuts out the state as the intermediary, as is the case with the OECD Guidelines for Multinational Enterprises (Abbott and Snidal 2009: 506). This "civil regulation" constitutes a patchwork in which the state's role is mostly indirect (Newell 2001b).

The ways in which regulation is conceived, adopted and implemented are changing: first, regulatory efforts use market mechanisms to implement regulations. Second, regulation has become transnationally anchored rather than reliant on individual states for implementation. Third, it encompasses new actors. Whereas previously regulation was the domain of state agencies, private actors and civil society are increasingly important regulators, both in their own right and as groups that push those vested with traditional authority to adopt and implement regulation. Fourth, standard-setting is moving away from "command-and-control schemes" and is rather becoming a deliberative process that includes regulators, regulatees and third parties. It is dynamic, in the sense that softer forms of regulation (such as the OECD Guidance in the case of conflict minerals, see below) may eventually become enshrined in hard law (Vogel 2008: 265). Fifth, regulation is not only applying formal, legal sanctions but also relying on social pressure and learning to achieve its aims (Abbott and Snidal 2000; Schneiberg and Bartley 2008).

Regulation to promote responsible supply chains differs from conventional extractive industry regulation, where multinational companies with a large degree of control over extraction and other operations are the target of regulators. The regulatee (i.e. the importer or manufacturer in the Global North) is not directly involved in mineral extraction, and the buck of compliance is passed towards the beginning of the supply chain. Importers subject to reporting requirements under the Dodd-Frank Act or the EU Conflict Minerals Regulation are compelled to manage the externalities of their business decisions. Conflict minerals regulation enacted in the Global North often imposes certain due diligence obligations but stops short of holding companies that import 3TG accountable for human rights abuses committed in the process of mineral extraction and trade. Emerging regulation is also a reflection of the notion that companies are responsible not only for the impact of their operations but also for the actions of those they do business with as well as of their wider stakeholders (Donaldson and Preston 1995). These newer forms of regulation are becoming more prominent: co-regulation, in which standards are developed by the private sector and governments only provide a sanction mechanism for non-compliance; self-regulation, in which the private sector alone sets standards and codes of conduct; and, finally, multi-stakeholder regulation, in which actors from different constituencies join to develop a regulatory framework (Haufler 2003).

Self-regulation originally referred to the adoption of industry standards but now also applies to the social and environmental domains (Haufler 2001) and comes in many varieties. Gunningham and Rees (1997) distinguish different forms, such as "social self-regulation", which is undertaken to limit the negative externalities of corporate behaviour, as opposed to "economic self-regulation", which maintains order in markets or facilitates them. Self-regulation also does not necessarily exclude governments: in "mandated self-regulation", the application of rules may be monitored and enforced by governments (Gunningham and Rees 1997: 365). Self-regulation might be in the interest of industry, simply to give the appearance of regulation and thus pre-empt more formal government regulation (Gunningham and Rees 1997: 370), but it can also serve to complement state regulation (Vogel 2008: 275). The inclusion of third parties such as NGOs improves the effectiveness of regulation (Nielsen and Parker 2008). Third parties may have enforcement capacity even if they are not endowed with formal authority. For self-regulation to be effective, there needs to be an overlap between public and private interests – e.g. in the case of minerals clean supply chains and reputational concerns – as well as oversight by governments, third parties or a combination thereof (Gunningham and Rees 1997: 406).

The United Nations Guiding Principles on Business and Human Rights recommend that states should consider a smart mix of measures – national and international, mandatory and voluntary – to foster business respect for human rights (United Nations 2011: 5). While the Guiding Principles imply business interaction with state governance, others more explicitly argue for non-state participation in supply chain governance. For example, Gunningham and Grabosky (1998) first mentioned a smart mix consisting of contributions from a variety of actors, levels of governance or institutional structures as well as optional private participation. More recently, van Erp et al. (2019: 50) defined smart mixes to consist of "various regulatory and governance instruments, both public and private and both international and local, [combined] into sophisticated mixes of complementary instruments and actors, tailored to the specific needs of the situation". While the primary focus is on regulation in its various forms, accompanying measures that build required capacity are part of a smart mix. Among them are on-the-ground projects by multi-stakeholder partnerships as well as development cooperation strengthening governance institutions and oversight.

Conflict minerals regulation in the DRC

Conflict minerals regulation in and around the DRC and the wider Great Lakes Region illustrates the interplay of actors and governance approaches attempting to curb the trade with mineral resources in zones of conflict. The United Nations already started in 2001 to investigate the links between the trade in natural resources and conflicts and continued to do so for more than a decade. The UN Report of the Panel of Experts on the Illegal Exploitation of Natural Resources and Other Forms of Wealth of the Democratic Republic of the Congo (United Nations 2001) proposed an embargo on Congolese minerals and targeted sanctions against those involved in the trade.

In 2006, the Heads of States of the International Conference on the Great Lakes Region (ICGLR) signed the Protocol against the Illegal Exploitation of Natural Resources, in which they committed to curbing the illegal exploitation of natural resources. This was followed by the 2010 launch of the Regional Initiative against the Illegal Exploitation of Natural Resources (RINR). The Regional Initiative has at its centre a Regional Certification Mechanism (RCM) which is intended to curb the illegal exploitation of and trade in the 3TG minerals. Only minerals extracted from mines certified as not benefiting armed groups and free from forced or child labour may be legally exported from the region.

In parallel, attention shifted towards due diligence. Companies in the Global North were held responsible for ensuring that their supply chains were free of minerals contributing to conflict (Geenen and Custers 2010). The issue was taken up by policymakers internationally: the G8 Summit Declaration of 2007 emphasised the role of natural resources for development and conflict. It also made reference to the OECD Guidelines for Multinational Enterprises and existing efforts to break the link between minerals and violence, such as the Kimberley Process. The G8 summit also saw the launch of initiatives for development cooperation. The Summit

Declaration called for the development of certification systems, which in turn led to the development of a standard on Certified Trading Chains by the German Federal Institute for Geosciences and Natural Resources (BGR) which was eventually adopted into Congolese law.

Between 2009 and 2011, the OECD, the then 11 member states of the International Conference on the Great Lakes Region as well as representatives from industry and civil society developed the OECD Due Diligence Guidance for Responsible Supply Chains of Minerals from Conflict-Affected and High-Risk Areas (OECD 2013). This document would eventually become the core standard for conflict minerals due diligence. It has become the leading global due diligence standard often referred to by other initiatives and included in relevant pieces of legislation. The OECD Guidance, the recommendations of UN Security Council Resolution 1952 of 2010, as well as the RCM were incorporated into the national law of the DRC (Government of the DRC 2011, 2012a, 2012b). Besides being given formal legal status in the DRC, the Guidance gained further relevance with the adoption of the EU Conflict Minerals Regulation. The latter appropriated the OECD model and links binding law with voluntary standards in implementation, effectively creating a legal obligation to apply the OECD Guidance.

The OECD Guidance is not an isolated document, but the result of several initiatives and processes aimed at promoting responsible business conduct. The Guidelines for Multinational Enterprises were originally devised in 1976 and contain recommendations on responsible business conduct. They were revised in 2011 to include due diligence guidance, based on the UN Guiding Principles on Business and Human Rights and the ILO Tripartite Declaration of Principles Concerning Multinational Enterprises and Social Policy (International Labour Organization 2006; Buhmann 2015).

The OECD Guidance stipulates that companies must take certain precautions to ensure that their supply chains do not include inhumane working conditions, forced labour, the worst forms of child labour or other serious human rights violations. The same applies to any direct or indirect support of non-state armed groups through the mining, transport, trade or export of minerals.

The Guidance contains recommendations for companies that source minerals from conflict-affected and high-risk areas on how to approach due diligence for responsible supply chains. The OECD five-step framework consists of 1) establishing a management system to engage with suppliers and facilitate transparency and reporting in the supply chain; 2) identifying and assessing supply chain risks in terms of human rights abuses, direct or indirect support of armed actors or security forces as well as extralegal taxation, bribery or money laundering; 3) designing and implementing risk-mitigation strategies, with disengagement from suppliers as the last resort; 4) carrying out an independent third-party audit of the supply chain and 5) publicly reporting on the company's due diligence practice.

While the conflicts in the Great Lakes Region led the OECD to adopt the Guidance, its scope extends beyond the Great Lakes Region. The Guidance applies to "conflict-affected and high-risk areas" worldwide, and in its current third edition it applies to all minerals, not only the 3TG.

Besides legislation there are also private regulatory approaches aimed at tackling the issue of conflict minerals. In 2008, private sector actors founded the Conflict-Free Smelter Initiative, which has since become the Responsible Minerals Initiative. This was intended to certify the conflict-free nature of mineral supply chains via the smelters. The smelters and refiners were to instruct their producers and suppliers to promote and trade raw materials in compliance with the OECD Guidance. Likewise, the International Tin Research Institute (ITRI) created the ITRI Tin Supply Chain initiative iTSCi, a traceability and due diligence programme to ensure traded minerals are "conflict-free".

These self-regulatory efforts are not without problems: Global Witness (2010) noted that "a major tin industry 'traceability' scheme, which aims to trace minerals from the mine to the refinery, risks rubber-stamping conflict minerals coming from mines controlled by national military units". In 2014, a traceability system had only been put in place at about 40 mine sites out of a total of 900 in the South Kivu province. Prices had dropped for minerals sourced from these sites, not least because the cost of implementing the traceability schemes fell on producers (Radley and Vogel 2015). Also, fraud had become widespread, and there were many instances where "illegal material" was introduced at iTSCi sites to get tagged or where iTSCi tags were brought to non-iTSCi mines (Vogel and Raeymaekers 2016: 1113). The UN Group of Experts on the DRC also noted the initiative's shortcomings and "documented several breaches of the chain of custody for mineral trade in North Kivu Province as well as the ongoing sale of tags on the black market in the Democratic Republic of the Congo" (United Nations 2017: 2).

Ultimately, the creation of the RCM at the level of the ICGLR was a reaction to private-led initiatives. It meant to ensure that conflict minerals regulation did not rest exclusively with the private sector. In the RCM, mines are certified according to a traffic-light system, based on inspections by member state officials. Exports are allowed from those assigned green status and provisionally from those assigned yellow status. (A blue status allowing exports from mines not yet visited was introduced in 2019.) Between 2017 and October 2020, IPIS (2020) counted 833 3TG mine sites in Eastern DRC, most of them for gold (570). While armed actors were observed in 362 of them, only 4 had been assigned the „red" status (i.e. exports from that mine were forbidden).

In 2009, a resolution to address the issue of conflict minerals was introduced in the US House of Representatives, but it never became law. However, provisions regarding conflict minerals in the DRC found their way into the Dodd-Frank Wall Street Reform and Consumer Protection Act in July 2010. Section 1502 of the Act stipulates that publicly traded companies must report whether they source 3TG minerals from the DRC and report on the steps taken to ensure that the minerals are "conflict-free". The Dodd-Frank Act was the first major piece of legislation to address the issue of conflict minerals. It became the tipping point for the emergence of minerals supply chain due diligence as a norm, prompting other countries to create corresponding legislation.

In the wake of the Dodd-Frank Act, there were a number of – sometimes abortive – bids to adopt conflict minerals or supply chain regulations at the national level. In 2014, the China Chamber of Commerce of Metals, Minerals & Chemicals Importers & Exporters (2014) launched a Chinese version of due diligence guidelines for responsible mineral supply chains for Chinese companies active in the minerals trade abroad. These guidelines were developed in consultation with the OECD, Global Witness as well as the European Commission. Whereas a Canadian bill that would have required companies to comply with the OECD Guidance failed in 2014, the French duty of vigilance law of 2017 requires companies to identify and prevent risks in their supply chains. The French law served as precedent for a number of human rights due diligence laws in other countries that are not limited to the extractive sector. In 2021, Norway and Germany adopted mandatory supply chain due diligence laws after years of negotiations. A Swiss initiative for responsible business was narrowly rejected in a national referendum in late 2020. The EU is also working on a directive on corporate due diligence and corporate accountability focusing on both human rights violations and environmental impacts. While these regulatory efforts have a wide and general scope for supply chain due diligence, other countries have adopted topic-specific laws in recent years. In 2017, the United Kingdom adopted its Modern Slavery Act, and the Netherlands passed its Child Labour Due Diligence Law in 2020.

In 2017, the EU adopted its Regulation on due diligence obligations for 3TG minerals originating from conflict-affected and high-risk areas. Three years of intense debate within the EU institutions, mainly on whether or not the Regulation would mandate self-regulation, had preceded the agreement. The European Commission had originally, with the support of the European Council, proposed a system of voluntary self-regulation of importers of unprocessed minerals from these areas that included provisions for voluntary self-certification. However, the European Parliament (backed by many civil society organisations) regarded the Commission's voluntary approach as far too weak and ineffective. Instead, the Parliament proposed mandatory third-party audits of all EU smelters and refiners as well as obligatory due diligence and reporting requirements for importers and downstream companies. These amendments met strong resistance on the part of the Council and the Commission. Following an inter-institutional "trilogue" between Council, Commission and Parliament, a compromise was reached to adopt a binding regulation that, for the moment, does not include companies further downstream in the scope of the Regulation (van der Velde 2017). From 1 January 2021, EU importers of 3TG, excluding downstream firms that process minerals and produce final consumer products, have to carry out checks on their supply chain following a five-step framework based on the OECD Guidance. The process requires a management system (Art. 4), identification of risks as well as risk management (Art. 5), a third-party audit (Art. 6) and reporting (Art. 7).

The deliberations on the Regulation's design were informed by the lessons learnt from implementing the Dodd-Frank Act. The Act had negative economic effects in the DRC (see below). To some extent, these effects were caused by introducing the legislation without having created the required infrastructure for its implementation. By introducing a three-and-a-half-year transition period, the EU gave European companies and relevant states sufficient time to prepare for fulfilling the Regulation's requirements. The EU is also providing funds in support of small and medium-sized enterprises as well as ASM mining, thus trying to avoid the pitfalls of the preceding US legislation.

In its approach, the EU Regulation differs from the Dodd-Frank Act in that the latter uses financial markets as a lever, whereas the EU Regulation focuses on physical trade. The US Act – whose enforcement was suspended by the Trump administration – applies to all companies listed on US stock markets that import and/or use 3TG in certain quantities. A further notable difference is the geographic scope. Whereas the Dodd-Frank Act applies to minerals originating from the DRC and its neighbouring countries, the EU Regulation uses OECD terminology covering 3TG minerals from conflict-affected and high-risk areas, albeit without defining these precisely (Koch and Burlyuk 2020). The Commission published an indicative list of these areas in December 2020 (RAND Europe n.d.). A further difference is that the EU Regulation applies only to companies that import or refine and smelt 3TG minerals (around 600–1000 importers, plus 500 smelters), whereas the Dodd-Frank Act is broader and applies to any US-listed company using these minerals.

The EU Regulation is an attempt to learn from past mistakes. Both the Regulation and the OECD Guidelines (as its core element) have been developed in consultation with the affected countries in the Global South. The legislation will be accompanied by measures of technical assistance to improve the modes of mineral extraction in producing countries. Part and parcel of the above-mentioned agreement on the legal nature (and some other features) of the Regulation was that the effectiveness of the Regulation will be evaluated in 2023. The question of whether or not EU downstream companies like end producers will also be subject to binding due diligence requirements will then be reopened. This will include thinking about possible sanctions by member states against companies violating their due diligence obligations. The evaluation might not only lead to an expansion of the Regulation to the entire supply chain (upstream and downstream). Given that the Regulation is seen to have important precedential value, it is conceivable that its scope will also expand to other minerals such as cobalt or copper and include other sustainability issues (such as wider human rights or environmental issues).

One of the accompanying measures to support effective implementation of the Regulation is the European Partnership for Responsible Minerals (EPRM). This multi-stakeholder partnership, founded in 2016, aims to create better social and economic conditions for miners and local mining communities. Its objective is "to increase the proportion of responsibly produced minerals from conflict-affected and high-risk areas (CAHRAs) and to support socially responsible extraction of minerals that contributes to local development" (EPRM n.d.). The EPRM's establishment was based on the assumption that the EU Conflict Minerals Regulation must be accompanied by an effective development policy if it is to have any substantive impact in the producing countries. Otherwise, there would be a risk that mining countries will be excluded from relevant value chains or that alternative business relationships will be entered into with buyers who circumvent the required standards. The EPRM funds projects for responsible sourcing of 3TG minerals from conflict-affected and high-risk areas worldwide. The partnership follows a three-pronged approach to reach its objectives. It supports work on ASM mine sites with a view to responsible production and supports miners in getting access to formal markets nationally and internationally. It also supports mid- and downstream actors in improving their due diligence practices in sourcing responsibly, for example through the "Due Diligence Hub" online portal. Third, the EPRM works to improve linkages between responsible sourcing and production by strengthening alliances between different supply chain actors in order to facilitate trade from ASM sites in conflict-affected and high-risk areas worldwide. Projects are financed by a multi-donor fund following frequent calls for proposals. Like the EU Regulation itself, the EPRM will also be evaluated in 2023.

Much ado about nothing?

Whether or not regulation aimed at curbing the illicit trade in 3TG minerals has served its purpose is subject to considerable debate. The conflict in Eastern DRC involves complex issues such as land rights and citizenship. This made it too difficult to mount an effective advocacy campaign that could successfully attract the attention of and mobilise an audience of Western consumers and policymakers. Pressure groups oversimplified the Congo crises to make the issue resonate. They tied the minerals extracted in Eastern DRC to consumer electronics, which depend on 3TG for critical components such as capacitors and integrated circuits. The civil society campaign reduced the complexity of the situation to create a narrative that resonated with audiences in the Global North (Seay 2015). While activists in the Global North often take up grievances of local organisations and amplify them for their audiences to effect change in the Global South in a so-called "boomerang effect" (Keck and Sikkink 1998), the campaign appears to have been supply-side driven. Nonetheless, the campaign was so successful that it eventually led to the adoption of conflict minerals legislation in the US.

The rationale behind the campaign was that consumers could pressure companies to procure conflict-free minerals; companies would then be obliged to either not source the minerals from the DRC or conduct due diligence of their supply chains. This, in turn, would ensure that no minerals were traded whose extraction had benefited parties to conflicts. The desired effect was to cut off financing to armed groups and hence to impede them from committing human rights abuses (Prendergast 2009; Seay 2015: 120).

However, the passage of the Dodd-Frank Act is a lesson in unintended consequences. The Act was adopted in 2010, but the Securities and Exchange Commission (SEC) only finalised its rules for the implementation of reporting requirements under Section 1502 in 2012. In the interim, the Congolese government had shut down artisanal 3TG mining activities in the Eastern provinces of Maniema, South Kivu and North Kivu. In addition to cutting off armed groups from potential revenue sources, the government's stated aim of the ban was to establish control of the informal mining sector and to fight fraud (Geenen 2012). At the same time, companies from the Electronic Industry Citizenship Coalition (EICC) responded to the uncertainty regarding the implementation of the Act by instituting a de facto embargo to halt sourcing from smelters that could not demonstrate that their minerals were "conflict-free".

Despite the mining ban, rebel groups continued mining activities in areas that were already under their control. They also made recourse to alternative sources of financing such as illegal logging. Mining also continued in areas under government control. The army and other government actors such as the mining police provided access or protection for miners – in exchange for payment. Yet overall, the ban led to a decline of gold production by 80 % (Geenen 2012). The blanket ban also affected mine sites with no involvement of armed groups at all.

The de facto embargo caused serious economic damage and had considerable impact on people's livelihoods. The focus on technical solutions such as traceability and formalisation of the Congolese ASM sector as a response to international regulation ignored this impact and worsened the situation for mining communities (Vogel and Raeymaekers 2016). ASM is a poverty-driven activity (Bryceson and Jønsson 2010; Hilson 2010) and is the only employment opportunity for hundreds of thousands of people in the DRC. Once established in the activity, artisanal miners face considerable exit barriers, i.e. cannot easily switch jobs, for instance because of indebtedness (Perks 2011). Those dependent on ASM don't always work in the extraction of minerals themselves, but are often petty traders or craftspeople conducting their business on and around mine sites. Following the ban, rates of school attendance declined, as parents could not afford school fees, and malnourishment increased. The mining ban severely limited purchasing power in the region (Geenen 2012). Moreover, there is evidence that the ban led to increased child mortality as a result of loss of income and access to healthcare (Parker, Foltz and Elsea 2016). Faced with unemployment, some miners moved into gold mining (which lends itself to smuggling much more readily than the 3T minerals) or even joined militant groups (Seay 2015).

Seay (2015) notes that there is no evidence that any armed group ceased operations because of the Dodd-Frank Act. In fact, the mining ban initially led to an increase in the militarisation of mining activities, as the Congolese army took control of mines in Walikale Territory immediately after its announcement. Instead of enforcing the ban, soldiers made agreements with miners, who would then pay for protection and access to mine sites (Geenen 2012). Moreover, it was found that the ban and the Act were followed by a period of increased looting and violence against civilians and a shift of conflict to territories that were not subject to the Dodd-Frank provisions (Parker and Vadheim 2017; Stoop, Verpoorten and van der Windt 2018).

Without disputing these negative impacts, some analysts caution against exaggerating these unintended consequences (Koch and Kinsbergen 2018). They focus in particular on the de facto embargo that persisted beyond the self-imposed mining ban and was putatively the result of the importers' efforts to avoid scrutiny. While the adoption of the Dodd-Frank Act coincided with a reduction of tantalum and tin imports, trade rebounded after the SEC's publication of the final rules for implementation (Schütte 2019).

On the positive side, the Dodd-Frank Act served as a "wake-up call" for those involved in mining in Eastern DRC. It highlighted the need for reform in the sector and led to the creation of a number of certification and traceability initiatives on the ground. They aim at facilitating due diligence and intend to improve the livelihoods of those engaged in the production of minerals. The Act also helped change the position of manufacturers and other economic actors, who started considering responsible supply chains as an integral part of their social responsibility (Cuvelier et al. 2014).

While some success can be noted relating to curbing illegal trade in 3T minerals, there is little progress on gold. With its low weight-to-value ratio, it is more readily smuggled and has not been in the focus of regional cooperation. Gold continues to be illicitly traded across the borders between the DRC on one side and Ruanda and Uganda on the other, and from there onwards towards the United Arab Emirates and India (United Nations 2017; IMPACT 2020). While the illicit trade with conflict minerals continues at somewhat lower levels, there is a shift towards gold, for which the development of traceability and certification schemes is more challenging. Trade flows of gold are becoming increasingly illicit due to tax evasion rather than the financing of conflicts. To improve the situation, policymakers, the private sector and development practitioners have recently started to address the issue of gold smuggling – for instance through the publication of a supplement on gold by the OECD in 2012, the Canadian-funded Just Gold pilot project, a pilot implemented by the BGR and the Congolese ITOA initiative. To date, traceability schemes for gold are still in the pilot stage, and while ASM production in the DRC is estimated at around 14–20 t, only 200–300 kg of exports are declared (Neumann et al. 2019).

Conclusion

Civil society pressure, corporate social responsibility and a susceptibility to consumer pressure, paired with expert reports addressing the "resource curse", provided fertile ground for various regulatory efforts and initiatives on conflict minerals. The creation of a considerable body of hard and soft law on the topic serves as a showcase example of norm emergence. It is also an important precedent towards broader responsible supply-chain governance. In industrialised countries, responsible supply chains are swiftly becoming a paradigm that goes beyond "conflict-free" minerals. The aim is to minimise and mitigate the negative effects of mining and to maximise the benefits for the mining countries and the affected populations. Responsible sourcing requires compliance with due diligence obligations along the entire supply chain to prevent human rights violations such as child labour or exploitation as well as unmitigated environmental damage.

Norm emergence must be understood as a process, not as an end. While the EU Conflict Minerals Regulation is a recent major effort to curb the trade in conflict minerals, more recent initiatives such as a European due diligence law are becoming broader in scope. There is a general shift in focus away from conflict towards sustainable and responsible supply chains involving a plethora of issues relating to human rights, the environment and governance. The scope of minerals considered has also broadened. While so far mainly the 3TG minerals have been subject to regulation, many other minerals mined artisanally and informally (e.g. cobalt) have meanwhile come under scrutiny. While they may not be linked to violent conflict per se, they are associated with child labour, modern slavery or environmental degradation – all issues of serious concern and high media attention.

The impact of existing regulation also remains to be determined: it is already difficult to disentangle the effects of the Dodd-Frank Act from changes in trade in minerals and the security situation in Eastern DRC, and the jury is certainly still out on the EU Regulation, given the starting date of its implementation in January 2021.

Regulatory policy in the Global North leaves dealing with policy outcomes largely to resource-rich countries in the Global South. Choking off trade in minerals mined under conditions of violence and serious human rights abuses is one thing, improving the situation on mine sites another. Both the EU Conflict Minerals Regulation and the Dodd-Frank Act pass responsibility up the supply chain to actors involved in mineral extraction. This means that the costs of compliance are generally borne by suppliers in producing countries and might ultimately fall on the miners. Neither the Dodd-Frank Act, nor the EU Regulation mandates specific actions by the regulatees at the sites or areas of extraction. The OECD Guidance and, by extension, the EU Regulation focus on risk mitigation and corporate compliance. However, with European importers as the target group of the Regulation being physically absent from the region, the arm's length nature of the supply chains favours disengagement from high-risk sources rather than working towards the improvement of the situation in areas of extraction. On-the-ground work to improve the human rights situation in conflict-affected and high-risk areas as a reaction to regulatory changes is mostly left to local actors. This remains so in general, even though policy learning over the past decade brought with it more consultation with and support for governments in producing countries to match new regulation with on-the-ground support for implementation.

The regulatory objective to end conflict in the DRC and the wider region by curbing illegal or illicit trade in 3TG minerals has not been achieved. Although these minerals are linked to the conflicts, they are not the sole driver of Eastern DRC's conflicts, as the norm entrepreneurs had initially claimed. The focus should not lie on "conflict minerals" but rather follow the OECD diction of conflict-affected and high-risk areas globally. Risks exist far beyond Eastern DRC, and there is much to be improved in terms of the responsibility and sustainability of supply chains. Using an arbitrary definition of conflict minerals that at any rate have only tenuous links to the persistence of conflict in the region falls short of a smart approach.

These observations do not imply that the emerging regulatory regime to fight the illicit trade with conflict minerals was established in vain. Whether conflict exists or not, the supply chains must become (more) responsible. Both the Dodd-Frank Act and the EU Conflict Minerals Regulation are important precedents for many laws and initiatives to come that work towards responsible supply chains within the extractive sector and beyond. At the same time, the fight against the illegal trade in minerals from zones of conflict continues, though it remains far from clear whether existing frameworks are effective in tracing and certifying mineral shipments, let alone in pacifying Eastern DRC.

The authors would like to thank Constanze Ely for research assistance.

References

Abbott, Kenneth/Snidal, Duncan (2000): "Hard and soft law in international governance". In: International Organization, 54, pp. 421–456.

Abbott, Kenneth/Snidal, Duncan (2009): "Strengthening international regulation through Transnational New Governance. Overcoming the orchestration deficit". In: Vanderbilt Journal of Transnational Law, 42, pp. 501–578.

Autesserre, Séverine (2010): The trouble with the Congo. Local violence and the failure of international peacebuilding. Cambridge: Cambridge University Press.

Autesserre, Séverine (2012): "Dangerous tales. Dominant narratives on the Congo and their unintended consequences". In: African Affairs, 111, 443, pp. 202–222.

Ballentine, Karen/Sherman, Jake (2003): "Introduction". In: Ballentine, Karen/ Sherman, Jake (eds.): The political economy of armed conflict. Beyond greed and grievance. Boulder and London: Lynne Rienner, pp. 1–15.

Bryceson, Deborah Fahy/Jønsson, Jesper Bosse (2010): "Gold digging careers in rural East Africa. Small-scale miners' livelihood choices". In: World Development, 38, 3, pp. 379–392.

Buhmann, Karin (2015): "Business and human rights. Understanding the UN Guiding Principles from the perspective of transnational business governance interactions". In: Transnational Legal Theory, 6, 2, pp. 399–434.

China Chamber of Commerce of Metals, Minerals & Chemicals Importers & Exporters (2014): "Guidelines for social responsibility in outbound mining investments". At: http://www.cccmc.org.cn/docs/2014-10/20141029161135692190.pdf (accessed 2 September 2021).

Collier, Paul/Hoeffler, Anke (2004): "Greed and grievance in civil war". In: Oxford Economic Papers, 56, 4, pp. 563–595.

Cuvelier, Jeroen/Van Bockstael, Steven/Vlassenroot, Koen/Iguma, Claude (2014): "Analyzing the impact of the Dodd-Frank Act on Congolese livelihoods". At: https://www.ssrc.org/publications/view/analyzing-the-impact-of-the-dodd-frank-act-on-congolese-livelihoods (accessed 2 September 2021).

Cuvelier, Jeroen/Vlassenroot, Koen/Olin, Nathaniel (2014): "Resources, conflict and governance: A critical review". In: The Extractive Industries and Society, 1, 2, pp. 340–350.

Donaldson, Thomas/Preston, Lee (1995): "The stakeholder theory of the corporation. Concepts, evidence, and implications". In: The Academy of Management Review, 20, 1, pp. 65–91.

EPRM (n.d.): "The European Partnership for Responsible Minerals". At: https://europeanpartnership-responsibleminerals.eu (accessed 8 November 2020).

Finnemore, Martha/Sikkink, Kathryn (1998): "International norm dynamics and political change". In: International Organization, 52, 4, pp. 887–917.

Florini, Ann/Simmons, P.J. (2000): "What the world needs now?". In: Florini, Ann (ed.): The third force. The rise of transnational civil society. Washington, D.C.: Carnegie Endowment for International Peace, pp. 1–15.

Geenen, Sara (2012): "A dangerous bet. The challenges of formalizing artisanal mining in the Democratic Republic of Congo". In: Resources Policy, 37, 3, pp. 322–330.

Geenen, Sara/Custers, Raf (2010): "Tiraillements autour du secteur minier de l'Est de la RDC". In: Marysse, Stefaan/Reyntjens, Filip/Vandeginste, Stef (eds.): L'Afrique des Grands Lacs. Annuaire 2009–2010. Paris: L'Harmattan, pp. 231–258.

Gillies, Alexandra (2010): "Reputational concerns and the emergence of oil sector transparency as an international norm". In: International Studies Quarterly, 54, 1, pp. 103–126.

Global Witness (2009): "Faced with a gun, what can you do?" War and the militarisation of mining in Eastern Congo. London: Global Witness.

Global Witness (2010): 'The hill belongs to them': The need for international action on Congo's conflict minerals trade. London: Global Witness.

Government of the DRC (2011): "Note circulaire n° 002/ CAB.MIN/ MINES/01/2011 du 6 septembre 2011 relative à l'Application obligatoire des directives et recommandations du Guide du Devoir de diligence de l'OCDE et de la résolution 1952 (2010) du Conseil de Sécurité de l'ONU dans le secteur minier Congolais". At: https://cdn.globalwitness.org/archive/files/library/note_circulaire_oecdguidelines_06092011.pdf (accessed 2 September 2021).

Government of the DRC (2012a): "Arrêté ministériel n° 0057/CAB.MIN/ MINES/01/2012 du 29 février 2012 portant mise en œuvre du mécanisme régional de certification de la Conférence Internationale sur la Région des Grands Lacs « CIRGL », en République Démocratique du Congo". At: https://www.mines-rdc.cd/fr/wp-content/uploads/documents/Arrete_0057_2012.pdf (accessed 2 September 2021).

Government of the DRC (2012b): "Arrêté ministériel n° 0058/CAB.MIN/ MINES/01/2012 du 29 février 2012 fixant les procédures de qualification et de validation des sites miniers des filières aurifère et stannifère dans les provinces du Katanga, du Maniema, du Nord Kivu, du Sud Kivu et de la Province Orientale". At: https://www.mines-rdc.cd/fr/wp-content/uploads/documents/Arrete_0058_2012.pdf (accessed 2 September 2021).

Gunningham, Neil/Grabosky, Peter (1998): Smart regulation. Designing environmental policy. Oxford: Oxford University Press.

Gunningham, Neil/Rees, Joseph (1997): "Industry self-regulation. An institutional perspective". In: Law & Policy, 19, 4, pp. 363–414.

Haufler, Virginia (2001): A public role for the private sector. Industry self-regulation in a global economy. Washington, D.C.: Carnegie Endowment for International Peace.

Haufler, Virginia (2003): "New forms of governance. Certification regimes as social regulations of the global market". In: Meidinger, Errol/Elliott, Christopher/Oesten, Gerhard (eds.): Social and political dimensions of forest certification. Remagen: Kessel, pp. 237–247.

Haufler, Virginia (2009): "The Kimberley Process certification scheme. An innovation in global governance and conflict prevention". In: Journal of Business Ethics, 89, pp. 403–416.

Hilson, Gavin (2010): "'Once a miner, always a miner': poverty and livelihood diversification in Akwatia, Ghana". In: Journal of Rural Studies, 26, 3, pp. 296–307.

Hoffmann, Kasper/Vlassenroot, Koen/Marchais, Gauthier (2016): "Taxation, stateness and armed groups. Public authority and resource extraction in Eastern Congo". In: Development and Change, 47, 6, pp. 1434–1456.

IMPACT (2020): "The intermediaries. Traders who threaten the Democratic Republic of Congo's efforts for conflict-free gold". At: https://impacttransform.org/wp-content/uploads/2020/09/The-Intermediaries_Sept-2020_EN-web.pdf (accessed 2 September 2021).

International Labour Organization (2006): "Tripartite declaration of principles concerning multinational enterprises and social policy". Fourth Edition. At: https://ilo.org/public/libdoc/ilo/2006/106B09_303_engl.pdf (accessed 27 September 2021).

IPIS (2020): "Artisanal mining in DR Congo – IPIS open data dashboard". At: https://ipisresearch-dashboard.shinyapps.io/open_data_app/ (accessed 2 September 2021).

Keck, Margaret/Sikkink, Kathryn (1998): Activists beyond borders. Ithaca and London: Cornell University Press.

Koch, Dirk-Jan/Burlyuk, Olga (2020): "Bounded policy learning? EU efforts to anticipate unintended consequences in conflict minerals legislation". In: Journal of European Public Policy, 27, 10, pp. 1441–1462.

Koch, Dirk-Jan/Kinsbergen, Sara (2018): "Exaggerating unintended effects? Competing narratives on the impact of conflict minerals regulation". In: Resources Policy, 57, pp. 255–263.

Le Billon, Philippe (2000): "The political ecology of transition in Cambodia 1989–1999. War, peace and forest exploitation". In: Development and Change, 31, 4, pp. 785–805.

Neumann, Martin/Barume, Bali/Ducellier, Benoît/Ombeni, Alain/Näher, Uwe/Schütte, Philip/von Baggehufwudt, Ulrike/Ruppen, Désirée/Weyns, Yannick (2019): Traceability in artisanal gold supply chains in the Democratic Republic of the Congo. Lessons learned from the Kampene gold pilot project. Hanover: Bundesanstalt für Geowissenschaften und Rohstoffe.

Newell, Peter (2001a): "Environmental NGOs, TNCs, and the question of governance". In: Stevis, Dimitris/Assetto, Valerie (eds.): The international political economy of the environment. Boulder and London: Lynne Rienner, pp. 85–107.

Newell, Peter (2001b): "Managing multinationals. The governance of investment for the environment". In: Journal of International Development, 13, pp. 907–919.

Nielsen, Vibeke/Parker, Christine (2008): "To what extent do third parties influence business compliance?". In: Journal of Law and Society, 35, 3, pp. 309–340.

OECD (2011): OECD Guidelines for Multinational Enterprises. 2011 Edition. Paris: OECD Publishing.

OECD (2013): OECD Due Diligence Guidance for Responsible Supply Chains of Minerals from Conflict-Affected and High-Risk Areas. Second Edition. Paris: OECD Publishing.

Oliviero, Melanie/Simmons, Adele (2002): "Who's minding the store? Global civil society and corporate social responsibility". In: Glasius, Marlies/Kaldor, Mary/ Anheier, Helmut (eds.): Global civil society 2002. Oxford: Oxford University Press, pp. 77–107.

Parker, Dominic/Foltz, Jeremy/Elsea, David (2016): "Unintended consequences of sanctions for human rights. Conflict minerals and infant mortality". In: The Journal of Law and Economics, 59, 4, pp. 731–774.

Parker, Dominic/Vadheim, Bryan (2017): "Resource cursed or policy cursed? US regulation of conflict minerals and violence in the Congo". In: Journal of the Association of Environmental and Resource Economists, 4, 1, pp. 1–49.

Perks, Rachel (2011): "'Can I Go?' – Exiting the artisanal mining sector in the Democratic Republic of Congo". In: Journal of International Development, 23, 8, pp. 1115–1127.

Prendergast, John (2009): "Can you hear Congo now? Cell phones, conflict minerals, and the worst sexual violence in the world". At: https://enoughproject.org/files/Can%20Your%20Hear%20Congo%20Now.pdf (accessed 29 September 2020).

Price, Richard (2003): "Transnational civil society and advocacy in world politics". In: World Politics, 55, 4, pp. 579–606.

Radley, Ben/Vogel, Christoph (2015): "Fighting windmills in Eastern Congo? The ambiguous impact of the 'conflict minerals' movement". In: The Extractive Industries and Society, 2, 3, pp. 406–410.

RAND Europe (n.d.): "Indicative, non-exhaustive list of conflict-affected and high-risk areas under Regulation (EU) 2017/821". At: https://www.cahraslist.net/cahras (accessed 7 September 2021).

Ross, Michael (2004a): "How do natural resources influence civil war? Evidence from thirteen cases". In: International Organization, 58, 1, pp. 35–67.

Ross, Michael (2004b): "What do we know about natural resources and civil war?". In: Journal of Peace Research, 41, 3, pp. 337–356.

Schneiberg, Marc/Bartley, Tim (2008): "Organizations, regulation, and economic behaviour. Regulatory dynamics and forms from the nineteenth to twenty-first century". In: Annual Review of Law and Social Science, 4, pp. 31–61.

Schütte, Philip (2019): "International mineral trade on the background of due diligence regulation. A case study of tantalum and tin supply chains from East and Central Africa". In: Resources Policy, 62, pp. 674–689.

Seay, Laura (2015): "Conflict Minerals in Congo. The consequences of oversimplification". In: de Waal, Alex (ed.): Advocacy in Conflict. Critical Perspectives on Transnational Activism. London: Zed Books, pp. 115–141.

Stoop, Nik/Verpoorten, Marijke/van der Windt, Peter (2018): "More legislation, more violence? The impact of Dodd-Frank in the DRC". In: PLoS ONE, 13, 8.

United Nations (2001): "Report of the Panel of Experts on the illegal Exploitation of Natural Resources and Other Forms of Wealth of the Democratic Republic of the Congo". At: https://www.undocs.org/S/2001/357 (accessed 2 September 2021).

United Nations (2011): Guiding Principles on Business and Human Rights. New York and Geneva: United Nations.

United Nations (2017): "Final report of the Group of Experts on the Democratic Republic of the Congo". At: https://www.undocs.org/S/2017/672/Rev.1 (accessed 2 September 2021).

van der Velde, Steffen (2017): "The end of conflict minerals on the EU market?", ASSER Policy Brief No. 2017–01. At: https://papers.ssrn.com/sol3/papers.cfm?abstract_id=2930215 (accessed 7 September 2021).

van Erp, Judith/Faure, Michael/Liu, Jing/Karavias, Markos/Nollkaemper, André/Philipsen, Niels (2019): "Introduction. The concept of smart mixes for transboundary environmental harm". In: van Erp, Judith/Faure, Micheal/Nollkaemper, André/Philipsen, Niels (eds.): Smart mixes for transboundary environmental harm. Cambridge: Cambridge University Press, pp. 3–24.

Vogel, Christoph/Raeymaekers, Timothy (2016): "Terr(it)or(ies) of peace? The Congolese mining frontier and the fight against 'conflict minerals'". In: Antipode, 48, 4, pp. 1102–1121.

Vogel, David (2008): "Private global business regulation". In: Annual Review of Political Science, 11, pp. 261–282.

The authors

Lorenzo Bagnoli is a journalist and board member of the Italian centre for investigative journalism IRPI. He is a member of the Global Initiative against Transnational Organized Crime.
Contact: lo.bagnoli@gmail.com

Stefan Bauchowitz, PhD, is working for the German development agency GIZ as an advisor in a project on economic development in the mining sector in the Democratic Republic of the Congo.
Contact: stefan.bauchowitz@giz.de

Dr Dyhia Belhabib is a principal investigator on fisheries at Ecotrust Canada and executive director and co-founder of Nautical Crime Investigation Services.
Contact: dyhia@ecotrust.ca

Daniel Brombacher is the head of the Global Partnership on Drug Policies and Development (GPDPD), a global programme at the German development agency GIZ.
Contact: daniel.brombacher@giz.de

Inga Carry works as a researcher in the project "Research Network Sustainable Global Supply Chains" at the German Institute for International and Security Affairs (SWP) in Berlin.
Contact: inga.carry@swp-berlin.org

Peter Fabricius is a freelance journalist and analyst. He regularly writes for the Institute for Security Studies (ISS) in Pretoria and the Daily Maverick, a South African online and printed journal covering foreign affairs and Africa.
Contact: apfabricius@gmail.com

Gerardo Damonte holds a PhD in anthropology from Cornell University. He is a professor in the Department of Social Sciences at Pontificia Universidad Católica del Perú (PUCP).
Contact: gdamonte@pucp.pe

Dr Nhomsai Hagen is a research pharmacist at the Institute of Pharmaceutical Sciences of the University of Tübingen. Her PhD thesis was on the quality of medicines for maternal health in Malawi and Rwanda.
Contact: nhomsai.hagen@uni-tuebingen.de

Dr Cathrin Hauk completed her PhD on the problem of substandard and falsified medicines at the Institute of Pharmaceutical Sciences of the University of Tübingen. She has been continuing this line of research at the Centre for Tropical Medicine and Global Health of Oxford University since April 2022.
Contact: cathrin.hauk@ndm.ox.ac.uk

Prof Dr Lutz Heide is a senior professor at the Institute of Pharmaceutical Sciences of the University of Tübingen. His research and teaching focuses on pharmaceutical global health.
Contact: heide@uni-tuebingen.de

Prof Dr Philippe Le Billon is a professor at the University of British Columbia with the Department of Geography and the School of Public Policy and Global Affairs.
Contact: philippe.lebillon@ubc.ca

Prof Dr Günther Maihold is deputy director of the German Institute for International and Security Affairs (SWP) in Berlin and professor for political science at Freie Universität Berlin. He was head of the project "Research Network Sustainable Global Supply Chains".
Contact: guenther.maihold@swp-berlin.org

Fatjona Mejdini is a journalist and researcher. She is the Western Balkans coordinator for the Global Initiative against Transnational Organized Crime.
Contact: fatjona.mejdini@globalinitiative.net

Dr Melanie Müller is a senior associate with a focus on Southern Africa at the German Institute for International and Security Affairs (SWP) in Berlin and the head of the research project "Transnational Governance of Sustainable Commodity Supply Chains".
Contact: melanie.mueller@swp-berlin.org

Dr Bettina Schorr is a political scientist and the programme director of trAndeS – Postgraduate Program on Social Inequalities and Sustainable Development in the Andean Region at Freie Universität Berlin.
Contact: bettina.schorr@fu-berlin.de

Detective Chief Superintendent Jan Schubert is head of a police station of the Bavarian State Police with experience in the field of transnational organised crime and has worked for several German institutions, including the Federal Foreign Office (AA).

Ina Tessnow-von Wysocki is a PhD student in the ERC project MARIPOLDATA at the University of Vienna with a focus on science–policy interfaces for ocean protection.
Contact: ina.tessnow-vonwysocki@univie.ac.at

Dr Leopold von Carlowitz currently works as senior advisor for the CONNEX Support Unit. Previously, he was senior advisor for the GIZ sector programme Extractives for Development, where he led the workstream on responsible mineral supply chains.
Contact: leopold.carlowitz@giz.de

Dr Judith Vorrath is a senior associate in the International Security Division of the German Institute for International and Security Affairs (SWP) with a focus on transnational organised crime.
Contact: judith.vorrath@swp-berlin.org